The Virgin's Baby

BEVIS HILLIER was educated at Reigate Grammar School and Oxford University, where he was Gladstone Prizeman at Magdalen College. He later joined *The Times*, became editor of *The Connoisseur*, editor of *The Times Saturday Review*, and a columnist on the *Los Angeles Times*. He is an authority on eighteenth-century English ceramics and Art Deco and has written more than 30 books, including the very highly acclaimed official biography of the Poet Laureate, John Betjeman, published in three volumes, 1988, 2002 and 2004 by John Murray. For some years he was the lead book reviewer of *The Spectator*, and he is still a regular contributor.

He is a Fellow of the Royal Society of Literature and a Commander of the Italian Order of Merit, for 'services to the arts'.

The Virgin's Baby

The Battle of the Ampthill Succession

BEVIS HILLIER

HOPCYN PRESS

© Bevis Hillier 2013

First published in Britain in 2013 by Hopcyn Press Limited.

Hopcyn Press
42 Russell Rd
London W14 8HT
Tel: +44 (0) 20 7371 6488
Email: info@hopkinpress.com
www.hopkinpress.com

ISBN: 978-0-9572977-0-8

Manuscript typed by Secret Genius, Winchester, SO23 8GH
www.secretgenius.co.uk

Design and layout by Ian Hughes, www.mousematdesign.com

Printed and bound in Great Britain by Berforts Information Press Ltd.

HAMLET Do not believe it.

ROSENCRANTZ Believe what?

HAMLET That I can keep your council and not mine own. Besides, to be demanded of a sponge! What replication should be made by the son of a king?

ROSENCRANTZ Take you me for a sponge, my lord?

HAMLET Ay, sir...

WILLIAM SHAKESPEARE, *HAMLET*

It has been more than a divorce case. It has been an intimate drama with the curtain rising and falling on climax after climax.

ILLUSTRATED SUNDAY HERALD, 18 MARCH 1923

If ever there was a family, seemingly blessed by fortune, where the birth of a child was attended by an evil spirit bearing a baneful gift liable to frustrate all the blessings, it was the Ampthill Russells. ... The most private and embarrassing marital intimacies were investigated and extensively regaled to a salacious public...

LORD SIMON OF GLAISDALE, HOUSE OF LORDS, 1976

Dedications

WITHLOV	ANDWITH	SINCETH	THENOVE	FURTHER	FINALLY	OHIHAVE	SINCEAL
EANDGRA	FONDMEM	EFOREGO	LISTELI	ASANAFT	MYWARMT	FORGOTT	LTHEFOR
TITUDET	ORIESOF	INGDEDI	ZABETHJ	ERTHOUG	HANKSAR	ENTOSEN	EGOINGW
OJOHNAN	OURSOME	CATIONW	ANEHOWA	HTIMUST	EDUETOD	DWARMTH	ASWRITT
DANNHEA	TIMEBOS	ASWRITT	RDWROTE	THANKAN	RSTEPHE	ANKSALS	ENANNHE
LDFROMT	SCOLONE	ENDAVID	TOMEIN2	THONYRU	NCRETNE	OTOANJE	ALDHASS
HEAUTHO	LPHILIP	RUSSELL	011GIVI	SSELLFO	YFELLOW	LICAHUS	ADLYDIE
RBEVIST	HARDING	HASSUCC	NGMEPER	RLETTIN	OFALLSO	TONWHOW	DMYSINC
OWHOMTH	OFTHETI	EEDEDAS	MISSION	GMEQUOT	ULSCOLL	ROTEDOW	ERECOND
EYHAVEG	MESSPEC	THEFIFT	TOQUOTE	EFROMHI	EGEOXFO	NFORMEH	OLENCES
IVENSOM	IALSUPP	HBARONA	ACRESOF	SMEMOIR	RDFORKI	ERVIVID	TOHERHU
UCHHELP	LEMENTS	MPTHILL	HERWRIT	IAMVERY	NDLYSEN	MEMORIE	SBANDJO
ALSOBES	AMENTOR	ONTHEDE	INGSABO	GRATEFU	DINGMEC	SOFHERF	HNFORME
TWISHES	ANDAMEL	ATHOFHI	UTHERFR	LTOHIMA	OPIESOF	RIENDCH	RLYCHAI
ANDMANY	IORATOR	SFATHER	IENDCHR	NDHISWI	HISADMI	RISTABE	RMANOFT
THANKST	FATHERF	GEOFFRE	ISTABEL	FECATHE	RABLEWO	LLADYAM	HEBETJE
ODAVIDA	IGUREAN	YTHEFOU	AMPTHIL	RINEFOR	RKSONSI	PTHILLI	MANSOCI
NDTIARU	DAJUDGE	RTHLORD	LWHOMSH	SOMEENJ	RJOHNWI	HOPETHA	ETYANDS
SSELLFO	OFMERIT	THERUSS	ESAIDIT	OYABLEL	THERSAN	TONEDAY	TILLONE
RTHEIRH	HEHADFA	ELLBABY	WASAJOY	UNCHESI	DTHEREP	AFILMWI	OFITSLE
ELPANDK	ITHINME	HIMSELF	TOKNOWW	NWINCHE	ORTINGO	LLBEMAD	ADINGME
INDNESS	WHENSOM	INEVERY	HENSHEE	STERAND	FDIVORC	EOFTHER	MBERSAN
ANDWELC	EDIDNOT	WAYHEWA	LIZABET	LONDONT	ECASESE	USSELLB	DAVICEP
OMEATTH	SALVEAT	SHELPFU	HJANEWA	HATBOOK	GTHERUS	ABYSTOR	RESIDEN
EIRHOME	QUEVALE	LANDGIV	SYOUNGS	OFHISIS	SELLONE	YANDTHA	TOFITHE
MYLOVEA	MARINER	INGHEHA	OIHAVED	SUPERBL	SIADMIT	TSHEWIL	HASTHEF
LSOTOST	LYINGAT	NDEDMER	RAWNONH	YWRITTE	HISFIND	LPLAYCH	INESTCO
EPHENJE	SHROTON	ICHLYDE	ERAUTOB	NANDIAM	INGSAND	RISTABE	LLECTIO
SSELOUR	INTHECO	TAILEDS	IOGRAPH	CONFIDE	HISCLEA	LINHERI	NOFMODE
OLDALLI	UNTYOFD	TRIKING	YANDHER	NTTHATI	RANALYS	RISHDAY	RNFIRST
ANCEWIL	ORSETWH	STORIES	ADMIRED	TWILLBE	ISOFTHE	SWHENSH	EDITION
LNOTPER	EREHISF	OFHISBI	SERIESO	COMEACL	MHAVEPR	EKNEWHE	SINHISH
ISHMYDE	AMILYON	RTHANDT	FCAZALE	ASSICOF	OVEDMOS	RSOWELL	OMEATGU
ARCHINA	CELIVED	IMESRIP	TNOVELS	ITSKIND	TUSEFUL	TALLYHO	ILDFORD

Contents

Pedigree of the Russell Family

AMPTHILL

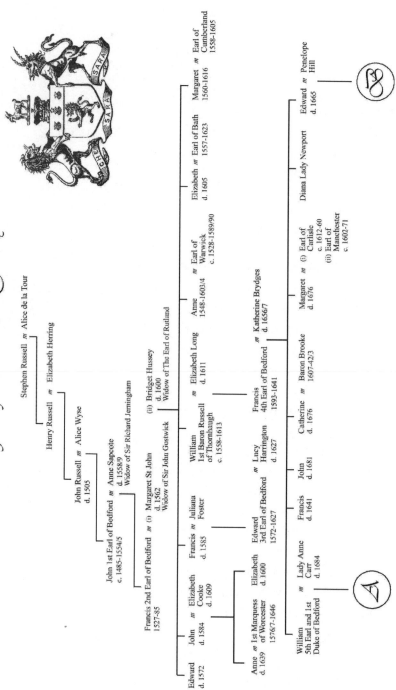

Stephen Russell *m* Alice de la Tour

Henry Russell *m* Elizabeth Herring

John Russell *m* Alice Wyse
d. 1505

John 1st Earl of Bedford *m* Anne Sapcote
c. 1485–1554/5   d. 1558/9
Widow of Sir Richard Jerningham

Francis 2nd Earl of Bedford *m* (i) Margaret St John   (ii) Bridget Hussey
1527–85   d. 1562   d. 1600
Widow of Sir John Gostwick   Widow of The Earl of Rutland

Edward   John *m* Elizabeth   Francis *m* Juliana   William *m* Elizabeth Long   Anne *m* Earl of   Elizabeth *m* Earl of Bath   Margaret *m* Earl of
d. 1572   d. 1584   Cooke   d. 1585   Foster   1st Baron Russell   d. 1611   1548–1603/4   Warwick   d. 1605   1557–1623   1560–1616   Cumberland
  d. 1609   of Thornhaugh   c. 1528–1589/90   1558–1605
  c. 1558–1613

Anne *m* 1st Marquess   Edward *m* Lucy   Francis *m* Katherine Brydges
d. 1639   of Worcester   3rd Earl of Bedford   Harrington   4th Earl of Bedford   d. 1656/7
  1576/7–1646   1572–1627   d. 1627   1593–1641

Elizabeth
d. 1600

William *m* Lady Anne   Francis   John   Catherine *m* Baron Brooke   Margaret *m* (i) Earl of   Diana Lady Newport   Edward *m* Penelope
5th Earl and 1st   Carr   d. 1641   d. 1681   d. 1676   1607–423   d. 1676   Carlisle   d. 1665   Hill
Duke of Bedford   d. 1684   c. 1612–60
  (ii) Earl of
  Manchester
  c. 1602–71

Ⓐ

Ⓑ

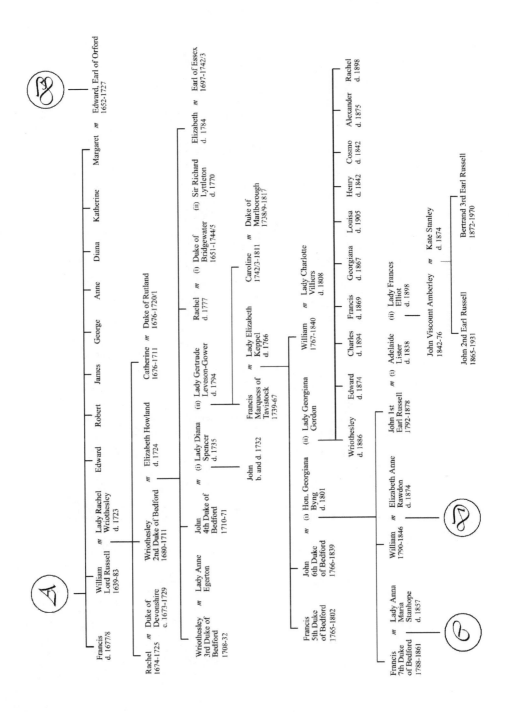

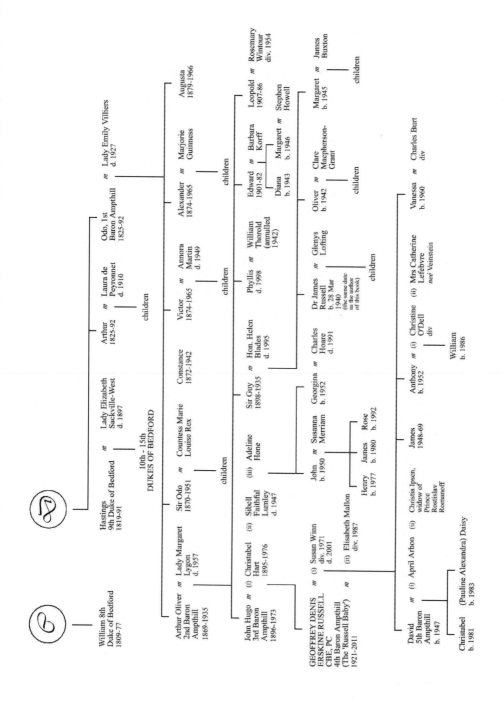

List of illustrations

20. Christabel in Ireland, not long before her death in 1976. *Stan Shields.*
21. Christabel, in characteristically striking dress, at a society wedding.
22. Geoffrey and Vanessa celebrating his victory in the House of Lords hearing of 1976.
23. Lord and Lady Ampthill with 'Jack Russell'.
24. Geoffrey in James Bond mode in the Bahamas in the 1960s.
25. *Evening News*, 25 February 1976. Geoffrey had been paid £30,000 to relinquish any right to the Ampthill estates – though not to the title.
26. *The Guardian*, 27 February 1976: the juxtaposition of photogtraphs of Geoffrey and John Russell suggests a strong family resemblance, especially comparing the mouths.
27. Pocket cartoon by Osbert Lancaster, *Daily Express*, 25 February 1976. The reference is to the womanizing philosopher Bertrand Russell (Earl Russell, 1872-1970).
28. Pocket cartoon by Osbert Lancaster, *Daily Express*, 13 April 1976.
29. Cartoon by 'JAK', *Evening Standard*, 25 February 1976.
30. Victory: Geoffrey Russell in April 1976 after the Lords' Committee for Privileges decided he was the rightful Lord Ampthill.

Colour plates

1. Hans Holbein the Younger, *John Russell, 1st Earl of Bedford. By gracious permission of Her Majesty the Queen.*
2. 'Spy' cartoon of the 1st Lord Ampthill, *Vanity Fair*, 28 July 1877.
3. 'Spy' cartoon of the 2nd Lord Ampthill, *Vanity Fair*, 21 March 1891.
4. 5. 6. The 2nd Lord Ampthill claimed he was 'almost ruined' by the costs of the *Russell* v. *Russell* divorce trials; but he still had enough money left over to institute a silver cup and medals for the London Rowing Club in 1930.
7. Sir William Orpen, *Sir Henry Duke (Lord Merrivale)* – who presided over the first *Russell* v. *Russell* divorce trial. *The Benchers of Gray's Inn.*
8. Lady Margaret Ampthill with two of her sons, John Hugo Russell, later 3rd Lord Ampthill (*right*) and Guy Russell.
9. Oakley House, Bedfordshire, where it is assumed the Russell baby was conceived in December 1920.
10. Sir John Lavery's portrait of the 1st Earl of Birkenhead, whose judgement was so critical in winning Christabel her case.
11. Etienne Drian, *Lady Baillie* (centre) *and her two daughters, Susan* (left) *and Pauline, at Leeds Castle, Kent.* The portrait was painted in 1948, two years after Susan's marriage to Geoffrey Russell.
12. Leeds Castle, Kent.
13. Christabel's Dunguaire Castle, Kinvarra, Co. Galway, Ireland.
14. Geoffrey's second wife, Elisabeth (*née* Mallon).
15. Geoffrey Ampthill as Lord Chairman of Committees at the House of Lords.

Prologue

In 1971 I was asked by *The Times* to cover an exhibition at Woburn Abbey, the seat of the Dukes of Bedford. It was a show about Henry Holland, the architect who in the 1750s designed a large part of the palatial house. The buxom French Duchess showed us round. There were plans, elevations and models, and letters from Holland to his foreman, Mr. Gotobed – a name which provoked a saucy aside from Her Grace. (Before she had become the 13th Duke's third wife in 1960, she had been Nicole Milinaire, a Paris television presenter. In later life she wrote a racy memoir, *Nicole Nobody*, in one passage of which she described a wild sexual encounter she had had in a hotel room with a handsome man whose name she never learned.)

The press were given champagne and canapés, and then the Duchess made a speech, in her very French accent. She spoke the Queen's English; but unfortunately it was the English of Queen Marie Antoinette. The speech began: ''Enry 'Olland was one of the great architects of the eighteenth century...' I'm afraid I typed her words exactly like that in my report for *The Times*[1]. So far from being offended by such mimicry, the Duchess was amused. The day after my piece appeared in the paper, she telephoned me: 'Mr 'Illier, all my friends asking, "Why you not learn to spik English properly?" Would you like to come and stay at Woburn next wikend?' Of course I accepted.

I and my suitcase were met at the local railway station, Flitwick, by a huge brown chauffeur-driven Bentley with the number plate DOB1. The Duchess welcomed me at the Abbey and said, 'We've given you the Gainsborough Room.' Sure enough, the room was hung with Gainsborough portraits. It overlooked the deer park. I had met Nicole's husband, John, Duke of Bedford (known to his friends as 'Ian'), at the Holland exhibition. He was the man who – following the lead of his friend, the Marquess of Bath, at Longleat – had turned Woburn into a successful tourist attraction.

It was the beginning of a long friendship with the Bedfords. I often stayed at Woburn. My visits ended when Ian and Nicole made over the Abbey to his son, the Marquess of Tavistock, who was born the same year as I (1940) and married the beautiful debutante Henrietta Tiarks (now Dowager Duchess); but I kept in touch with Ian and Nicole after they moved to New Mexico. Ian wrote to me, characteristically: 'We opened a friend's new bookshop the other day. A long queue of people was waiting to be presented to us. All the women curtseyed, and so did one of the men.' Nicole wrote – also characteristically: 'We are enjoying sun, sand and ...'

The Henry Holland exhibition of 1971 that led to this friendship contained not only the architect's designs for Woburn, but also those for the alterations he made to Oakley House, a hunting-box of the Dukes on the banks of the Great Ouse, at Oakley, Bedfordshire. In 1757-58, on instructions from the fifth Duke, Holland added to the seventeenth-century building an elegant chinoiserie verandah, with detailing reminiscent of the Chinese dairy at Woburn.[2] In April 2008 this house was put on sale by its owner, Chris Kilroy, a former High Sheriff of Bedfordshire. *The Sunday Times* chose it as one of its 'Houses of the week' –

The editorial feature ended with a mysterious comment:

...our receptions and a photographic darkroom. Its 15 acres include a cottage, a pool and river frontage. It is four miles from Bedford, which is 40 minutes by train from London
Agents: Savills; 01223 347000, www.savills.com. Knight Frank; 020 7861 1078, www.knightfrank.com
They say: Extremely pretty Georgian house in English hunting country
We say: Scandalous past: the house was the centre of a notorious divorce case in the 1920s

I doubt that one in a million of the newspaper's readers knew to what scandal that sentence referred; but I did. For the past five years I had been writing a book about it – the book you have just begun to read.

Preface

I had never heard of the Russell Baby case until 2002 – eighty years after it scandalized Britain in the London divorce courts. If, before then, you had asked me which was the most sensational divorce case of the twentieth century, I would probably have suggested that of the Duke and Duchess of Argyll in 1963, with its photographs of a nude 'headless man' and the other titillating elements that hogged the headlines when I was in my early twenties. But the Russell Baby case was at least as notorious in its time. The scabrous details published in the press outraged King George V; the destiny of a young child was at stake; and as a direct result of the case English law was changed.

I first encountered the story by accident: my mother, who had some of the more benign attributes of a witch, would have said it was 'meant'. In 2002 I was out of a job and rather hard up. I was wondering what book I could create quickly to bring in some money. The answer could be an anthology: arranging Other Men's Flowers, in effect getting others to write my book for me. I had been a journalist on *The Times*, the *Los Angeles Times* and elsewhere, and had written several books. It occurred to me that, drawing on both disciplines, I could compile (if the Oxford University Press showed willing) an *Oxford Book of Fleet Street* or perhaps, with the American market in mind, an *Oxford Book of Press Anecdotes*. When journalists retire – hacks put out to pasture – they often write their memoirs. Writing is their trade; they can relate the full stories they were unable to tell in their careers for fear of libel suits; and there is much humour. I began riffling through their books for golden nuggets, and found plenty.

I also gave thought to the illustrations that might be used. Obviously one would have portraits and photographs of leading journalists – De Blowitz and William Russell of *The Times*, Lords Northcliffe and Beaverbrook, William Randolph Hearst ('Citizen Kane'), Walter Winchell and so on. But I also decided to show sample front pages of newspapers from the seventeenth century to the present – ranging from the *Ipswich Journal* of 1620 to the infamous issue of the *Sun* which appeared after the Argentine cruiser *General Belgrano* was sunk by the Royal Navy in the Falklands conflict of 1982, with the front-page headline 'GOTCHA'. I went to a specialist dealer in vintage newspapers in Covent Garden and came away with a large clutch of papers. Among them was the *Daily Sketch* of 31 May 1924. This was its front page:

I wondered what all *that* was about. So I read the *Sketch*'s story and found it fascinating. Then I went to the files of *The Times* for a much fuller and more accurate account. To summarize very briefly, this is what I learned. In 1915, through a personal advertisement placed in *The Times* by three midshipmen, a young woman called Christabel Hart met John Hugo Russell, son and heir of the second Lord Ampthill, a cousin of the Duke of Bedford. In 1918 she and John Hugo were married. In 1921 she was told that she was pregnant. At first her husband was overjoyed; but soon, goaded by his formidable mother, he was adamantly denying that the expected baby was his. On the eve of their marriage, he had reluctantly accepted his wife's plea that there should be no sex, at least for a long time. In his view he had kept to the bargain. He had been allowed 'incomplete relations', with emissions on her body, but he did not think they could have led to the pregnancy. Christabel said they must have done, as she had had no sexual relations of any kind with another man. Complicating the mystery further, the doctor who told her that she was five months pregnant also declared that she was still, technically, a virgin – a judgement confirmed when she was examined by other doctors. In October 1921 a son was born, Geoffrey Denis Erskine Russell (later 4th Lord Ampthill).

In 1922 John Hugo sued Christabel for divorce, citing two named co-respondents and 'a man unknown'. The jury dismissed the evidence against Christabel in connection with the two co-respondents but disagreed as to whether she had committed adultery with the 'man unknown'. The judge therefore ordered a new trial. That took place in 1923. Now a man called Edgar Mayer was named as a co-respondent. The jury found Christabel not guilty of adultery with him, but guilty of adultery with an unknown man. She appealed to the High Court, but lost. In 1924 she scraped together all the money she could and appealed to England's then supreme court, the House of Lords. By three votes to two, she won: that was the victory blazoned on the front page of my *Daily Sketch*. As a result, her son Geoffrey became next in succession to the Ampthill peerage, after John Hugo.

I discovered that there was no satisfactory book on the Russell case. Two books had touched on it. The first, of 1973, was a biography of Christabel – Lady Ampthill, as she had become – by Eileen Hunter (Mrs Petrovitch), written in a women's-magazine sort of style. She had been a friend of Christabel and had interviewed her for her book in the late 1960s; but Geoffrey Ampthill says, 'My mother was, I'm afraid, rather losing her marbles by then – she had a hopeless memory for what had happened.'[3]

The other book was *The House of Lords* (1977) by John Wells, best known as a comedian who did amusing impersonations of Denis Thatcher and John Betjeman and co-wrote the 'Mrs Wilson's Diary' and 'Dear Bill' columns in *Private Eye*. In researching his book, Wells had had lunch in 1992 with Geoffrey Ampthill, who had by then risen to be Chairman of Committees, the highest office in the House of Lords under the Lord Chancellor. On the way out of the restaurant, Wells asked Ampthill why he did the job. 'He thought about it for a moment. "Well, I feel I ought to take it seriously, really, after all the trouble I'd had getting in."'

Wells had no idea what Ampthill was talking about, but did some research and found out. As a result he included in his book a highly coloured and highly inaccurate chapter headed 'Incomplete Relations'. This is how it began:

'It was only when I was looking through the newspapers for references to the

House of Lords after the First World War that I understood Lord Ampthill's words about his mother having been a virgin when he was conceived. Lord Ampthill was the Sponge Baby. The story took various forms, but all involved a child having been born after his mother had employed a sponge in an intimate capacity in the bath, unaware that it had been used for some unworthier purpose by a recent male occupant.

'According to a later story, accepted with a joyous guffaw in aristocratic circles, the young Geoffrey Ampthill had been staying in a country house for the weekend when a friend found him unpacking his wash bag. As he took out his sponge, his friend said, "Ah, I see you've brought your father with you!" '[4]

Lord Ampthill was disgusted by these paragraphs. ('No friend of mine would ever have spoken to me in that way,' he said.) He set his solicitors on to Wells and the offending passage was cut when the book was published by Sceptre as a paperback in 1998 – 'though it is still chock-full of mistakes,' Ampthill told me.

I felt that here was an extraordinary story to which justice had never been done. In March 2003 I wrote to Lord Ampthill saying that I would like to write a book on the Russell Baby case. I added: 'In the 1970s I used to stay with your cousin, "Ian" Bedford, at Woburn.' The next day (Ampthill never wasted time), I found a message on my telephone answer-machine.

'Geoffrey Ampthill here. I'm absolutely *delighted* that you want to write about the Russell case. I thought I was going to have to do it myself – and, as a result, you'll be glad to know, I have had copies made of all *The Times* law reports, and some of the tabloid accounts too.

'I can't talk for very long, as I'm due on the Woolsack in a moment or two; but I've looked up your long list of publications on the House of Lords computer. Would you care to have lunch with me here, at the House of Lords? Are you free next Tuesday?'

The voice was unexpectedly youthful for the age I knew he must be (eighty-one in March 2003). Of course I accepted the invitation. We got on. Equally important, we seemed to have the same ideas about the projected book. 'I've read the preface to your second Betjeman volume,' he said. (The second part of my biography of John Betjeman had been published the year before.) 'I only needed to read that to see that you have a sense of humour. Facts are facts and you will need to record them; but I think that if anybody approached this subject without a sense of humour, the result would be disastrous. It is a story of incredible accidents, ludicrous misunderstandings, amazing characters and wonderful repartee in the courts. It just can't be written about with a po-face.' Initially, I was surprised at his willingness to co-operate on a book about the kind of scandal that some families might want to keep firmly locked in the closet; but I quickly realized two things. First, that Geoffrey Ampthill was a man of great integrity and straightforwardness; and second, that, repelled by John Wells's travesty, he wanted to have the record put straight, once for all.

The lunch at the House of Lords was followed by many Saturday sessions in his Westminster flat, in which I interviewed him on my tape-recorder. He lent me a mass of trial transcripts, documents, intimate letters and family photographs. But for them I would have had to put in months of work at the British Library's newspaper collections at Colindale. I was being presented with the story as Salome requested the head of John the Baptist – on a platter.

More than eighty years on, the Russell Baby case has faded from the public's memory; but the *cause célèbre* entered English literature. Nancy Mitford, in *The Pursuit of Love* (1945):

'On Saturday the blow fell.

' "Linda and Fanny, Fa wants you in the business-room. And sooner you than me by the look of him," said Jassy, meeting us in the drive as we came in from hunting. Our hearts plunged into our boots. We looked at each other with apprehension.

' "Better get it over," said Linda, and we hurried to the business-room, where we saw at once that the worst had occurred.

'Aunt Sadie, looking unhappy, and Uncle Matthew, grinding his teeth, confronted us with our crime. The room was full of blue lightning flashing from his eyes, and Jove's thunder was not more awful than what he now roared at us:

' "Do you realize," he said, "that, if you were married women, your husbands could divorce you for doing this?"

'Linda began to say no they couldn't. She knew the laws of divorce from having read the whole of the Russell case off newspapers with which the fires in the spare bedrooms were laid.'

When, in Graham Greene's novel *The End of the Affair* (1951), the narrator Maurice Bendrix comes across the inquiry agent Parkis in the British Museum reading-room, he asks him what he is working on.

' "This isn't work. It's my day off, and the boy's back at school today."

' "What are you reading?"

' " *The Times* Law Reports, sir. Today I'm on the Russell case. They give a kind of background to one's work, sir. Open up vistas. They take one away from the daily petty detail. I knew one of the witnesses in this case, sir. We were in the same office once. Well, he's gone down to history as I never shall now." '

James Lees-Milne encountered Geoffrey in 1986 and wrote in his diary for 6 July:

'We attended a dinner at the Warrenders[5] last night for about twenty people. Didn't enjoy it much. Full of lords and ladies, yet A[6] and I given place d'honneur. I suppose being the oldest present. It is good of them not to observe the absurd formal precedence at meals. On my right was Lord Ampthill, a man in his fifties[7] whom I much liked. I think he must have been the baby in the famous Russell Baby case, whose mother Christabel became a pen-friend of mine to whom I wrote when she was ill in Ireland (addressing my letters to the Cavalry Hospital until she told me it was Calvary). Geoffrey Ampthill is Deputy Speaker of the House of Lords, who sits on the Woolsack when the Lord Chancellor is absent. Says the House is the best club in the world...'

Woodrow Wyatt alludes to the case in his diary of 1995.[8] John Mortimer mentions it (rather inaccurately) in his memoir *The Summer of a Dormouse* (2000); and in March 2005 Ferdinand Mount wrote this in the *Daily Telegraph*: 'At supper with a neighbour once, we met a silver-haired elderly gent. This was a few years ago and he must have then been in his late sixties. During the war, he had served as a captain in the Irish Guards. Later he had run newspapers and theatre companies. He was crowning his career as Deputy Speaker of the House of Lords. He could not have been more charming. Yet all I could think of saying as soon as we shut the front door behind us was: "Do you realise that was the Russell baby?" For the benefit of readers not yet approaching senility, let me explain... [Mount then summarized the 1920s trials.]'

Among the reasons that the Russell Baby case attracted so much publicity was that it involved one of the great aristocratic families of England. Like the Howards, the Percys, the Cavendishes and the Cecils, the Russells, headed by the Earls (later Dukes) of Bedford, had been eminent in social and political life, and in wealth, for centuries. Ian Bedford had told me: 'With their thousands of acres, they thought themselves slightly grander than God.' Geoffrey Ampthill said: 'Of the families which have been well-known for five hundred years or so, the Cecils are the ones who are considered to have made the greatest contribution. The only giggle is that John Russell [first Earl of Bedford] was made Lord Privy Seal by Henry VIII exactly fifty years before the Cecils reached that pinnacle. (See colour plate 1). And that's the only reason – if the Cecils were to get uppity – that I think we might have a marginal edge. Both families produced a great Prime Minister.'

Lord John Russell (first Earl Russell, 1792-1878) was the Prime Minister; his grandson was the philosopher Bertrand Russell (3rd Earl Russell, 1872-1970). Geoffrey Ampthill, too, was descended from Dukes of Bedford. His great-grandfather was Lord Odo Russell (1829-84), who as British Ambassador to Berlin was known as 'Bismarck's favourite Englishman'. He was ennobled as the 1st Baron Ampthill in 1881. (Colour plate 2).

His son – Geoffrey's grandfather – (Arthur) Oliver, 2nd Baron Ampthill (1869-1935) was a celebrated rowing Blue at Oxford (colour plate 3); he became private secretary to Joseph Chamberlain at the Colonial Office; at thirty-one was appointed Governor of Madras; at thirty-five, acting Viceroy of India while Lord Curzon was on extended leave. He married Earl Beauchamp's daughter, Lady Margaret Lygon. John Hugo, their eldest son, was born in 1896.

I thought that the reader would want to know what happened to the Russell Baby after the 1920s trials. His life was adventurous, romantic and high-flying; and in 1976 there was the drama of a new *Russell* v. *Russell* case, after John Hugo died and the Hon. John ('Johnnie') Russell[9], Geoffrey's half-brother by a third marriage, challenged him for the peerage – unsuccessfully. Absorbing though Geoffrey's record is, the person who takes centre stage for much of the book is his remarkable mother, Christabel, Lady Ampthill. Hers is the story of a beautiful, brave and clever (if sometimes selfish and wilful) woman who wiped the floor with some of the leading barristers of the day – a story which seems almost predestined to be made into a Hollywood film one day. (She took part in a film – alas, lost – in 1925, and Anjelica Huston, who knew her in Ireland in the 1950s, based on her a bravura performance in the movie adaptation of Evelyn Waugh's *A Handful of Dust*.)

By Chinese whispers over the years, the truth about the Russell Baby case has been obscured by lewd legends and journalistic sensationalism. My aim has been to get at the truth and to write the book to end all books on the Russell affair. That I should succeed in this was Geoffrey Ampthill's prime object too. I know that he was absolutely candid with me; and he supplied the best jokes in the book.

During the time that I was researching and writing the book, the novelist Louise Doughty contributed a series of articles to *The Daily Telegraph* on how to write a novel. In 2007 these were collected in her book *A Novel in a Year*. I bought it, thinking that I might perhaps have a stab at fiction after almost half a century as a writer of non-fiction. It is full of good advice, none of which I have yet had time to follow. Not far into the book, Doughty pays qualified tribute to an earlier 'how to' book, Basil Hogarth's *The Technique of Novel Writing* (1934).

'Old Basil's book makes for interesting reading, not least because of the insouciance with which he refers to well-known contemporaries who have now sunk into relative obscurity. "According to Frank Norris, famous writer of *The Octopus...*" That aside, much of his advice is the same practical stuff that any sensible writer would give a novice today – bar, perhaps, his insistence that "the disputed succession is a plot device that has been done to death and is therefore to be avoided." '

Doughty is right and Basil Hogarth was wrong. The theme of disputed succession never loses its potency. Wars have been fought over it: the Wars of the Roses; the War of the Spanish Succession; the War of the Austrian Succession. *Hamlet* and *King Lear* are based on it. So are Wilkie Collins's *The Dead Secret* (1861); Ibsen's play *The Pretenders* (1864), Trollope's *Is He Popenjoy?* (1878) and Frances Hodgson Burnett's *Little Lord Fauntleroy* (1886). *Fauntleroy* uncannily foreshadows the Russell Baby case.

'The Earl had been uneasy for some time during the evening, as he glanced at Mr Havisham, and when he was uneasy he was always ill-tempered.

' "Why do you look so at the boy?" he exclaimed irritably. "You have been looking at him all the evening as if – See here now, why should you look at the boy, Havisham, and hang over him like some bird of ill-omen! What has your news to do with Lord Fauntleroy?"

' "My lord," said Mr Havisham, "I will waste no words. My news has everything to do with Lord Fauntleroy. And if we are to believe it – it is not Lord Fauntleroy who lies sleeping before us, but only the son of Captain Errol..." '

(As in the Russell case, the boy proves to be the rightful heir.)

With Louise Doughty's imprimatur, her trainee novelists will feel free to mine the rich lode of disputed succession. And the story of the Russell Baby is proof that truth is stranger than fiction. In his summing-up at the House of Lords hearing in 1976, Lord Simon of Glaisdale (who was still living, in his nineties, when I began writing this book)[10] invoked the fairy tale of the Sleeping Beauty:

'If ever there was a family, seemingly blessed by fortune, where the birth of a child was attended by an evil spirit bearing a baneful gift liable to frustrate all the blessings, it was the Ampthill Russells. Its curse was litigation. In the early 1920s there were two long hearings in the Divorce Division of the High Court, in the first of which the jury disagreed. Some of the most famous and expensive counsel of the day were briefed for the petitioner, for the respondent and (ultimately) for no fewer than three named co-respondents. The most private and embarrassing marital intimacies were investigated and extensively regaled to a salacious public...'

Though it had a happy ending, the Russell Baby case was no fairy story. It is time that its truths should be disentangled from the web of myth.

1

Consulting the Oracle

You can only predict things after they have happened.
EUGÈNE IONESCO, *LE RHINOCÉROS* (1959)

At 9.45 a.m. on Friday, 17 June 1921, Christabel Russell rang the front doorbell of No. 21 Hanover Street in Mayfair. She had come to see Mrs Mary Naismith, a fashionable fortune-teller. It was unusually warm: the next day *The Times* reported that even the King of Spain, in England for the last day of Ascot, had thought it 'very hot indeed'. Christabel was wearing a close-fitting dress of her own jazzy design – 'It was that summer when frocks were rather tight,' Mrs Naismith later recalled in court.

Mrs Naismith did not care to be referred to as a fortune-teller, a phrase suggestive of grubby diddicoys and palms crossed with silver. She was not even happy with 'clairvoyante'. She preferred the title 'psychological expert'. Her deductions, she insisted, were scientific, based on 'vibrations of hormones'. In court in 1922 and 1923, the lawyers were to have fun at her expense over these high-falutin pretensions.

Christabel could have walked to Hanover Street from her dressmaking shop and flat in Curzon Street, also in Mayfair. Today not much is left of the Hanover Street of 1921. The street still runs from Hanover Square (with Vogue House to one's right) and leads into Regent Street, opposite the windows of the former Dickins & Jones, an old-fashioned department store which closed down for good in 2005. No. 21 is the last door before you reach Regent Street. But the building Christabel found on this site was not this fascistic 1930s block. It was much more like the Belle Epoque edifice at No. 10.

Though Christabel often consulted clairvoyants, it was her first visit to Mrs Naismith, a woman of forty-five who had been recommended to her by a mutual friend. The introductory formalities over, Mrs Naismith gave her full attention to Christabel's hormones. After a few minutes of profound concentration, eyes closed, she peered into her client's eyes and asked, 'Do you know that you are five months pregnant?'

Christabel's immediate reaction was amusement. Not only was she unaware she was pregnant; because of her unusual marital arrangements, she was sure it was impossible. But Mrs Naismith was unwavering in her opinion. This in spite of the fact (as she later testified in court) that Christabel's figure – compressed by her tight frock – gave no hint of her condition.

Christabel took the view that there was small point in consulting an expensive clairvoyante if one dismissed her conclusion out of hand, however preposterous it might seem. So, four days later, she went to see a general practitioner, Dr John Baird McKenzie, at his consulting-rooms in Bedford Square, part of a building put up and owned by the Russell family. On examining her, McKenzie confirmed that she was indeed five months pregnant. (In court, asked what Christabel's reaction had been, he replied: 'To the best of my recollection she laughed and said something about she did not understand it.') When Christabel told the doctor that she had already had the news from a clairvoyante, he said, 'I could use her services!' But McKenzie's examination also revealed something that Mrs Naismith had not divined: that Christabel was still technically a virgin.

The lawyers might mock Mrs Naismith and her telltale hormone vibrations; but the proof of the pudding is in the eating. She did not gaze into a crystal ball, read runes and tea-leaves, or cut decks of Tarot cards; but she made an assertion which proved to be true. Mrs Naismith's clairvoyant (or scientific) reading marked the first time that the 'Russell Baby' affair was brought – however confidentially – into the open.

The soothsayer in *Julius Caesar* and the witches in *Macbeth* spoke prophecies darker than a childbirth, and Mrs Naismith predicted no murders; but if Christabel could have known the searing train of events of the next fifty-five years, to which Mary Naismith's opinion was the discreet prelude, she might not have giggled so lightheartedly on 17 June 1921.

2

Young Christabel

Bedtime!

Sitting there, she could recall with sudden strange clearness the days of her own childhood: the little old house in Sussex, with its two gables and the eaves beneath which martins used to make their nests. Always when she went to bed in the summer she had been able to hear, from just above her window-sill, the gentle conversation of the birds in their little mud houses. And, thinking now of those carefree, unfettered years, it seemed that there came back to her the scent of mignonette and tobacco-plant and briar which, on those still evenings, used to crowd up from the untidy, old world garden...

CHRISTABEL RUSSELL, *AFRAID OF LOVE*, 1925

Christabel Hart was born in 1895 at Hawley House, Tadley in Surrey, the second daughter of John and Blanche Hart. Her father, Colonel of the Leinster Regiment, was in his late forties. Christabel, whose fiery litigation would ensure that her son one day became a lord, had some blue blood of her own. Her mother, *née* Blanche Anstruther Erskine, was the granddaughter of a baronet, Sir David Erskine. His grandfather, the ninth Earl of Kellie, had sired a bastard Erskine son by a Swedish countess. In 1821 George IV had thought it best to regularize the situation with a baronetcy.

One of the nineteenth-century Erskines had received a telegraph announcing that the ancestral home of Cambo, Fife, had burned down. He telegraphed back: 'Rebuild at once and make it the largest house in Fife.' The result was a vast, sprawling mansion which Christabel considered 'one of the ugliest buildings for miles around'. Her opinion is endorsed by John Gifford, who in the entry for Cambo in his 1988 book on Fife, describes it as: 'Huge-scale suburbanish villa of the faintly Italianate Georgian-survival type', noting with further distaste the 'Frenchy plaster enrichment' on the drawing-room ceiling and a 'soggy acanthus leaf cornice' in the billiard room.

Blanche had been brought up in Paris and Brussels and spoke fluent French and German. She and John Hart married in 1892 and spent their honeymoon in New Zealand, where John had once thought of emigrating. While there they bought Hawley House sight unseen, on the strength of a flattering photograph sent out by an estate agent. The house turned out to be smaller and less distinguished than the photograph suggested, but it had a large garden, with a field and paddock. The elder child was born there in 1894. She was christened Gwenydd but was usually known as Gwen. (Blanche had Welsh ancestry, as well as Scottish.) Christabel followed eighteen months later. The family remained at Tadley until 1898, when they moved to The Cottage, Swallowfield, in Berkshire, a small Georgian house. The Harts were not particularly well off. Blanche made the girls' clothes, including a riding habit for Christabel, who learned to ride when she was five. She hunted for the first time at six, riding dashingly astride – though for the rest of her life she almost always rode side-saddle. It was the beginning of a lifelong passion. Already she tended to gallop out of view of her mother and the groom, careering recklessly across the fields and jumping high fences.

The girls attended no school but were taught at home by a grey-haired governess, Miss Twirt. The girls called her 'Twit'. They put a grass snake in her bath and a mouse in her flannel combinations. 'Poor old Twit!' Christabel recalled. 'She was so *feeble*. Fancy kneeling down to lace our boots and drinking coffee when we had stirred mud into it!' Colonel Hart, who referred to Miss Twirt as 'that sterile blancmange in the schoolroom', added to her miseries by insisting that she should teach the girls about 'comparative religions'. The son of a Devonshire parson, he felt he had had an overdose of Christianity in childhood. Miss Twirt was upset at being asked to bring up her charges as 'little heathens'. Gwen was studious, but Christabel took no interest in lessons. Though intelligent, she did not learn to read until she was twelve. She tried every stratagem to escape from the classroom. One day she tied together the frills of her knickers, trimmed with Madeira lace, and staggered round the room crying out that she was paralysed and could not walk.

Christabel got most of her education from her father. She plied him with endless questions and, when she was eighty, recalled that he was never lost for an answer. Miss Twirt's most congenial task was to teach the musical Gwen to play the piano. More than once, too, 'Twit' accompanied the 'cellist Madame Suggia, the subject of a famous Augustus John portrait. Blanche had known Suggia in her Paris days. The 'cellist came to stay at Broadhurst, a house between Burwash and Mayfield in Sussex, to which the Hart family had moved when the girls were in their teens. Impressed by Gwen's performance on the piano, Suggia allowed her to try the 'cello and she managed to coax some notes from it. Suggia suggested that she should come to Paris and study with her. The plan was not acted upon at once; but in 1912 John Hart died of pneumonia and Blanche decided to take up Suggia's offer. Gwen left for Paris and took lodgings with a family who were old friends of Blanche's.

Christabel was desolated by her father's death. She had learnt country lore from him – the names of wild flowers, how to recognize bird-songs or listen for the sucking plop of a rising trout. Now there was no one to answer her questions. However, Miss Twirt was replaced by a severe German Fraülein. One day she was so infuriated by Christabel's inattentiveness that, seeing her mouth gape into an enormous yawn, she jabbed the back of her throat with a penknife. Christabel quickly began to pay attention and to read books more challenging than her favourite, *Black Beauty*.

A year after Gwen went to Paris, Blanche and Christabel joined her. They moved into a small flat in Nôtre Dame des Champs, on the corner of the Boulevard Raspail. It was the Paris of Post-Impressionism and of newly liberated fashions for women. Hector Guimard's iron Métro entrances, with their sinuous green tendrils, still looked new. Gwen was continuing her lessons with Suggia. (A later family tradition suggests that she was also taught by Pablo Casals, who was for a time Suggia's lover.) Christabel enrolled in an art school. Her career as a fashion designer had its origin in the life classes. She would bring home her drawings of nude men and women and paint clothes on them. She was particularly intent on covering 'the malodorous hirsuteness' of men, with smart costumes – a practice which suggests that possibly a sort of revulsion against the animal physicality of men was already part of her character.

Most nights the girls went out dancing, in modish dresses made by their mother or themselves. Waltzes and polkas had given way to turkey-trots and tangos. Christabel performed exhibition dances in a local café with a fellow student, and taught the tango to make some extra money. The girls flirted but did not 'go steady' with any man. Eileen Hunter wrote in 1973:

'Mrs Hart ... did once ask Christabel what she knew about sex and received the emphatic reply that she "knew *all* about it". The reason for this inaccurate statement was given to me lately in her own words: "Neither Gwenydd nor I *wanted* to know, and in consequence we had years of *blissful* ignorance, and how thankful I have always been for them, for they were *such* happy years!" '

Here again one gets the sense of a disinclination to think about sex, let alone to indulge in it. Geoffrey Ampthill's view was that 'My mother was not very keen on what goes on in the bedroom.' The nearest to a kiss that she would allow her French admirers was a touch of the lips on a hand or a proffered cheek, or a 'butterfly kiss' – heads close enough to brush eyelashes. She did briefly accept a proposal of marriage from a young American student – not because she was in love with him or he had seduced her, but because he had stirred her imagination with tales of wild horses roaming the prairies. The engagement was broken off when he went back to the United States for the summer vacation.

In the summer of 1914 the three women returned to Broadhurst, with every intention of settling in Paris again after the holiday. Not all the neighbours wanted their daughters – still less their sons – to mix with the 'Frenchified' Hart girls. Christabel in particular, with her sleeveless tennis tops, shaven armpits and talk of tango teas, was thought 'fast'. But the girls took part in tennis parties, gymkhanas and dances. They went to London to see Basil Hallam, the matinée idol of the moment, in *The Passing Show* and – more to Blanche's taste – Chaliapin as Ivan the Terrible.

The First World War broke out and there was no question of going back to Paris. Blanche gave refuge to displaced foreigners, headed by Suggia and an emaciated lover twenty years her junior. ('Hide the spoons!' Blanche said.) Some Belgian refugee children also joined the household. Gwen's career as a 'cellist fizzled out when she fell in love with a young officer called Hilton Welford. They were married in 1915 with a guard of honour forming a canopy of crossed swords at the entrance to the church. Before the marriage, Blanche discussed the possible problems of a wedding night with Gwen, in Christabel's hearing. But Christabel did not want to hear.

Her ambition to be a fashion designer was put on hold. During the war, young society women like Lady Diana Manners became nurses; but Christabel went to make munitions at Woolwich Arsenal for a wage of 25s a week. She lodged at a nearby hostel, rising at five o'clock every morning. The Arsenal had changed little from the 'formidable town for manufacturing instruments of destruction' described by Robert Smiles in an 1890s article on 'Great industries of Great Britain'. It occupied 350 acres, with fifteen streets, eight avenues, four miles of normal railway track and seven of 18-inch track on which fifteen 'Little Wonder' locomotives pulled anything up to twenty tons of goods. About 14,000 hands were employed. There were long, low sheds, warehouses and furnaces, and innumerable machines for 'shearing, planing, shaping, slotting, boring and facing, mortising and tenoning, drilling and rifling'. Christabel was photographed in a leather apron, her hair tightly coiled round her head. She made double the number of shell caps in a day that the other women produced. She was promoted to be inspector of gun carriages.

Hard as she worked in the day, Christabel was always ready for a night out on the town. When her cab turned into the little cul-de-sac that leads off the Strand to the entrance of the Savoy Hotel, it seemed to her 'like turning into my own driveway'. Young officers bought her caviar and *foie gras* at Kettner's, Oddenino's or the Café Royal. Often she danced with them at the Grafton Galleries, where a 'negro band' played until three in the morning. Occasionally she stole a day's hunting on officers' chargers or was smuggled into Knightsbridge Barracks at night to give carrots to the troop horses. Sometimes the officers hired launches to take her back to Woolwich by river. There was no commitment on her part. Eileen Hunter writes:

'She hardly knew what it was to pay for a meal – "I almost began to think that girls never had to buy *food*." In addition many of her beaux proposed to her, and all were accepted: "I *never* refused an offer, though I was never in *love* with any one of them for more than three days at the *most*." So often was marriage urged on her in the dimly lit secluded sitting-room on the left of the main entrance in the Savoy – it still exists – that she named it "The Proposal Room". This frivolous attitude towards matrimony, which was not at all uncommon in those feverish wartime days, did not, as might have been expected, involve her in dramatic scenes of injury or heartbreak or, indeed, in any definite repudiation of the gaily undertaken engagement: "They just realised I didn't care any more when I began to refuse invitations and simply *drifted* away." '

Christabel's 'no strings attached' lifestyle could have continued for the rest of the war; but in April 1915 a lonely-hearts advertisement in the Personal columns of *The Times* changed her life for ever.

3

Small Ad: Big Consequences

'... there is nothing more distasteful to me than the idea of feeling
as one person with anyone ...'
CHRISTABEL RUSSELL TO JOHN RUSSELL, 1920

The origin of the Russell Baby scandal was a jolly jape by a group of midshipmen who put a lonely-hearts advertisement in *The Times* in 1915. In that year, the Hon. John Hugo Russell, heir to the barony of Ampthill, was an eighteen-year-old midshipman on the cruiser HMS *Defence* at Scapa Flow. He was nicknamed 'Stilts' because of his height (six foot five). He and his comrades Gilbert Bradley and Hugh Stevenson had served their time as midshipmen and were being posted as sub-lieutenants to take part in the Great War. Bradley and Stevenson were to be destroyer men and Russell was eventually going to submarines. The three men were granted ten days' leave before their new postings. How were they to kill that time? They had led very closeted lives, having gone to the Royal Naval College at Dartmouth when they were fourteen.

It was Bradley, a live-wire, who hit on the idea of placing an advertisement in the agony column of *The Times*. It read: 'Lost in the North Sea mist – three young midshipmen serving in the Grand Fleet would like to correspond with young ladies – Reply to Box No .... ' Stevenson recalled in the *Daily Mail* (26 February 1976), as an eighty-year-old lieutenant-commander:

'Hundreds of replies were received: extra mailbags were delivered to the gunroom. The commander visited the junior officers' mess to inquire what was going on with so much extra mail arriving.

'Many of the young ladies sent clippings of their hair or small portions of clothing, even petticoats, which was pretty daring then.

'Of course an advertisement like this would have been unthinkable before the war, but nice young girls were expected to do their bit and be jolly companions to beardless officers who were probably going to die anyway. [HMS *Defence* was sunk at the Battle of Jutland with no survivors a week after the three men left her.]

'It was terribly non-sexual. I suppose we had thoughts of sex at the back of our minds but really that wasn't something that occurred with girls of your own class until you married.

'What we wanted was companionship and jolly good fun – in fact, one nice girl to have fun with us all. But who were we to choose?'

First, the men eliminated all the girls who had not sent photographs of themselves. Then the young officers got together in the gunroom to choose a winner by a majority vote. Christabel's letter, with its photograph, won her the date. The sailors wrote to her and she promised to meet their train at King's Cross on 21 May, a month after they had put in the advertisement.

Standing at a prearranged place at King's Cross and wearing the colours she had promised, Christabel was first spotted by Hugh Stevenson. 'I thought what a stunning girl she was,' he recalled, adding, 'Much to my disappointment my mother was waiting and whisked me away to our home in Keston, near Bromley.' But he escaped from his family the next day and joined Russell, Bradley and Christabel. His two friends had installed themselves in the Waldorf Hotel.

'What a ten days we had [Stevenson told the *Mail*]! I don't think we slept very much – we went to every smart nightclub in town. We dined at Romano's in the Strand and used to go to those mildly wicked places like Murray's Club and Lady MacFarlane's place in Leicester Square. The entry used to be 5s and you could have a really good night out for £2.

'Russell paid all our expenses with his allowance from his father. It was the first time he'd ever really let his hair down. He'd led a very protected life and a rather dull one.

'His father [the second Lord Ampthill] had been Governor of Madras Province in India and then had come back to Oakley, the family seat in Bedfordshire, and had hardly ever moved away from there.[11]

'He didn't even rag Bertie, the Prince of Wales's younger brother who was below us at Dartmouth. I'm afraid we used to make fun of Bertie's stutter although I'm delighted that he was able to overcome that when he became King [George VI].'

When the young men's leave was up, Stevenson realised it was not he or John Russell who had made the biggest impression on Christabel. 'At the end of those ten days,' he told the *Mail*, 'she was deeply in love with Bradley. I'm absolutely sure of that.' Given Christabel's dizzy love-life, 'deeply in love' was probably an exaggeration; but there is no doubt that, of the three men, she found Bradley the most winning. She saw Hugh Stevenson half-a-dozen times in the next year, and Russell occasionally escaped from his family to take her out to dinner when on leave. But she spent most of her spare time with the debonair Bradley. He seemed able to wangle more leave, to obtain unobtainable theatre seats and to be led by head waiters to unbookable tables in exclusive restaurants. He was a favourite of the notorious Rosa Lewis of the Cavendish Hotel, 'the Duchess of Duke Street'. He took Christabel to the Cavendish to meet her, pointing out such celebrities as Nancy Cunard, Viola Tree and Lady Diana Manners with Duff Cooper ('They say she's going to marry him').[12]

Commander Stevenson recalled that 'during one leave [Bradley] even managed to get permission for both him and Christabel to go across to Paris - quite a difficult thing with the war on. When they came back they had decided to marry.' Christabel had already shown herself to be unorthodox in replying to the *Times* advertisement. To be going to Paris with an unmarried man was still more daring, even though they occupied separate rooms in their hotel. If in London it was 'Flick' Bradley who knew all the best places to dine and dance, in Paris Christabel took the lead. She knew the city intimately and had perfect command of the language. It is not surprising that in this setting she followed her habitual practice of accepting a proposal. Her mother and sister often helped her to write a 'Dear John'. Gilbert Bradley later said ruefully that he was 'never sure if we were engaged or not'. Like the other suitors, he was soon given his *congé*.

John Hugo Russell, after leaving HMS *Defence*, was first posted to a sloop in the Mediterranean, then served for the rest of the war in submarines, even though his height was a disadvantage in the cramped conditions. He was unaware of how much Christabel had been seeing Bradley. John Hugo would take her out to dinner, gaze at her adoringly and pay her shy compliments. She teased him but also flattered him. With her knowledge of munitions, she was up to asking him about the diving mechanism of a submarine. Though he did not dance with anything like the fluency of Flick Bradley, she enjoyed his company and felt affectionate towards him. She invited him to Broadhurst for weekends.

For John Hugo, the relaxed atmosphere of the Sussex farmhouse was soothing after the stiff formality of his parents' home. At Oakley, the butler would sound the dressing gong on the dot of seven o'clock; at Broadhurst John Hugo could just slip on a smoking jacket. And, when Christabel was out riding, he found Blanche Hart much easier to talk with than his own starchy mother. He confided in Blanche that he was in love with Christabel and wanted to marry her. But was Christabel in love with him? Nobody knew, least of all Christabel herself.

In December 1917 John Hugo proposed. Christabel accepted him, of course, in the way she accepted most proposals. Exultant, he left to rejoin his submarine. Back at Broadhurst for her next free weekend, Christabel told Blanche that she could not go through with the marriage. Stilts was not her kind of man: didn't ride much, didn't dance well enough. In January 1918 the usual tactful letter was concocted to tell Russell the engagement was off. He wrote back brokenheartedly, saying Christabel must let him know if she ever changed her mind.

One reason for Christabel's turning John Hugo down was that she still had feelings for Flick Bradley. He got in touch with her on his every leave. He was always fun to be with. He teased her about leading his friend Stilts up the garden path. 'You're a wicked siren,' he said. 'You'll have to settle for some common cad like me in the end.' Christabel decided to marry Bradley. At their next meeting, she told him she wanted to elope with him – *immediately*. He was happy to agree. Both thought that Scottish law countenanced instant marriage – everyone said so. Not Gretna Green, of course, but a respectable register office in Edinburgh. All they would need were their birth certificates. They took the night train the next day.

Sleepers on the train were occupied by brass-hats. Passengers overflowed from the compartments to sit on their suitcases in the corridor. Finally room was made for Bradley and Christabel in a compartment filled with rowdy Australian soldiers. There were whistles and winks when Christabel let slip that they were eloping. John Hugo shared a bottle of grog with the Anzacs and played cards with them. (Christabel was always teetotal.)

In Edinburgh the two made a disconcerting discovery: they could not marry without two weeks' residence in Scotland. Bradley was angry – not least because Christabel seemed rather relieved. In their circle, news leaked out about their excursion and their return unwed. They made light of the adventure but it did nothing to tone down Christabel's reputation for 'fastness'. She scraped up enough money to buy her own car, a little open tourer, and drove up to Northumberland to visit her sister Gwen, with Blanche in the passenger seat. Gwen's husband, Hilton Welford, had been invalided out of the army and they had gone to live at his home, Craig Hall, near Morpeth. By the end of the weekend Christabel had begun to make jokes about her elopement, which had been hanging in the air as a forbidden subject. Everyone agreed that, dashing and amusing as Flick Bradley was, he was not husband material: Christabel had had a lucky escape.

She was busy throughout the summer of 1918. Her little car gave her more opportunity to go riding and fox-hunting, although many packs had had difficulty in hanging on during the war. George Smith Bosanquet, who had started his own pack at Potter's Bar in 1908, had become one of her best friends. While he was away at the war, she often went to his kennels to give a helping hand and to exercise his horses. In September she received an unexpected letter. It was from John Hugo Russell. He told her how difficult he had found it to stay away from her, as she was seldom out of his mind. He had heard rumours that she had thought of marrying Flick Bradley but had changed her mind. Would she change it again and marry him? He loved her deeply. He was sure he could make her happy.

Christabel gave the proposal a lot of thought. The war was severely depleting the supply of eligible men. The mild and malleable Stilts would be a quite different proposition from Bradley, who had shown that he could be domineering. John Hugo she could manage. He would not 'bother' her if she did not want him to. He was clearly besotted: he would give in to her every whim. Besides, he really was rather endearing. And it in no way told against him that one day he was going to be a lord. On 4 October she wrote to him saying that if he was still of the same mind she would marry him. He was rapturous. He telegraphed immediately that he still loved her. He applied for special leave and a special licence and ignored his parents' protests: who was this nobody of a girl? Were the nasty rumours about her true? What was the hurry? Had he got her pregnant? He need not think they would attend the wedding.

The wedding took place at St Jude's Church in Kensington on 18 October 1918 – a small private ceremony, not a society splash. Blanche, Gwen and a small group of friends attended; Lord and Lady Ampthill did not. John Hugo and

Christabel caught the train to Harwich, his submarine base, where the first few days of their honeymoon were to be spent. After that, he was to take her to Oakley for a weekend to visit his parents: to that extent the Ampthills had relented. Like most young men, John Hugo's fellow officers found Christabel captivating. 'On one frolicsome occasion,' Eileen Hunter writes, 'she was pushed half a mile along a railway line in a truck by a round dozen of them.' No doubt John Hugo had to endure a lot of teasing, smirks and innuendoes from his friends when he left his submarine to spend some nights in a local hotel with his new wife. What the friends did not know was that on the day before the wedding Christabel had exacted a promise from him that they would not have children for at least a year or two. She had made it clear that during this period there was to be no sex.

Then came the visit to Oakley. 'We received her,' Lady Ampthill said later. It was a chilly reception. Christabel 'quite liked' her father-in-law but did not care at all for her mother-in-law. The dislike was entirely mutual. Lady Ampthill was the daughter of the sixth Earl Beauchamp and Woman of the Bedchamber to Queen Mary. It was said that her position at court and her friendship with the Queen had made her dream of an alliance between her son and the Princess Royal. Christabel could be considered a lady; but her Bohemian upbringing and her absolute indifference to convention did not recommend her. Lord Ampthill was rather taken with her and taught her to scull on the Great Ouse river which flowed through the Oakley estate. Christabel enjoyed that, but was indignant when Ampthill expressed strong disapproval of her going into the paddock and catching, saddling and bridling her own horse. Those were tasks for a groom, he said. Lady Ampthill looked sceptical on hearing of Christabel's fox-hunting experiences and said she was surprised that 'a girl of that kind' had gone hunting at all. She sniffed at mention of Bosanquet and Potter's Bar. *Potter's Bar!* You might as well go hunting in Hyde Park!

One habit of her father-in-law Christabel especially disliked. After lunch or dinner he would suddenly sound A on a tuning-fork and invite those present to join in a rollicking sea-shanty or folk-song. He sang horribly out of tune; the company winced. At the end of the visit, Lady Ampthill made one big concession. She said she would present Christabel at court so that she could take her proper place in society. One suspects that was more for Lady Ampthill's benefit than Christabel's, but John Hugo took it as a seal of approval of the marriage. He hoped that his mother would not discover that his dressing-room bed had been slept in – Christabel had turfed him out of their four-poster bed when his embraces had become over-ardent.

After the honeymoon, the couple moved into a small house in Lincoln Street, a demure Regency tributary of the Kings Road in Chelsea. John Hugo rejoined his submarine at Harwich. Until the war ended in November, he saw Christabel only when on leave. She enjoyed her new status. Although the Hon. Mrs John Russell received as many invitations to dine and dance as Miss Christabel Hart had done, they were not followed by propositions and proposals. She found the social scene just as much fun and a lot less bother. On Armistice Day she joined riotous celebrations in London, while John Hugo was leagues under the sea. Soon afterwards he applied for discharge from the Navy, but it was more than a year before he was released to take up a job he had been promised in the naval engineering branch of Vickers. On his infrequent leaves, he found Christabel was often too busy to spend much time with him. Entertaining as ever in the drawing-room, she was still a dead loss in the bedroom. She would not discuss the problem; she hardly acknowledged that there was one, beyond complaining to a friend, 'Every time I am nice to him, he behaves like an *animal!*' She seemed to be disgusted by the idea of the sexual act, and to regard the promise she had exacted from John Hugo as binding *sine die*. He sent her a copy of *Married Love* by Marie Stopes, in the hope it would convince her that sex within marriage could be enjoyable for a woman, even ecstatic. She wrote back:

'I am afraid pandering to the lower side of nature would in no way make me fonder of a person, and there is nothing more distasteful to me than the idea of feeling as one person with anyone. One's separate soul is the thing to aim at, and I'm afraid all the "beauty" which is attributed to sex relationship in "Married Love" is camouflage and self-justification.'

It was mystifying to John Hugo that the same woman could write to him a week or so later:

'I'm miserable without you and want to howl, how I wish you were here to put your arms around me and kiss my tears away ... I love my funny old angel of a husband and would kiss him sixty-five times ...'

4

Living (but not Loving) above the Shop

'It was very definitely haunted.'
LORD AMPTHILL IN INTERVIEW, 2003

As if the Great War had not taken a sufficient toll, a lethal influenza – 'Spanish 'flu' – swept through England, Europe and America just after it, killing more than had died in combat. 'In flew Enza' ran the refrain of a black-comedy song. The disease caught up with Christabel in September 1919 and turned into a serious and stubborn pleurisy. Her mother persuaded her not to go back to a job she had taken with Whitworth Engineering. Swiss air was considered the answer to lung complaints, so in December 1919 a small chalet was rented for Christabel near Lausanne and a temporary tenant was found for the Chelsea house. Soon Christabel was feeling much better and writing cheerful, loving letters to John Hugo telling him how beautiful the scenery was and what a good time she was having. The letters tended to begin 'Darlingest' or 'Darling old bean' and to end 'Your lovingest' or 'I love the nicest husband in the world' and to suggest that he should join her. She wrote incessantly and teasingly of the men she met. In one letter, she told him: 'I've a very nice man in tow ... one Buchanan, who is simply topping. We have formed a lifelong friendship. He has a wife and several large children. These he tactfully leaves behind.' In another letter, of March 1920, she told him:

'Darlingest Old Thing ... The people here are too cheery and priceless for words. I need hardly say your wife has a vast following of adoring young men. There are several of the type after my own heart – sleek Greeks and Argentines. There is a professional dancer, and I do tangos with him almost every night. I've four young men in the Bucks Light Infantry. They are priceless and so naughty and so is wife! I am so in love with a dago young man. You'd have spotted him as my future fate the moment you set eyes on him. He looks very ill, his hair is beautifully marcel waved and his clothes fit like gloves. He is very slim and has lovely hands ...'

After reading that, John Hugo hotfooted it to Switzerland. He enjoyed the days with Christabel, on sleighs and in bierkellers. In the nights, she was as aloof as ever. This time her excuse was that the bunks in the chalet were too narrow for even a cuddle. He had to admit this was true, and suffered tortures trying to fit his lanky frame into a sleeping position. When Christabel was well enough to return to England, she could not at once go back into the Chelsea house: the tenant's lease had not yet run out. So she accepted an invitation to stay in Redcliffe Square with Maud Acton, a woman she had known for some years. Miss Acton was amazed by, and perhaps envious of, Christabel's jazzy social life. In court later on, she was to be a hostile witness.

Lady Ampthill kept her promise and presented Christabel at court, in satin and ostrich feathers. But Christabel had no interest in 'taking her place in society' – doing the season at Epsom and Ascot, Henley and Lords. ('Though she loved fox-hunting, she loathed horse races,' her son remembered.) But still she enjoyed the good life, which cost more than John Hugo could provide with his salary from Vickers and his £100 allowance from his father. Money problems caused friction between the two young Russells. Christabel had an answer to the problem. In September 1920 she and her mother opened a dress shop at No. 1 Curzon Street, Mayfair, opposite what was later the Mirabelle restaurant.

The Ampthills were predictably appalled. Christabel's father had been a perfectly respectable army officer; but now his daughter was 'going into trade'. (It was just about this date that the parents of Hugh Gaitskell, the future Labour leader, refused to invite his prep-school friend John Betjeman to tea because his father was 'in trade', a cabinet-maker.) Other society ladies were to follow Christabel's lead: Mrs Dudley Coats opened her shop 'Audrey'; Poppy Baring launched 'Poppy'; Barbara Cartland's hat shop was 'Barbara' and Lady Dean Paul, mother of the notorious socialite Brenda Dean Paul, first worked in Baroness d'Erlanger's dress shop, then set up as a society dressmaker and tailor in Yeoman's Row, where Queen Mary and the Prince of Wales were among her clients. But Christabel Russell Ltd was a serious and successful enterprise which eventually employed almost forty people. It took some money to start. Christabel begged some of John Hugo's Naval gratuity, and borrowed from the bank. It *had* to be Mayfair. Among her admiring men friends was an American called Edgar Mayer who lived not far away, in Half Moon Street. He was an experienced businessman who gave her advice on setting up her company and became a director. Mayer was to figure prominently in the Russell Baby scandal.

The workrooms were presided over by Miss Cole, who was Christabel's right-hand woman for many years. Christabel designed most of the clothes herself, but they were cut by Mr Kuhl, a first-class tailor who also became a permanent member of the team. Christabel went to France for stocks of exclusive materials. Before long, business was booming. The Russells' attic private apartments were the last part of No. 1 to be completed. They were made comfortable and well decorated at Christabel's direction; but John Hugo was pained to discover that she had allotted them separate bedrooms. Already irritated by this situation, he made an angry scene when he found there was no hot water. Edgar Mayer, who heard of the difficulty, pressed both the couple to use his bathroom round the corner in Half Moon Street – a gesture that was to-be insinuatingly commented on in court.

When Geoffrey Russell was young, No. 1 had to be exorcized. 'It was very definitely haunted,' he recorded.

'The two famous chaps of the time for clearing ghosts out of places were a bus driver and his conductor. Chris pounced on them. They came and we both – my mother and I – felt clammy hands being put on our faces, *independently*. I was the one who first mentioned it – she said, "Well, that's exactly what I felt, too." These blokes came and did whatever they did; and they said that a footman had committed suicide. It makes sense, because where we lived was at the top of a big house, in the part where a footman would have been parked. Whether the suicide story was true or not, I don't know; but after the bus driver and his mate went away, we never felt the clammy hands again.'

In addition to Geoffrey Ampthill's memories, we have three vivid evocations of Christabel and her shop. Though they represent her in the 1930s, rather than in 1920, she had not changed in character; the shop was still at No. 1 Curzon Street; and Miss Cole and Mr Kuhl were still helping her run the business. In her biography of Christabel, Eileen Hunter remembered her first visit to the shop in 1934, when she (Eileen) was twenty-six. 'In those days,' she wrote, 'Curzon Street was not intruded on by blocks of flats and offices but maintained its strange and I thought haunted character throughout its length and breadth.' (Perhaps she had been told about the exorcism.) 'Small, elegant modistes and milliners, a few fine town houses, furnished flats and chambers that seemed designed for assignations, a hairdresser, an old-fashioned chemist, a florist, one or two shady hotels.' She further wrote of Curzon Street:

'It was bounded at the Berkeley Square end by the sinister and now vanished Lansdowne Passage – a descent of steep dark steps that never caught the sunlight ... It contained, as it still does, beautiful Crewe House, set back within a court-yard, and Sunderland House, but with the difference that they then belonged to and were lived in by their aristocratic owners and not, as today, to an industrial holding company and a bank respectively. Because of this change in ownership, which applies also to Lord Curzon's ivy-covered mansion, now a gaming club, and the house where Disraeli died, now tenanted by several advertising firms, these buildings though outwardly unaltered have all lost heart ...'

Eileen Hunter also recalled 'an odd run-down hotel, the Curzon, since demolished, where a waxen-faced porter sometimes took the air on the grimy steps' and the archway leading to Shepherd Market, 'where smart prostitutes leaned, or sauntered on high heels' *(Tout ça change ...)*.

Entering Christabel Russell's shop, she found herself in 'a thick-carpeted amber gloom', facing heavy velvet curtains which masked fitting-rooms. Hunter knew all about the Russell Baby case; and the severe-faced woman with shingled hair who came out to attend to her was not her idea of the Christabel she had read about. (Neither was she Christabel.) Hunter tried on several dresses. When she had made her choice, the fitter was summoned – 'dressed in black and with brilliant hennaed hair'. A young assistant entered Hunter's measurements in a notebook.

Swatches of material were riffled through and debated. Hunter was handed an estimate of the cost, and left the shop disappointed at having not met its owner.

On her second fitting, the fitter exclaimed, 'This looks so nice on you, Madam, I wish Mrs Russell could see it.'

'The assistant disappeared. I continued studying myself in the mirror when suddenly behind me, in reflection, the curtains parted and there – unmistakably – she was: tall, long-legged, Scandinavianly fair with tresses wound about a shapely head, a thrusting chin, high cheek bones, wide-open blue-grey eyes, splendid teeth and a quite exceptional personal elegance.'

That was in January. In June, Hunter's diary recorded, 'Tea Russell' and, eight days later, 'Party Christabel'. At the parties Hunter increasingly attended, Christabel was escorted by 'a selection from amongst the train of men who still surrounded her'. They would dine and dance 'in an atmosphere of enchanting frivolity'.

'She had a way of building intricate towers of verbal absurdity and then toppling them in a plangent drawling voice that was irresistibly comic ... and though she never smoked or drank, her enjoyment, although she worked hard all day, never faltered. Because she expected people – not only men – to do things for her, they did, lending her a car, a house, a horse, or bringing a cold soufflé to one of her parties made by their cook from a recipe she had admired. "Such a kind little man," she would say dreamily of an admirer who had placed a fully-staffed villa in the South of France at her disposal, and of another, "Every day he sent me a *green* orchid, won-der-ful at first, but after *weeks* one thought, oh *no*, not that awful *orchid*!" '

In spite of this luxurious lifestyle, Hunter noted that Christabel was personally frugal. 'She had made herself responsible not only for the education of ... Geoffrey, but also for her sister's four children, whom the death of their father had left in difficult circumstances.'

The second 'speaking likeness' of Christabel is in *Slipstream,* the autobiography of the novelist Elizabeth Jane Howard. Christabel was a friend of Howard's parents – a well-off timber merchant married to a daughter of the composer Arthur Somervell, who turned A.E. Housman's poems into sublime songs. Howard, who herself became a celebrated beauty, was much of an age with Christabel's son: Lord Ampthill said: 'I know I was madly in love with her at about the age of ten.' Howard was introduced to Christabel at one of her parents' dinner-parties.

'She was the personification of glamour – always beautifully dressed, with a perfect figure and hair immaculately set in the little flat ram's horn curls that were the fashion then. She spoke with a 1930s drawl, and her face was in keeping: She wasn't beautiful, but each feature was groomed to maximum effect: eyebrows plucked to perfect arches, dark blue mascara and eye shadow, and scarlet lips set in a smooth powdered expanse. She looked and spoke like a Noël Coward heroine, but there was far more to her than that. She was unlike anyone I'd ever met before. She treated me not as a child but as an equal; she wanted to know what I thought and listened when I told her. On top of that, she was very funny. Her attitude to everything wasn't quite like anyone else's, and was infinitely more interesting. Very gladly did I join the ranks of people who would do – and were often persuaded to do – anything for her.'

Christabel took Elizabeth Jane Howard in hand.

'When I was fourteen she told me I should not frown or wrinkle my forehead, "or you will have deep and completely unnecessary lines". I looked at her glamorous, smooth face: her large eyes, fringed with midnight blue mascara, that looked back at me with a penetrating intelligence that belied the drawl and make-up.'

Christabel also took Howard riding. She told her that every time she pulled on the reins she was hardening her pony's mouth. 'Talk to your horse, and use your knees,' she said. When Howard got to know her better, she concluded:

'Her appearance conformed to the fashion and good grooming of her time, but inside that was a formidable free spirit; she was utterly without fear, didn't give a damn about what anyone thought of her, remained herself in all circumstances, and with everyone. She enjoyed herself and everybody enjoyed being with her – a real and unusual life-enhancer.'

In the 1990s, Elizabeth Jane Howard made Christabel a leading character in her cycle of four novels, *The Cazalet Chronicle*. She appears as Hermione, Lady Knebworth, who is divorced, with one son, has a dress shop in Curzon Street, holds glamorous parties and loves riding. We first encounter her in *The Light Years*, Book One of the sequence, when the heroine Viola ('Villy') is being seduced into buying several dresses in the Curzon Street shop.

' "I think that is rather *you*."

' "It is lovely. It's just that I've never worn this colour."

'Villy was arrayed in one of Hermione's bargains: a dress of lime green chiffon, the bodice cut in a low V edged with gold beads and a little pleated cape that floated from the beaded shoulder straps. The skirt was simply cut in cunning gores that lay flat on her slim hips and flared out to a tremendous floating skirt.

' "I think you look divine in it. Let's ask Miss MacDonald what she thinks."

'Miss MacDonald instantly materialized. She was a lady of indeterminate age – always dressed in a grey pin-striped flannel skirt and a tussore silk blouse. She was devoted to Hermione, and ran the shop for her during Hermione's frequent absences. Hermione led a mysterious life composed of parties, weekends, hunting in winter and doing up various amusing flats she bought in Mayfair and let at exorbitant rents to people she met at parties.

'Everybody was in love with her: her reputation rested upon the broad front of universal adulation. Whoever the current lover might be was lost in a crowd of apparently desperate, apparently hopeless suitors ...'

We must bear in mind that this is fiction; but it meshes convincingly with the pen-portrait of Christabel in Howard's autobiography. As the same scene in the novel develops, Howard depicts Christabel as a canny businesswoman.

'Villy, standing in a kind of trance in the diaphanous frock that seemed to have turned her into some fragile exotic stranger, realised that Miss MacDonald was registering appreciation.

' "Might have been made for you, Mrs Cazalet." "The midnight blue would be more *useful*."

' "Oh, Lady Knebworth! What about the *café-au-lait* lace?" "That's brilliant of you, Miss MacDonald. Do fetch it."

'The moment Villy saw the coffee lace she knew that she wanted it. She wanted all of them, and them included a wine-coloured moire with huge puff sleeves made of ribbon rosettes that she had tried on earlier.

' "It's utter agony, isn't it?" Hermione had already decided that Villy, who had come in for two frocks, should buy three of them, and knowing Villy, it was essential that she should forgo one. Stage whispers ensued.

' "How *much* are they?"

' "Miss MacDonald, how *much?*"

' "The moire is twenty, the chiffon is fifteen, the lace and the midnight blue crêpe could be sixteen each. Isn't that right, Lady Knebworth?"

'There was a brief silence while Villy tried and failed to add things up. "I can't have four, anyway. It's out of the question."

' "I think," said Hermione consideredly, "that the blue is a bit on the obvious side for you, but the others are all perfect. Supposing we made the moire and the lace fifteen each, and threw in the chiffon for ten? How much does that come to, Miss MacDonald?" (She knew perfectly well, but she also knew that Villy was bad at sums.)

' "That comes to forty, Lady Knebworth."

'And before she knew it, Villy had said, "I'll take them. It's wicked of me, but I can't resist it. They're all so ravishing. Goodness, I don't know what Edward will say."

' "He'll adore you in them. Have them packed, Miss MacDonald. I'm sure Mrs Cazalet will want to take them with her." '

Whether or not Christabel was that smart an operator, she was a single mother with expensive tastes and other people to support. One has to admire her resourcefulness and energy in running a successful business for nearly forty years.

5

A Shattering Surprise for 'Stilts'

'It seems inexplicable that you should be having a baby,
and it's very hard to keep rotten thoughts out of my mind.'
JOHN HUGO RUSSELL, LETTER TO CHRISTABEL RUSSELL, JUNE 1921

John and Christabel Russell had few friends in common. One such was Gilbert Bradley – surprisingly, perhaps, in view of Christabel's dalliances with him in Paris and Edinburgh before her marriage. There seemed to be an acceptance that the best man had won and that 'honour among officers' would preclude any amorous advances from Bradley. After all, if anybody knew how resistant Christabel was to sexual propositions, it was John Hugo.

Bradley enjoyed the company of both, but seldom together. He would spend a quiet evening at Curzon Street having a drink with John Hugo and playing cards, while Christabel was off dancing with another man. Or he would be Christabel's dance partner for the evening. They would whirl their way from the Carnival Club to the Silver Slipper to the Florida with its revealing glass floor, lit from below. Or they might join the Bright Young People at one of Ma Meyrick's clubs, hoping there would not be a police raid, and only call it a night at 2.0 a.m. or later.

One day, after Bradley had driven her home to Curzon Street, Christabel could not find her door keys. She and Bradley repeatedly rang the doorbell and thundered on the knocker, with no effect. John Hugo must have been out, or deeply asleep. It was impossible to ask for a room in a hotel at that late hour, with no luggage, and they did not want to rouse Christabel's mother, who had been ill. There was nothing for it but to go back to Bradley's flat in Onslow Place, South Kensington. By their account, he lent her his bed and dossed down on two chairs in the sitting-room.

In the morning, Bradley telephoned John Hugo, who said he would come round at once, bringing some day clothes for Christabel. The three of them had breakfast together, joking about the awkward predicament of the night before. Nobody suggested that anything improper had happened. When Christabel played truant from the shop in the daytime, it was mainly to go riding and fox-hunting. Here again John Hugo was out of the picture. She was often accompanied by a twenty-three-year-old artillery officer called Lionel Lesley Cross, whom for some reason she called George[13]. He was stationed near Salisbury, and from time to time (with her customary indiscretion) Christabel would stay at the County Hotel, Salisbury, in a room next to his. The next day she would hunt with him or check on the progress he was making with a young horse he was schooling for her. As a bonus, he was, she said, 'a divine dancer'. He was impressionable. When she spoke of her frequent buying trips to Paris and noticed his admiration, she suggested he might come along some time. The prospective jaunt was discussed in John Hugo's presence. He seemed to find nothing strange about their plan and raised no objection. He even saw them off at Victoria Station. Christabel and Cross stayed in the same Paris hotel – the Hôtel Chatham[14] – in separate rooms.

John Hugo found his own bizarre amusements. He liked to attend fancy-dress parties in drag. With his great height, he was never likely to be mistaken for a woman; but he spent a long time getting ready. First, he applied elaborate *maquillage* to his face. Then he would put on a ruched taffeta dress with a sash. A velvet tam o'shanter topped his dark curly wig. He was specially proud of having found a pair of pink velvet pumps with diamanté buckles, that fitted his huge feet. 'They must have belonged to a giantess,' he said. Christabel was revolted when he came to her bedroom after a party and left a sticky lipstick imprint on her cheek. Sometimes he tried to take things further; but she continued to insist that he must content himself with cuddles. She did not understand his frustration and despair.

Yet the same Christabel could take a great interest in other people's problems and aspirations. When buying a tie in Selfridge's one day she got chatting to a young salesman, Billy Milton. He poured out his troubles, telling her that his real ambition was to be a musician. His father, disapproving, had made him take the Selfridge's job at £1 a week, as soon as he left Lancing College (where he had been a schoolfellow of Evelyn Waugh and Tom Driberg). Christabel asked him to play and sing at one of her parties. Liking his performance, she advised him to give an audition at Chez Henri Club in Long Acre – a street once owned by the Russell family. She said she would organize the whole thing and would take along a large party of friends to give him support. In his 1976 memoirs, enviably entitled *Paradise Mislaid,* Milton recalled:

'Hastily I put an act together: songs, piano solo and finishing with a dance. To my delight the audition was a success and resulted in my first professional engagement. Salary ten pounds a week. The Houston Sisters (Renée and Billie) were the stars of the Chez Henri cabaret and I appeared each morning at 1.00. Both acts were accompanied by the house band, Charlie Kunz and his Orchestra.'

Thus Christabel launched Milton's successful career. Soon he attracted the notice of the French dancer, singer and actress Mistinguett (Jeanne Marie Bourgeois), who asked him to be her regular accompanist at the Café de Paris, London. As Mistinguett was in her fifties (she had been a mistress of Edward VII) and Milton was in his twenties, a gossip columnist commented: 'Grandma has discovered a new grandson.' Milton never forgot Christabel's kindness to her, nor her 'compelling beauty'.

Figure 1 Cartoon by Tor: Billy Milton accompanies Mistinguett

In August 1920 occurred an incident which brought the worsening feeling between John Hugo and Christabel into the open. John Hugo drove down to Broadhurst one day. He found that Christabel had arrived before him and that she was out motoring with Flick Bradley. Angered by this, he later took Bradley aside and allegedly demanded: 'Are you playing hanky-panky with my wife?' Bradley replied enigmatically: 'It would be much better if Christabel had children.' (John Hugo could not have agreed more.) From the time that she heard of this interview, Christabel would not even allow her husband to kiss her – or so it was later claimed. John Hugo's frustrations boiled over in the later months of 1920. Christabel's maid constantly heard him shouting, making scenes and slamming doors. Christabel thought he was becoming thoroughly deranged. One night he crashed into her bedroom as she slept, waved a shotgun around and threatened to shoot her, her cat or himself. He told her of the nights he had lain in his own bed with the gun's barrel pointing at his head, the stock between his feet and his toes on the trigger ready to blow his brains out. After the threats, he broke down into sobbing entreaties and apologies. He later wrote to her: 'I feel so sorry for you, as life with a "mad" husband at No. 1 [Curzon Street] must have been awful,' adding in a postscript: 'Tell me if I ever start "going cracked" as I did at Curzon Street.'

Neither of the couple at this stage had discussed any problems with family or friends. They did not ask for separate rooms when staying in other people's houses. In public they treated each other with affection. Yet Blanche Hart could see that all was not well with the marriage; and Lady Ampthill felt a deepening resentment towards Christabel for the same reason. John Hugo and Christabel were to stay with the Ampthills just before Christmas 1920. They arrived, bearing presents, on 18 December, and were assigned a large guest room with an adjoining dressing-room. When bedtime came, after an evening of frosty conversation, John Hugo emerged from his dressing-room and told Christabel she had no choice but to let him share her bed, as the one in the dressing-room had not been made up. What happened in that bed, during the nights the young Russells were at Oakley, was to be the subject of acrimonious dispute in court. The holiday ended with little overt hostility, though Lady Ampthill acidly remarked that she thought Christabel's dressmaking talents would be better employed making a layette for a baby, than clothes for society women.

Relations between John Hugo and Christabel deteriorated still further after they returned to Curzon Street. Any attempt by him to enter her bedroom was repulsed. They spent no more weekends together. But on 24 February 1921 the couple dined with the Ampthills in London. Lady Ampthill was bristling with antagonism towards Christabel. She had been interrogating her son, on one of his solo visits to Oakley, and had a pretty clear idea of what was happening – or rather, not happening – in the marriage. She noticed that Christabel had stopped wearing her wedding-ring. (Geoffrey Ampthill thought there was a good reason for that: his mother was embarrassed at the way her work in munitions had roughened her hands, and did not want to draw attention to them.) At the end of the dinner, Lady Ampthill asked Christabel why she had taken marriage vows before God and witnesses and had not kept them. Her meaning was quite clear. Christabel, furious that John Hugo had, as she saw it, betrayed their intimate secrets, replied that she had made the vows with calculated reservations. She left no doubt in Lady Ampthill's mind that she was not having normal marital relations with John Hugo, and, in effect, told her mother-in-law to mind her own business.

After this, everybody concerned, including John Hugo and Christabel, began to talk about ending the marriage: John Hugo reluctantly, Christabel negligently, Blanche and Lady Ampthill seriously. Both the mothers understood that the marriage had not been consummated: John Hugo was being 'denied his rights'. Annulment was suggested, and discussed by the two mothers on 22 March 1921. But of course it was up to John Hugo to take proceedings, and he was still hoping for a happy ending. By this time he had moved more or less permanently to Oakley. Christabel joined her mother in Harrington Gardens, South Kensington, the flat which Blanche Hart, economizing, had bought after selling Broadhurst in Sussex.

Lady Ampthill nagged John Hugo and never lost an opportunity of asking him when he was going to set about getting rid of 'that woman'. He felt he would not be able to think straight unless he could live somewhere on his own, preferably in the country. When a suitable cottage within commuting distance from London came on to the market, he viewed it and wanted to buy it, but did not know how to finance the purchase. His father refused to help him; so, astonishingly, John Hugo turned to his commercially successful wife. The approach ended in a blazing row. Christabel may have regretted her words, as she wrote to John Hugo on 20 May 1921: 'Awful pity to be so venomous with each other and bad for general tempers.' She said she was laying out her 'points' to him 'so that you can be quite clear and get them into your thick cranium'. She could not afford to share a cottage in the country. Even with combined resources they could not pay for a house in London. 'We are both too extravagant and would leave it all to maids and get rooked – besides which, I am never going to put myself in the position of being dependent on you or your family for one penny, as after the very charming things they have said about me and my extravagance I am taking no further risks.' (It is not clear why the couple were no longer able to live at Curzon Street: possibly the business had expanded into the private apartments.)

In the letter Christabel told John Hugo how happy she was living with her mother. 'She is never jealous of my friends, which in you infuriates me.' She referred to the 'ridiculous scenes of melodrama at Curzon Street' and continued:

'If you want a divorce you must take the necessary steps to get it ... I can do nothing to oblige you in that way! You must do what you think right and best. You know my present feelings ... Things could change but probably not worth waiting for. If I were you I'd get a job abroad for a few years. I might be rich enough when you came back to share a place in the country, but if you prefer the idea of divorce you must do that.'

She could never resist ending her letters on a jocular note; but he replied seriously: 'I repeat, I want to remind you that any time you are ready to take up married life properly, I am only too ready to do everything possible; but I have felt so messed about for the past year that my patience is running out. I may have to see my lawyers.'

After much heart-searching, he did decide to see his solicitor. That happened on 21 June 1921; but he suddenly remembered that the next day was Christabel's birthday; so instead of telling her what he had done, he sent her fruit and flowers. She wrote to thank him, saying that she must see him *most* urgently and asking him to lunch with her on 23 June. She signed off with the usual teasing aside: 'Do try not to wear a soft hat and have a hole in your elbow: it does cause me such grief.' John Hugo agreed to lunch with her, and found her in amiable spirits. He did not discover her reason for wanting to see him so urgently until they went for a walk afterwards. The news she broke stopped him in his tracks: *'I am over five months pregnant.'* She told him about her meetings with the clairvoyante and Dr McKenzie. With John Hugo, incredulity turned into delight. He did not suggest that there was any question over the baby's parentage: something very strange must have taken place without his and Christabel's being aware of it. For her part, Christabel said she was surprised by feeling thrilled at the idea of having a baby. John Hugo said he felt the same, and suggested that the Duke of Bedford might be godfather. They parted with a warm embrace.

Before returning to Oakley that day, John Hugo wrote Christabel a long, enthusiastic letter, telling her how pleased he was about the baby. They must get together to give it a real chance.

'We must forget the past ... [he wrote]. Happiness is all important. I would be perfectly happy if only I could feel you were happy too ... I will always love you but didn't enjoy being on chance acquaintance terms, there's no use pretending it was anything else; but for the baby's sake I'll keep my distance if that's what you want. It's your move, old thing. I will try to do all I can to make you happy.'

In his mood of qualified euphoria, John Hugo was unprepared for the disbelief and scorn with which his mother greeted his news. She was certain that Christabel had been unfaithful, and planted strong doubts in his mind. He now wrote to Christabel (24 June):

'It seems inexplicable that you should be having a baby, and it's very hard to keep rotten thoughts out of my mind. I have come to the conclusion that a mistake has been made. I wish to heaven we could have a baby ... I would have been overjoyed. Darling thing, I've been through hell.'

He followed this up with another confused letter.

'It is quite impossible under the circumstances for us to have a baby, as nothing short of a miracle would have made it possible for us to have had conjugal relations unawares ... That miracle may have occurred but it is extremely unlikely, so if you are going to have a baby *I am not the father.*'

After this flat statement came an anguished concession: 'I absolutely believe in you and know that you are as honest and straight a person as ever was.' He ended the letter, 'It's just inexplicable,' and sent her his best love.

Blanche Hart was sure that the baby was John Hugo's. She had been to see Dr McKenzie with Christabel and heard him say that conception was possible from partial intercourse. She had been full of hope when Christabel had let her see John Hugo's first letter. When Christabel showed her the two follow-up letters from Oakley, both women were in no doubt as to who was influencing John Hugo. Christabel replied to him that she could not understand his recent letters. Would he please come and see her and explain exactly what he meant?

He telegraphed that there was no point in his coming to see her until he had seen her doctor. He had made an appointment – he quoted the day and time – and would meet her at the surgery if she wished. Christabel immediately went to see Dr McKenzie and showed him John Hugo's letters. It was arranged that both of the couple should be at his consulting rooms the next day, 29 June. John Hugo duly arrived, but accompanied by his solicitor, Richard Taylor. It was Taylor who asked the doctor all the questions, and he did not allow Christabel to be present. Obviously put out by this procedure, McKenzie answered Taylor's questions as briefly as possible. He afterwards said he thought it a breach of professional conduct to discuss a patient with a third person; but he did reply to John Hugo's query as to whether it was possible to conceive by partial intercourse with a curt, 'Barely possible.'

In July 1921 the Russell family declared war on Christabel. She was formally notified by John Hugo's solicitor that he would be sending her a petition for divorce on account of her adultery. Hilton Welford, Christabel's brother-in-law, went to Oakley to make an appeal to John Hugo, with whom he was on friendly terms. John Hugo spoke to him frankly and miserably: 'There is an awful fuss on between me and Chris.' Welford said he had heard Christabel's side of the story and had come to see whether he could 'straighten things out'. John Hugo confided that he had many times attempted sexual relations with his wife. He showed Welford a memorandum listing occasions when he and Christabel had shared a bed. He included in the list 18 and 19 December 1920, but added a note that he could not remember what had happened between them then.

Welford's comment on this was that he must have been more successful than he thought, as he was undoubtedly the child's father. John Hugo said it might be so, but would not directly admit it. He did admit that he could not name anyone as co-respondent and that he believed Christabel was 'absolutely straight'. He told Welford he was most anxious to meet her again. He exchanged telephone numbers with him with the idea of arranging the meeting with Christabel. When they parted, he handed him the memorandum of dates, saying, 'My father would kill me if he knew I was giving you this.' Welford did not succeed in organizing a meeting between John Hugo and Christabel, although she was receptive to the idea. The Ampthills intervened implacably and insisted that all further dealings must be through solicitors. Later Christabel wrote to her friend Elfrida Shorten, 'I wonder if John realised he could make things alright forever by just one step nearer me?'

Christabel saw that the time had come for her to consult a solicitor. Withers & Co were selected. She developed a rapport with Mr (later Sir John) Withers.[15] He recommended as counsel Patrick Hastings KC, who agreed to take on the case. The preparation of the brief was deferred until after the baby was born, as apparently the case could not be heard until the following summer, almost a year ahead. On 4 July Christabel wrote Maud Acton a letter of bravado and barbed levity.

'Accy, darling ... I'm having a priceless time. John, after evincing the greatest delight over the child, and deciding that the Duke of Bedford was to be Godfather, is now trying to divorce me! As I've never done anything he hasn't been aware of, and since I always told him, if only to provoke him, of all my flirtations and frivolities, and he knows of my weekends and other indiscretions, I don't see that he has a leg to stand on.

'I'd rather the devil himself was the father ... and if I produce a horror with sticking out teeth and adenoids we'll feel pretty sure about its parentage!

'My Solicitors are priceless and I long for the fray. You will come daily and take a box, or whatever it is ... If only I could take it seriously it would be more seemly, but for the last few days I have been in the wildest hysterics over it! Everyone knows of it now so I see no point in keeping it dark.

'Do think of the rows of "Co's" [co-respondents] lined up for trial!'

On 15 October 1921 Christabel gave birth to a 10? lb boy. To her own surprise she was enchanted with her baby. Blanche was amazed at the change in her daughter. If only John Hugo could see her and the child, surely he would change his mind. After consulting Withers, she suggested that Christabel should write once more to appeal to John Hugo. The solicitors vetted and edited the letter, but Christabel hoped it still had enough of her in it to touch his heart.

'Dear John,

I understand from my Solicitors that you are denying the baby is yours. Don't you think it is rather absurd to take this line? I know that you don't in your heart really and truly believe it. If nothing else I have always been straight. We'll have to do something drastic for the sake of the baby (he is an awfully nice one). This sort of situation is absurd, and it's up to us to make an effort.

'It is extraordinary how it changes one's outlook having a baby. I feel quite different about it all now, and we have got to think of him.

'Will you, for his sake, if you don't still like me a bit, start afresh?

'We've both got to chuck pride to the winds and try and make a decent sort of home for the boy.

'All the past must be washed out, and we must both try all we can. I am prepared to do so if you will. You can't have forgotten that you once did like me a lot. I, too, don't forget that the baby must have a lot of you in him. You only have to see him to see how exactly like you he is.

'Yours sincerely, if you will –
Chris'

It was no use. To have had any chance of persuading John Hugo to relent, Christabel would have needed to tell him she was ready to accept normal conjugal relations; and in any case it is doubtful if, at this stage, he would have made any move without his parents' blessing. There was no response to the letter. Christabel's hopes faded. She wrote sadly to Elfrida Shorten.

'I've got to vindicate myself and my baby before the world. I sometimes wonder whether Stilts really thinks the baby isn't his ...

'I wonder if I love my son more than other people? Now that I have to fight for him I suppose it is only natural.

'I think having a child is the most wonderful thing in the world. Fancy me saying that and being just an ordinary sentimental woman.

'Every time I look at that baby I see Stilts coming out in him. I adore him and he's got to have his rights ...'

Nine months elapsed between the birth of the baby – Geoffrey Denis Erskine Russell – and the divorce trial. Christabel was busy with the shop – its clientèle swollen by the curious. She and the infant continued to live with Blanche in South Kensington, and Christabel took her solicitor's advice not to be seen out alone with any man. Indeed, some of her former escorts were not too keen to be seen out alone with her, as the scandal slithered its way into gossip columns and ribald banter in clubs and pubs. Gilbert Bradley and 'George' Cross were horrified and angry to find that they were being cited as co-respondents.

As the date set for the trial drew nearer, Christabel's attitude hardened. She would fight to the death, convinced that right would prevail in the end. At the same time, she was becoming aware of the degree to which she had left herself open to criticism, and wrote with rueful humour to Maud Acton.

'Darling Accy

'Of course Stilts can make up a thousand things against me without going an inch out of his way.

'Every weekend I've spent with George Cross ... I spent one night at Gilbert's flat and Gilbert had to telephone to Stilts to bring my clothes so that I could get home again ... and various others; all these John knows about so he has all the evidence he requires.

'However, I have a maid as witness that he used to burst into my room at all hours of the night and he has been found out already in two flagrant lies to the Solicitors, so on my side my case is frightfully strong. But I've been so indiscreet all my life that he has enough evidence to divorce me about once a week! ...'

6

'Is this a Man or a Jelly?'

'She added that her husband had behaved like a Hun, and that he walked in his
sleep, and said: "Isn't it curious? That's how it happened." '
MRS MORESBY-WHITE, TESTIFYING ABOUT CHRISTABEL RUSSELL
IN THE CASE OF *RUSSELL* V. *RUSSELL*, 1922

John Russell's suit for divorce – the case of *Russell* v. *Russell, Bradley, Cross and a
man unknown* – opened on 7 July 1922. The setting was a courtroom in the Probate,
Divorce and Admiralty Division of the Law Courts in the Strand – known in the
legal profession as 'Wills, Wives and Wrecks'.

The public had been well informed about the hearing in advance, in titillating
paragraphs in the newspapers. The gossip columns hinted at upper-class scandal,
adultery, deviant sex, medical abnormalities and suicide attempts. The heroine (or
was she the villainess?) was a beautiful young woman fighting for her reputation
and for the right of her baby to inherit a title. The hero (or was he the villain?) had
served with bravery in the late war.

The queue of people wanting to attend the trial stretched down the Strand.
Chauffeur-driven limousines dropped off elegantly dressed ladies and debutantes,
who jostled against shop girls and housemaids. Gentlemen left their clubs and
joined lawyers, City businessmen and cabbies in the crush. People fought their way
in; the public gallery was full to bursting point. The press were there in force,
shorthand notebooks at the ready.

The *News of the World* set the scene for its readers:

'Day by day since the hearing began, fashionable women and blasé young men
have clamoured for admission to the court, as though it were some popular place
of entertainment. The result is that those with legitimate business there have
difficulty in getting inside. The seats at the rear and in the gallery are always
uncomfortably crowded. No less attractive setting could be found for an enthralling
matrimonial drama. Around its dull oak-panelled walls are hundreds of musty law
books behind wire netting. In addition to these a score or more are ranged at a table
at the right hand of the President, Sir Henry Duke, who conducts the hearing.

'Prominent on the wall behind him is a golden anchor, the symbol of the
Probate, Divorce and Admiralty Division. A much begrimed map of Jutland and

the North German coast which hangs aslant behind the jury box gives a further suggestion of maritime affairs...

'The President leans back in his chair most of the time taking copious notes, glancing up occasionally through horn-rimmed glasses with a word of advice to counsel to confine their questions strictly to the point or to explain some technical matter to the jury.'

The 'special jury' consisted of ten men and two women. No one was quite sure for what qualities they had been selected. Experience in the marital bed? Medical knowledge? More probably for their uprightness, suggested by their membership of religious organizations or Conservative clubs.

All were bidden to stand as the President, Sir Henry Duke, entered, an imposing figure in his wig and robes (Colour plate 7). The Clerk of the Court intoned the petition:

'The Hon. John Hugo Russell of Oakley House, Oakley, Bedfordshire, son and heir of Lord Ampthill, prays in this suit for the dissolution of his marriage with the Hon. Christabel Hulme Russell, whose maiden name was Hart. He alleges that she has committed adultery with Gilbert Murray Bradley and with Lionel Lesley Cross, and also that she has committed adultery with a man unknown, who is the father of her child born on October 15 last.'

The respondent (Christabel) and both co-respondents, by their answers, denied the allegations of adultery.

The Ampthills had procured for Stilts the best legal team that money could buy: Sir John Simon KC, Douglas Hogg KC, Robert Bayford KC and the Hon. Victor Russell. (Bayford had known Stilts's father when they were both leading Oxford oarsmen in the early 1880s; Victor Russell was a younger brother of Lord Ampthill.) Christabel, with the takings from her dressmaking business and some help from her mother, had managed to recruit a good brace of counsel: Patrick Hastings KC and Digby Cotes-Preedy, later a county court judge. The two co-respondents were represented by Sir Ellis Hume-Williams KC and Richard Bush James, a thirty-three-year-old Old Harrovian who had served in the Great War and become a captain in the Royal Horse Guards.[16]

Hume-Williams was a very experienced barrister who had taken silk in 1899 and been elected Conservative MP for the Bassetlaw Division of Nottinghamshire in 1910. We know from his memoirs exactly how he was drawn into the Russell case.

'I well remember the first I heard of it. It was in August 1921. The House [of Commons] was still sitting and I was consequently detained in London, and like every other member of the House was very tired and bad-tempered. There arrived one day a prominent solicitor, a partner in a large and important firm, who had said he wished to see me, at the House if necessary, as the matter was urgent. He arrived at the House, sent for me and began by saying, "A client of ours is about to have a baby." It really seemed to me not worth getting me out of the Chamber into the Lobby to make such a statement, and I expect I was rather bad-tempered. "Which of the partners – " I began, but was instantly stopped by their outraged representative who said, "You mistake. That is not the importance of the information, the interesting fact is that the lady who is about to have the baby is a virgin." I remember saying, "Well, really, on a hot day like this, and when we are all tired out, to come down and make a statement of that sort to me is more than human patience can stand." The gentleman, however, assured me it was a fact, and indeed added that he spoke on the testimony of a well-known doctor.

'So the matter had to be considered, and I, of course, said what was obvious, namely, that if it were so, and if the lady were threatened with trouble in consequence of her condition, she must be taken at once to the most prominent gynaecologists in London in order that they might verify the fact, and I mentioned the names of several eminent gentlemen whom I had come to know very well during my practice in the Divorce Court. It is curious that during the long course of the trial, the statement which so surprised me was about the one thing as to which there was, and could be, very little dispute. Indeed, the various gynaecologists who were called treated with contempt the astonishment of the laymen at such a condition of things, and proved that in their practice the condition of the lady, although "virgo intacta", was far from being so astonishing, and was indeed not a very unusual event.'

For this first *Russell* v. *Russell* trial, there exist no official transcripts of court proceedings; but *The Times* published reports after each day (so detailed that they upset King George V);[17] and these are reinforced by those of the *Daily Mail* and other newspapers, which often printed more prurient revelations, omitted by *The Times* as beneath its Olympian dignity. Even the American papers took an interest: this was England as they liked to picture her – aristocracy and sexual inhibitions.

Sir John Simon made the opening speech. He was, without doubt, a Brain: he had taken a First in Jurisprudence at Oxford and was a Fellow of All Souls. But he was often called 'shy', sometimes 'cold'; and he made it a little too obvious that, for him, the law was never more than a stepping-stone towards a career in politics. In his favour, it has been written: 'In court his strength lay in his ability to analyse and clarify issues of great complexity. His preferred style was to persuade a jury through logic and reason rather than oratory or histrionics.'[18]

Simon accused Christabel of having concealed her pregnancy from her husband for months; 'and when it could no longer be hidden she told him a fantastic story'. He implied a social disparity between John Hugo and Christabel. 'Mr Russell was the eldest son of Lord Ampthill, and any son of his might become entitled in time to bear the honoured name of Baron Ampthill.' Simon added: 'If this child, as we propose to establish before you, was not a child of which Mr Russell was the father, then you will see that there is a duty upon you which you will have to discharge with the greatest care and circumspection.'

He outlined John Hugo's naval service and said the young man had met Christabel in 1915. No mention was made of the *Times* personal ad: the jury might have thought less of a man who found a wife by that means. Nearly every part of Simon's opening speech was intended to show Christabel in a bad light.

'The petitioner and the respondent became engaged in December, 1917, at Broadhurst, Sussex, where Mrs Hart was living, and Miss Hart was at that time employed on war work at Woolwich. She was a year older than Mr Russell, who was then an officer in a submarine based at Harwich. Almost the first thing that happened was that she broke off the engagement, saying that she was not "a marrying sort", and she added that there was no question of another man. Mr Russell was deeply grieved. Soon afterwards Miss Hart went to Scotland with Mr Bradley, one of the co-respondents, with the apparent intention of getting married there. A good many people appear to be under the impression that if a couple desire to be married secretly and expeditiously, the best place for the ceremony is Scotland. That romantic view does some injustice to the cautious Scots character. Miss Hart and Mr Bradley came back next day without having been married. There was then an interval until October, 1918, when Miss Hart wrote to Mr Russell and said that she was willing to marry him if he still wanted to marry her. He telegraphed "Yes", and as soon as his naval duties permitted he obtained leave, and they were married on October 18, 1918. The match was not approved of by Lord and Lady Ampthill.'

Sir John Simon paused, before delivering a *coup de théâtre*. 'Let me tell you at once', he continued, 'that there has never been a consummation of that marriage.' He explained how, the day before the marriage, Christabel had told John Hugo that she was most anxious not to have children at first. 'She extracted a promise from him, which he has loyally kept.' The cold, damning recital continued.

'Although Lord and Lady Ampthill knew of the marriage, they were not present at the wedding. They regarded the marriage as imprudent. Two or three days after the marriage Mr Russell had to return to his life at sea, and he saw his wife only when he was able to obtain leave. On those occasions his wife did not always welcome him. When he came home first, she said – perhaps out of temper or petulance – "I wish to God I hadn't married you"; but, on the whole, she maintained an affectionate demeanour.'

At this point, the jury might have thought: 'Well, Sir John is trying to be fair to Mrs Russell' – but his next sentence was a slamming repetition of what he had already revealed: 'The marriage was not consummated: the wife insisted that the agreement come to before the marriage should be adhered to.' Simon described how John Hugo had sent Christabel Marie Stopes's book *Married Love*, in the hope that it would convince her that her attitude was not justified. 'Afterwards the petitioner and the respondent had some talk about the book, and Mrs Russell criticized it. She said that she did not like the idea of the use of preventives of conception, and Mr Russell said that he did not, either.'

There was a sudden commotion in the jury box. The President was handed a message from one of the two women jurors. The unmarried woman was distressed by the increasingly graphic nature of the case, and asked to be discharged. Sir Henry Duke sympathetically agreed that she should be released and that the case should be determined by ten men and one woman, although he felt that the presence of women, in such a 'difficult' case, could be very helpful. He asked the remaining woman if she felt she could cope. 'I will do my best,' she replied.

Resuming, Sir John Simon recounted the visit to Switzerland and the problem of the narrow bunks. 'Mr Russell suggested that they should sleep in another room, but Mrs Russell refused.' Simon spoke of Russell's job with Vickers and the couple's move to Lincoln Street in Chelsea. 'There, the husband found that his wife had arranged to sleep in a room by herself.'

'Mrs Russell was constantly indulging in dancing. She was a good dancer, and Mr Russell was not, and she continually attended dances with male friends. When Mr Russell protested, he used only to get as an answer that he was interfering unjustifiably with her amusements. Mr Bradley was one of the friends who used to take her out to those dances.'

Simon went on to describe the weekend in August 1920 when John Hugo visited Broadhurst and found that Christabel was out motoring with Bradley. It was that incident that had allegedly provoked John Hugo's question to Bradley, 'Are you playing hanky-panky with my wife?' to which Bradley had given the oblique reply, 'It would be much better if Chris had children.' John Hugo had agreed with that; when Christabel heard of the conversation she was furious and from that time, allegedly, did not allow him to kiss her. 'The child was born in October, 1921,' Simon continued, 'and Mr Russell said that, whoever was the father, it was not he, for there was no form of affection between him and his wife from August, 1920, and the birth of the child.'

Simon mentioned the move to Curzon Street. There was more than a touch of disdain in his comment: 'As Mrs Russell was a good needlewoman and clever with her fingers she conceived the plan of setting up shop and providing gowns for ladies.' Christabel, he added, 'continued going to dances and staying out very late at night'.

'Between October, 1920, and March, 1921 [Simon added], they occupied separate rooms at Curzon Street, and Mrs Russell declined to allow her husband to enter her bedroom, except when he used to take her breakfast in bed, and she told him that she intended going out when, where and with whom she pleased. She refused to go out with him when he invited her, and his life was very unhappy. She seldom dined with him, and when she did she was wont to go out to dances afterwards. Mr Russell put his case to her, and she answered: "I don't love you, and I don't want to be married." '

Simon suggested it was suspicious that Christabel had two keys, one for Curzon Street, the other for her mother's flat in Harrington Gardens. 'So if she did not return to Curzon Street on any night she might be supposed to be at her mother's flat.' With maximum innuendo, he then referred to the night Christabel had spent at Bradley's flat on the pretext that she had lost her key; though Simon must have been aware that this piece of evidence was weakened by the telephone call to John Hugo, asking for her day clothes to be brought over to Bradley's flat. Immediately after this anecdote, Simon said: 'Mr Russell had not the slightest notion that his wife was to bear a child until he had an interview with her in June, 1921.' He added that John Hugo had told others about the circumstances of his married life, and that 'a question arose as to the possibility of annulling the marriage on the ground of the lady's refusal to consummate it'.

Simon then read out Christabel's long letter to John Hugo of 26 May 1921, after he had asked her for money to live in a separate cottage. Part of the letter read: 'I am never going to put myself in the position of being dependent on you or your family for one penny ...' Counsel put the worst construction on the letter. 'It was written in May by a woman who was going to have a child in October ...' Simon also read out, emphasizing its pathos, John Hugo's letter to Christabel of 10 June 1921, in which he repeated that he was willing to try to make a success of the marriage if she were willing to sleep with him; but if she were not, he would be forced to see his lawyers. Simon rounded off this part of his speech by quoting Christabel's flippant reply: 'Dear J ... Don't go to the same lawyers as me, or they may send you my bill by mistake!! ... P.S. Awful haste. Just off to M[other].'

Simon moved on to the critical events of the latter part of June 1921. He told the jury that although John Hugo had consulted a solicitor about nullity proceedings, he had not wanted the blow to fall upon his wife before her birthday, and had sent her some fruit and flowers. It was in her letter of 21 June, thanking him for this gift, that she asked urgently to see him. The lunch, the walk and the revelation about her pregnancy had followed on the 23rd. At first, though very surprised, John Hugo was overjoyed and had written her a letter to that effect from the St Pancras Hotel before returning to Bedfordshire. But after talking with Lady Ampthill at Oakley, he had thought things over and decided the child could not possibly be his. He had written to Christabel on 24 June to say so. Simon described Christabel's reply as a 'laconic note' –

'Dear John, – I think your second letter is absolutely inexplicable, to say the least of it. You had better come up and see me so that you can explain exactly what you mean. Wire me when you are coming. CHRIS.'

With obvious implications, Simon turned straight to Christabel's friendship with Lionel Lesley Cross.

'Mr Cross had been an Artillery officer quartered on Salisbury Plain. Mrs Russell on two occasions went down to Salisbury to try a horse of Mr Russell's which Lieutenant Cross was training. It now appeared that on December 30 and 31, 1920, Lieutenant Cross occupied a room at the County Hotel, Salisbury, next to Mrs Russell's bedroom; and exactly the same thing happened on January 15 and 16, 1921. That fact was never mentioned to Mr Russell.'

It was clear what Simon wanted the jury to think: that these circumstances were compromising, and that a baby due in October 1921 was more likely to have been conceived in Salisbury on 30 or 31 December 1920 – or in mid-January 1921 – than at Oakley on 18 or 19 December 1920.

With this Parthian shot, Simon handed over to another of John Hugo's counsel, Douglas Hogg KC. Fifty in 1922, Hogg was to become Bonar Law's attorney-general later that year, and was a future Lord Chancellor. After Eton he had spent eight years with the family firm of sugar planters, partly in the West Indies and British Guiana, and had been wounded and decorated in the second South African war. He had been called to the Bar in 1902 and taken silk in 1917. Sir John Simon (later Lord Simon), who led him in the Russell case, wrote that:

'Hogg had all the qualities that go to make a leader at the bar: an accurate grasp of complicated facts, a clear view of the principles of law which had to be applied to them, a sturdy attitude in the face of the situation with which he had to deal, and a manner which was genial and conciliatory with a persuasive force behind it well calculated to win assent from the tribunal he was addressing. He was never at a loss, and no counsel was more adept at preparing the way to meet the difficulties of the case.'

John Hugo entered the witness box. Hogg took him through much of the history that Simon had already covered; but some new facts, apparently damaging to Christabel, also emerged.

'In January 1921 [John Hugo recalled] I went away to a dance at Elstree, and on my return I suspected that someone had occupied my room [in Curzon Street]. About that period my wife ceased to wear a wedding ring. She said that it did not suit her finger. At the end of January I made a communication to my mother, and afterwards I told my wife that my people now knew the position between us. My wife said that I was a fool. Afterwards she showed me a letter which she had received from my mother, in which my mother said that she would like to see her making a trousseau for her grandchildren.[19] On May 21 I had a conversation with my wife in a boat. She said, "If your people still want annulment of our marriage, I am quite agreeable." '

The first day's hearing ended with a short exchange between Hogg and John Hugo.

Mr DOUGLAS HOGG: 'You desired to be the father of a child in June 1921?' – 'I did.'

'Did you read in *The Times* of the birth of a child to the respondent on October 15, 1921?' – 'I did.'

'Are you the father of that child?' – 'No.'

There was a break over the weekend. The Sunday papers went to town on the case. Headlines in *The People* (9 July) blared: 'PEER'S HEIR SUES FOR DIVORCE ASTOUNDING ALLEGATIONS.'

The hearings were resumed on 11 July. Now Christabel's leading counsel, Patrick Hastings KC, cross-examined John Hugo. Eight years younger than Sir John Simon, Hastings had worked his way up from relative poverty to being one of the busiest barristers in London, 'with all the cases that I wanted and perhaps more than I could do'. The son of a solicitor and a quasi-Pre-Raphaelite woman painter, he had hated his prep school and Charterhouse – for the discipline, the games and the, to him, useless classical curriculum. Like Simon, he had had work experience before the Bar (as a mining engineer in Wales) and had served in the second South

African war. He was called to the Bar in 1904 and took silk in 1919. Disillusioned by the feud between Asquith and Lloyd George, he quit the Liberal Party and became a Labour candidate, winning a seat in Northumberland in December 1922, after the first Russell divorce case. (In 1924, like Simon, he became attorney-general.) Hastings was not an intellectual. 'His reading was largely confined to law reports and thrillers such as those of his friend Edgar Wallace.'[20] It would have appealed to Christabel that he was a good horseman, a first-class shot and a keen fisherman. But he was quick-witted, famous for his brilliance in cross-examination. He had learned that art primarily from Sir Edward Carson, the counsel who had worsted Oscar Wilde in the dramatist's court battle with Lord Queensberry. From Carson he had adopted brevity and the trick of getting under a witness's skin with the first question, then pursuing his case ruthlessly and relentlessly, firing questions in rapid succession. All these forensic talents he now brought to bear on John Hugo, together with theatrical disclosures that must have made the jury gasp.

Mr PATRICK HASTINGS: 'When did you first come to the conclusion that your wife had committed adultery?' – 'After she made the extraordinary statement to me on June 23.'

'If I proved in this Court that the child is yours, would you be glad or sorry?' – 'You never could.'

'Answer my question. Would you be glad or sorry?' – 'The child is not mine; I should be sorry.'

John Hugo said that he had been to see Dr McKenzie, the general practitioner Christabel had consulted, and asked him certain questions. McKenzie had suggested that Mrs Russell and her mother should properly be present when he answered those questions.

HASTINGS: 'Supposing that I am able to prove to you that in June, 1921, your wife was a virgin, would that affect your view?' – 'Not in the least.'

One up to John Hugo.

Under further cross-examination, John Hugo told the court that his wife had had an unconventional upbringing and was rather spoilt. 'Throughout our married life she has been very secretive about her movements.' He spoke of the marriage and of the agreement about no sexual relations for a while. He read out some of Christabel's affectionate letters to him. He had asked her how she could reconcile her attitude to him with such letters; 'and she answered that she was only acting'. John Hugo added: 'She said that she did not think that she had ever been in love with me except for two or three days. That was why she would not kiss me or let me kiss her. I do not believe that she was in love with me when I married her.' Until he had heard of the child he had no suspicion of anyone, though he had had occasion to speak to Bradley in August 1920 'because he was always about with my wife and had an unsettling effect on her'. His wife had been brought up in Paris in Bohemian circles, and had been a student in the Latin Quarter.

Patrick Hastings was preparing to launch another of his sensational revelations at the jury.

'You were a little unconventional yourself when you lived at Curzon Street?' – 'I don't think so'.

John Hugo was shown a photograph of himself dressed as a woman at a fancy-dress ball (see Plate 7), and he told the court that his commanding officer and his wife went with him, the wife dressed as a man.

HASTINGS: 'I make no imputation against the lady, but you went about with her a good deal?' – 'I dined with her and her husband.'

'But she was living apart from her husband?' – 'Part of the time.'

'You were fond, when at Curzon Street, of dressing up as a woman?' – 'I did so sometimes.'

'Did you dress up as a woman in this lady's flat?' – 'Yes, before a fancy-dress ball.'

'If Mrs Russell had done some similar thing, you would not have hesitated to accuse her of adultery?' – 'It would depend on circumstances.'

Again John Hugo was showing that he was no pushover; but Hastings's questioning became still more insinuating and deadly.

'And you were found alone with Mrs S in her bedroom in the dark?' – 'I don't remember whether she was there.'

'And if your wife had been found alone in the dark with one of her dancing partners, you would not have hesitated to accuse her of adultery?' – 'It depends on circumstances.'

'But when you found her in Mr Bradley's flat and you brought her clothes, you did not accuse her of adultery?' – 'I believed my wife; but since she has had a child – '

'Then it all goes back to the child? Would you believe that she had committed adultery if she had not had a child?' – 'I accepted her story at first. If she had a child and I was not the father of it, it is quite obvious she has committed adultery.'

'Obvious. And you cannot discover who is the father of the child?' – 'No.'

John Hugo said that he had believed in his wife's innocence when she visited Bradley's flat, because Bradley had been his shipmate, and because of his faith in her. He had since picked out that occasion, and one when his wife visited Bradley when he was ill at his flat, as occasions on which he charged adultery. He himself had not attempted to consummate the marriage in Curzon Street.

'But did you know of no occurrence in December which might account for the child?' – 'I could not understand. I was in love with her and all her words were as gospel true. She asked me whether I remembered one night when she found me in my pyjamas, walking in my sleep, in Curzon Street. I had never heard of such a suggestion. I said, "No." Then my wife told me that she had consulted a fortune-teller, who informed her that she had a remarkable married life, and asked her whether she realized that she was going to have a baby. My wife then set herself to persuade me – who never doubted her fidelity – that I and she were about to become the father and mother of a child in consequence of a connexion of which neither was conscious at the time. When faced with that amazing fact, I was persuaded that some such thing could happen.'

He admitted that it was when he returned to Oaldey and told his mother what had happened, 'representing my wife to her as a faithful wife', that Lady Ampthill's forcefully expressed views had made him change his mind.

Lady Ampthill was brought into the witness box, Examined by Sir John Simon, she delivered her sour version of events.

'I first heard of my son's intended wedding on the day before it took place. He wrote to me and told me. I begged him to postpone it. Neither I nor Lord Ampthill attended the wedding. We decided "to make the best of it", and we treated our daughter-in-law in every way with affection. My son and his wife called on me the day after their wedding, and I received them. In 1920 I knew that my son was often left alone. In December of that year I noticed that Mrs Russell was not wearing a wedding-ring during a visit. I did not speak to her about it. I first heard of the state of affairs about January 25, 1921, in a letter from my son, and I went up to see him next day. I found him very unhappy. On February 24, 1921, my son and Mrs Russell dined with us. Afterwards I asked Mrs Russell why, after taking vows before God and witnesses, she had not kept them. Mrs Russell replied that she had made the vows with mental reservations, and she never for a moment denied the suggestion made to her that she was not living with my son on the ordinary terms of husband and wife.'

Next, Miss Edith Jane Pond, who had been nurse to Lady Ampthill's children, was called to the stand. John Hugo had been nineteen months old when she took charge of him.

COUNSEL: 'He had not done much sleep-walking up to that time, then?' [*Laughter*] – 'No.'

'Did he ever disturb you with violent scenes at night?' – 'Certainly not.'

'If anybody told you Mr John walked in his sleep, would you believe him?' – 'No.'

Then Lieutenant Francis Wylie RN, examined by Douglas Hogg, testified that he had first met John Hugo in 1909 and had often served with him on different ships. In 1918 he had met him again. 'The petitioner never walked in his sleep, nor did he ever do acts while in an unconscious state.'

The court again adjourned, to be reconvened two days later. John Hugo was further cross-examined by Hastings on that day, 15 July. He was asked to recall the day in July 1920 when he had been visited at Oakley by Hilton Welford, the husband of Christabel's sister Gwen. Welford had come on a mission, to see whether there was any chance of reconciling the couple. At the meeting, John Hugo had handed Welford a memorandum of the dates and places at which the couple had slept together (though without full intercourse). Hastings pointed out to John Hugo that the memo contained one passage which had been struck through in pencil and also in ink: 'Chris slept Sat. night at Bradley's fla[t] in S. Kensington as she was locked out of Curzon Street.' Hastings asked if John Hugo remembered writing that sentence. He did.

HASTINGS: 'When he read that, did Mr Welford say: "Surely you don't believe that Chris has committed adultery with Bradley," and did you say, "No, of course I don't'?" ' – 'I don't remember saying that ...'

'The passage is struck through, as you see. Have you any doubt that you struck it out because Mr Welford said: "If you don't believe it, strike it out"?' – 'I have no doubt that I did strike it out, but I did so because it had no bearing on the matter I was discussing with Mr Welford.'

'When Mr Welford left you, was not your attitude that you believed in your wife and desired a reconciliation?' – 'No; my attitude was that it was impossible for me to be the father of the child. I suggested that that was a dreadful blow to me, because I absolutely trusted my wife ... If any good could be done by a meeting, I was agreeable that there should be a meeting, but I insisted that the legal advisers of both sides should be present.'

Hastings read out a letter that Welford had sent John Hugo on 12 July 1921, after returning to his home, Craig Hall:

'Dear Stilts, – Sorry not to have telephoned or written you sooner ... After seeing you I saw Chris, who was quite willing to meet you and talk things over with you. I certainly think a meeting should take place, and I am waiting to hear that one has been arranged. – Yours, Hilton.'[21]

No meeting ever took place.

In answer to the President, Sir Henry Duke, John Hugo added that he said to Welford: 'It is bad enough for a man in a cottage for his wife to have a baby of which he is not the father; it is worse for me, because I have four brothers and sisters and an honourable name to keep untarnished.' Welford huffily commented that his name was equally honourable, and that the proceedings would bring equal disgrace and shame on his family.

Next on the witness stand was William Wood Shorten FRCS, of Edinburgh. Examined by Robert Bayford, he said he had known John Hugo since 1918. He had attended him in November 1920: 'he was perfectly normal physically and mentally'. Then Miss Maud Acton, of Redcliffe Square, London, took the oath – Christabel's former friend, apparently turned traitor. She was gaunt, sombrely dressed and above middle age. She said she had known Christabel slightly since she (Christabel) was a little girl and intimately in the last eight years.

'I frequently saw Mr and Mrs Russell together in the early days of their married life; Mrs Russell treated her husband in quite a friendly way. At the end of 1919 Mrs Russell went to Switzerland, and in the following September she came to stay in Redcliffe Square for four weeks. During that time she spent one evening at home and spent the others in dancing and dining out. I also saw Mrs Russell very often at Curzon Street. Mrs Russell told me that she was "always out" in the evenings. I noticed that Mrs Russell was not treating Mr Russell in the same way as she did in the early days of their married life; she treated him almost with dislike. At an interview which I had with Mrs Russell at Redcliffe Square between January 8 and 31, 1921, Mrs Russell said to me, "I never slept with John as his wife, and I never mean to; if I have a child it won't be his." At a later meeting, when I knew that a baby was coming, I reminded Mrs Russell of that conversation, and repeated it to her, and said, "Don't you remember what you said to me in my flat?" She replied: "Yes, but you don't remember the date." I answered, "I do not." Mrs Russell said that there were Hunnish scenes, but I said, "Please don't tell me that, being the woman you are, you would have stayed in the house with a man after the Hunnish scenes. Why, you would have left him." She replied: "I could not make a scene." '

The phrase 'Hunnish scenes' – meaning sexual advances by John Hugo – became part of the folklore of the Russell Baby case, ribaldly repeated in clubs, salons and saloons. The word 'Hunnish' was of course a relic of the First World War, so recently over – a word full of loathing. Nothing could have shown Christabel's antipathy to sex more clearly than her use of this highly charged expression.

Christabel's letters to Maud Acton were read out in court: the one of 4 July 1921 in which she joked that if the baby had sticking out teeth and adenoids, they'd know who was the father; and the undated one which ended: '... I've been so indiscreet all my life that [John Hugo] has enough evidence to divorce me about once a week!' There was laughter in court at this passage, but the President looked stern and said: 'The court would be better for the absence of people who take an amused interest in the case, and I will see that such persons are absent if such conduct is continued.'

It could perhaps be claimed for Miss Acton that she was simply telling the truth, the whole truth and nothing but the truth, as she knew it; but Christabel regarded her as a snake in the grass, and Acton came under pointed questioning by Patrick Hastings. She told him that she was an unwilling witness – 'I am very fond of Mrs Russell.'

HASTINGS: 'Did you ever find out anything which she had not voluntarily told you?' – 'No.'

'Everything she did was done perfectly openly?' – 'Yes.'

'Until you heard of the coming of the child did you ever think that Mrs Russell was an immoral woman?' – 'No.'

'Do you now?' – 'I am frightfully sorry, but I am bound to say that she must have misconducted herself once.'

'Is that because of the birth of the child?' – 'Yes.'

'If it had not been for the birth of the child in the circumstances as we know them, would you still regard her as a moral woman?' – 'Absolutely moral.'

'Was she a woman who used the wildest form of expression in everything she said and wrote?' – 'Yes.'

'Are you surprised that she wrote in this style?' – 'No.'

'Is she a woman of absolute courage, afraid of nothing and of no one?' – 'Yes.'

'And absolutely truthful in everything she says?'

Miss Acton was not to be caught out by that question. She replied: 'I don't know.'

'Has she ever told you a lie?' – 'There was the birth of the child ...'

'Apart from that, have you found her fearless and truthful?' – 'Yes.'

'The substance of what she told you in January, 1921, was that nothing which had happened could result in the birth of a child?' – 'Yes.'

Under further cross-examination by Hastings, Miss Acton described how her friendship with Christabel had broken down. At her 'interview' with Christabel in July 1921 she had 'reminded Mrs Russell that she had warned her against being alone with a man, as she might be overpowered'. Christabel had replied: 'You were right, and I was wrong, for I have been assaulted by my husband.' To that, Miss Acton had asserted: 'I do not believe it.' Later, she had received a bitterly reproachful letter from Christabel:

'Curzon Street, Mayfair
'Ac. dear, – No doubt from what you think you know you are right in forming such an opinion and if you did not happen to know me, too. When the truth is known, which at present is only known by myself, my mother, my lawyers and John, you will change your opinion,

'I have always made the mistake of telling everyone I've liked and trusted all my doings, but there are some things one does not discuss. If you were married you would know this. Theory and practice in matrimony are very different things.

'I am sure Gilbert [Bradley] would be very glad that you have such implicit faith in him, and I share your opinion. Neither he nor any man I have ever met has ever let me down or even hinted at such a thing, which is a boast very few women of 26 could make. The only man who has failed me utterly is John, and the only women who have failed me are you and Freda.[22] Funny that the three I've had most to do with outside my family should all fail – and I was so fond of you, Accy. – CHRIS.'

Sir Ellis Hume-Williams, representing Bradley, questioned Miss Acton about him. 'I have known Mr Bradley for about eight years,' she said. 'I regard him as an honourable man. I have never had the slightest suspicion that there was any impropriety between him and Mrs Russell.'

Next to testify was Mrs Moresby-White, whose brother had married a sister of Blanche Hart. She had known Christabel for several years.

'On June 23 of last year I met Mrs Russell, who told me that a fortune-teller had said that she was seven months advanced in pregnancy.[23] A day or two later, I met Mrs Hart and had a conversation with her, and, on the day after, I had tea with Mrs Russell. Mrs Russell said to me: "I have never done anything of which I am ashamed. I don't mind having an illegitimate child: I would rather it was anyone's but John's. I told him when I married him that I would not alter my way of living, and I don't intend to." She added that her husband had behaved like a Hun, and that he walked in his sleep, and said: "Isn't it curious? That's how it happened." '

Cross-examined, Mrs Moresby-White said she had not known what to make of the conversation with Christabel: 'It left me hopelessly bewildered.'

Richard Taylor – a partner in the firm of Messrs Taylor and Humbert, John Hugo's solicitors – was called next. He described how he had gone with John Hugo to see Dr McKenzie on 29 June 1921. McKenzie told Russell that Christabel was five and a half months advanced in pregnancy. He said that Christabel was then in the house and asked whether John Hugo would see her. On Taylor's advice, John Hugo refused. The young man asked McKenzie whether a child might be conceived without complete sexual intercourse, and McKenzie replied that it was 'barely possible'.

Taylor was cross-examined by Hastings: 'Mrs Russell was in the house. Do you not think that it would have been useful if the husband and wife had met together before the doctor and both had told him exactly what had happened?' Taylor replied, evasively and lamely: 'I am not prepared to say that.' (Geoffrey Ampthill always maintained that, if at that stage John Hugo had been told about Christabel's 'signs of virginity', he would not have felt able to sue for divorce.)

Mrs Mary Stevens, caretaker at Onslow Place, South Kensington, where Gilbert Bradley had his flat, testified that Christabel had spent a Saturday night there. Cross-examined by Hastings, she agreed that no attempt had been made to conceal the fact that Christabel had stayed overnight. Then Charles Henry Boulton, proprietor of the County Hotel, Salisbury, stated that Christabel and Lionel Cross had stayed in the hotel on 30 December 1920 and on 15 January 1921. 'Mr Cross slept in Room No. 1, and Mrs Russell in Room No.2.'

Concluding the petitioner's case, Douglas Hogg questioned Sir Maurice Craig, a specialist in mental illness. Craig said that Christabel's story that she had found John Hugo walking in his street in his pyjamas, had taken him upstairs and put him to bed while he was sleepwalking, was 'impossible'. Her husband would certainly have awakened.

Mr DOUGLAS HOGG: 'Would it be possible for a healthy man and woman to procreate a child without knowing it?' – 'No.'

On the same day, Patrick Hastings opened the case for Christabel with a display of contemptuous invective on the Carson model. He began politely enough, but as the speech rasped on, John Hugo was deluged by wave after wave of personal abuse. If uttered outside the privilege of the courtroom, Hastings's jibes would probably have provoked a libel action.

Everything, Hastings first suggested, turned on what had happened on a few nights in December 1920. 'The petitioner's case was that he was not, and could not be, the father of the child. As the case was opened, on the first day, the impression left on the mind of the jury must have been that the petitioner had done nothing which could have resulted in the birth of a child. The truth was that not once, but scores of times, Mr Russell had partial intercourse with his wife which might easily have resulted in the birth of a child. He did not know that it might so result, and she did not, but it now appeared that the risk of conception was very great. The petitioner had not dared to call one doctor to say that what had happened ... could not have resulted in the birth of a child. The only doctor [who had been called] in

London, which teemed with gynaecologists, was a mental specialist, who was completely unable to answer questions on that subject. Sir John Simon had dismissed with a sneer the suggestion that Mrs Russell had first learned of her pregnancy from a fortune-teller. He (counsel) would call before the jury – infinitely against her will – the woman who had told her that.

'If the petitioner's suggestions about Mrs Russell's life were correct, she was little better than a prostitute. [Here was a characteristic Hastings tactic: to exaggerate the opposition's case against his client, the better to knock it down.] When it became clear that Mr and Mrs Russell were not to be allowed to meet again, Mrs Russell was examined by an eminent gynaecologist, Mr Stanley Dodd, who would tell the jury that her condition was such that he was positive that no man had ever had complete intercourse with her. She showed, although she was five months advanced in pregnancy, all the marks of virginity. In his (the counsel's) submission, the petitioner was the father of the child beyond all possible question.'

Hastings thought it odd that not one of John Hugo's advisers, no member of his family, no friend who had been called had ever seen Christabel's baby. He (counsel) was going to ask his Lordship to allow the child to be produced, and it would be for the jury to say whether there was not an amazing resemblance between the child and its father, the petitioner.

Hastings moved in for the kill.

'Mrs Russell is a remarkable, perhaps an unhappy, product of modern education. She is a woman who has no such enemy in the world as herself. There is no shadow of evidence against her which she has not supplied. She is a woman absolutely fearless – frightened of nothing – a woman to whom public opinion means nothing; spoilt by admiration; spoilt by her independence, just the sort of girl who wants to marry a man. Instead, she married the petitioner – day after day querulous, complaining – asking for what he ought to have taken, beseeching where he ought to command. Cannot the jury imagine her thinking, "*Is this a man or a jelly who behaves like this*? Why can he not do anything which will make me feel that I respect him?" There he was, making futile scenes about her going out with other men, speaking to the young men about her, begging and imploring to be accorded what he had the right to demand – is there a girl in the world who could respect a man like that? If only he had taken her and said, "You have married a man, and not a mouse; this will have to stop," she might have respected him, but in the circumstances, was there any wonder that they drifted apart?'

These are words to make any modem feminist see red; Hastings is doing nothing short of recommending marital rape. But it must be remembered that the people he needed to convince were ten men and one woman of 1922 – people to whom the idea that 'A man is master in his own house' was likely to be axiomatic. In any case – as with Churchill – Hastings's mastery of the English language and genius for picking the *mot juste* could make even unenlightened ideas sound enthralling.

He continued to deploy a gleeful sarcasm.

'As to the visit to Paris – was Mr Cross going to imagine people would go about saying that he had committed adultery with Mrs Russell when her husband saw them off at the station?

'Everything depends on one thing. Do the jury believe that what happened before, happened on December 18 and on two or three subsequent occasions? It is obvious that it was Mr Russell's desire. On December 18 they slept in the same bed. Neither of them had the slightest idea that what had happened before might result in the birth of a child, and they were both wrong.

'It is a question of law – and his Lordship will direct the jury upon it – but if a child is born to parents who at material dates were living together the presumption is that the child is the husband's, and, in many cases, he could not be heard to give evidence against that presumption.'

This was the first time in the case that anybody had invoked the rule – enunciated by Lord Mansfield in the case of *Goodright* v. *Moss* (1777). Mansfield had said: '[It is] in the interests of decency, morality and public policy that the husband shall not be allowed after marriage to say that he has not had connexion with his wife and that therefore the offspring is spurious.'

7

Christabel Takes the Stand

The Russell case, with its strange revelations as to the generation of babies, is the favourite topic of conversation in these last hours of the season. Sir J. Simon, who cross–examined 'the Hart', seems to have been heavily scored off by her. When he asked her (very foolishly) whether it wasn't 'unusual' for a young married woman to use the bathroom of a bachelor, she replied at once: 'Well, Sir John, isn't it better to be indiscreet than to be dirty?'

H. H. ASQUITH, LETTER TO MRS HILDA HARRISON,
20 JULY 1922, PRINTED IN *H.H.A.:*
LETTERS OF THE EARL OF OXFORD AND ASQUITH TO A FRIEND,
SECOND SERIES 1922–1927, LONDON 1934

There was a buzz of anticipation in the court as Christabel was summoned to be questioned by Hastings. The *News of the World* reporter observed 'a craning of necks as Mrs Russell was called into the witness-box'.

'A slim, supple figure, she replied to questions with her left hand poised assuredly on her hip, her fashionable open sleeve revealing a bare arm. She wore a black satin dress with boat-shaped neck cut on long loose lines that suggested excellent taste. Its severity was relieved only by a deep band of blue and red embroidery. Her ribbon-edged black hat hid most of her hair – only two tightly-rolled, golden-tinged tufts were seen – and its broad brim cast shadows across her pale, girlish face. Her woman's wit was matched against Sir John Simon's keen legal intellect in a fascinating cross-examination that vividly recalled to mind the famous scene in "A Butterfly on the Wheel".'[24]

Hastings took Christabel through her parentage ('My father commanded the Leinsters'), her education, her three winters in Paris and her war work ('I had two thousand people under me'). At the end of the Great War, she was working at Whitworth's on a salary of £400 a year. She had continued in that job until September 1919. Her husband made her no allowance: she lived on what she earned. Hastings asked her about her married life.

'On the night of our marriage, my husband went to sleep at once. There was a compact between us about children. It had been agreed that there should be no children at first because I wanted to go on with my work. There was, however, no agreement that we should never have children. At the time of our marriage I was very devoted to my husband.'

HASTINGS: 'Was there any reason except affection why you should marry him?' – 'Well, I thought it would be nice to be no longer pestered by men to marry them. I thought it would be peaceful. I was rather surprised that on the first night my husband did not even want to kiss me. About three days after the marriage he attempted incomplete intercourse, and this incomplete intercourse took place frequently afterwards. I never thought that it could result in the birth of a child. My feeling of affection for my husband gradually decreased. It decreased because his attitude generally annoyed me, especially as regards my men friends. Moreover, he never stood up for himself.'

'Did he ever insist on your giving way to his wishes?' – 'He tried to insist, but not sufficiently to enforce his views.'

'Did he ever say that he was going to give you a shaking or a beating?' – 'No. I think I should have admired him more if he had.'

'Do you think in your married life that you deserved it?' – 'I should have been perfectly furious with my wife, if I had been a man, and she had behaved as I did. I very often went out dancing in the evenings. I realize that my behaviour was indiscreet, but everyone always knew everything that I did.'

The next day, Christabel was grilled by Sir John Simon.

'Do you represent to the jury that your unconventional proceedings with Mr Bradley and Mr Cross are not different from your unconventional behaviour with other gentlemen?' – 'Exactly.'

'Do you suggest that you have been away with other gentlemen to hotels, occupying adjoining rooms?' – 'I have.'

'Do you suggest that Mr Russell was ever told of that?' – 'I do.'

'You say there were other gentlemen. There were several?' – 'Yes.'

'Will you take a pencil and paper and write down the names of the gentlemen with whom you went to hotels and who occupied adjoining rooms to your own?'

[The witness wrote down four.]

Sir JOHN SIMON:'There may be more, I suppose?' – 'No, those were the only occasions.'

'Mr Bradley was in love with you?' – 'That is a question for him to answer.'

'At the moment, madam, it is a question for you to answer. Did he tell you that he loved you?' – 'Yes.'

'After you were a married woman, did he kiss you?' – 'No.'

'Then your unconventionality did not go to that length?' – 'No.'

Simon interrogated her about the night she had spent in Bradley's flat. Why had she been driven to take refuge there when she lost her key? 'It seemed the most obvious place to go,' she replied. 'There was nothing else to do but sit on my own doorstep. One could hardly go to a hotel in the middle of the night with no luggage, and I had not the key of my mother's flat.'

'The Curzon Hotel is near to your flat?' – 'It is exactly opposite my house.'

'Why shouldn't you have gone to the Curzon Hotel?' – 'In the first place I was then only recently at Curzon Street, and I did not think they would know me, and, in the second place, it seemed more reasonable to go back with Mr Bradley ...'

'Had you really lost your key?' – 'It appears so.'

The PRESIDENT: 'That is not what the learned counsel asked you.' – 'I had really lost my key.'

SIMON: 'When did you find it again?' – 'I don't know that I ever found it again ...'

'You had no night clothes. What did you sleep in?' – 'I don't remember. Probably I took off my dress and slept as I was. I went to bed in Mr Bradley's room after we made a bed for him in the sitting room.'

'What time did you go to bed?' – 'About 2 or 3 o'clock'

Simon next turned to Christabel's friendship with Lionel Cross. She emphasized that Bradley was a greater friend of hers, but added, 'Mr Cross was an exceedingly good dancer.'

SIMON: 'Some people might call him a "divine dancer"?' – 'I did.'

'Sometimes when you danced with him, would you put your head against his cheek?' – 'That was the fashion at one time. It has gone out now.'

'You followed the fashion?' – 'Implicitly in dancing.'

In answer to questions about her trips to Paris with Cross, Christabel said that a porter at the Paris hotel had booked them berths on a *wagon–lit*. They had not realized they were to share the same compartment. And no, Mr Cross had never kissed her. She decidedly got the better of Simon by one of her quick, pert answers. She had told him that Cross lay in the bunk.

'And you?' – 'I went to bed. I removed my shoes and hat. I did not otherwise undress.'

'Why not?' – 'How could I possibly? Mr Cross was there.'

Simon taxed Christabel with the evidence that her supposed friend Maud Acton had given about her.

'You heard Miss Acton say that in January you told her that you had never slept with your husband as his wife, and that if you had a child it would not be his?' – 'I don't remember that conversation. It seems highly improbable.'

'Miss Acton was a friend who had your confidence?' – 'Yes.'

'In July she reminded you of that conversation?' – 'I heard her evidence, but I have no recollection of the conversation. I do not think that it ever took place.'

'Had Miss Acton warned you about what might happen if you allowed your men friends to be too familiar?' – 'She used to warn me about that, but I always laughed at her, and I still laugh at her.'

'She may have been a prudish maiden lady?' – 'She was not at all a prudish maiden lady.' 'You claim always to tell the truth?' – 'Yes, I am distressingly truthful.'

'Listen to your letter to Miss Acton. Does that contain the truth? You say: "I have Johnson (my maid at Curzon Street) as a witness that he used to burst into my room at all hours of the night." Was that true?' – 'My maid Johnson told me that she used to hear him coming into my room at night.'

'Is your maid here?' – 'She is.'

'Your letter goes on: "and he [John Hugo] has been found out already in two flagrant lies to the Solicitors". What were they?' – 'I have been trying to remember since I heard the letter read, but I cannot.'

The next day's hearing began with some discussion as to whether, and if so when, the baby might be shown to the jurors. Hastings wanted that to happen; significantly, John Hugo's counsel did not. Douglas Hogg pointed out that in the *Slingsby Baby* case of 1915 – in which Duke had taken part – the eminent sculptor Sir George Frampton (creator of the Peter Pan statue in Kensington Gardens), had 'sat on the Bench as a sort of assessor, and the impropriety of such a mode of trial had been commented on by the Court of Appeal'[25]. Duke interrupted Hogg to say that was not the only case to be considered. He referred both counsel to the Irish case of *Pagot* v. *Pagot* and said he would consider Hastings's request when both sides had had time to read the relevant report.

Hastings continued his questioning of Christabel, attempting to neutralize the impression that Simon's interrogation might have left.

'I want to deal with one act of indiscretion: you returned from Paris [with Cross] by night?' –'Yes.'

'How did you travel?' – 'By *wagon–lit.*'

'Who engaged it?' – 'We sent the hotel people to engage it ...'

'Looking back at it now, do you think that that was indiscreet?' – 'Yes; but it never entered my head at the time.'

'Have you ever committed adultery with Mr Cross?' – 'No.' 'Have you ever committed adultery with any other man?' – 'No.'

In reply to further questions from Hastings, Christabel said that she had no idea that the relations which she had had with her husband might result in the birth of a child. She had been absolutely convinced that they could not. Hastings led her on to the meeting with John Hugo after her visit to the clairvoyante. She said she had heard his account of what had happened at the meeting. She did not agree with it. About the pregnancy, she had said to him then: 'Perhaps it is something that we don't know about that accounts for it.' He had replied, 'We don't do things of which we are unaware.' It was then that she had asked him whether he was aware that once she had found him, as she thought, walking in his sleep in his pyjamas just outside the front door of the house in Curzon Street.

'He said, "No; I have no recollection of it," and he asked why I had not told him about it at the time. I said that I imagined that he was walking in his sleep, and he used to tell me about his young brother who used to walk in his sleep. I then asked him whether he remembered that he had been lying on his bed with his gun between his feet and his toes on the trigger, to blow his brains out if I did not consummate the marriage.'

By introducing this new, sensational revelation, Christabel was showing her awareness that she was now in a gladiatorial battle, no holds barred. After this attack, she could not expect much gentleness from Sir John Simon, as he interrogated her about the sleep-walking incident. First he rained down sharp little questions upon her, trying to trip her up over the facts –

'Did you speak to him?' – 'No ...'

'Were his feet bare?' – 'I cannot remember.'

'When you had led him to his room, what happened?' – 'I led him to his bed and he got into bed.'

In the sneering verbal assault that followed, Simon tried to manoeuvre Christabel into endorsing the absurd suggestion, already planted in the jury's mind, that the baby had been conceived when John Hugo was in some sort of trance.

'Until you found that you were going to have a baby, did you ever tell anybody the sleep-walking story?' – 'No.'

'Did you tell Mrs Moresby-White, referring to your pregnancy: "I found John walking in his sleep. Isn't it strange? That is how it happened"?' –'I heard her say that, but I regret to say that it is untrue. I never said it.'

'You heard your husband's evidence about the occasion when you told him of your pregnancy. What was the point of an honest wife's beginning by telling her husband this sleep-walking story?' – 'I did not begin by telling him that. He has stated fairly accurately in his evidence what was said, but in the wrong order. I only referred to the sleep-walking after I had told him that I was going to have a child, and we were going through all that had occurred to see whether there was anything that could account for it. I never suggested that the child was begotten while he was sleep-walking. I only referred to that to show that there might have been occurrences of which he was himself unconscious.'

Simon also mocked Christabel's melodramatic phrase 'Hunnish scenes'. She said that the expression referred to the occasions when there had been incomplete relations between John Hugo and herself. She was now told that the child had been begotten as the result of those relations, and she did not suggest that there had been relations between them of which her husband and she were unconscious.

'I never saw anyone so overjoyed as my husband was when I told him that I was going to have a child. He rejoiced and I rejoiced.'

'Did you rejoice that your husband might become the father of the child?' – 'I rejoiced that I was going to be the mother of a child; it was my child as well as his.'

'You have a contempt for your husband?' – 'Yes.' 'You despise and dislike him?' – 'I will not say that.' 'But do you?' – 'No, I do not.'

'By July 4 were you writing: "I'd rather the devil himself was the father?" '– 'By that time I knew that my husband was trying to divorce me. I thought that it was no honour to my child to have a father like that.'

'You also wrote: "If I produce a horror with sticking-out teeth and adenoids, we'll all feel pretty sure about the parentage"?' – 'I was furious with my husband when I wrote that.'

Asked as to the truth of Mrs Moresby-White's evidence, Christabel said emphatically: 'I very much regret to say that Mrs Moresby-White's untruthfulness is a byword in London.' She was more charitable about Maud Acton. 'I do not suggest that Miss Acton is telling lies; I think she has misremembered what took place.'

Sir John Simon harried Christabel on the subject of her wedding-ring. Why had she left off wearing it in December 1920?

'Because my husband gave me at Christmas the present of a large ring which he had had designed for me by a friend. We agreed that it was impossible for me to wear it with my wedding-ring, and we agreed that I should give up wearing the wedding-ring.'

'Where is this ring?'

[The ring was produced and handed to the witness.]

SIMON: 'Put it on your right hand.'

[The witness did so, and said:] 'Have you ever shaken hands, sir, with anyone with a large ring on the right hand?'

'Did you tell your husband that the wedding-ring did not suit your finger?' – 'I said that rings in general did not suit my hand. Nor do they, because I have very ugly hands, and rings draw attention to them.'

Having been effectively beaten in this exchange, Simon switched rapidly to another topic, on which he fared no better.

'Did you have a bath in a bachelor flat, when the tenant was there, and the blinds were drawn?' – 'I have no recollection of any such occurrence, and I have not the faintest idea what you are driving at.'

'Do you know 42, Half Moon Street? Who lives there?' – 'Mr Mayer. Now I know what you are driving at. When we were moving into Curzon Street, Mr Mayer kindly said that if my husband and I would care to use his bath at any time he would be delighted. As a matter of fact, we never did avail ourselves of his very kind offer, as the bath at Curzon Street was working.'

As we have seen, Edgar Mayer was an American director of Christabel's dressmaking company. In a letter of July 1922 (quoted in the epigraph at the head of this chapter) the former Prime Minister, H.H. Asquith, relayed to a woman friend a telling exchange between Simon and Christabel –

'Is it not unusual for a young married woman to use the bathroom of a bachelor?' – 'Well, Sir John, isn't it better to be indiscreet than to be dirty?'

That sounds like Christabel; but the banter appears in none of the newspaper reports; and as Christabel denied having used Mayer's bath, the story may be apocryphal. It could be significant that in his letter Asquith refers to Christabel as 'the Hart'. A subtle pun might be intended – the analogy of a deer's being hunted;[26] but possibly, too, he was closing ranks with the aristocracy – to which, three years later, he would be admitted – by declining to link the honoured name of Russell with somebody whom in 1922 he probably regarded as a Scarlet Woman. Christabel's maiden name was in common circulation now, if only because her mother, Blanche Hart, was in court. Asquith evidently expected his correspondent to know whom he meant.

Sir Ellis Hume-Williams examined Gilbert Bradley. In his memoirs, eight years later, he misremembered him as 'a young soldier' *(sic,* for sailor) – 'a nice, clean, English lad'. Interviewing Bradley in his chambers before the courtroom hearing Hume-Williams found his naïvety breathtaking.

'It appeared that one night, when Mrs Russell was living in Curzon Street, they had been to a dance together. On returning, Mrs Russell found that she had lost her key (and I cannot imagine why any woman is ever entrusted with one) and they were consequently unable to get in. Whereupon, the young man, anxious to make the lady as comfortable as possible under the circumstances, took her back to his own flat, and there she slept in his room, while he slept on the sofa in the neighbouring sitting-room. This seemed to me to be rather a difficult proposition to deal with, and, I confess, I felt extremely nervous as to what view the jury might take. However, I said to the young man, "But what happened in the morning?" To which, with complete simplicity he said, "Well, you see, it was rather awkward, because the lady had nothing but evening dress, and could not very well leave in that attire." "Well" said I, "then what did you do?" "What did I do?" said the young man in astonishment; "why, of course, I did the obvious thing, I telephoned to her husband." "Did *what?*" I said. "I telephoned to her husband, told him that she was with me, and was still in evening dress, and that he must pack up and bring her day clothes at once." "And what," said I, "did the husband do?" "Why," said the young man, "of course he did what I suggested. Brought her clothes, waited while she changed, had some breakfast, and took her away!"

'The jury looked a little doubtful, but I think I clinched the matter in my final speech by one single observation, which was this: "Members of the Jury, if the husband did not mind, why on earth should we?" '

Rumpole of the Bailey couldn't have put it better.

Cross–examined by Douglas Hogg, Bradley spoke about the incident at Broadhurst in August 1920.

[After the trip to Edinburgh and the broken engagement] 'I saw Mrs Russell once or twice during 1919, but I was no longer in love with her: I put all that aside when I knew that she was married to a brother officer. I left the service in March 1920. I never stayed with the Russells at Lincoln Street, but I went there for tea. I went to Broadhurst on three occasions. On one occasion Mr Russell asked me into the garden for a talk. Mr Russell said that Mrs Russell gave him the impression that she had been in a bad temper. There was certainly no question of Mr Russell's saying anything about my "playing hanky-panky" with his wife.'

Re–examined by Sir Ellis Hume-Williams, Bradley said that he was very surprised when he was cited as a co-respondent. There was not a vestige of truth in the charges against him. No one had told him that Mr Russell was going to make these charges against him. Until the papers were served no one had made any such suggestion. When Mrs Russell went to Paris she went on business, and she paid her own bill.

As Bradley left the witness stand, the other named co-respondent, Lionel

Lesley Cross, entered it. He too was questioned by Hume-Williams. He said he was a lieutenant in the Royal Field Artillery. He was twenty-three years old. He had first been introduced to Mrs Russell by Maud Acton at Redcliffe Square in October 1920. He saw her again on 7 November. 'A friend took me to tea. Mrs Russell was in bed, and I was taken up to her bedroom, and was there first introduced to Mr Russell.' He became friendly with the Russells and agreed to look after a horse of Mrs Russell's. He was asked about the occasion on 15 January 1921 when he and Christabel had occupied adjoining rooms at the County Hotel, Salisbury.

'Mrs Russell [Cross said] had come down to see the horse. The rooms were booked by my soldier servant. Mrs Russell and I had been to a dance at Southampton and I stayed at the hotel instead of returning to my quarters, which were five miles from Salisbury ... The first occasion on which Mrs Russell came to Salisbury was on December 30, 1920, when she came for a dance. I had invited her to come, as I knew no one to dance with. There was no secrecy about the arrangements and no attempt to conceal them from the husband. Mrs Russell came about 8 p.m., we had dinner, and we returned from the dance about 1 a.m. Rooms had been engaged at the hotel by my servant. In the morning Mrs Russell returned to town. There is no truth in the suggestion that I committed adultery with Mrs Russell either at the Salisbury hotel or anywhere else.'

Dealing with the visits to Paris with Christabel, Cross said that John Hugo had been present when the idea was first mooted, and had joined in the discussion. Cross and Christabel had stayed at the Hôtel Chatham. He had a room on the fourth floor; Christabel's room was on the sixth floor. They never entered each other's rooms.

'[On the second day] we were going to the theatre in the evening and made arrangements for our luggage to be sent to the Gare du Nord. The porter was instructed to take places on the train and, if possible, to reserve two sleeping berths. On reaching the station, we were conducted to the sleeping car by the attendant, and we found that we had been allotted berths in one compartment. It was my first experience of a *wagon-lit*, and I was unaware that any such arrangement had been made. I told the attendant that some other arrangement must be made, but the attendant said that the train was full and there was no other accommodation. I spoke to Mrs Russell and she agreed that we should make the best of it and treat the compartment as an ordinary railway carriage. Neither of us undressed.'

Sir ELLIS HUME-WILLIAMS: 'Looking back on your friendship with Mrs Russell, have you anything with which to reproach yourself?' – 'Seeing now what construction has been put on what I regarded as absolutely harmless incidents at the time, I suppose I must have been indiscreet, but no such thought crossed my mind.'

Questioned by Sir John Simon, Cross told the court that he had been married after the *wagon–lit* episode, and that his wife knew about it.[27]

SIMON: 'Was there an occasion when Mr Russell was present and you danced with Mrs Russell with your head against her cheek?' – 'I think it very unlikely. The occasions when I danced like that were extremely rare, and only with people who were very keen on following the exact fashion.'

Dr John Baird McKenzie MB, BCh, Edin. now appeared – the general practitioner Christabel had consulted after her visit to the clairvoyante. He described her visit to him of 21 June 1921. He had never seen her before. She had mentioned her meeting with Mrs Naismith. 'I found that Mrs Russell was rather more than five months advanced in pregnancy, and I told her so. In examining her I found that she showed signs of virginity. I could get no information from her about the date when conception might have taken place.' About eight days later, McKenzie had seen John Hugo.

McKENZIE: 'Mr Russell asked whether it was possible that he might have had relations with his wife while he was asleep. I told him that I had never heard of that happening. I then questioned him closely in order to ascertain the date when the child was conceived. He told me that he had not slept with his wife for quite a long time. I questioned him further, and then he told me that he had spent a weekend shortly before Christmas with his wife at his father's house. He said that they shared the same bed, and admitted that he had attempted intercourse on that occasion.'

McKenzie added that he had engaged a room in a nursing-home for Christabel's confinement for a week between 20 and 27 September 1921. He had based those dates on a computation from the date in December supplied to him by John Hugo. He had no doubt that an 'attempted intercourse' of the kind described by John Hugo might result in the birth of a child. It was quite certain from Christabel's condition that she had not had complete intercourse with any man. Dr Stanley Dodd of Wimpole Street, a gynaecologist, agreed with that opinion. Cross-examined by Simon, Dodd said it was exceptional for a woman to be unaware of her pregnancy so long, and that it was exceptional for a woman to conceive as the result of incomplete relations. But here Sir Henry Duke chipped in with a question, and Dodd said: 'I have in my own experience met with several cases in which conception has occurred without penetration.'

At the next day's hearing on 19 July, Patrick Hastings renewed his application for the baby to be inspected by the jury. John Hugo's lawyers were still much opposed to this.

SIMON: 'It might be proper to have the child produced in a case where a woman palmed off a child as her own, but there was a distinction where there was a question of the paternity of a child. Such a case could not be decided by inspection and in *Slingsby* v. *Attorney-General,* the House of Lords characterized such a proceeding as "loose and fanciful"[28]. It was a process of suggestion. There was no reported case in which a child was used as an "exhibit" ...'

The PRESIDENT: 'The *Slingsby* case was heard by a Judge, and the assent of the parties was given.'

SIMON: 'In the *Slingsby* case the child was about four years old, and at that age the resemblance was easier to trace.'

The PRESIDENT: 'That goes to value, not to admissibility.'

Duke asked Hastings what application he intended to make: was it for the child to be an exhibit or to tender evidence for cross-examination? Hastings replied: 'I make both applications. The question is analogous to a case of alleged handwriting – whether a document had been written, say, by the petitioner or the respondent. The documents would then be brought before the Court.'

This argument did not wash with Duke. 'That would be an analogy', he said, 'if it were a question of the paternity of two children. It is not a true analogy. The question is whether the evidence is admissible to prove a likeness.' Hastings riposted: 'My strong case is the *Slingsby* case.' Duke: 'If you desire to show the child to the jury you may do so at a convenient opportunity. If you wish to tender evidence, I will deal with it when it arises.' Duke then directed that the baby should be seen by the jury in the jury-room at two o'clock that day. Lady Ampthill would also see it.

By the time the next day's session opened (20 July), the jury had seen the baby. On Sunday, 23 July, The *News of the World* described the 'extraordinary precautions' that had been taken to shield the little boy from public gaze.

'He was conveyed to the court in a cab in charge of a nurse wearing a dark uniform and veil, arriving there when most of the public had dispersed for the luncheon interval, and hardly anyone suspected what was taking place. The nurse hurried with her tender burden through the main entrance to the new wing, up the staircase, and along a private passage leading to the judge's room.

'The actual inspection took place in the jury's private room under the court. What the privileged few saw was a plump, healthy-looking child, nine months old, with light hair, brown eyes, and a fair, pale face. It had on a short coat, and during its journey was closely wrapped in a white woollen shawl with a tasselled hat of the same white wool, closely pulled over its ears so that hardly an inch of flesh could be seen.'

The child remained for three-quarters of an hour, 'cooing happily', until he could be smuggled out of the judge's entrance, still with the nurse. During that wait, Christabel came down to see him.

Sir Ellis Hume-Williams once more took Gilbert Bradley through the night Christabel spent at his flat. Bradley stated that when John Hugo brought round Christabel's day clothes in the morning, '[he] uttered no word of surprise or complaint during that time'. Bradley also recalled staying with Christabel at the Hôtel Chatham, Paris. They went to the races at Longchamps together; but in the hotel he was never in her room, neither had she been in his.

By the time the next day's session opened, the jury had seen the baby; but Sir Henry Duke, a stickler for legal formalities, pointed out that the child had not yet been identified (as Christabel's baby). Hastings retorted that Christabel could be recalled or the nurse could give the necessary evidence; but Simon politely interrupted to say he did not seek to dispute the identity. What resemblance, if any, the jury had observed between young Geoffrey and John Hugo remained known only to them. Lady Ampthill was biding her time.

Dr McKenzie was recalled and produced his books, with the records of

Christabel's several visits to him. Cross-examined by Simon about his reserving a room at the nursing-home, he said it was impossible to forecast the date of delivery of a child without a considerable margin of error. 'Three weeks' error in computation was not unusual, even when the date of a particular occasion when intercourse last took place was known.' Dr Thomas Eden, a gynaecologist, was questioned by Hastings. He said:

'In the case of *Gaskill* v. *Gaskill*, tried recently before the Lord Chancellor, where a question of the duration of pregnancy arose, I was one of three experts called on behalf of the Crown. I have made a lifelong study of these questions. I found myself completely in accord with Dr Stanley Dodd when he gave evidence that conception might result without penetration, after incomplete relations of the kind described by Mrs Russell. The normal period of gestation varies and cannot be stated with accuracy. The average period is 280 days, calculated from the first day of the last preceding menstrual period. The longest period I have known in my own experience was 308 days, but longer periods are known to science. Assuming relations on December 18, there was nothing inconsistent with the child's being born on October 15 of the next year.'

Cross-examined by Sir John Simon, Eden said:

'I understand that it is common ground that Mrs Russell has given birth to a child and that the question for the jury is: who was the father? I do not suggest that I can give evidence which will assist them in arriving at that conclusion. I am not laying down the proposition that conception may occur as the result of incomplete relations only when the father of the child is the woman's husband.'

Re-examined by Hastings, Eden said that he had had in his own experience two cases in which women had appeared to be ignorant that they were going to have a child until they were far advanced in pregnancy. He was followed on the witness stand by Dr Trevor Berwyn Davies, obstetric surgeon to Queen Charlotte's Hospital, who said he had seen Christabel immediately after the birth of her baby. He also saw the baby, which weighed 10½lb. 'The child was exceptionally well developed, and seemed to be well beyond the average of a full-term child.' He, too, agreed with Dr Dodd about the possibility of conception after partial intercourse. Pressed by Simon, he conceded that the dimensions of the child did not necessarily mean that it had been carried for more than the normal period.

For those of the public in court who, to Duke's annoyance, were treating the case as a piece of theatre (or, to deploy an anachronism, a soap-opera), there were two treats in store this day: appearances by Christabel's mother, Mrs Blanche Hart, and by the clairvoyante, Mary Naismith. Like Christabel, Blanche was not easy to intimidate: a clever, sophisticated woman who gave as good as she got. Examined by Sir Ellis Hume-Williams, she said:

'My daughter, Mrs Russell, has lived a very independent life. I have never had the slightest cause for suspicion of her conduct with Mr Bradley and other young men. I know Mr Bradley very well, and like him very much. At Broadhurst there was a large number of guests who were regular visitors.

Plate 1; Christabel, a studio photograph by Madame Yevonde.

Plate 2; Studio photograph of Christabel by Madame Yevonde. Christabel inscribed it for her boyfriend Charles de Beaumont (see plate 12).

ODO RVSSELL BARON AMPTHILL

Plate 3; Odo Russell, 1st Lord Ampthill. As British Ambassador to Berlin,
he was known as 'Bismarck's favourite Englishman'.

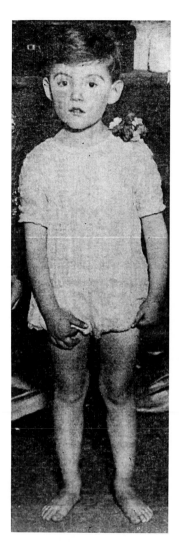

Plate 4; Geoffrey Russell in 1926, when he was five. That was the year Christabel had him formally declared legitimate.

Plate 5; 'I was never really taught to ride. But Chris would criticize me.' Christabel and Geoffrey, *c.* 1928.

Plate 6; Blanche Hart with Gwenydd
(Gwen) and Christabel (*left*).

Plate 7; John Hugo Russell in drag.
(*The Daily Mirror*, 13 July 1922).

Plate 8; John Hugo with his father, Oliver,
2nd Lord Ampthill.

Plate 9; Oliver, 2nd Lord Ampthill.

Plate 10; Sir Edward Marshall Hall.

DAILY SKETCH.

No. 4,504   Telephone (London—Holborn 6510, Manchester—City 6501.)   LONDON, SATURDAY, MARCH 3, 1923.   (Registered as a Newspaper.)   ONE PENNY.

THE £ s. d. OF THE RUSSELL DIVORCE CASE

Mr. Edgard Jacquard Mayer, who is the new co-respondent cited in the Russell case.

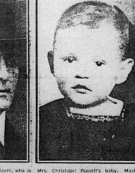

Mrs. Christabel Russell's baby, Master Geoffrey. His parentage is the big question involved in the case.

The Hon. John Russell said in evidence that he failed to see the baby's likeness to himself.

Mr. Justice Hill, the Judge, enjoying a pipe in an interval of the case.

Mrs. Christabel Russell, described by her counsel as "an unconventional, lively woman, without fear, and popular."

Mrs. Christabel Russell is still carrying on business in Mayfair as a dress designer. Some of these gowns displayed by mannequins this week are her own designs.

The Hon. John Russell disclosed yesterday that his previous suit cost £10,700, of which he had to pay £5,700 to Mrs. Russell for her costs. He formerly earned £550 a year at Vickers', but for two years had tramped the streets in search of a job. He and his father, Lord Ampthill, had had to raise money to contest the case.

Plate 11; *Daily Sketch*, 3 March 1923.

Plate 12; Charles de Beaumont, the champion fencer who became Christabel's boyfriend.

'There were no opportunities for adultery at Broadhurst, as my daughter was too good a hostess and was engaged in looking after her guests, and a visit to a bedroom at night was impossible. I did not see Mr Bradley going about alone with my daughter any more than any other young man did. I knew all about the visit to Mr Bradley's flat. I saw Mr and Mrs Russell and Mr Bradley together after that incident. They joked about it. I knew all about my daughter's visit to Salisbury with Mr Cross, except, perhaps, the sleeping in adjoining rooms. I discussed Mr Cross with Mr Russell, who did not object to Mr Cross except that he was jealous of him, as he was of all the other boys. I heard the Paris visit discussed in the presence of Mr Russell, who never at any time made any complaint.'

Simon cross-examined her.

SIMON: 'Have you ever contemplated that nullity proceedings might be taken between Mr Russell and your daughter?' – 'We have.'

'On March 22, 1921, you had some discussion with Lady Ampthill about it?' – 'I did.'

'Of course at that time you had no notion that your daughter was going to have a child?' – 'No.'

'Did you then agree with Lady Ampthill that annulment would be much the best thing?' – 'I did.'

'That was because you knew that they had never lived properly together as man and wife?' – 'It was.'

Under further questioning, Blanche said she had first learned of Christabel's pregnancy on 17 June 1921, the day on which her daughter had consulted the c1airvoyante. On 28 June she (Blanche) had telephoned Lady Ampthill at Oakley House. By then Blanche had seen the two letters from John Hugo to Christabel.

Sir John Simon pounced.

'Did you say to Lady Ampthill: "Has John told you about Chris?" ' – 'That is not how the conversation began. It began by my telling Lady Ampthill that I wanted her to tell John not to write such idiotic letters to Chris.'

'Did Lady Ampthill say: "It cannot be Jack's child, and therefore he thinks it must be nerves"?' – 'Lady Ampthill may have added, "I am putting it in the hands of my solicitors." I was so enraged at the imputation of my daughter that I said, "It is the best thing you can do," and I hung up the receiver.'

'Did you say: "I hold a letter from Chris that acknowledges that he is the father and suggests a godfather"?' – 'That had been earlier in the conversation.'

'Where is the letter that suggests a godfather?' – 'I don't know.'

'Did you say: "Cannot the annulment be hurried on?" ' – 'No, I did not.'

'Do you swear that?' – 'I do. How could it be annulled when a child was on the way?'

'Did Lady Ampthill reply: "Annulment? If you say it is John's child, he will take divorce proceedings"?' – 'I do not remember her saying that. The only thing I remember is her saying that she would put the matter in the hands of her solicitors.'

'I suggest that you replied to that remark by saying: "Oh! Divorce? We'd rather have anybody but John as the father of the child"?' – 'That's a lie.'

Simon asked Blanche to cast her mind back to August 1920, when John Hugo used to come to Broadhurst at weekends, and Bradley also stayed there.

'There is no doubt that Mrs Russell did at times neglect her husband and give her time to her men friends?' – 'I think that she divided herself among my guests.'

'Did Mrs Russell give her time and companionship to her husband in the way that you might expect?' – 'I don't think she had time. She was working all the day and her relaxation in the evening was dancing, and her husband could not dance.'

'When Mr Russell came down for a weekend in August, did he speak to you about your daughter and Mr Bradley?' – 'He did.'

'Did he ask you whether you didn't think that they were too thick in friendship to be entirely playing the game?' – 'I don't think he did. The only thing I remember is that once, when my daughter had been out in a car with Mr Bradley and was rather longer away than she expected, Mr Russell seemed rather cross, and kept saying, "I wish they'd come back." I said to him, "Why, instead of 'grousing' to me, don't you grouse to Bradley himself?" '

'Before that weekend was over did you ascertain whether he had seen Bradley?' – 'I heard no more about it.'

'You say that your daughter's spending the night at Bradley's flat was treated as a joke?' – 'Yes.'

'Is that your idea of a joke?' – 'It was treated as a joke by all her friends, Mr Russell included.'

Re-examined by Sir Ellis Hume-Williams, Blanche said:

'Down to June, 1921, my daughter took much violent exercise and made no difference to her usual mode of life. She went on with her work until the night before the child was born, and she resumed work three weeks afterwards. In my interview with Lady Ampthill in May, 1921, I think I said that if Mr Russell was firm their little troubles would come to an end. [This was possibly an oblique reference to what is said to newlyweds: 'May all your troubles be little ones.'] Lady Ampthill said that they always thought that Mr Russell was a man of firm will. Lady Ampthill added that if he beat her and locked her up in a room it would be better, at which I laughed. We came to no conclusion at that interview.'

Now Mary Frances Naismith, the clairvoyante, came to the witness box. Examined by Digby Cotes-Preedy, she said she was a 'psychological expert' and an artist. She was *not* a fortune-teller. She had passed examinations conducted by a medical man, and had formed a society. She remembered Christabel's visit to her on 17 June 1921, when she told her of her physical condition.

Cross-examined by Sir JOHN SIMON – 'And you told her that she was $7^1/2$ months in the family way?' – 'No, I think that I told her that she was five months gone.'

The witness said that, although Mrs Russell showed no sign of coming motherhood, she was able to diagnose her condition from the vibrations of the hormones. A comedy double-act ensued, as Simon and Duke indulged in some gentle teasing.

SIMON: 'Is that Latin or Greek?' – 'It is a very good word.'

'What is it?' – 'It has to do with a very deep subject; it has to do with psychology and physiology.'

The PRESIDENT: 'You need not be afraid that Sir John's mental powers will give out.'

SIMON: 'I am holding on as well as I can. Can you tell me whether psychological science has yet advanced to the extent that you can tell from it who the father of the child is?' – 'It could in time.'

'In the meanwhile we shall have to depend on the verdict of the jury.'

On the next day, friends of Christabel's were called to vouch for her character. Mrs Laing, the wife of Lieutenant-Colonel Laing, said she had known her for seventeen years. (Christabel had been a bridesmaid at her wedding.)

'Mrs Russell is rather unusual: she is very clever, energetic and independent. I have heard the suggestions made against her. I have never seen anything which would lead me to suppose that there could be any truth in such suggestions.'

The PRESIDENT: 'Did you ever see on Mrs Russell's part any undue familiarity with men – any caress, anything that would lead you to suppose that she desired intercourse with men?' – 'I have never seen anything of the sort. She always treated all men exactly the same.'

In answer to a question from Sir Ellis Hume-Williams, Mrs Laing added:

'I do not believe that Mrs Russell would allow any man to kiss her. She is the most unsentimental person I have ever come across.'

She came under tougher questioning by Sir John Simon.

'You suggest that Mrs Russell never conducted herself otherwise than as a modest married woman should?' – 'Certainly.'

'Do you suggest that a modest married woman may properly spend the night in a bachelor's flat with its occupant?' – 'No, certainly not.'

'You would not do it, I suppose?' – 'Not if I could possibly avoid it.'

'Would a modest married woman dance with her face against the face of her partner?' – 'I have never done it myself, but I don't follow fashion. At one time it was the fashion brought over from America to dance with your face against your partner's.'

The PRESIDENT: 'Is there still a fashion of that kind?' – 'I don't think so.'

SIMON: 'One was not ostracized from Society or forbidden to go to Court because one did not follow that fashion, I suppose?' – 'Oh dear, no!'

Captain Robert Buchanan was called to give evidence on the saucy letters about him that Christabel had sent John Hugo during her stay in Switzerland. He said he had met Christabel and Mrs Hart in January 1920. He could take exception to nothing that he had seen in Christabel's behaviour.

Cross-examined by Douglas Hogg, he said he had first met the two women in the boat or train: they were in the same train between Paris and Lausanne.

HOGG: 'Did you not stay in Paris with them?' –'I cannot remember.'

'Listen to what Mrs Russell writes to her husband from Paris: "I've a very nice man in tow – one Buchanan, and he is spending all day with me. We met on the boat and he goes on to Switzerland with us tonight." And from Lausanne she writes: "Our friendship with Buchanan progresses apace. He is simply topping and is still with us. We have formed a lifelong friendship ... He has a wife and several large children. These he tactfully leaves behind." '

Buchanan explained that his wife had intended to travel with him, but had unfortunately contracted measles, and so was unable to come.

HOGG: 'Are the statements in those letters true?' – 'She was writing an amusing letter to her husband and expressed herself very extravagantly in order to be amusing. Her statements bore very little relation to the truth.'

Mr DIGBY COTES-PREEDY: 'I think my friend ought to read the next passage.'

HOGG: 'Certainly. "It is too priceless, no one will believe I am married. All the servants and people call me Mademoiselle, and when one of them found out somehow I was married she nearly fainted and said I looked so young! One up for your elderly wife." '

The WITNESS: 'I knew that Mrs Russell was married.'

Re-examined: 'Did you ever see any sign of familiarity between Mrs Russell and any man?' – 'No.'

Perhaps to give the jury a more balanced impression of Christabel's letters to John Hugo from Switzerland, Sir Henry Duke then read out two more of them. One ended: 'I love the nicest hub in the world and kiss him sixty-five times'; the other ended: 'Your lovingest Chris'.

Mrs Crutwell, Christabel's aunt, called next, said that she regarded her niece as 'a super-woman'. (The expression, here used over fifty years before Shirley Conran's book *Superwoman*, was presumably an adaptation from Bernard Shaw's *Man and Superman*, 1903, though it was Nietzsche who first wrote about the Übermensch or superman.) 'She is so superior to most other women. She is extremely clever, extremely lively, and extremely good. She is a very good sister, a very good daughter and a very good friend.' Hogg jabbed in the irresistible rejoinder: 'And a very good wife?' Mrs Crutwell answered carefully: 'I knew very little of her married life.' But Hogg was not to be so easily sidestepped.

'Are you excluding her married life when you give her that testimonial?' –'No.'

Miss Caroline Erskine, Mrs Crutwell's sister (who, as we shall see, was a great figure in Geoffrey Ampthill's early life), said that in the summer of 1920 Christabel and John Hugo had spent a day with her at Great Bookham, Surrey. 'They were like two children: they seemed so affectionate, playing about in the garden with the dog.'

Michael Webb, Lionel Cross's soldier servant, confirmed that he – off his own batman's bat, as it were – had booked the adjoining rooms for Christabel and Cross in the County Hotel, Salisbury. A deposition from one of that hotel's chambermaids was read out. She said she had seen nothing to lead her to suppose that there had been any impropriety.

Now the redoubtable Lady Ampthill was recalled for an encore. Sir John Simon told her: 'I desire to put to you some conversations you had with Mrs Hart.' Hastings objected, but the President admitted the evidence.

SIMON: 'Lady Ampthill, Mrs Hart has told us that she had a conversation with you on the telephone?' – 'Yes. The conversation took place about 9.30 p.m. on June 28, 1921.'

'Did you make a note of the conversation?' – 'Yes.'

'When?' – 'Directly after it occurred. I have the note in court.' 'Is this the note?' – 'Yes.'

'Did you say to Mrs Hart, "It's not Jack's child?" ' – 'Yes. She gave me Dr McKenzie's address during the conversation.'

'When you said that, what did Mrs Hart say?' – 'She said, "I hold a letter from him in which he acknowledges the fatherhood, and inquires about a godfather." '

'What did you say?' – 'I replied: "It is not Jack's child, and he will do nothing without consulting his lawyers." Mrs Hart then said, "Cannot the annulment be hurried up?" I replied: "Annulment – when you say it is Jack's child! What he will probably do is take divorce proceedings." '

'Did you see the baby when the jury saw it?' –'Yes.' 'Mr John Russell is your eldest son?' – 'Yes.'

'Do you remember what he was like when you nursed him?' – 'Oh, yes.'

'Do you see any resemblance between the baby whom you saw and what you remember your son was like?' – 'No.'

John Hugo was recalled and said that his wife never told him a word about the *wagon-lit* incident, neither did she tell him that she and Cross had been staying in the Salisbury hotel or that she and Bradley had stayed in the hotel in Paris.

A woman who taught dancing gave evidence that the fashion of dancing cheek to cheek came in during 1921 and 'still obtains among decently minded people'. Cross-examined, she said she was not surprised that some husbands should object.

Sir Ellis Hume-Williams made his closing address to the jury on behalf of the co-respondents, Bradley and Cross.

'Members of the jury: to do justice you must put yourselves into the atmosphere surrounding the people concerned. Mrs Russell is a curious product of the age. The war has produced in women effects which would undoubtedly have astonished, and perhaps would have shocked, our ancestors. Women did men's work during the war; they dressed like men and were working in conditions in which sex was subordinated and forgotten. That had a profound effect on their manners, though not on their morals. Lady Ampthill will have no difficulty in appreciating that fact, as she rendered great services during the war in directing and controlling the activities of a number of women war-workers. No woman who lived that kind of life during the war could entirely shed it when she came out of it, and, therefore, to such women must be applied a different standard from that applied by Anthony Trollope or Thackeray when writing of the well-behaved, though possibly somewhat insipid, women of that day. [Hume-Williams seems to have forgotten the very spirited Becky Sharp in *Vanity Fair*.]

'When Mr Russell married a woman of that kind, he was not in the dark. He knew that she had been engaged to Bradley. He knew that Bradley and she had gone to Edinburgh to be married, and then, in the curious haphazard way of modern days, there wasn't time and they did not do it. It is not for you, Members of the Jury, to decide whether you approve of Mrs Russell's conduct, but whether adultery has been committed.

'I must point out that the two co-respondents are uninterested in the parentage of the child, which is the main question in this case.'

Hume-Williams reviewed in detail the evidence relating to the charges against the two co-respondents. At the end of his speech the court adjourned until the next day, when Patrick Hastings addressed the jury on behalf of Christabel.

Besides the husband and wife, Hastings emphasized, the child was vitally interested in the verdict. That 'little chap' did not realize now that they were deciding his fate for him; but if the verdict went against his mother, when he grew up he would be regarded by all who remembered the case as a bastard.

'Mr and Mrs Russell are still young – there is hardly any person concerned who is over twenty-five years of age. You might wonder what might have happened on that day in July when Mrs Russell was in one room at her doctor's and Mr Russell and his solicitor in another room – he distrustful, and she angry at being distrusted – had they been allowed to meet. Perhaps if that had happened the case might never have been heard. It is just possible in the event of a particular result of the case that the two young people might – without the intervention of their solicitors – come together again. I am not going to say a word which might tend to keep them for ever apart.'

Here Hastings made some amends for the aspersions he had cast on John Hugo's virility in the 'man or jelly?' attack. (He may well have worried that his punishing comments had made the jury feel sympathetic towards the young man.)

'If I have suggested weakness and lack of determination on the part of Mr Russell, no doubt his youth was the cause. Mrs Russell's own youth must be borne in mind, also. It is easy to suggest that she has treated her husband harshly, and even cruelly; there can be no doubt that her behaviour distressed him immeasurably; that he was wronged by what she did cannot be questioned.'

Having all but apologized for his taunting of John Hugo, Hastings turned all his fire on to Sir John Simon. He charged that a very unpleasant atmosphere had been created by the way in which the case for the husband was opened.

'At the end of the opening speech, you, members of the jury, must have asked yourselves: "Why on earth is the respondent wasting time in contesting what Sir John Simon has told us must be practically an undefended case?" Why was the case opened in that way? Was it because if it had been put in the true way it would never have been successfully launched at all? In the opening speech it was stated that the marriage had never been consummated and that therefore Mr Russell could not be the father of the child. Not one word of reference was made to the fact that relations which might easily have resulted in pregnancy had admittedly occurred until August, 1920, and that the wife who was being accused of adultery showed all the signs of virginity long after the child was conceived. The suggestion now made that Mrs Russell had submitted to relations with men other than her husband which fell short of complete relations was invented at the last moment by the cleverest advocate that Mr Russell's family could find. It is admitted that on December 18, the date on which it is suggested that the child was conceived, the husband and wife occupied the same bed. Mr Russell, when he was asked whether relations had taken place between them, merely said: 'I do not remember that they took place on that occasion.' Formerly, if a husband were sharing the same bed, the husband could not be heard to say that relations had not taken place between them. The law as it stands at present was stated in *Bosvill* v. *The Attorney-General* (1887) as follows:

"The presumption of law, which is that a child born in wedlock is the child of the husband, is not lightly to be repelled. It is not to be broken in upon or shaken by a mere balance of probability: the evidence for the purpose of repelling it must be strong, distinct, satisfactory and conclusive."'

The evidence against Christabel, Hastings implied, had none of those qualities.

Sir John Simon was given an immediate chance to hit back, in his summing-up of the case for John Hugo. He began by stating with great simplicity: 'Members of the jury, if you believe Mr John Russell the case is proved.' He then drove home every fact, alleged fact or half-fact that helped to denigrate Christabel and undermine her case.

'The child was born on October 15, 1921, and the normal calculation of 273 or 280 days carries us back to a date of conception in January. Mr Russell has said that from the previous August or September he and his wife had been on such terms that she had not even permitted him a kiss. Nothing that happened before August, 1920, has the slightest importance with regard to the birth of the child. A relevant period to begin at is August, 1920. Did anything happen then, and, if so, what was it? Mr Russell said that though he married Mrs Russell because he loved her he never attempted relations with her because he owed her that degree of respect which some people might call chivalrous, quixotic, or even foolish. She was a girl of extraordinarily strong will. Until August, 1920, Mr Russell had allowed her to go her own way with her then men friends, hoping that by reason of the kindness which he showed her she would change. But at Broadhurst in August he found her going motoring with Mr Bradley, and he spoke to Mrs Hart and he determined to see Bradley, and Mrs Hart said that was the best course to pursue. Mrs Hart corroborated his account. He spoke to Mr Bradley; and his wife, when she found out, was furious. He felt that he must protest, and he did so. If that is true, and if it is true that she was furious at her husband's taking independent action against one of her friends, the date of August, 1920, becomes all-important, for from that date she never kissed him or allowed him to kiss her. She said that she did not love him and could not, and that she ought never to have married him.'

Inevitably, Simon harked back to Christabel's staying the night at Bradley's flat and to her sharing the sleeping compartment with Cross. But cunningly – aware that by now the jury probably did not regard those episodes as proof of adultery – he added: 'I do not mention these incidents as proving misconduct, but as showing how unlikely that relations were resumed in December. Mr Russell, who had shown considerable restraint, must have changed his nature – or was it the lady who had changed *her* character?'

At this point Sir Henry Duke interrupted Simon with a stern question.

'The burden is on Mr Russell to show that relations did not take place. Do you agree, Sir John?' – 'Yes.'

Responding to the rebuke, Simon said it was for John Hugo to satisfy the jury that there was no effective intercourse in December 1920.

'Sooner or later [he continued], Mrs Russell realized that she was with child, and on June 21 Dr McKenzie confirmed her impression and told her that she was five months gone. Had there been any intercourse on December 18, how was it that the doctor was wholly unable to get from her any date to account for the conception?'

Simon could not resist mentioning Christabel's 'attempt to persuade her husband that he was a sleep-walker'.

'You may consider [he told the jury] that a woman who made that nonsensical suggestion had something to hide. That impudent invention about the sleep-walking was tried by Mrs Russell not only upon her husband, but also upon some of her closest women friends. To Miss Acton, an old and close friend, she made the suggestion in July that the child had been conceived as the result of relations into which she had been forced by her husband. The war, among its many results, has apparently provided counsel for the respondents and the co-respondents in the Divorce Court with an ever-ready explanation of every possible irregularity.'

Simon asked why Hilton Welford had not been called as a witness. John Hugo had been cross-examined at length about his conversation with Welford, and Hastings had said that Welford would be called. Why had he never been called? Simon suggested a reason: 'because Mr Welford would have had to say that, at that interview in July, Mr Russell told him that there were no attempted relations between him and his wife on December 18'.

At the end of his summing-up, which lasted three hours and fifty minutes, Simon launched into his hammering peroration.

'Members of the jury: before the respondent's case can be accepted you will have to assume the occurrence of a series of improbabilities superimposed one on another. I will enumerate some of these. In the first place, you would have to assume that a child, born on October 15, was the result of incomplete relations in December of the preceding year – a matter not impossible, but highly improbable; secondly, that relations took place in December, although Mr Russell denied that they had, and it was against all the undisputed facts in the case; thirdly, that Mrs Russell was unaware of the pregnancy until June 17; fourthly, that she learned of it for the first time from a "psychological expert"; fifthly, that when Mrs Russell consulted the doctor she had entirely forgotten the attempted relations in December; sixthly, that Mrs Russell, associating as freely as she did with men, spending the night in a bachelor's flat and in a *wagon-lit* with a man, had never in the course of her married life been kissed; seventhly, that John Russell, who longed for a child, had repudiated his own baby after admitting to Dr McKenzie that he might be the father; and eighthly, that Miss Acton's evidence was a piece of invention. I submit that this painful inquiry has established the tragic fact that Mrs Russell is an unfaithful wife.'

On the same day Sir Henry Duke began his charge to the jury – who might have felt that they deserved a rest, after almost four hours of Sir John Simon. Even if they were not tired, they had every reason to feel perplexed. The petitioner, the respondent and the two co-respondents had all seemed engaging and sincere; but they couldn't all be right. John Hugo and Christabel were represented by two of the most eloquent advocates of their time, or any time. It was a duel on the lines of Pitt versus Fox, Ingres versus Delacroix, Gladstone versus Disraeli and Pevsner versus Betjeman: chill mastery faced exotic showmanship. Simon and Hastings had both advanced formidable cases for their clients. If the jury found for John Hugo, they were condemning the 'little chap', the infant Geoffrey, to a lifetime of being despised as illegitimate, and branding Christabel as a loose woman. If they found for her, they would be pillorying John Hugo – already ridiculed as a bedroom wimp – as a man who had put his wife through a cruel and futile ordeal. How were they to vote? Fortunately, before they retired to reach their verdict, they had Duke's magisterial summing-up to guide them.

In 1916, after the Easter Rising, Asquith had appointed Duke (later Lord Merrivale) chief secretary for Ireland; and he had been as successful in that rôle as anybody could hope to be.[29] In court he had 'a commanding presence' – 'There were no "scenes" in his court, no bandying of jokes, no laughter during the hearing of a case.'[30] He began his charge to the jury:

'You have before you as difficult a task as I have ever known during a long career at the Bar and on the Bench, in a case painful to a degree that it does not require words to emphasize. You have to deal with things proven and to pronounce upon things proven. The mere balance of probabilities and conjecture is in the main a misleading guide ...'

He accepted that at times the jury might be compelled to have recourse to probability rather than certain fact; but, as a rule, they must rely on what was proven beyond reasonable doubt. As was his way, Duke did not traffic in airy generalities, but vividly reminded the jury of what they had actually seen and heard in the courtroom. 'In order that your minds may be properly balanced, you must recall at what period of the case it was that we first became aware of the extraordinary character of the problem before us.' That 'we' seemed to draw the jury into a cosy alliance with him – as when a doctor breezily asks a patient, 'And how are we feeling this morning?' He had shared an emotional experience with them.

'I wonder whether any one of you during the first day of this case had any idea that in truth and in fact this young woman, three years after her marriage, and when more than five months advanced in her pregnancy, had never been known by any man in what is ordinarily described as sexual intercourse. It is the outstanding fact in this case in my judgment, and you should review the case in the light of it to ensure the balance of your minds and to adjust any impressions you may have had before you were aware of it. Another matter which you must similarly consider is that it is not disputed that such an approach by a man to a woman as the petitioner from time to time made to his wife may be the cause of the conception of a child.'

In that passage, we can observe two things. First, that although some of Duke's language is as delicately euphemistic as one might expect from the Victorian he was (born 1855), he does not flinch from getting down, immediately, to brass tacks. And secondly, the two circumstances he chooses to mention this early are both in Christabel's favour (in respect of the charge of adultery) rather than John Hugo's.

Once again, Duke made it clear that the onus was on John Hugo to satisfy the jury beyond reasonable doubt that the child was begotten by some man other than himself. He added:

'The effect of your verdict in favour of the petitioner on this question will be to cast the gravest possible stigma upon the child, but in order that there may be no misapprehension I must tell you that in this country questions of legitimacy have an appropriate mode of procedure in which the child is represented by his guardian. Do not misunderstand me: it is true that your verdict for the petitioner will indirectly brand the child as a bastard; but you must not suppose that it will finally dispose of the matter. I do not say that in any degree to minimize the gravity of the decision which you have to take.'

In his next words, Duke was severe on Christabel's behaviour, but once more what he said was rather in her favour than in her husband's.

'No one can help seeing that the self-willed, disordered conduct of the respondent has produced the whirl of trouble into which the petitioner and his parents, and she and her parent, have been launched. But you must not allow your minds to be swayed by resentment. The respondent is not being tried for wildness or indiscretion, but for adultery. You must also exclude from your minds, as influencing your judgment, the sympathy you will undoubtedly feel with the petitioner and his family and perhaps with the young officers who are charged as co-respondents in the suit.'

Duke urged the jury to weigh the characters of the parties. He offered a fair-minded portrait of each of them. First, John Hugo:

'Try to recall the impression made upon your minds by the petitioner when he gave evidence nearly a fortnight ago. Contempt has been poured upon him from some quarters because he was not man enough to master the respondent, and various people have suggested, some of them without knowing much about the matter, that if he had been man enough these troubles would not have occurred. It is not from that point of view that you are to judge him, but you must consider: Is this a man who speaks the truth and regards the sanctity of an oath? I did not hear much criticism of him in this respect. It does not appear to be disputed that he bound himself on his wedding eve not to overmaster the will of his wife, and, in spite of his passion and distress, he thought that, as a man of honour, he must stand by his word. That seems to be regarded in some quarters as fantastic quixotry. Does it bear on his readiness and desire to speak the truth and on the question whether you can rely on his word? You must also consider whether the horrible circumstances in which he was placed may have affected or warped his memory.'

Clearly, Duke is favourably impressed by John Hugo; but, while he does not think he is lying, he feels that his experiences may have distorted his memory of what happened.

Duke turns to Christabel's character.

'You must also consider the respondent: her veracity and her memory. And in this connexion you will not put out of your minds the tribute of many of her friends. Because, in spite of the errors which have brought her here, she has gathered round her a number of friends who have given her an extraordinary testimonial on the point of veracity, if not as a virtue, then as a habit. Tributes to her veracity have been paid to her by Miss Acton and by the petitioner himself, who said that before these questions arose he would have staked his life on her truth. Her wilful conduct towards her husband in refusing the obligation to which she vowed herself with a mental reservation must also be borne in mind in considering whether she is an honest mother or an adulterous wife.'

Duke did not stop there in his assessment of the kind of woman he took Christabel to be. With wisdom and an open-mindedness that one suspects was rare among the senior judiciary of the day, he urged:

'Another matter which you must carefully consider is the nature of the respondent as a woman. She is charged here with adulteries which might almost be described as promiscuous; and in relation to those charges you must consider whether she was a lustful and wanton woman, or whether she had a resentful distaste and dislike for anything in the nature of sexual intercourse. On that point there is a good deal of evidence. Her husband – whom I regard as a deeply injured husband – said that the approaches which he made to her were regarded by her with distaste and revulsion. Miss Acton gave her view, and said that but for the birth of the child she would still be of the opinion that the respondent was absolutely moral. I asked some of the witnesses whether they had ever seen any indication of a lascivious temperament in the respondent, and I could not hear of it. You must come to a conclusion on the evidence whether her nature and desires were lustful or whether she was a woman whose inclination it was to reject any sexual approach, to repel it, resist it, and resent it.'

It was pretty clear what Duke's opinion was; but he added:

'If you should find, however, that she permitted any man other than her husband to approach her in the same way as he has approached her, with a similar possibility of the conception of a child, I direct you that that would undoubtedly amount to adultery.'

The next day, 22 July, Duke concluded his address to the jury. There were some facts in the case, he said, 'and perhaps the most important', that were not in dispute: for example, that Christabel, when thirty-three weeks advanced in pregnancy, bore the evidences of virginity. He thought it very unfortunate that she had not had the advantage of being able to tell her husband that fact. Why had that fact been left to emerge from questioning by Mr Hastings – 'received with incredulity and amusement'?

'Counsel know, and solicitors know, and medical men know, that where there is no obligation of secrecy there are things which should spring to the lips, and I search my mind why there was not a communication of it at an earlier stage in this case ...'

Duke could be very down to earth; but he could also, when he chose, rise to the cadence of an Old Testament prophet.

He asked the jury to consider the position of John Hugo in June and July 1921. 'On his side there was, of course, a revolted incredulity when he was told that the wife who had refused to give herself to him was found pregnant and ... there was at that time a fateful silence as to the all-important fact of her bodily state.' There were inevitable conclusions by him and his parents. Duke felt that Lord and Lady Ampthill had come to the case with an honest resolve to seek the truth. He allowed himself an ironic aside:

'Something has been said about their attitude to this young woman. The petitioner said that his parents did not approve of his marriage. Parental wisdom is at a discount in these days, but I do not know that you will conclude that in this instance parental wisdom was at fault.'

Duke saw no indication that Christabel was received at Oakley other than with kindness and consideration.

He thought there was no real controversy about the period from conception to delivery. It was common knowledge that the ordinary period was nine months, but the medical experts had said – and it was not challenged – that the time could be much extended. The jury would have to make up their own minds whether John Hugo had had incomplete relations with Christabel in December 1920.

Duke turned to the allegations against Bradley and Cross, the co-respondents. These he regarded as less important than the earlier part of the case, which was 'fraught with consequences grave beyond measure'. Had Bradley been 'warned off' by John Hugo in August 1920? After Christabel slept in Bradley's flat, John Hugo had still treated him as a man of honour. The petitioner knew about his wife's stay in Salisbury with Cross, but said he did not know about the adjoining rooms at the hotel. 'If she had told him that they had occupied adjoining rooms, how would that have advanced the matter?' As to the incident of the *wagon-lit*, Cross thought that when he ordered two berths he was going to have two separate sleeping-car berths, and was amazed when he arrived at the station and found that the berths were in the same compartment.

Duke then gave the jury his final direction.

'If the petitioner satisfies you that he made no sensible approach to the respondent in December, 1920, or later, you ought to find her guilty on this part of the case. If the respondent satisfies you by her evidence or any corroborative fact that the petitioner did approach her in December at Oakley House and there was the sort of intercourse that had previously taken place between them, then it will be your duty to say that she is not guilty of that alleged adultery. If, on consideration of pure fact, you are left in doubt – if you cannot be reasonably sure – whether that abortive intimacy did not take place, then it is your duty to say that she is not guilty. That is what the law requires.'

Duke added that if the petitioner satisfied them that the respondent was guilty with either Bradley or Cross, it was their duty to say so. If the petitioner did not convince them, or they could not be sure, their verdict must be one of not guilty. After these common-sense observations, Duke moved into his loftier manner for his last words to the jury.

'The law does not ask impossible tasks of a jury. A judge, sitting alone, would have to decide a question of fact. The task is one which he is competent to fulfil; here you find the facts, and, just as a judge would have to decide them in other circumstances, you have to decide them here; you are competent to do so, and I ask you to agree upon your verdict.'

Duke concluded his address at 12.40 p.m. and the jury retired at 12.45. They returned twice for advice from the President on particular points. At 5.34 Duke said there was a majority and a minority on the jury. He asked whether counsel were prepared to accept a majority verdict.

Mr ROBERT BAYFORD: 'No. We have considered that point.'

Mr DIGBY COTES-PREEDY: 'Both of us agree not to accept it.'

At 5.35 the jury finally returned into court. They found that Christabel had not committed adultery either with Bradley or with Cross: the two men were innocent. But the jury disagreed as to whether Christabel had committed adultery with a man unknown.

The PRESIDENT: 'Is there any possibility of any agreement?'

The FOREMAN: 'Not the slightest.'

The jury were discharged. The two co-respondents were dismissed from the case, with costs.

What had fascinated the press was the battle of wits between Christabel and Sir John Simon. The *Daily Express* asked James Douglas, the editor of the *Sunday Express*, to cover the trial. Douglas was often vindictive. (It was he who later wrote of Radclyffe Hall's 1927 lesbian novel *The Well of Loneliness*, that he would sooner put a phial of poison in a young girl's hand.) But he was clearly very taken with Christabel – almost enraptured.

'It was a battle [he wrote] between an intellectual giant and a fragile wisp of a woman. The flexible steel of the advocate met the flexible steel of the wife and mother, and the duel was equal.

'I make no comment upon the combat. All I can say is that the duellists were marvellously matched. Wife-wit, mother-wit and woman-wit on the one side; on the other all the intellectual powers of an archmaster in dialectic. Amazing!

'Pale, slim, graceful, her head poised like a flower on her slender throat, Mrs Russell stood for hours almost immobile and almost emotionless, with every feature and every limb and every nerve under perfect command and control.

'The play of her mind was subtlety sharpened to the uttermost point of simplicity. It foresaw and anticipated every flash of the dangerous rapier that searched for an opening in her wary defence. Its swiftness was dazzling. In sheer intellectual artistry it was miraculous. What a brain! Often it beat its skilled and experienced antagonist and foiled his veiled craft.

'Sir John Simon's voice is pure masculine music. Mrs Russell's voice is pure feminine music. It is low and clear, and beautifully modulated. Its tones express every fine shade of irony and scorn and contempt. The printed word conveys no hint of its suave and sinuous inflexions. At times the sensitive face of the great lawyer seemed to wince and wilt under the tension. He looked more haggard than his quarry.

'And the duel between their four eyes watched the duel between their keen minds.

' "You have been standing for two hours," said the grave judge, almost pleadingly. But the willowy shadow of a woman refused to sit down. We were all weary, but she was unweariably proud. Her thin, white arms and long, pale hands stole out of her soft black sleeves, but there was no tremor of indecision in their quiet, slow movements. Strange arms and hands, whose quietness matched the quiet eyes and the quiet voice! Arms and hands of steel!

'The delicacy of the profile is almost unearthly. And yet there is no touch of weakness in the pallid, clear features. The strength is hidden, but it is felt. And it is utterly unconscious in its reserves and stores of resource. A prodigy of self-mastery!

' "Sir," she sibillated, and the syllable said volumes. "No – o – o," she drawled, and the long, open vowel echoed through the hushed court. For once I felt that Sir John Simon had met his match, and more than his match, in dialectical brilliancy. A marvellous witness!'

On 16 July, *Lloyd's Sunday News* gave further coverage to the case under the headline 'BABY CAUSES A GREAT LEGAL BATTLE'. 'One felt,' the reporter wrote, 'that here was a very Inquisition upon Love himself.' He added:

'Once or twice the judge, clean shaven and handsome, peered at the witness over tortoise-shell spectacles, and addressed her in a reverberating, solemn voice.

'Then Mrs. Russell turned towards the black-robed figure beneath the gold anchor, her determined chin uplifted, the Lesbian curls of her bobbed hair ebony against the pallor of her cheeks.'

Under the headline 'RUSSELL JURY FAIL TO AGREE ON ONE POINT', *Lloyd's Sunday News* of 23 July 1922 reported on the closing day.

'Mrs Russell sat in her accustomed place, in front of her counsel, at the solicitors' table. Beside her were her mother and her sister.

'Throughout the hearing, Mrs Russell, a slim figure dressed entirely in black, has borne herself with great dignity. But as the case drew towards the close something of the terrible strain showed in the intense pallor of her face.

'Beside his parents, Lord and Lady Ampthill, sat Mr. Russell, a slight, boyish figure in a brown lounge suit.

'During the summing-up, whilst Mrs Russell sat absolutely immobile, Lady Ampthill frequently covered her face with her hands...

'Mrs Russell is a problem for the psychologist. Her duel with Sir John Simon KC, during her cross-examination, was a performance unparalleled in that court.

'In a conversational tone, without gesture, and with a certain smoothness of voice, Sir John Simon started that long list of questions. In a voice of perfect enunciation and clarity Mrs Russell gave her answers.

'Standing there in the only place on the floor of the court uncovered by humanity, Mrs Russell gave battle to the greatest lawyer at the Bar. And as the duel of intellects went forward it became very much like some form of exquisite torture.

'Yet never once did this woman with the boyish figure, white, wide-eyed face, flinch, but, utterly mistress of herself and utterly unafraid of this grey-haired man, in silk gown and horsehair wig, whose success meant the loss of her baby's heritage, she made her answers slowly, deliberately, haughtily.

'And so it went, through that heavy afternoon, the vivisection of a human soul, the utter and absolute exposure of the most intimate details of a young couple's marital relations.

'Only an extraordinary woman could have come through that ordeal unscathed. Mrs Russell did.'

On 25 July, before the President and a special jury, the question of Christabel's costs was raised. She was allowed her full costs on the two main issues on which she had succeeded – the allegations of adultery with Bradley and Cross. On the issue of 'adultery with a man unknown', she was allowed her costs up to the amount covered by the security her counsel had applied for. The *Daily Mirror* estimated that the Ampthills would have to pay counsels' fees of £4,000.

Four months later, on 23 November 1922, Patrick Hastings applied to the President for a ruling that the rehearing of the suit should not be taken before 14 December, as Mrs Russell had to meet an entirely new case: a further co-respondent had been brought into the suit. He was Edgar Jacquard Mayer of Half Moon Street, London.

8

'Disgusted, Buckingham Palace'

The King was deeply interested in the [Russell] case
but quite unable to grasp the final result.
THE HON. ARTHUR PONSONBY TO HIS WIFE, DOROTHY, 6 MARCH 1926

On 15 July 1922, George V's private secretary, Lord Stamfordham, wrote to the Lord Chancellor, Lord Birkenhead, to say how outraged the King was 'by the detailed newspaper coverage of the *Russell* v. *Russell* divorce case.

'You will not be surprised [he wrote] to hear that the King is disgusted at the publication of the gross, scandalous details of the Russell divorce case.

'His Majesty doubts whether there is any similar instance of so repulsive an exposure of those intimate relations between man and woman which hitherto through the recognition of the unwritten code of decency indeed of civilization have been regarded as sacred and out of range of public eye or ear. The pages of the most extravagant French novel would hesitate to describe what has now been placed at the disposal of every boy or girl reader of the daily newspapers.

'His Majesty asks whether it would be possible in future to try such cases in Camera.'

The King's indignation could be represented as a little hypocritical. Kenneth Rose, author of the standard biography of George V, has told me: 'He was quite fond of a bit of smut – gossip and scandal. He liked British ambassadors abroad to write to him about the private habits of kings and prime ministers – for example, one prime minister who was addicted to sodomy.' But, as the father of the nation, the King took a paternalistic view of what his subjects might allowably be exposed to.

The King's disapproval was not ignored. The sort of views he expressed through Stamfordham gained increasing political currency during the 1920s, culminating in the passage of the 1926 Judicial Proceedings (Regulation of Reports) Act, which forbade the publication of graphic reports of the testimony in divorce cases. Historians acknowledge that the Act was precipitated by, and the direct result of, the frank reporting of the *Russell* v. *Russell* cases; but, long before the 1920s, there had been a demand for such a curb on reporters.[31]

In the eighteenth century, pamphlets and magazines which lubriciously covered cases of sexual misconduct were a profitable part of the publishing industry. Many of the stories were about the civil suit known as 'criminal conversation' ('crim. con.'

for short), by which a husband sued his wife's seducer for damages. In the eighteenth century, such coverage was an erotic entertainment; in the nineteenth century, the aristocracy's outrage at the scandal and publicity surrounding crim. con. litigation engendered support for the 1857 Divorce Act, which abolished crim. con. suits.

Discussing crim. con. during the debate on the Divorce Bill, the Marquess of Lansdowne pointed to its discreditable heritage: 'One of the earliest of such cases occurred in the reign of Charles the Second, and that monarch is stated to have attended every day's proceedings and to have declared that he found it quite as entertaining as a play.' Lansdowne suggested that winks and grins by the nation's rulers made it impossible to maintain the solemnity necessary to render justice and teach moral lessons. Dr Gail Savage observes:

'Those who sat in the House of Lords had more than a theoretical interest in this issue, since a crim. con. proceeding was one required step of the cumbrous procedure by which the most persistent and highly motivated of estranged spouses obtained a parliamentary divorce. Lord Lyndhurst, speaking on behalf of the Bill, reminded his colleagues of how a particular case had recently occupied the House of Lords for three full days, "in the course of which most indecent details were given, to the great disgust of your lordships". Legislators optimistically anticipated that the enactment of the Divorce Bill would bring an end to the unsavoury publicity given sexual transgression by obviating the need for crim. con. action.'

Of course, that was not what happened. A commentator in the *Saturday Review* wrote:

'The great law which regulates supply and demand seems to prevail in matters of public indecency as well as in other things of commerce. Block up one channel, and the stream will force another outlet: and so it is the current demand up in Holywell Street flings itself out in the divorce court.'

As early as January 1859, less than two years after the passing of the Divorce Act, Lord Campbell, after hearing some lurid divorce cases, confided to his journal: 'Like Frankenstein, I am afraid of the monster I have called into existence.' In the House of Lords he suggested, as George V was to do over half a century later, that such cases should be heard behind closed doors 'so that the details of cases of a certain character should not be made public'. Lord Redesdale (father of Nancy Mitford's 'Uncle Matthew') strongly objected to the *in camera* proposal: he thought the courts' business should be conducted 'in the most public manner' so that couples would think twice before applying for divorces. In any case, the idea of secret tribunals was contrary to the tradition of English jurisprudence. (When Voltaire wrote a pamphlet on the Elizabeth Canning case in 1754, he praised the open system of English justice, contrasting it with the closed French system.)[32] In the Commons, there were misgivings about an apparent attempt to censor the press.

Queen Victoria was exercised about the titillating coverage of divorce cases. She wrote to the Lord Chancellor about the possibility of suppressing press reports, using words uncannily similar to those of the 1922 Stamfordham letter – 'None of the worst French novels from which careful parents try to protect their children can be as bad as what is daily brought and laid upon the breakfast–table of every educated family in England, and its effect must be most pernicious to the public morals of the country.'

In 1860, Lord John Manners, who had been a leading member of the Young England party, with Disraeli, in the 1840s, again proposed that the divorce court be given the power to conduct its business *in camera*. He thought the publicity given to divorce cases was more damaging than out-and-out pornography. If somebody wanted to purchase pornography, he argued, he had to seek it out; but, with divorce reports, 'details equally corrupt and disgusting' were spread broadcast 'wherever the English language was read or understood'. An opponent suggested that, on the contrary, the reporting of divorce cases was 'one of the great means of operating upon the public morality' – presumably, as a Horrible Warning. Manners was defeated by a majority of 185 votes.

So the graphic reports continued. In the 1870 *Mordaunt* case, the Prince of Wales testified about his relationship with a baronet's wife who had been declared insane after confessing to several adulteries. In 1886 the Campbell case offered further entertainment. The blighted careers of Charles Parnell and Sir Charles Dilke showed what could happen to you if you challenged the conventions of monogamy.

By the turn of the century, attitudes had changed. Dr Gail Savage has identified three distinct strands of opinion which worked together to press for a re-evaluation of divorce law. Feminists resented the inequity of the sexual double standard of the law. Other people chafed at the way a restrictive statute intruded upon the individual's freedom to lead a life according to private inclinations rather than the requirements of the state. And judges and other lawyers increasingly felt the hardships suffered by those who did not qualify for the law's protection. Arnold Bennett's 1906 novel *Whom God Hath Joined*, depicting the agonizing dissolution of two marriages, was a powerful instrument of propaganda. Also in 1906, E.S.P. Haynes, a solicitor, helped to found the Divorce Law Reform Union (DLRU), which demanded a Royal Commission to study the whole question of divorce law.

In his summing-up in *Dodd* v. *Dodd* – again in the critical year 1906 – Gorel Barnes, President of the Divorce Court (known as a 'wife's judge'), fiercely criticized divorce law as it stood. In 1909 the Liberal Government appointed a Royal Commission on divorce, with Barnes as its chairman.

The issue of press reports on divorce cases was one of the Commission's specific terms of reference. Many witnesses described the suffering that callous reporting had caused them. Newspaper moguls opposed legislation that would restrict freedom of the press, though Charles Moberly Bell, the managing director of *The Times,* thought that ridicule and contempt were deterrents from divorce comparable to the death penalty as a deterrent from murder. Sir Lewis Dibdin, one of the Commission's members, spoke for many when he expressed concern about the 'practical corruption' caused when 'the young of the poorer classes' read about divorce. Lord Alverstone, the Lord Chief Justice, was hot against the publication of what he called 'lady's maid evidence'. Harold Hodge, editor of the *Saturday Review,* suggested that if the lower classes were allowed to read about the goings-on among aristocrats, they might conclude that these activities 'were not so very wicked after all'. (The Education Act of 1870 had created many more working-class readers.) In its findings, the Royal Commission supported the view that newspaper reports of divorce proceedings ought to be limited by law.

When Stamfordham wrote to the Lord Chancellor in 1922, Birkenhead asked his Permanent Secretary, the brilliant lawyer Sir Claud Schuster, to reply.[33] Schuster knew that he must both appease the King with soothing words and diplomatically smack down any idea of eroding the liberty of the King's subjects by *in camera* hearings. He wrote to Stamfordham on 29 July 1922:

'The Lord Chancellor fully shares the view expressed in your letter as to the impropriety involved in the publication of many of the details of the Russell case which have appeared

'There would be obvious advantages in causing cases, in which evidence of this nature must necessarily be given, to be heard in secret, and the natural impulses of healthy-minded people would be to pronounce in favour of that course. Very weighty reasons, however, exist on the other side, and have commended themselves practically to all those who have long experience in the matter.

'In the first place, it is to be observed that it by no means follows that because a trial takes place in public all the details which are necessarily given in evidence or discussed in the speeches of Counsel and the summing-up of the Judge should be published in the press. In the past it has been found possible to rely upon the discretion of the editors of newspapers to omit repulsive details from the report. There is no doubt that in this, as perhaps in some other things, the discretion of the press is exercised less wisely at present than in former years. Perhaps this is in part due to a general change in public feeling, which in itself contains elements both of good and of evil, and in a greater readiness to face the facts of life, and to treat publicly and openly subjects which only a few years ago were hardly mentioned or at the most spoken of in privacy.'

Schuster pointed out that judges could, at their discretion, hold parts of trials in secret. But, he added, the belief that public hearings were on the whole the wisest and safest course was 'based upon a fundamental principle of English Justice'.

'The disadvantages of secrecy will be readily apprehended ... The public must know with what crimes the prisoner is charged. It is of vital importance that the public mind should be assured that the proceedings have been conducted with propriety, that no partiality for the prisoner and no prejudice against him have influenced the course of justice. Secrecy in legal proceedings inevitably engenders suspicion and, even at the cost of a certain shock to the modesty of many, it is imperative that the confidence of the public in the unflinching impartiality of justice should be preserved.

'The strength of the feelings entertained on this subject by the present judicial bench is shown by a recent incident. The Punishment of Incest Act, 1908, contains a direction that all proceedings under the Act are to be held *in camera*. Those judges who have most experience in trying cases under that Act have again and again represented to the Lord Chancellor that this provision was a hindrance to the ends of justice, and that by reason of it the Act largely failed of its effect. I believe that this view, acquired by these Judges by experience on the Bench, is shared by all their brethren, and last year during the passage through the House of Lords of a Bill, which for reasons unconnected with this subject, suffered shipwreck in the House of Commons, a clause was introduced repealing the section of the Act to which I have referred.'

Schuster's letter could be summed up in the 1923 adage of Lord Justice Hewart, 'Justice should not only be done; it should manifestly and undoubtedly be seen to be done.' Schuster concluded: 'The minds of men are so framed that they inevitably associate secrecy with the idea that there is something wrong.'

In 1923, when the Conservative MP Sir Evelyn Cecil introduced a private member's Bill to regulate the reporting of divorce proceedings, Schuster recommended that it be sent to a select committee for study – a standard delaying tactic. In the autumn of that year Cecil wrote to the Lord Chancellor asking for his support in easing the Bill through Parliament, reminding him of the need to avoid allowing 'too long time to elapse between the Russell case and legislation'. In spite of this plea, the matter rested there until 1925, when the 'nauseating' press coverage of *Dennistoun* v. *Dennistoun* rekindled the King's indignation.

The *Dennistoun* case was not actually a divorce. It concerned a woman who was claiming damages from her divorced husband: he had failed, she said, to give her the promised support, which he could well afford. During the litigation, it became clear that Mrs Dennistoun had had an affair with a well-placed military officer, General Sir John Cowans, in order to advance her husband's career. It was this aspect of the case that most appalled George V.

On 6 March 1925, Stamfordham wrote to the Lord Chancellor (by now Viscount Cave): 'The King deplores the disastrous and far-reaching effects throughout all classes and on all ranks of the Army of the wholesale press advertisements of this disgraceful story.' Cave sent a sympathetic reply and suggested the reintroduction of Evelyn Cecil's Bill. The Home Secretary, Sir William Joynson-Hicks ('Jix' – the man who, three years later, banned Radclyffe Hall's lesbian novel, *The Well of Loneliness*), enthusiastically brought the matter before the Cabinet, which decided to give the Bill strong backing. The rather vain and pompous Conservative MP Sir Ellis Hume-Williams, who, as we have seen, had defended the co-respondents in *Russell* v. *Russell*, to his credit opposed the measure (as he had also done before the Royal Commission), adamant in his belief that justice required courts open to public scrutiny.

The Judicial Proceedings (Regulation of Reports) Act was signed into law by the King on 15 December 1926. It made it unlawful to publish 'any indecent matter' in relation to court proceedings, and more specifically confined the reporting of divorces to such neutral matters as the names and addresses of the parties and the summing-up of the judge. Some of the judges greatly disliked the Act, among them Mr Justice Rigby Swift, who had an important rôle in the Russell affair.[34] On 27 September 1929, the *Evening Standard* published an article under the headline 'Ever-Growing Divorce: More than 4,000 Cases This Year'. The piece quoted Swift, who, faced with a long divorce list, had complained: 'People seem to be breaking up their family life very calmly. If the public knew what is going on and what is being done in this court there would very quickly be some reform of the Divorce Court.' In the same issue of the paper, the Londoner's Diary commented:

'But the public cannot know what is going on except through judicial utterances. Since the publication of evidence in divorce cases was forbidden an obscurity has descended on the courts, and the general public remains calmly unaware of how the changed regulations are working.'

There is further mention of George V's interest in the Russell case, in a letter of 1926 from the former and future Labour MP, Arthur Ponsonby, to his wife Dorothy, a daughter of the composer Sir Hubert Parry. Ponsonby was a son of Queen Victoria's private secretary, Sir Henry Ponsonby, of whom he wrote a fine biography. Once a page to Victoria, he joined the Diplomatic Service but resigned to become a radical MP. He was a minister in the second Labour Government and was created Lord Ponsonby of Shulbrede in 1930. Pacifism was his great crusade. He inspired and almost single-handedly distributed 35,000 copies of his pacifist manifesto 'Peace Letter to the Prime Minister' (Stanley Baldwin). The 1926 letter to his wife is handwritten on stationery with the printed heading PEACE LETTER TO THE PRIME MINISTER, from 40 Smith Street, Chelsea. Ponsonby and Dorothy addressed each other by nicknames. He signs the letter 'Your own Taylor' and calls her 'Darlingford' (in preference to his more usual 'Dolly'). He tells her:

'I was at the Speaker's dinner last night. I found my legs rather chilly in breeches. I had a lot of talk with Patrick Hastings. He is a curious mixture of crudity, shrewdness, coarseness of mind and wit. He is certainly entertaining. We talked of *Scotch Mist* and he said the Bishops were awful and he disputed that it was improper. He also spoke about the Russell case and said how perfectly awful [the second Lord] Ampthill was. He said she [Christabel] spoilt her case by her utter inability to say anything nice about the family. When she saw Ampthill in court she lost her head. What she objected to in John [Russell] was that he would not wash – he never washed his testes and she had to burn his underclothes! Of course there was no question about her baby being his. The King was deeply interested in the case but quite unable to grasp the final result.'

If this letter were taken at face value, three interesting new facts could be derived from it: that Christabel hated her father-in-law; that she found John Hugo unhygienic; and that George V was mystified by the final ruling of the House of Lords. All these things are possible; but the information rests on the most unreliable kind of hearsay evidence. Two-thirds of it depend on what Christabel has told Hastings, Hastings has in turn told Ponsonby, and Ponsonby has relayed to his wife. Chinese whispers! Hastings is clearly out to be amusing, in a men's smoking-room sort of way. And Ponsonby – out to divert his wife, who was snowed up in their house – was an offbeat, quirkish, unpredictable man, a political maverick. He resigned from the Diplomatic Service because he thought the Foreign Office 'an obsolete institution'. He was a turncoat who left the Liberals to join Labour. In 1908, as Liberal MP for the Stirling burghs, he voted against his Party on the King's visit to the Tsar. As a result, Edward VII disliked him so much that he left him off a list of MPs invited to a royal garden-party, causing a big row. Ponsonby attacked the 'Liberal Imperialism' of Asquith and Grey. He joined the Independent Labour Party, experiencing the invidious position of an aristocratic socialist who was 'in the Party but not of it'. His monomaniac zeal for pacifism made him unpopular in both world wars. George V told Ponsonby's sailor brother, John: 'I

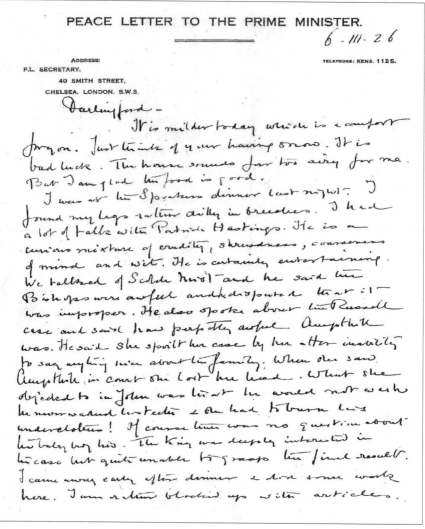

Figure 2 The beginning of Arthur Ponsonby's 1926 letter to his wife Dorothea.
The letter, filed under 'Letters from Arthur Ponsonby to his wife Dorothea' at Shulbrede Priory,
Haslemere, is reproduced by kind permission of the Hon. Laura Ponsonby.

know before I open my *Times* in the morning that I shall see Arthur's name doing something wrong.' We may choose to keep Ponsonby's gossipy revelations at the back of our mind; but they would not have stood up in a court of law.

Scotch Mist, mentioned in Ponsonby's letter, was a play by Patrick Hastings, published and performed in 1926. Concerning a failed marriage, it starred Tallulah Bankhead (who, two years later, seduced six Eton boys in a Berkshire hotel). In one scene it was made quite clear that a married woman spent a night with her lover while her husband was in the same Scottish house. Arthur Winnington-Ingram, Bishop of London, denounced the play from the pulpit as 'utterly immoral'. The outburst ensured a rise in ticket sales at the theatre; the play ran for 117 performances.

As the play was written only a couple of years after Hastings had acted for Christabel, it is not surprising to find in it a number of strident echoes of the Russell case. There is a general flippancy about the dialogue that would be likely to offend bishops.

Mary Denvers: 'Have you got any relatives?'

Freddie Lansing: 'Not officially.'

Mary: 'I have. They come and lecture me once a year on my morals.'

Freddie: 'That must take some time.'

Or again:

Jonathan Waterhouse: 'You two have taken to separate rooms.'

Mary [*laughs*]: 'Why not?'

Jonathan: 'Why not. When a husband has a single room in his own house, he is generally looking for a double one somewhere else.'

And again:

Mary [*indignantly*]: 'There would not have been any children.'

Jonathan: 'That seems very probable, from what I can see.'

The relationship between Mary and Freddie becomes more explicit:

Mary: 'And what would have happened then?'

Freddie [*in a whisper*]: 'I should have kissed you.'

Mary: 'You have done that before.'

Freddie [*with as much passion as is in him*]: 'But not as I should have kissed you then.'

Mary [*looks up at him*]: 'And afterwards?'

Freddie [*leans down – in a whisper*]: 'I should have asked you for a great deal more.'

Mary's husband, Sir Lawson Denvers says:

'You are one of those charming people who promise so much, but never give anything.'

Mary: 'What have you ever given to me? Does life consist of nothing, but just a living, hoping for the days to pass? I do live for these amusements you despise.'

Act 2:

David Campbell [*angrily*]:' Do you ever try and drive a man mad?'

Mary [*laughs*]: 'Often. I am married.'

One can almost hear Christabel saying that. Later in Act 2, there is a more direct echo of the Russell trials:

Freddie: 'You and I know her so well.'

David: 'Do we?'

Freddie: 'We ought to. We were both engaged to her at the same time.'

Further on, Freddie tells David that, but for him (David), Mary would be going with him to France.

David [*slowly*]: 'It is just as well Dick [nickname of Mary's husband] did not hear you say that.'

Freddie: 'Oh. He would not mind.'

David: 'Do you mean to tell me that Dick knew you asked her to go abroad?'

Freddie: 'Of course. We tell our husbands everything nowadays.'

That is a piece of business snitched straight from the Russell trials.

The Judicial Proceedings (Regulation of Reports) Act, though since amended, has never been repealed and remains in force to this day – the unhappy outcome of an unhappy episode. Dr Savage, who has given the Act and its cultural context more careful consideration than any other historian, concludes her findings with these severe words:

'The passage of the 1926 Act extended a state-sanctioned veil of privacy to everyone caught in the marital extremis. It did so, not so much to protect the individual's privacy from public scrutiny and so extend the scope of the individual's freedom of personal conduct, but in order to preserve the public decorum crucial for the maintenance of hierarchies of class, gender and age.'

However, Dr Stephen Cretney, whose observations on the Act were published in the same year as Dr Savage's, warns us not to overestimate its force.

'What, then, has been the effect of the 1926 Act? First, it is clear that the prohibition on publication of indecent matter added little to the law and has, in the context of press reporting, been effectively a dead letter.

'Secondly, although the 1926 Act prevented the daily press from giving detailed verbatim accounts of sensational divorce cases, the direct effect of the restrictions on reporting divorce cases was never great, and the press proved well able to make copy, even in undefended cases, from the materials which the 1926 Act allowed to be published ...

'But the most important reason why the Act ceased to serve any useful purpose is because of the dramatic changes which have taken place over the past seventy years in the law's approach to divorce and other matrimonial causes. The view, almost universally accepted in 1926, that the public had a legitimate interest in the trial of matters affecting the status of the marriage and the family, has come to be gradually (albeit with little or no public discussion) supplanted by the view that family matters are essentially private and that this privacy is to be respected by the legal system.'

Dr Cretney adds that for all practical purposes, with the coming into force of

Part II of the Family Law Act 1996 the effect of the 1926 Act would have become 'well and truly spent'. It was not spent in time for Parkis, the enquiry agent in Graham Greene's *The End of the Affair*. He morosely comments: 'The law that forbade the evidence in divorce cases being published was a blow to men of my calling. The judge, sir, never mentions us by name, and he's very often prejudiced against the profession.'

9

Enter Sir Edward Marshall Hall

Of divorce, and of the linking of divorce with the Admiralty, the late judge's opinion may be gathered from his now famous saying that he had 'one foot on the sea and one in a sewer'. Undoubtedly the most famous trial in divorce over which he presided was the second hearing of 'Russell v. Russell', which aroused great public interest and controversy.

THE TIMES, OBITUARY OF SIR MAURICE HILL, 7 JUNE 1934

On 27 September 1922, two months after his defeat in the divorce hearing, John Hugo Russell begged leave of the High Court to amend his petition. He wanted to add these further charges:

'That the said Christabel Hulme Russell has frequently committed adultery with Edgar Jacquard Mayer; [and] that on divers occasions from about March 1920 till the date of the Petition namely the 17th day of November 1921 at 42 Half Moon Street Piccadilly in the County of London the said Christabel Hulme Russell committed adultery with the said Edgar Jacquard Mayer.'

John Hugo swore before a Commissioner for Oaths in Field Court, Gray's Inn, that he first received 'certain information' towards the end of June 1922 which led him to have further enquiries made. But it was not until September 'that the result of such enquiries was so far completed as to enable me to make the fresh charges suggested above'. John Hugo was also persisting in accusing Christabel of adultery with a man unknown.

The new case, *Russell* v. *Russell and Mayer,* was heard before Mr Justice Hill and a special jury, beginning on 1 March 1923. We know something of Edgar Mayer beyond the bald court transcript, because Christabel's biographer Eileen Hunter had met him and developed a crush on him when she was a schoolgirl. She was on holiday in Norfolk with her mother and three younger sisters. Mayer was introduced to them as a friend of Eileen's uncle and aunt, Noel and Ethel Hunter.

'He was of medium height, dark-haired, of fair complexion and with blue-grey eyes, but it was his expression and his voice that I loved particularly. He seemed to be perpetually amused as though he found life always gay and sometimes entrancing. His eyes really did sparkle and his voice brimmed with laughter. He had a good figure and was always elegantly dressed. I can remember still, from the

Norfolk holiday, his perfectly creased white flannels and a gold cigarette case that flashed in the sun and was inscribed inside "To darling Edgar" – clearly from a woman, I had thought unenviously – and the dazzling white buckskin shoes banded by brown broguing, "co-respondent shoes" they used to be called.'

Mayer was born in Cincinnati in the United States and had first worked on the New York Exchange. He had come to England and in 1910 became a naturalized British subject. In 1907 he had married a Miss Abrahams. They had separated in 1917 and in 1921 his wife had obtained a divorce from him because of an affair he had had in Paris. But the couple stayed on good terms and saw each other for the sake of their daughter, born in 1910. Mayer had moved from Half Moon Street to Cork Street in 1922.

The Mayers' daughter and Eileen Hunter were both at schools in Eastbourne, and Eileen saw him again at the Grand Hotel there.

'With my uncle and aunt ... and others he formed part of a good-looking dashing group who, it appeared to me, spoke their own language, had many private jokes, and glided elegantly over the dull surface of taking their children out from school, doing it with style in a carefree manner and without becoming involved in the rather stodgy atmosphere of Eastbourne, as though they were reserving their main forces for deployment elsewhere.'

In another house Eileen's mother rented for the holidays, at Rye, in Sussex, the schoolgirl found nine copies of *The Times* relating to the Russell trials. 'Recalling it now,' she wrote in 1973, '... I see again the closely packed type tinted by the peculiar pinkish brown glow, I hear the dry crackle as I turn the pages, sniff the frowsty, cloying smell and feel my brow bead with sweat in that airless room where I dared not open a window for fear of being discovered.' As she read on, Eileen was amazed when the name Edgar Jacquard Mayer suddenly started out of the page at her. She wanted to know more about the origins of the *Russell* case, 'in which I was now passionately interested because of my romantic attachment to Edgar Mayer'.

The citing of Mayer as a co-respondent was not the only novelty in the court hearing of 1923. John Hugo Russell had lost the services of Douglas Hogg, who had been made attorney-general; and Sir John Simon was 'unable to appear for other reasons' – some thought because after one bruising encounter with Christabel he was 'chicken'. John Hugo's solicitors sought advice from Hogg as to the choice of another counsel. He replied: 'Well, there's one man at the Bar who might pull it off and win a brilliant victory for you – or he might make a terrible mess of it. That's Marshall Hall.'

Sir Edward Marshall Hall was the most famous barrister of his day – perhaps of any day. At first he refused the brief on the ground that it had been 'hawked around the Temple'. A direct appeal to him by Lady Ampthill changed his mind. Marshall Hall was sixty-five in 1923, the year in which he fought his two most famous cases: in civil law, the *Russell* case; in criminal law, defending Marguerite Fahmy, a beautiful Frenchwoman who had shot her sadistic Egyptian husband in the Savoy Hotel.[35] Legends accreted round Marshall Hall. They are perhaps best distilled in the 1966 biography of him by Nina Warner Hooke and Gil Thomas, and in the memoirs of Sir John Mortimer, who in part based on him the character of Rumpole of the Bailey. Hooke and Thomas write:

'Nothing pleased Marshall more than to throw open the court door as the jury was being sworn. On the threshold he would stand poised, his head upflung, sniffing the air as a warhorse smells the battle. His junior clerk would precede him into court with his medicaments – pills, smelling salts, nose and throat sprays – a shagreen instrument case containing compasses, rulers, magnifying glass, etc., his air cushions and adjustable footstool.

'The throat spray must have been an instrument of torture to opposing counsel, for somehow – quite innocently and by coincidence of course – it would happen that just as counsel was making an impression on the jury in a closing speech or asking a pertinent question of a witness, Marshall Hall's throat would become troublesome. Out would come the throat spray, and as he operated it there would be a disconcerting hissing of the spray, accompanied by a gargling sound from the sufferer, to the distraction of both counsel who was speaking and the jury who were listening. Often I've seen the fascinated eyes of the jury turn to watch the spray at work. And if it were not the throat spray, then there would be the adjustment of the footstool to give comfort to his painful leg, or else the blowing up of the air cushion.'[36]

Mortimer gives a complementary version of the Marshall Hall legend, told to him by his barrister father, who had seen the great man in action.

'[He] was always preceded into court by three clerks, one carrying a pile of clean handkerchiefs, the next with a carafe of water and the third bearing an air cushion. If the prosecution evidence was impressive he would blow his nose, a loud and terrible trumpet, on the handkerchiefs. If it got more dangerous he would knock over the carafe of water. If it looked like being fatal he would slowly and deliberately blow up the air cushion and so attract the jury's undivided attention.

'Marshall Hall's acting technique was old-fashioned but wonderfully effective. He would end his final speech by holding out his arms to represent the Scales of Justice. "Evenly balanced until you put in one side that small feather, the presumption of innocence. And then," here one arm sank, "the scales come down on the side of the defence." On one occasion, the judge, a merciless dramatic critic, told the jury that he was always pleased when Sir Edward Marshall Hall came to his Scales of Justice act, "because that means his speech is almost over".'[37]

Marshall Hall suffered from phlebitis and was often allowed to sit while conducting a case in court. The cartoonist Harry Furniss drew him in that posture.

If you want to get an idea of what Marshall Hall was like in action, watch the 1957 film *Witness for the Prosecution*, in which Charles Laughton, as Sir Leonard Robards, defends a murderer played by Tyrone Power. Sir Leonard is obviously based on Sir Edward, down to the lines of pills laid out in front of him, his thermos flask (allegedly cocoa, possibly brandy) and his being allowed to stay seated while cross-examining. Marlene Dietrich is Power's bigamous wife, who appears as the

Figure 3 Sir Edward Marshall Hall by Harry Furniss.
NATIONAL PORTRAIT GALLERY

eponymous witness for the prosecution. She is an art deco beauty comparable to Christabel; when Laughton interrogates her, both his melodramatic accusations and her coolly insolent replies give some impression of what it must have been like to witness the courtroom battles of 1923.

Marshall Hall knew all about marriages that went wrong. His own first marriage was to a young woman who did not love him and who died in 1890 of a criminal abortion, having been made pregnant by another man.

Proceedings began on 1 March 1923 with Marshall Hall examining his client, John Hugo.

'I think you are a son of Lord and Lady Ampthill, who are sitting here in Court in front of me?' – 'Yes.'

As in the first trial, a tactful fib veiled the way that John Hugo and Christabel had met.

'When did you meet the present Mrs Russell, Miss Hart as she then was?' – 'About September, 1915.'

'Where did you meet her?' – 'I met her in London.'

'Were you introduced to her?' – 'I was introduced to her by a shipmate.'

'How much did you see of her on that occasion?' – 'My shipmate and I took her to lunch and a matinee, and then we had to rejoin our ship by train that evening. We just saw her one afternoon.'

No mention of the *Times* personal advertisement. No mention of the high old time that Commander Hugh Stevenson was to recall in his newspaper interview of 1976. ('What a ten days we had! don't think we slept very much – we went to every smart nightclub in town ...') Marshall Hall took John Hugo through his service on submarine *C. 25* and his and Christabel's engagement and broken engagement. Then he moved on to Christabel's relationship with Gilbert Bradley, making a damaging new allegation about her.

'Was Mr Bradley an old shipmate of yours?' – 'Yes.'

'He had been to sea with you and to college with you too?' – 'Yes.'

'Did you find that you had both been engaged at the same time?' – 'Yes, that is what it came to.'

Marshall Hall covered Christabel's trip to Edinburgh with Bradley; her broken engagement to him and her offer to marry John Hugo if he still wished to marry her. It was Marshall Hall's way to coax his witnesses into being very specific. He managed to get John Hugo to give an account far more graphic than in the first trial, of what had happened after he returned to England from his duties at sea on 16 October 1918.

'On the 17th October did you see Miss Hart and have an important conversation with her?' – 'I did.'

'I will not lead you as to that: I prefer you to tell the jury what that conversation amounted to.'

John Hugo told how, after dinner with Christabel on 17 October, on the way back to her mother's flat in Harrington Gardens, she had asked him to promise that at first, at any rate, they would not have children; and how he had given his promise.

'At that time had you ever had any intercourse with a woman in your life?' – 'No, none at all.'

'And that was the agreement – that you should not do anything that would result in her having children?' – 'Yes.'

'I think the next day, Friday, at 2 o'clock, you were married in St Jude's, Kensington?' – 'Yes.'

'Your father and mother did not come to the wedding?' – 'No.'

'Did Lady Ampthill ask you both to lunch the following day, and did you in fact go to lunch the following day?' – 'Yes'.

'I am very sorry, but I must ask you what took place. First of all, where did you sleep the night you were married?' – 'We slept in the same bed, in the same room, in a suite of rooms that we had taken for this short honeymoon, at a place called Kensington Palace Mansions.'

'Where did you dine?' – 'We dined at the Berkeley and I took her to a play and then we went back there.'

'When you went to bed, what happened?' – 'We both went to sleep pretty quickly, because I was very tired after my fourteen days at sea, and she was tired, too; but very affectionate; we kissed one another and that before we went to sleep, and she went to sleep more or less in my arms; my arms were round her. About 3 o' clock in the morning I woke up to find her awake; I do not know whether she had woken me up or not; she may have done. She said to me: "Is this all that marriage means?" So I then took her in my arms and I said, "Well, yesterday I promised you that we should not have children at the beginning of our marriage because you desired it to be like that; but if you are agreeable, I am quite ready to swing that agreement and go ahead"; and with that I made a move to take down her pyjama trousers, but she said, "No, no" and so I stopped at once, and then she kissed me and said she was very glad; she had not realized a man had so much restraint, and she wanted me to keep that promise; and there the matter ended.'

'But for that promise, would you have consummated your marriage at that time?' – 'Yes.'

'I am sorry to have to ask you this question, once and for all. Have you ever consummated your marriage in the full sense of the word of having physical possession of your wife's person?' – 'No. I have never consummated my marriage in the full sense of the word; I have never had penetration.'

Marshall Hall established that Lord and Lady Ampthill, though disapproving of the marriage ('They said you were too young at the time?') had been kind to Christabel after it, inviting her often to Oakley. He turned to Christabel's two-day visit to John Hugo at Harwich. ('Where did you stay?' – 'Parkestone Quay Hotel'.)

'Then the Armistice came in November and I think you got Christmas leave in December, 1918?' – 'Yes, ten days' Christmas leave.'

'Part of that did you spend with her and her mother at Harrington Gardens; 46D was her mother's flat?' – 'Yes.'

'And the remainder of the time did you go to Craig Hall, near Malvern?' – 'Yes.'

'I want you to tell me what happened during that ten days' leave. How did things get on?' – 'She was very kind and we were very affectionate and kissing and that, and in bed, one night there, we were kissing and fondling, and she was in my arms, and my passions arose and I had the first emission I had had in my married life. Her pyjamas were not down, nor were mine, so in consequence there was a good deal of mess, which I apologized for. I said: "I am sorry I have made such a mess." She said: "Oh, that does not matter; I do not mind; I did not notice." That was the first time, really, that there was anything of that nature between us.'

'Was she affectionate to you?' – 'Yes'.

'And when she said she did not mind, did that seem really to convey her opinion?' – 'Absolutely.'

'Did that occur once or more than once during that ten days' – 'I do not think it occurred more than twice.'

After the ten days' leave, John Hugo recalled, he had to rejoin, but early in 1919 he got four weeks' peace leave. His then submarine was at Chatham for a refit. He had spent the four weeks with Christabel at Harrington Gardens.

'Occupying the same bed?' – 'Yes.'

'Did the same sort of thing happen again there, but with a difference?' – 'Yes.' 'What was the difference?' – 'She had her pyjamas down.'

'Did she, or did you take any precautions with regard to the result of an emission of this kind – about the bed?' – 'Yes.'

'Did you or did she?' – 'It was a little later on than this, but at her suggestion, when she thought these things might occur she used to have a bath towel spread on the bed underneath.'

'Did she ever complain about it?' – 'No, not at that time.'

'What sort of position were you in when these acts took place?'

'We were on our sides. I was on my left side, and she would be on her right side.'

'Did you ever assume another position, of being on the top of her?' – 'Only once.'

'What happened then?' – 'There was no actual emission during that one, and afterwards she said that it hurt her, and she would never let me assume that position again.'

Pressed further, John Hugo said that when the emissions were imminent, Christabel withdrew herself. There was never, from first to last, any penetration. 'Not in the slightest degree, ever.'

'About this time I think once or twice she got a little angry about something. What did she say?' – 'The first night of that four weeks' leave early in 1919, when I arrived at the flat she told me that she wished to God she had not married me.'

'Then later on I think she withdrew that attitude and said something different?' – 'She said she was pleased she had married me; she had got used to me again ...'

'That lasted for four weeks?' – 'Yes.'

'During that four weeks did you have a disturbance with her, a little bit of a quarrel or something?' – 'Yes, I did.'

'Just tell the jury what that was. You need not mention any names.' – 'She was working all day, and in the evening when she came in I had expected we were going to have dinner at home, but just before dinner she said she had to tell me something, and that was that she was going to go out dancing directly after dinner; and I got very angry and said that it was not right, that I was on leave and it was not right for her to go rushing off with other men, leaving me behind; and also the sort of man who would ask her to go out dancing like that when he knew me and knew that I was only on short leave from my ship, was no sort of man for her to go about with. She got very angry; there was a lot of squabbling, and she went, and she came back late that night.'

Questioned further by his counsel, John Hugo said that Christabel had never given in to any wish of his about going out. He remembered her contracting pneumonia in 1919. He was stationed at Greenock then, and took her to Wemyss Bay to recover. When she got better, they shared the same room. 'It was a very happy time, and really the only happy time of my married life.'

Marshall Hall was quick to exploit the implications of that remark.

'Up there, of course, we know that there were not very many friends at Wemyss Bay. There was only the hotel society?' – 'Yes.'

'Was she dancing much up there?' – 'She went to one or two – not more.'

John Hugo recalled that Christabel's sister had come to stay at Wemyss Bay. So had his commanding officer, Commander Marrack, and his wife.

'You and your wife saw a good deal of each other?' – 'Yes.'

'During that time was she living a quiet life?' – 'Yes, a very quiet life.'

Marshall Hall was skilfully drawing a contrast between a tethered Christabel – she happy in her husband's company and he happy in hers – and the flighty metropolitan Christabel, seizing every chance to play truant from the man she had sworn (if with reservations) to love, honour and obey. By drawing from John Hugo intimate human details that the aloof, academic Sir John Simon would not have thought, or not have deigned, to make explicit, Marshall Hall was presenting John Hugo as a far more sympathetic figure than he had cut in the first trial. And he was not done.

'As far as you could judge, did she dislike this sort of semi-marital intercourse that took place between you? Did she ever express any annoyance or disgust at it?' – 'No, not at all.'

'Did she express any pleasure in it?' – 'I have only known her really express pleasure in it as if she was really enjoying it, once.'

'We will deal with that in a moment. Was that an incident that took place on the night of 23rd December, 1919?' – 'Yes.'

'You were going to take her up to Northumberland?' – 'I was taking her across from Wemyss Bay to Craig Hall, which is near Morpeth.'

'Was it necessary to spend one night in Glasgow?' – 'Yes, we spent one night in Glasgow to break the journey.'

'Did you stay in an hotel?' – 'We stayed at the Railway Hotel.'

'You shared a bed with her?' – 'Yes.'

'Did this sort of marital embrace take place again?' – 'Yes.'

'On that occasion did she pull herself away, as you have told us she usually did?' – 'No. She said: "Go on: go on."'

'Is that the occasion you are referring to when you say that was the one occasion that she expressed pleasure?' – 'Yes; but I could not go on.'

'At the time when she said: "Go on," had in fact your emission taken place?' – 'Yes, it had.'

'Did nothing more take place that night?' – 'No, nothing at all.'

'Then the next day, I think, you went to Morpeth?' – 'Yes.'

'You left her at Craig Hall, her sister's house, on Christmas night?' – 'Yes.'

'How did you part?' – 'She was obviously very sorry at my going and I was very sorry, too, and it was the only time in my life I have ever seen her with tears in her eyes.'

'Whether she was or was not, of course, you cannot say, but did she appear to be very fond of you?' – 'She did, very fond of me.'

Marshall Hall then turned to Christabel's stay in Switzerland: she and her mother had gone to Diablerets in January 1920. John Hugo had joined them on 4 March and stayed for nine days. Christabel was very pleased to see him, and affectionate. But there was the problem of the bunk beds, impossible for two people to sleep in.

'Did you make any suggestion or overture towards resuming the existing relations?' – 'I suggested we should move to the downstairs bedroom which I was using as a dressing-room, and sleep there where there were two small beds, but they were side by side.'

'What did she say to that?' – 'She said "No", and I said, "Why?" and she said that the maid would laugh.'

'You stayed there nine days?' – 'Yes.'

'During those nine days was there any resumption of the old relations?' – 'No, none at all.'

When John Hugo returned to England, Christabel had written him several letters, including one which Marshall Hall sardonically labelled 'the "screed of passion" letter'. Marshall Hall asked him what he had written to her to provoke this letter.

'I wrote to her and explained that I had been very annoyed about the sleeping arrangements in Switzerland, and why I was annoyed was because I could not have any relations with her; and in this letter I said they were only natural; I mean, relations between man and wife were perfectly natural things, and nothing to be ashamed of or disgusted about, and it made it exceedingly difficult for me if I was deprived of them, and kept away from her. So really she must try and understand that she must help me as much as she could about this. And then I also said if the relations between man and wife were looked at in a proper way they were a very sacred and wonderful thing, and there was nothing whatsoever in them to be ashamed of or disgusted with.'

Marshall Hall then read out part of Christabel's reply:

'Your lengthy screed re passion leaves me unmoved. I'm afraid pandering to the lower side of nature in no way makes me fonder of a person, and there is nothing more distasteful to me than the idea of feeling as one person with anyone or that anyone should feel merged into one with me.

'One's separate soul is the thing to aim at, and I'm afraid all the "beauty" as attributed to sex relationship in married life by ardent husbands (and I daresay wives too) is in camouflage, and self-justification. Everyone must realize it is the beastly side of one's nature, and they all try to hide it behind some blithering rot or other. I think I look at it in its true light, and am not ashamed of doing so or admitting the possibility of such weakness in myself. Having delivered this short and eloquent speech, I turn to lighter matters.'

'Then,' Marshall Hall scathingly added, 'she goes on to give you details with regard to her black knickers having a yellow and blue butterfly on one leg.' He was taking a risk in reading out this letter. While it might prejudice some of the jurors against her, as an 'unnatural', obstructive wife, it was hardly the letter of a woman likely to leap into adulterous affairs. Marshall Hall went on to imply that Christabel was mercenary and spendthrift, her husband of value to her only as a supplier of cash: it was on her insistence that, when the Admiralty offered him a choice between going on half-pay or accepting a lump sum of £1,200, he had accepted the latter. Most of it was spent on a Hammond coupé motor-car and a fur coat, both for her.

John Hugo recalled how he and Christabel had taken two rooms at 46E Harrington Gardens when she recovered from her illness. The 'incomplete relations' were resumed – surprisingly, at her suggestion.

Sir EDWARD MARSHALL HALL: 'By the way, was it about this time that you first saw Mr Mayer?' – 'Yes, it was while we were staying in these rooms.'

'I had better break off a moment to deal with that. When had you first heard of Mayer?' – 'I first heard of Mayer in 1919.'

'Did she tell you where she had met him?' – 'She told me she had met him on one of her visits to or back from abroad on business.'

'Tell us all she said about him.' – 'She said that he was full of admiration for her business capacity, and for the work she was undertaking for this Company, and he was very friendly and nice. She also told me that he called her "Peggy". I said, "That is pretty quick work. Why does he do that?" She said, "Well, he told me that he thought I ought to be called 'Peggy' before he spoke to me, and he would call me 'Peggy' whether it was my name or not." She said, "It is all right. I call him 'Mr Mayer', and I don't see him very often." '

'And did she tell you anything about the need for jealousy, or anything of that kind?' – 'Yes, she told me there was no need for jealousy, that he was a respectable elderly man, and there was nothing to fear.'

This testimony was damaging to Christabel, because before long Mayer was to appear in court and the jury would see that he was in fact a man in his prime – the Adonis admired by Eileen Hunter.

Marshall Hall asked John Hugo about a day when he had met Mayer in the Harrington Gardens flat the couple had rented.

'You came back one afternoon and you went to your room, and your wife was not there. Where was she?' – 'She was giving Mayer tea in the landlady's sitting-room that she had borrowed for that purpose. I knew that she had done that.'

'And you found her there, and you went into the room?' – 'Yes.' 'Were you introduced to Mayer?' – 'Yes.'

'How long did you stay in the room?' – 'Just about time to be introduced to him; that is all. Did they say anything? – She said she still had some business to discuss, and it was evident that I was not wanted, so I left.'

'About twenty minutes afterwards, did Mayer go?' – 'Yes.'

'Did she say something about your coming in?' – 'She was very angry with me, and asked me what the devil I meant by coming in and interrupting a business conversation.'

Sir ELLIS HUME-WILLIAMS: 'When was this?'

MARSHALL HALL:'I think, as far as we can get it, it was about June, 1920.'

The WITNESS: 'This was at 46E Harrington Gardens, and it was about the end of April, or the beginning of May, 1920.'

The judge asked what the business was that Christabel was interested in. He was told it was a limited company at No. 1 Curzon Street, called Christabel Russell Ltd. Marshall Hall led John Hugo through the brief stay in Lincoln Street, Chelsea, and the unsatisfactory sleeping arrangements there from the end of May to September 1920. There was no renewal of sexual relations in Lincoln Street. However, the couple usually stayed with friends at weekends, and once or twice relations were resumed.

Counsel introduced the names of two women whose evidence was later to be important.

MARSHALL HALL: 'As a matter of fact, do you know Mrs Shorten?' – 'Yes.'

'Is that the lady who is called Freda or Frog?' – 'Yes.'

'That is your wife's pet name for her?' – 'Yes.'

'Did she come and stay at Lincoln Street while you were there?' – 'No.'

'Where does Mrs Shorten live?' – 'At that time she lived at 58 Redcliffe Square.'

'Did anyone else whom we know live there?' – 'Miss Acton.'

'Miss Acton and Mrs Shorten both lived at 58 Redcliffe Square. Amongst the weekend visits you paid did you sometimes go down to her [Christabel's] mother's house in Sussex?' – 'Yes.'

'And, generally speaking, what was the relationship between you and your wife during this period up to August?' – '[When she came back from abroad] it was friendly, and that; but it steadily got worse and worse, and she steadily paid less attention to me the more she began to get in touch with old friends and new friends and pick up the life of a gadabout in London.'

Marshall Hall asked John Hugo to bring his mind to Saturday, 7 August, the day of the Lewes races. That was the day Christabel went to the races with Bradley; then they had driven to Eastbourne, not returning to Broadhurst until one o'clock in the morning on 8 August. Bradley was staying in the house, sleeping on the drawing-room sofa. Mrs Shorten was staying in the house too. After dinner on 8 August Christabel (John Hugo recalled) took Bradley out in her car to return some empty bottles to a public house. These details were apparently not disclosed in the first divorce trial; but now Marshall Hall took John Hugo through his confrontation with Bradley in the garden, with its familiar punchline, 'Have you been playing hanky-panky with my wife?' Counsel's further probing produced a new revelation.

'Afterwards, did your wife speak to you?' – 'She did, yes.'

'What did your wife say?' – 'She asked me what I had been saying to Bradley.' 'Did you tell her?' – 'I did.'

'What did you tell her?' – 'I told her that I had asked Bradley if he had been playing hanky-panky with her, and that Bradley had said no; and I had then explained to Bradley that I thought he had been a good deal too much with her, and he had always had an unsettling influence upon her, and that was why I asked him the question, but I accepted his word that there was nothing wrong. He said: "The trouble is another fellow in the house is in love with her, and she is very miserable and unhappy about it." '

Mr Justice HILL: 'Did you say all this to your wife?' – 'Yes, I told her exactly what I had said to Bradley.'

HASTINGS: 'Might we know who the other fellow is?'

The WITNESS: 'His name is Woollan.'

HASTINGS [with heavy irony]: 'He has not been made a co-respondent yet, my Lord.'

MARSHALL HALL: 'Bradley had told you that that was the trouble, and you told your wife this?' – 'Yes.'

'That this young fellow Woollan was in love with her?' – 'Yes, and she was very worried about it, and did not know what to do, and so she had been asking Bradley's advice.'

'When you told that to your wife did your wife seem pleased, or angry, or what?' – 'She was very angry.'

'What did she do?' – 'She went down to Bradley and spoke to him.'

'Where did she go and see Bradley?' – 'He was still in the drawing-room.'

'Then, having seen Bradley, did she go up to bed?' – 'Yes.'

'Had you one bed there, or two?' – 'One.'

'Did you sleep in the same bed that night?' – 'Yes.' 'Did she tell you what she had said to Bradley?' – 'No.'

'Was she in a better temper, or was she still angry when she came up?' – 'She was very angry.'

'Were there any sort of relations between you that night? ...'

At that point, Patrick Hastings rose to make a forceful interruption, beginning: 'I have not taken the objection formally before, and I think this is probably the moment at which it is best I should take it...' He gave notice that he intended to argue that 'evidence is not admissible in this case as to the relations between a husband and wife – for my purpose it is enough to say husband and wife – who are in fact sleeping in the same bed'. He said that the principle on which he would be arguing was this: 'Evidence by a husband or a wife for the purpose of bastardizing a child born in wedlock when the opportunity for intercourse is admitted to have existed is not admissible.' Mr Justice Hill shot back: 'Do you say that that applies not merely to a case in which the issue is the legitimacy of a child, but to a case in which the issue is adultery?' Hastings replied that in his submission it did. There followed a series of legal arguments, with the citing of old cases. Hill was a judge who liked to spar with counsel and assert his supremacy; and the bruiser Marshall Hall soon joined in, though when he referred to the 1922 Russell hearing Hastings delivered a smart put-down: 'You will forgive me if I just remind you that you were not there.' Perhaps Hill was playing devil's advocate, but at times he could seem obtuse, as when disputing the relevance, in the present case, of 'Lord Halsbury's rule'.

HILL: 'The actual mother and the man who is her husband cannot be heard in a legitimacy case to give direct evidence that they did not have intercourse. How does that help us here, because that rule, you see, would make it wrong to do what we are doing every day in this Court. I suppose, during the last few years, when husbands returned from the war and found that there was a child born in their absence, there have been scores of cases in which a decree nisi has been pronounced upon this evidence alone: I was in France between such and such dates. I came home and found my wife had had a child. I could not be the father. Decree Nisi.'

HASTINGS: 'There is no doubt whatever that impossibility of access was always a ground for permitting the evidence. I would not suggest anything else.'

HILL: 'Now take this case. Supposing the husband called a medical man to prove he was impotent.'

HASTINGS: 'That would be impossibility of access. Directly you can prove *aliundi*[38] impossibility of access I would not suggest that the rule applies.'

Hill told Hastings that he would have to go a great deal further to satisfy him that the principle was one that applied to divorce proceedings, than a general statement of Lord Halsbury in a case in which the whole question was the legitimacy of a child. Hill treated the court to some further observations, halfway between knockabout humour and reactionary polemics.

HILL: 'It seems to me quite possible that when Judges of former days laid down these rules they had not contemplated a case in which a wife made it a condition of marriage that there should be no intercourse.'

HASTINGS: 'I am bound to say that I do not know. I am not quite prepared to express a view as to that.'

HILL: 'I think one hundred years ago they would have said: "Well, if a wife chooses to make such a condition nobody will pay any attention to her." '

HASTINGS: 'Except that they might have said that it was the husband's duty to put an end to such a position.'

HILL: 'That is what they would have said one hundred years ago.'

In that last exchange, Hastings was hinting at the point he had made so sneeringly explicit in the first trial: that John Hugo was a milksop who had weakly failed to take what was his by right; and perhaps Hill was hinting that that was not a very modern view. The badinage continued. When Robert Bayford, junior counsel for John Hugo, said the Evidence Act was 'the last survival of the rule that parties were not competent to give evidence at all on their own behalf', Hill commented: 'That is the law which kept Mr Pickwick out of the box.' But eventually Hill gave his decision:

'The point that Mr Hastings has made is to my mind a novel one. I do not think there is any authority in support of it, and I shall admit the evidence. What its weight is, is, of course, another matter, and where the onus is, is quite another matter. We are really deciding now whether it should be put before us, and I think it ought to be put before us.'

Marshall Hall resumed his questioning of John Hugo Russell.

'We had just got to Sunday night, the 8th August [1920], at Broadhurst.'

HILL: 'She went to bed, and she was very angry.'

MARSHALL HALL:'Then I had asked you this one question. Did any form of marital intercourse take place between you, and you said no?' – 'No, none at all.'

'My learned friend anticipated very shrewdly the next question: as a matter of fact from that night onwards had these marital relations which you have described ever been resumed?' – 'No, never since.'

HILL: 'Never since?' – 'Never since, my Lord.'

HILL: 'Would you mind getting the last time he says that this sort of relationship occurred?'

MARSHALL HALL:'I will ask him that very question, my Lord. [To the Witness:] Was the last time you had any relations with your wife at one of the weekend parties, or was it at Broadhurst?' – 'It would be during the weekend party in July, 1920; but where the weekend party was I do not know. It might have been at Oakley or Broadhurst.'

Mr Justice Hill's question was a gift to Marshall Hall, because the primary message he wanted to get into the jury's heads was this: John Hugo Russell had no sexual relations of any kind with his wife after July 1920. Ergo, he could not possibly be the father of a child born in October 1921. But the questioning of John Hugo continued: there was more dirt to dish on Christabel. He told how in July 1920 he had written her a letter saying 'It is rotten having all these rows and let us make it up' and had sent her a ring, which she returned. 'She said she could not accept it from me, and in any case I could not afford it.' Marshall Hall was always one for specifics. He wanted the jury to know exactly how sexual relations had come to an end.

The Hon. JOHN HUGO RUSSELL: 'I was beseeching her, and trying to explain to her how difficult it was for me to be deprived of marital relations of any sort, and to have no kissing, or anything like that at all, and so she turned round to me and she said, "I suppose if you insist I must submit to it." '

'What did you say?' –'I said to her under those conditions it was no earthly use to me, and I would have nothing to do with it at all.'

'And did you have nothing to do with it?' – 'No, I did nothing. From that day to this she has never kissed me or allowed me to kiss her.'

In reply to more questions, John Hugo recalled staying at Oakley on his own on 21 August 1920. He had driven to Maidenhead to meet Christabel at the Guards'

Club, and had tea with her. She drove him back from Maidenhead to Oakley (Bedford).

'On the way from Maidenhead to Bedford did she say something to you?' – 'Yes.'

'What did she say?' – 'She said she thought it would be a jolly good thing if I went abroad for a few years.'

'Did she give any reason for saying that?' – 'She said: "We don't seem to get on," and she was generally fed up with the whole thing.'

'At that time had she got all the arrangements ready for the business at Curzon Street?' – 'No, but she was well on the way to get it started; she had not actually opened.'

About that time, John Hugo said, he had asked Christabel about the affectionate letters she had sent him from Switzerland, which he had kept for sentimental reasons. He had asked, 'How can you account for those letters in face of your extraordinarily distant and beastly behaviour now?' and she had replied, 'At the time I wrote those letters I was weak and ill and bored, and I wrote them like that because of that.'

'Had you pointed out what her letters had said about her doings in Switzerland?' – 'No, I did not go through the letters with her.'

'I thought perhaps we had better get it out. You were really very much fed up with it all?' – 'Yes.'

'And you did threaten to do yourself in?' – 'Yes, I did.'

Once again, Marshall Hall was taking a risk. At the least, John Hugo's reply might suggest he was an unstable witness; and attempted suicide was still a criminal offence in 1923. No doubt these considerations were outweighed by the impression the young man's truthful answer would give, that he had been driven to utter despair by his wife's conduct.

As the hearing reached this emotional pitch, the court adjourned for a short time. When it reassembled, Marshall Hall questioned John Hugo further about the events from August 1920 onwards. On 30 August John Hugo had taken Mrs Shorten to the theatre. On 6 September he and Christabel had given up the Lincoln Street flat. They were invited to live with Lord and Lady Ampthill at Oakley until Curzon Street was ready. John Hugo had come to London occasionally to do some distempering and floor-staining at Curzon Street. Christabel in fact stayed in London most of the time, but came to Oakley twice. The first time, she asked him if he thought his mother would mind or worry if she found out the two of them had separate rooms. He had replied: 'I do not think my mother is likely to nose round and try to find out that sort of thing.' He had not told his parents anything about his married life until January 1921. But one of John Hugo's brothers had realized what was going on on 2 October 1920, when Christabel was staying at Oakley.

'That night did you occupy the same or separate rooms?' – 'Separate rooms.'

'And you can remember that night, because of a bulldog incident?' – 'I went to bed early in my own room, and the parlourmaid had not realized that I had turned in. She came in to put some hot water there, or something, and the bulldog, which was sleeping on the bed, got up and growled at her, and she went away and fetched my brother to quieten him, and it was only when my brother came into the room and switched on the light that they realized I was in bed in my own room.'

On 4 October, John Hugo said, he had gone to 46D Harrington Gardens, which was then empty. Christabel was staying at 58 Redcliffe Square, with Miss Acton and Mrs Shorten. Then came the move to Curzon Street, where Christabel had a large bedroom and he had a smaller one next to it. The dressmaking business was about to open. In answer to a question, he said that Mayer was a shareholder in the business. The episode of Christabel's staying the night at Bradley's flat, and her clothes being brought over, was rehearsed. He never went into his wife's bedroom at night; they talked through the door.

'Is it true that you ever burst into her room at night?' – 'No, it is an absolute lie.'

He had protested that she was spending more nights at Harrington Gardens than at Curzon Street.

'How did she treat you at Curzon Street?' – 'With absolute contempt, and ignored that I existed, unless there was a job wanted doing.'

When he had yet again remonstrated with her for not letting him kiss her or touch her in any way, she had said: 'If you want that sort of thing, you must buy it in Piccadilly.' He had replied: 'I will not buy it in Piccadilly for you or anyone else.'

Marshall Hall then brought him to the hotly disputed events of 18 December 1920. He made him spell out every detail: how at Oakley they were allotted the pink bedroom and dressing-room ('They are the best guest rooms'); how there was a large double bed in the pink bedroom; how he had found the dressing-room bed was not made up; how it was too late to ring for the maid, who would have gone to bed; how he slept in his wife's bed but made no advance to her of any kind. He had not had the dressing-room bed made up for the next night, as he wanted to sleep with his wife; but again there had been no relations. On 20 December he had gone to his office in Victoria Street, she had gone to the business at No. 1 Curzon Street. On 24 December the couple had gone to stay with her sister and brother-in-law at Craig Hall. John Hugo had slept in Hilton Welford's dressing-room, Christabel in a spare room some way off.

'Did you go into your wife's room at all there?' – 'I stood in her doorway once.'

'How did you come to stand in her doorway?' – 'On the Christmas night she and I had been alone in the drawing-room and she had talked to me and said that she was going to try and be nicer to me and make things go more smoothly, and she was altogether very pleasant and I thought that things were really going to go better. When we went up to bed that night, as she went into her room, I followed just into the doorway and offered to kiss her goodnight. She got very angry and said that the minute she was nicer to me I took advantage of it and wanted to kiss her, and she would not be kissed at any price.'

'Did she say what impression it produced upon her?' – 'She said it was disgusting.'

If the jury believed this, it was very unlikely that they were going to believe that John Hugo had had an emission on Christabel's body on 18 or 19 December, only a few days earlier.

To the outside world, the two were still behaving like a married couple early in 1921. They stayed with Lord Rochdale in the Lake District.[39] In February they spent a night with Major and Mrs Laing, at Aldershot. Back in Curzon Street, John Hugo had again taxed her about her affectionate letters.

'What did she say this time?' – 'She said it was all acting; she had been acting since the first day of her marriage and now she was fed up with it and was not going to act any more.'

Christabel still spent some weekends at Oakley. On one of them – 21-23 May 1921 – John Hugo took her out in a punt, while the rest of the family and their other guests were at church. 'And in this punt she said to me: "If your people still want the marriage annulled, I am quite willing to go on with it – I am quite ready for the annulment." So I said that it was hardly a question of whether my people still wanted to go on with the annulment; it was a question for me to decide; and I did not discuss the matter any further with her.' She had made no mention that she was pregnant. On the weekends she spent at Oakley, she had played many sets of tennis and had gone riding with him.

'On the 28th May I think you had an interview with Mrs Hart and your wife at 46D Harrington Gardens?' – 'Yes.'

'What sort of interview was it?' – 'I went to dine there with my wife and her mother, and I told them the results of the searches I had been making during the past few weeks for a suitable country cottage. I had two or three that I thought might do, but I was not prepared to take any more definite steps about taking one unless she said she would come and live there with me as my wife, and give me a reasonable proportion of her society. She got very angry and said that I was insulting her mother, for some reason, and ordered me to leave the flat; but as it was not her flat but Mrs Hart's, and Mrs Hart said I had not insulted her, I refused to leave. We had a lot more discussion, but she still would not agree to live with me as my wife, so there the matter dropped.'

'Did she call you a name of any sort?' – 'She called me a cad – all sorts of cads.'

Novelists know that specific detail gives their stories verisimilitude. Daniel Defoe, the first great English novelist, had Robinson Crusoe begin his story: 'I was born in the year 1632, in the city of York, of a good family, though not of that county, my father being a foreigner of Bremen, who settled first at Hull' – one sentence, five hard facts. The detail with which John Hugo, skilfully steered by Marshall Hall, was interlarding his narrative, made it difficult for the jury to believe that he was telling lies. This part of his testimony was damning to Christabel. It not only suggested she had been petulant and unreasonable; it reinforced, yet again, the impression Marshall Hall wanted to convey, that she was actively hostile towards her husband and immune to any overtures or blandishments from him, let alone sexual advances.

Marshall Hall then read out the letter John Hugo had written Christabel on 10 June 1921, in which he threatened to go to his lawyers if she would not 'take up married life with me properly'.

'Was it an honest genuine letter on your part?' – 'Yes.'

'Did you want her back?' – 'I did.'

'At that time were you in love with your wife?' – 'I was.'

'Physically?' – 'Yes. I was very angry at the way she had treated me, but I was in love with her.'

Marshall Hall then read out Christabel's flippant reply. On receiving it, John Hugo had consulted his uncle, Victor Russell, on 13 June. The next morning, John Hugo and Christabel bumped into each other in the Underground lift at Dover Street (a Tube station now extinct). She asked: 'What are you doing in London? Where have you been?' He told her he had stayed the night with Uncle Victor, but not why. On Victor's advice, he had decided to start proceedings to have the marriage annulled. Then came the revelation of 23 June, about Christabel's pregnancy.

Much of the territory covered in the first trial was now traversed again: Christabel's suggestion about sleep-walking; John Hugo's astonishment at the news she broke to him; and Christabel's question to him, 'Cannot you remember those Hunnish scenes at Curzon Street?'

'What did you say to her?' – 'I said: "But we have not had anything to do with one another since August" ... and she said: "I know." '

The couple had discussed the weekends they had been away together – 'and we came to a date we did not know. Neither she nor I knew it. It was a weekend just before Christmas [1920] when we had been at Oakley and we agreed we had been in the same bed but then nothing had happened. Then she said: "Well, what about the New Year visit to Lord Rochdale?" I said: "You must remember we had separate rooms there. I was never in your room at all – never in your bed there." '

Marshall Hall might not have been altogether happy at this reply. At least John Hugo was conceding that he and Christabel had shared a bed in late December 1920, even though he was denying that any kind of sexual relations had taken place.

'Having exhausted that topic, did she say anything more about "Hunnish scenes"? – Well, the conversation sort of kept on going round and round and we kept on coming back to it ...'

HILL: 'Did she explain what she meant by the word "Hunnish"?' – 'No, there was no explanation or anything. But since the War "Hunnish" or the word "Hun" is generally connected with violence or anything like that, and that is what I took it to mean.'

As far as John Hugo was concerned, there had been no sexual relations between the two of them since the row about Bradley in August 1920. Because of that, he had told Christabel, he was going to commence nullity proceedings.

'Just after that she said: "Of course people will say that I have gone wrong, but you know me well enough, and I give you my word that I have not gone wrong." So I said I believed her absolutely, but it was a very remarkable thing. It was shortly after that that she said: "Well, I do not know, I am sure, what has happened, unless I am another Virgin Mary." '

Marshall Hall asked him what his feelings were when she said that. He answered with painful honesty.

'Well, I was very puzzled about it, but I had not any doubt that there was nothing wrong. I was very surprised and very glad, because I wanted a child all along, and I was racking my brains to try and get something for her to tell the doctor.'

As they parted, she said to him: 'Goodbye, and thank you for being so nice about it.'

Marshall Hall read out the letters that had passed between John Hugo and Christabel, both before and after he told his mother about the pregnancy. Patrick Hastings tried to prevent Marshall Hall from questioning John Hugo about his visit to Christabel's doctor, Dr McKenzie, but Mr Justice Hill tartly rejected the plea:

'What does it matter if the evidence has got to come out? I do hate all this fencing. This witness has got at some time to give his evidence about the conversation with the doctor and the doctor is going to give his evidence about the conversation. What does it matter?'

Duly chastened, Hastings withdrew his objection. So Marshall Hall put to John Hugo some questions about his visit to Dr McKenzie. John Hugo remembered that the doctor had been very angry because Christabel had shown him one of his letters, in which he had written: '[Your doctor] should be exposed – it is nothing short of criminal lunacy to advise any woman, however strong, with a $7^{1}/_{2}$ months child, to carry on riding, dancing and racketing around'.[40] Marshall Hall knew how to play that one.

'It *is* a little annoying to say of a doctor that he must have been guilty of criminal lunacy, you agree?' – 'Yes.'

Maintaining the light touch, counsel then asked John Hugo what words the doctor had used about the fortune-teller.

'He said: "Yes, she [Christabel] told me that yarn." '

That was almost tantamount to suggesting that the meeting with Mrs Naismith was a cunning fabrication and a conspiracy.

John Hugo now came under gruelling cross-examination by Patrick Hastings, who seemed as keen on circumstantial detail as Marshall Hall. He asked him about the attempted relations with Christabel.

'I want just in a sentence, and as delicately as I can, to make it quite clear what those attempts consisted in. Did they result in emissions from you on the orifice of your wife's person?' – 'They resulted in emissions from me between my wife's legs.'

'I am sorry, I must ask you another question about it. You have given evidence in these proceedings before, have you not?' – 'Yes.'

'Tell me if this is accurate, and then I will not ask you another question about it. This is the question you were asked: "Your wife would be covered with your emission at the orifice of her person?" and your answer was "Yes." ' – 'Yes, if I had an emission between her legs that certainly would be a part.'[41]

'Mr Russell, I am sure you will see that, as far as possible, I want to put this part of the case as shortly as possible. Is that right or not? If it is, I need ask you no more about it.' – 'Yes, that is all right.'

'Then I will not ask any more about it.' – 'I do not differ at all.'

'At the time when those proceedings took place between you, were you satisfied that they could not result in the birth of a child?' – 'I did not think that they would result in the birth of a child ...'

'To the best of your belief at the time, was your wife equally convinced that they could not?' – 'Yes, as far as I know ...'

'You know now, do you not, that what you did with your wife might at any moment have resulted in the birth of a child?' – 'Yes, Dr McKenzie told me that it was just possible.'

Hastings also made John Hugo agree that he had heard Dr Dodd's evidence that 'all the signs of complete virginity were present when he examined her'. He was shown photographs of baby Geoffrey and asked if they resembled photographs of himself at the same age. Answer: no. But John Hugo agreed to obtain photographs of himself as a baby, from the servants at Oakley. Mr Justice Hill said he would not be happy to rely on newspaper photographs of Geoffrey: ' ... I have seen once or twice photos of people whom I knew and whom I could not recognize.'

By deft questioning, Hastings got John Hugo to admit that when he married Christabel he already knew her to be a woman with innumerable men friends, and knew also that she went about with them entirely alone and unchaperoned. He agreed that she was unconventional, lively and a little spoilt. Hastings teased him about having named Bradley and Cross as co-respondents in 1922 – both men had been acquitted, had they not? More aggressive questions followed.

'Mr Russell, have you raked every single spot that you can think of to see if you could find any evidence against your wife with anybody?' – 'My solicitors have made complete inquiries, but I myself have done nothing.'

'Do you know of a firm of detectives called Messrs Stockley?' – 'I believe they are inquiry agents employed by my solicitors.'

'Would you think that had charged thousands of pounds for the inquiries that they have made in this case?' – 'I do not know anything about it. I do not know.'

'Do you know that all round this house where your wife has lived has been picketed with innumerable detectives in the employ of Stockley's?' – 'No, I do not.'

Sir Edward Marshall Hall interrupted to say the detective firm had been paid less than £500. Hastings: 'All I can say is that you should go into the witness box. I asked this gentleman, and I do not accept that figure from you.' Turning again to John Hugo, Hastings asked if he knew that as many as ten detectives at a time had been employed. The judge intervened to help John Hugo off the hook: 'He very wisely left it to his solicitors, and he knows nothing about it.' But Hastings was still demanding that Stockley's invoices should be produced in court.

Hastings continued questioning John Hugo on the third day of the trial (3 March). As in the first trial, he was intent on suggesting that it was a lack of virility by Christabel's husband that had caused most of the trouble. 'Looking back, have you any doubt at all that with a girl of the nature that you have described, it was essential that her husband should be a man for whom she should have the utmost respect and not contempt?' – 'I really do not know about that.' Hastings also implied that John Hugo had been far too much influenced by his strong-willed mother, who had opposed the marriage from the start: here, he seemed to be telling the jury, was a feeble mummy's boy. And once again Hastings returned to the wedding night.

'Have you any doubt that when you ... woke up in the middle of the night that she seemed distressed and unhappy?' – 'She was distressed – hardly distressed, but she was a little – I expect she did not – it is rather hard to explain. Unhappy in a way explains it, but it was evident she was disappointed: put it like that.'

Hastings was only too willing to do so.

'She said to you, as I understand you to tell us: "Is this all that marriage implies?" ' – 'Yes.'

'Looking back, you agree that it would be difficult for a clean-minded girl to say much more to her husband in the nature of overtures?' – 'Oh, yes.'

'Looking back, does it strike you now that if you had then acted, shall I say, quite inoffensively, like a man, your married life might have been very different?'

For once, John Hugo hit back hard.

'Might have been; but it is no part of my code of honour to seize a woman and more or less rape her. That is what you are suggesting I should have done.'

John Hugo added that he had thought that perhaps Christabel was frightened of having children.

HASTINGS: 'Does it strike you that it may be a husband's duty to break down that barrier?' – 'Yes, certainly it is, by kindness and decent methods.'

Hastings tried a new tack: had John Hugo provided his wife with a penny? Presumably forgetting the money for the motor-car and the fur coat, John Hugo replied that up to the first trial he had provided no money because he had not been asked to; after it, Christabel had applied for alimony but the court officials had told her she was not entitled to it. Hastings painted a pathetic picture of Christabel's slaving away in her dress shop. The pathos was somewhat lessened by her 'dancing all night'. Hastings changed tack again. Did John Hugo make a habit of dressing up as a woman?

'I have dressed up as a girl, yes.'

HILL: 'That is not the question. Did you make a habit of it?' – 'I have done it lots of times, my Lord.'

HASTINGS: 'Did you keep a regular outfit in Curzon Street: stays and silk stockings and everything, so that if you wanted to, for any purpose of amusement, you could dress up as a woman?' – 'Yes.'

'Did it strike you that to a girl like this, that would increase her feeling of respect towards her husband for his manliness?' – 'I do not think it would make any difference. She is very fond of going to fancy-dress dances, and that sort of thing ...'

'Just look back at it. Do you think your life at Curzon Street was likely to appeal to a girl of this sort, with this kind of amusements, grumbling, dancing in that way, dressing up in that way? Look back at it!' – 'She was never there, so I really do not see it could have had any effect on her what I did.'

Hastings raced John Hugo on to the crucial date 18 December 1920, the pre-Christmas visit to Oakley.

'Did you have a very unpleasant night, the night you slept in your wife's bed?' – 'It was unpleasant in the sense that it is not much pleasure lying in bed there, aching all over for your wife, and seeing her lying there with her back towards you and taking no notice of you at all.'

'Then if your story is true that nothing took place between you that night, why did you not have the bed made up the next day, so that the next night you could sleep in the little bed?' – 'Because I thought that as I had shown restraint and had not done anything which she could take exception to on the Saturday night, I thought perhaps on the Sunday night she might be nicer to me.'

John Hugo swore that nothing had taken place between Christabel and himself during the Oakley visit. He told Hastings that he thought Christabel must have known she was pregnant some time before she told him she was. If that were so, Hastings suggested, wouldn't she have invited him to sleep with her 'to cover her tracks'? John Hugo: 'Yes, I think she certainly would have done, if she had any intelligence.' Hastings: 'Do you really mean to say that this lady ... was a woman of no intelligence?' John Hugo had to climb down on that one; but he riposted that by the time Christabel might have realized she was pregnant, from the baby's moving about, 'it would have been a little too late to do these covering up tricks, would it not?'

HASTINGS: 'You must not ask me what I think about it.' – 'I am sorry.'

Hastings asked John Hugo about his return to Oakley on 23 June 1921, after Christabel had told him she was pregnant. At first, he said, Lady Ampthill had told him that Christabel's story was 'moonshine'. Later that night she had sent for him again – she was in bed – and said, 'I do not believe Chris is going to have a baby at all; it is nerves.' He agreed that when his brother-in-law Hilton Welford came to see him at Oakley on 7 July 1921, Welford had told him that Christabel was 'furiously angry' with him because of his suspicions about her.

Sir Ellis Hume-Williams weighed in with a question on behalf of the co-respondent, Edgar Mayer, who had presumably retained him because he had done so well for the two named co-respondents in the first trial.

'Mr Russell, do you agree that if your wife has never had proper connection with any man and that the child is the result of the practices in which you indulged with her, and consequently that the child is yours, this woman is being put through a very cruel ordeal in this second trial?' – 'If it were the result of the practices I used to have with my wife prior to August, 1920, I should say that would be so, but I see no earthly reason why she could not have had the same practices with somebody else.'

'Is it your suggestion that some other man has been satisfied to do with your wife that which you did?' – 'As she is going to have a child which is not mine she has obviously committed adultery with somebody. Exactly what took place when she was committing adultery with that man I cannot tell you.'

While he was on his feet, Hume-Williams did not miss the chance to explore 'the way in which Mr Mayer has been brought into your family troubles'. First he reminded the jury of the way Bradley and Cross had been hauled into court for the first trial, and acquitted.

'Now it is Mr Mayer. Let us see about Mr Mayer. You knew something about Mr Mayer at the last trial, did you not?' – 'What I knew about Mayer has already been said, but during the last trial, after my case had closed, certain information came to us.'

'Oh, no, certain information came to you during the trial, did it not?' – 'After my case had closed.'

'During the trial, I said. – Yes, during the trial. Do I make myself clear?' – 'Yes.'

'Was Mrs Russell examined by Sir John Simon as to her relations with Mr Mayer?' – 'She was, yes ...'

'And did you supply to Sir John Simon information upon which the questions were put to Mrs Russell?' – 'When she was cross-examined?'

Hume-Williams was referring to the accusation, made by Simon in 1922, that Christabel had had a bath in Mayer's flat in Half Moon Street, when nobody else was present and the blinds were drawn – something she had denied. Hume-Williams thought that only John Hugo could have given Simon the information on which his question was based. John Hugo replied, 'No, the information was given to my solicitors which they naturally gave to Counsel.' He knew that Mayer had offered to let her use his bath, and he disliked the idea. 'I did not say very much about it, but I took jolly good care that the bath at home was all right, so that she should have no need to go there.' That was not the point, Hume-Williams objected. Since John Hugo was the petitioner, and he had named Mayer as co-respondent, why had he not mentioned the offer of the bath in his evidence-in-chief? John Hugo had two answers to that: first, that he could only answer questions his counsel put to him; and secondly, as far as he knew his wife never had taken a bath in the Half Moon Street flat.

Hume-Williams made a much stronger point when he showed that Mayer was being accused of committing adultery with Christabel at Half Moon Street from March 1920, when in fact he had not occupied that flat until October. 'It is rather a serious misapprehension for Mr Mayer, is it not? ... A little careless, was it not?' 'No.' As the *coup de grâce*, Hume-Williams reminded John Hugo that Christabel was abroad from December 1919 until May 1920. So how could she have been committing adultery with Mayer in March? He further pointed out how helpful Mayer had been to Christabel in the setting up of her dressmaking business – a business in which John Hugo and his parents had taken no shares. (He replied: 'I suggested to Mrs Russell that I should, and she said, "No, it will be a bad plan to put all our eggs into one basket."') Most of the money had been put up by Bradley and by Mrs Hart.

John Hugo said that what had prompted the inquiries into Christabel's relationship with Mayer was her statement in the first trial. She had testified: 'I remember Mr Mayer making this offer [about the bath]. He said he was out all day, and we could go there. There was a hall porter. We had a key to his flat, and I could go there at any time I liked.' John Hugo had been adversely impressed by the fact that Christabel 'said we had a latchkey of the flat and I could go there whenever I liked, and I certainly knew nothing about it. I had never seen a latchkey.' Hume-Williams was sure that the official shorthand writer had made a mistake and that 'we' should be 'he' (the hall porter) – that would leave Mayer in the clear.

Wilfred Crane was sworn, a valet attached to the 'bachelors' chambers' in Half Moon Street where Mayer had lived. He was thirty-five and had been twice wounded in the Great War – 'I had an exemplary character.' He was questioned by Robert Bayford, one of John Hugo's counsel. Asked whether Mayer had had any visitors, Crane replied: 'Several lady visitors.' Did he see any of those visitors in the present court? Crane indicated Christabel. He said he had seen her at the flats a dozen times or more, usually about tea-time. She would stay an hour or two hours. On one occasion it was more than three hours. She was never accompanied by anybody else. Crane also stated that Mayer had two photographs of Mrs Russell in his room, one of her in evening dress, the other in walking costume with furs. Sometimes Christabel had arrived when Mayer was not there: Crane would see her into the flat and make tea. Mayer had told him to let no one in if he were engaged. Mayer never had male visitors. Crane sometimes took notes from him to Curzon Street, nearby. He had noticed powder over Mayer's tortoiseshell hair brushes, and hairpins near them. Once, he took Mayer's evening dress clothes up to him. He heard bathwater running and knew that Mrs Russell was in the flat. Crane had gone out for about an hour. When he went up to Mayer's flat, it looked 'as if two persons had been in the bath with a cigarette at each end of the bath'. Mr Justice Hill: 'I do not know how a bath can show that.' On another occasion, Crane saw Mayer feeding Christabel sweets as she lay on a sofa.

Crane was cross-examined by Patrick Hastings, who soon elicited the fact that Crane's interest in the case had begun when he was approached by Stockley's, the detective firm. 'I did not want anything to do with the case.' However, during the 1922 trial he had accepted £8 5s a day to sit in court. He had been called in on either the first day of the trial or the second. His salary was £1 7s a week, with tips of perhaps £4 a week. Mayer had tipped him a pound or 10s every fortnight.

Hastings proceeded to demolish Crane's 'exemplary' character. First he showed that he passed as the husband of a Miss Walker of Lillington Street, London, under the name of William Walker. He had lately been allowing her £2 a week. Then a 'Miss H' was produced in court, a servant in the Half Moon Street flats. Hastings suggested that Crane had slept with her and had then written to a friend of his, named Ward, telling him not to marry her because he, Crane, had caught a venereal disease from her. He had had money from her. Crane admitted that he had left his holiday hotel without paying the bill, leaving a 'bogus bag' there. (The bag was shown in court.) At the end of his examination, Hastings asked Crane:

'Do you happen to know what your nickname is in the flats?' – 'No: I do not take much notice.'

'Did you know that you are known as Christopher Sly?'[42] – 'No.'

'Oh, come, Crane; put your hand down, if you do not mind, so that we can hear you. Do you mean to tell me that you do not know that you are known by that name to everyone in the flats?' –'No.'

Crane faced equally hostile cross-examination by Sir Ellis Hume-Williams, on behalf of Mayer. Hume-Williams also suggested that Crane's motive for giving evidence had been mercenary. He forced him to contradict himself. A man *had* been to Mayer's flat – Mr Hunter, accompanied by his wife. Mr Hunter was in court: Eileen Hunter's Uncle Noel.

At the start of the fourth day, 6 March, Phyllis Gower, who had been a housemaid at 42 Half Moon Street, was examined by Bayford.

'Did Mr Mayer have any visitors while you were there?' – 'Yes.'

'Ladies or gentlemen?' – 'Ladies.'

'Do you see any lady who visited Mr Mayer?' – 'Yes.'

'Where?' – 'She is dressed in black, sitting down there *[indicating]*.'

'Mrs Russell?' – 'Yes.'

Miss Gower said she had seen Mrs Russell about five or six times. Once, she recalled, she had entered the hall of Mayer's flat and he had come out of the bedroom and told her she could not come in yet. She heard someone splashing about in the bath, about eight o'clock p.m. Later, she saw Mayer and Christabel going out together, both in evening dress. Miss Gower went straight up to the flat. In the bedroom she found hairpins and powder, and an attaché case on the floor, 'big enough to get a lady's frock in'. In the bathroom, the towels were disarranged, the bath wet and warm. There was powder on the floor and a cigarette end on the bath.

HILL: 'How many towels do you say were disarranged?' – 'Two.'

Sir Ellis Hume-Williams suggested it might have been Mayer's cigarette in the bathroom, and that he might have used talcum powder after shaving there. Questioned by Bayford, Miss Gower said she had never heard Crane called 'Christopher Sly'.

Herbert Foster, who had been a valet at Half Moon Street, was called. He also recognized Christabel as one of Mayer's lady visitors: he had seen her a dozen times or more, usually about teatime. He or Crane would take up tea. He remembered seeing her first after Christmas 1920. Sometimes Mayer would send down word by Crane that he was not to be disturbed if a lady was there. Bayford said he could not accept that evidence unless Foster himself had had the order direct from Mayer. Foster said that once or twice the order had been direct to him from Mayer.

Ellen Maud Rayner entered the witness box. She had been housekeeper at Half Moon Street; her husband was the steward. She too remembered Mayer's visitors as 'Ladies, always.' Once she had served a *tête-à-tête* lunch to Mayer and Christabel: sole, cutlets and strawberries and cream. She and her husband had been dismissed from Half Moon Street. Hastings tried to get details but the judge said he would have to question the husband about those. Hastings suggested that her husband had been busy since he was fired, working for the Stockley's detectives. She said he had been about with the Stockley assistants 'because he has been followed about by Withers' assistants [employed by Christabel's solicitor] – as many as four at a time'. She denied she had been dismissed for drunkenness, adding, 'Impudence!' Kathleen Ellen Foster, who had been an under-housemaid at Half Moon Street, testified that she had seen Christabel in Mayer's flat.

Lady Ampthill was now examined by Bayford, who straight away flourished her credentials before the jury –

'Are you one of the Ladies-in-Waiting to Her Majesty the Queen?' – 'Yes.'

'Did you, in fact, present your daughter-in-law, Mrs Russell, at Court?' – 'I did, in the summer of 1919, at a garden party.'

She said of the couple: 'We were only too delighted to see them whenever they would come to us.' Details disclosed in the first trial were recapitulated: the non-wearing of the wedding-ring; John Hugo's unhappiness; the dinner at Oakley at which she had asked Christabel why she had not kept her wedding vows. She had been 'rather horrified' when Christabel admitted she had made the vows with a mental reservation. The old question about sleep-walking was asked once more: no, her son had never walked in his sleep. Then photographs of John Hugo as a baby were shown to her. She agreed they were of her son. Asked whether she saw any similarity between them and Christabel's baby, whom she had been shown, she replied: 'None whatever.'

Mr ROBERT BAYFORD: 'Something has been said about your son dressing up. Have you known him to dress up?' – 'Yes, I have on one or two occasions.'

'I do not know what the suggestion is here. Is he a person fond of manly sports or not?' – 'Yes, very; particularly fond of football; and if I may be allowed to make another statement, I should like to say that it was really a joke when he dressed up. It was a poor joke, but it was one. My son takes size 12 in shoes, size 10 in gloves, and stands 6ft 5in in height.'

While Bayford wanted to show that Lady Ampthill had been kind to Christabel, Hastings suggested quite the opposite.

'I daresay you guessed that your son would have liked you to be at the wedding?' – 'I am sure he would have.'

'Am I right in thinking that you purposely kept away?' – Yes, I purposely kept away.' 'Although you realized, of course, it must have been a great distress to both of them?' – 'I think it was a distress to my son. I never asked about the other.'

'Your daughter-in-law did not know you at that time, did she?' – 'Oh, yes; she had stayed with me in 1917 at my country house. I am obliged to say "me" because my husband was abroad at the time.'

'In that case it would have been all the more distressing to her?' – 'No, I do not think so.'

Mr Justice Hill told the jury they could see the photographs afterwards, adding: 'To my mind you will not attach too much importance to any similarity.'

Maud Acton was examined by Sir Edward Marshall Hall. She said she had known Christabel since she (Christabel) was a child; intimately since she was about seventeen.

'Was she a great friend of yours?' – 'Yes; I was very fond of her.'

'And you are still fond of her?' –' I was fond of what she was.'

Both before and after Christabel had married John Hugo she had warned her. 'I said I thought it was extremely dangerous of her, as she was so attractive, to go out with men at night, and subject herself to being assaulted, because I felt certain a man could overpower her if it came to a struggle.' What had Christabel replied to that? 'She said she could best any man.' Miss Acton said Christabel had treated John Hugo 'very badly indeed' when they lived in Lincoln Street. She thought she treated him even worse after the move to Curzon Street. About June 1921 she had noticed a change in Christabel's figure: 'She was much fatter.'

'What did you say to her?' – 'I said: "When are the twins coming, Chris?" '

'What was her reply?' – 'She said: "I am getting fat; I must take to wearing my corsets again." That was all. Then she changed the subject.'

By then Miss Acton was quite sure that Christabel was expecting a child. When she admitted it, Miss Acton reminded her of what she had said in January 1921: 'If I did have a child it should not be John's.'

'What else did she say?' – 'She said: "There are such things as Hunnish scenes," and I said, "Do you mean to say that John was violent – used violence to you? Do you expect me to believe that?" and she nodded. I said: "You would not have stayed under the roof an hour if he had attempted to be violent with you; certainly not for a night." '

'What did she say to that?' – 'She said something about: "We had an awful fortnight," or "There was an awful fortnight in January." '

Christabel had also said, 'I could not make a scene,' to which Miss Acton replied: 'You could have come to me.' When Miss Acton reminded Christabel of how she had warned her she might one day be overpowered, she said, 'You were right and I was wrong.'

Christabel had told Miss Acton how she had met Mayer, in Belgium. 'And when he was introduced to me,' Miss Acton added, 'I said: "I suppose he is in love with you" – as they all were; and she said, "I suppose so."' A month later, Christabel had said to her, of Mayer: 'He is getting too fond of me. I must not see so much of him' or 'I must drop him.' Asked what Christabel had told her about her relations with John Hugo, Miss Acton replied: 'It was always the same. She said, "His life or mine has got to be ruined, and it is not going to be mine."' After Geoffrey was born, Miss Acton had seen Christabel once more, in the nursing-home; but after that Christabel refused to have anything more to do with her – 'She saw that I doubted its parentage.'

Hastings, in his cross-examination, took her through the answers she had given him at the first trial. Yes, but for the birth of the child she would still have believed Christabel to be a moral woman. Yes, she knew Christabel was very fond of her. Yes, Christabel was a lovable girl; absolutely fearless and absolutely honest.

'And absolutely frank?' – 'When she wished to be.'

Christabel's letters to Miss Acton were once again read out, including the passage 'and the only women who have failed me are you and Freda'.

'Freda was this lady, Mrs Shorten. I think you used to live with Mrs Shorten?' – 'Yes.'

'And I think you know that Mrs Russell had had what was to her a very distressing dispute with Mrs Shorten?' – 'I do not know, not particularly.'

'Did you not know that Mrs Russell had taken a step which she thought was in the interests of Mrs Shorten, and which had caused a great cleft between them?' – 'Oh, yes, I do.'

'I thought you did. "Funny that the three I've had most to do with outside my family should all fail – and I was so fond of you, Accy." Did that letter touch you at all when you got it?' – 'No.'

Sir Ellis Hume-Williams took over the interrogation.

'Have you ever in your life heard one syllable about any improper relations between her and Mr Mayer?' – 'No.'

'Had you the least suspicion that there were any such relations?' – 'Not until she told me he was getting too fond of her.'

'Do you mean to tell my Lord and the Jury that when she volunteered the statement to you that he was getting too fond of her you understood from that that they had guilty relations?' – 'Not as far as that, but familiarities.'

Maud Cicely Moresby-White was sworn, the wife of Archer Moresby-White. As we have seen, her brother married a sister of Christabel's mother. Asked by Marshall Hall if she was attending on subpoena, she answered: 'Yes; I dislike it very much.' She had known Christabel since she (Christabel) was a small child. Christabel had telephoned her on the day she saw the fortune-teller, to announce 'a great piece of news', that she was going to have a baby. 'I said: "Isn't John delighted?" She said: "Yes; I told him today."' She repeated how Christabel had made, a few days later, the suggestion about sleep-walking. Hastings took over the questioning. He charged that Mrs Moresby-White was not really a friend of Christabel's at all: she disliked Christabel and Christabel disliked her. She replied:

'I was very fond of her before she married.'

'Do you see a Miss Erskine in Court? Just look round and see if you can see her.' –'I think I saw her this morning. I do not see her at this minute.'

'Did you ever chat over Mrs Russell, your friend, with Miss Erskine?' – 'I talked about her.'

'Did you know Mrs Benjamin?' – 'Yes.'

'Have you also chatted over your friend, Mrs Russell, with Mrs Benjamin?' – 'Yes, we discussed her.'

'Just see whether we agree as to what you told her. Mrs Russell, you say, was a very great friend?' – 'I thought she was then.'

'Did you tell Miss Erskine that Mrs Russell went to all the lowest night clubs in London indecently dressed?' – 'I told her I had heard it.'

'Well, that is a good start to increase your friendship. Did you then say that she had not a shred of reputation left?' – 'No, I did not say that.'

'And that she was the wickedest woman in London?' – 'No, certainly not ...'

'Now as to Mrs Benjamin. Did you tell Mrs Benjamin that Mrs Russell was living with a man to whom she had let the top floors of Curzon Street?' – 'No.'

Lord Ampthill came into the witness box, a stout, bearded figure. He told Marshall Hall that he had had to borrow heavily to defray the costs of the first trial: 'It means practically ruin to me.' Cross-examined by Hastings, he said he had liked Christabel when he had first met her, and had told her so; but in March 1921 had advised his son to make a press announcement that he would not be responsible for her debts. When Hastings suggested that Christabel was making more money than the £300 allowance John Hugo received from his father, Ampthill said: 'She had eaten up every penny of money he had.'

Elfrida Shorten was sworn. For many years before their quarrel, she had been a great friend of Christabel's, and she had invested £400 in her business. At one time she had been secretary to the business, in Curzon Street. She had met Mayer once or twice. She had first encountered him in October 1920 when he came to a dinner Christabel organized at Redcliffe Square when she was staying with Maud Acton and herself. Once, she had been to Half Moon Street with Christabel to look at some chintzes Mayer had bought. She knew that he called Christabel 'Peggy'. But she believed the relations between the two were 'purely business'. She had been at Broadhurst in August 1920 when Christabel took Bradley out in the motor-car.

MARSHALL HALL:'I want just yes or no to this. Do you know that something happened?' – 'Yes.'

'Did Mrs Russell tell you anything about it?' – 'Yes.'

'What did Mrs Russell tell you about it?' – 'She came into my bedroom that evening and said: "John is talking to Gilbert now in the garden," and she was very angry indeed, and she just said: "If Gilbert leaves the house tonight, I will go, too." '

'Gilbert was Bradley?' – 'Gilbert being Bradley.'

Mrs Shorten agreed that Bradley had not in fact left the house that night.

Marshall Hall asked her about the time John Hugo had taken her to the theatre.

'She used to be very keen for me to take him out, and keep him amused.'

'Can you tell the Jury what her exact words were when she said that?' – 'She used to say, "For heaven's sake, Rug,[43] take John out and keep his eye off the ball." '

'If you take your eye off the ball at golf, you lose your stroke, do you not?'

HASTINGS: 'Can she tell us who was the ball?'

MARSHALL HALL:'My learned friend wants to know who was the ball?' – 'I imagine Mrs Russell.'

Marshall Hall also made Mrs Shorten repeat what Christabel had told her about the Christmas 1920 visit to the Welfords at Craig Hall: how she had made an effort to be nice to John Hugo and how, as a result, 'The fool actually came into my room and wanted to kiss me.' Mrs Shorten thought that was said seriously. She also repeated what Christabel had said about the critical weekend at Oakley in December 1920 – 'Wasn't it awful? I had to spend last weekend sleeping in the same bed as John.' To which Mrs Shorten had replied: 'How dreadful. What did you do?' 'Got to the furthest side of the bed naturally and had nothing to do with him.'

She and Christabel had quarrelled in January 1921. Marshall Hall tried to find out the cause of the break, but received only a vague reply – 'She had become quite a different person.' They saw nothing of each other until after the baby was born in October. Then Mrs Shorten had sent flowers to the nursing home and Christabel had asked to see her. She had gone to the nursing home. Nothing had been said about the child's paternity.

Marshall Hall read out a letter from Christabel to Elfrida Shorten, undated but certainly written after the baby was born.

'Rug, darling,

You are right I don't understand but then that is where I have failed from the start I suppose ... Is Time going to heal it all or what? Are we to wait ten years and then will you have forgotten the hurt of it? If not, why is it best we should not meet now? I believe you said to Stilts or someone (I forget who now) that I'd failed you when you wanted me most. Don't you think Rug that I must be wanting you just desperately now when I've got to vindicate myself and my baby before the world? ... I've wanted you and I think you've thought I've got hard and not caring ... You're Rug and as such I've got certain rights to you!'

The letter was signed 'Tob'.

Another letter from Tob to Rug, read out by Marshall Hall, hinted at what might be the origin of their quarrel –

'Rug darling – I believe I see things at last in their true light. I suppose if you really love Reg I ought never to have said a word against him even if I thought I was helping you. If that is it, Rug, will you forgive me and let me apologise more deeply than I can ever say and will you understand that it was because I didn't realize that anyone could feel like that about a man? I suppose I'm hard or is it that I've never really been in love? ...'

Patrick Hastings, cross-examining, soon established that it was indeed Christabel' s 'interference' over Mrs Shorten and 'Reg' (whose full name was never revealed) that had caused the breach between them. She refused to concede that Christabel had been broken-hearted when she wrote the 'Rug, darling' and 'Darling Rug' letters after the baby was born. 'Mrs Russell was a woman with a very keen sense of humour and I cannot imagine her being broken-hearted about anything.' She thought that for the most part Christabel was merely laughing at her in the letters, though she accepted that the new mother was not being humorous when she wrote to her: 'My son can smile. Life's going to be wonderful, but I want there to be you in it. I shall burst soon if I don't talk to you and I want Rug to have some of the joy of Geoffrey.'

Hastings asked her if she had a bitter grudge against Christabel. 'I have no grudge at all against Mrs Russell.' What, then, was it that prevented her from resuming this friendship of years? She said she had lost her trust in Christabel. But hadn't it been courageous of Christabel to risk their friendship by trying to save her from Reg? 'She always is very courageous.' Was it because of the interference over Reg that Mrs Shorten had left Curzon Street? 'Oh, no; I left Curzon Street because I was obviously incapable of doing the work.' Why had she attended court every day during the first trial? 'Because I was frightfully interested in the case, knowing all the people so well.' Why on earth had she sat in court, day after day, in the first trial and apparently not realised the importance of what Christabel had told her about relations between John Hugo and herself on 18 December 1920? She had not realized it until too late.

Mrs Shorten was re-examined by Marshall Hall. He read out another of Christabel's letters to her, again about the baby.

'When can you come and see me? Any day this week for tea. The "new treasure", as he is referred to by all and sundry photographers who ask for sittings would like you to see him again and sends to say that after his Christening on Sunday he is going to be put into real coats and trousers. Won't he look rather an angel? I must be the most unnatural brute that ever lived as no one seems to think I like him a bit. You did not at first, did you, and on Saturday Dennis[44] asked most earnestly if I cared for him at all and today Gilbert [Bradley] and Marjorie French enquired. One can't go shrieking about like Mrs Soesch used to about her efforts.'

Before letting Elfrida Shorten step down, Marshall Hall said: 'I want you clearly to understand the suggestion that is underlying the cross-examination of both my learned friends. The suggestion is that you have invented this conversation with reference to the weekend at Oakley for the purpose of doing Mrs Russell down. Is there a word of truth in that suggestion?' 'None whatever.' She added that having to give evidence had been 'extraordinarily unpleasant'. With that, Marshall Hall rested his case.

AY NEWS.   FOOTBALL COMPETITION.—CASH PRIZE—SEE PAGE SEVENTEEN.   MA

FIGHT FOR A WOMAN'S HONOUR AND A BABY'S NAME.

All About the Russell Case.

THE CASE.

The Hon. John Hugo Russell petitions for a divorce on the ground of his wife's misconduct with Edgard Jacquard Mayer and with a man unknown.

He also alleges that the unknown man is the father of Mrs. Russell's son, Geoffrey, born on Oct. 15, 1921.

In a case heard last July Mr. Russell alleged misconduct with two named co-respondents and a man unknown. The jury found there had been no misconduct with the men named, but were not agreed as to the alleged misconduct with a man unknown.

Subsequently the petition was amended by the citation of Mr. Mayer.

"*PROBATE, DIVORCE, AND ADMIRALTY.—Court I. —Before Mr. Justice Hill.—At 10.30.—Special Jury: Russell v. Russell and Mayer (pt. hd.).*"

THERE is no place for romance or drama in the Daily Cause List. "Jones v. Jones and Brown," "White v. White and Black," or a thousand and one other names, the cold, unemotional legal machine sorts them over, puts them into different groups, and leaves them to await their turn—just so many *actions*.

In Mr. Justice Hill's list this case of "Russell v. Russell and Mayer" was just one of a number classified as a husband's petition against a wife on the ground of misconduct. It was not, as the world has come to regard it, a tense human drama in which the principal person concerned stands aloof, happily unconscious of the march of events which are destined to make or mar his future.

Jury's Terrible Task.

The Hon. John Russell has accused his wife of misconduct with Mr. Edgard Jacquard Mayer and a man unknown; Mrs. Russell and Mr. Mayer are contesting the charge each is fighting for honour. But the petitioner is also denying that he is the father of Geoffrey Russell, who was born in October, 1921. The unknown man, according to Mr. Russell, is Geoffrey's father.

Day after day these King's Counsel and six brilliant juniors are battling for the decision of the jury, those ten men and two women whose faces show signs of strain born of the knowledge of what their verdict must mean.

Either they must decide that this tragedy of domestic unhappiness must continue or the man must be given his freedom and the woman condemned.

Either that happy-faced, blue-eyed baby boy must grow to manhood, his head erect, his honour unsullied, the proud heir to the ancient Barony of Ampthill, or he must face the future branded with the stigma of illegitimacy, the nameless child of a dishonoured mother.

The Scene in Court.

With these essential features is it any occasion for wonder that queues of people have waited for hours in the hope of securing admission to the court? Is it surprising that the newspapers have devoted columns each day to the "Russell Baby Case"?

In the court itself the atmosphere is tense in the extreme. The jury, solemn and still, listening, watching, and wondering. In the well of the court the husband and the wife sitting within a few feet of each other, glancing first one way and then another, but seldom directly at each other. Just once or twice since the trial opened their eyes have met, but their features remained impassive.

The husband, slightly flushed, leans over from time to time to join in a whispered conversation with Lord and Lady Ampthill and his lawyers. On Thursday and Friday when he went into the witness-box there were slight traces of nervousness. Mrs. Russell, on the other hand, has sat hour after hour with a look of calm and confidence—an astounding example of self control. Even while Sir Edward Marshall-Hall was detailing the petitioner's case, and later when her letters were being read

All these *causes célèbres* have their moments when everyone in court catches his or her breath, when everyone seems to move just a couple of inches in the same direction, and when at the same moment everyone sighs, perhaps with relief, maybe with astonishment. These are called *sensations*.

The "Russell Baby Case" has already had more than its share. The first came during the opening speech when Sir Edward Marshall-Hall used these words:

The case for the petitioner is that before the marriage Mrs. Russell had stipulated and Mr. Russell had undertaken that she should not run any risk of having children, at any rate, for the first part of their married life. Mr. Russell made that promise to the lady who became his wife, and he will tell the jury that he had kept it.

"The question, then, that the jury has to decide is whether something occurred in December, 1920, which resulted in the birth of Mrs. Russell's child in the following October."

After detailing the husband's service in the Navy, Sir Edward dealt with the

GEOFFREY.

suggestion that Mrs. Russell was "dancing mad," and then went on to refer to certain letters written by the wife to her husband.

Astonishing Letters.

"Unless Mrs. Russell is an accom-

to revolting embraces against her will could have written this letter?

The next day, Friday, she wrote:—

My own darling old Angel.—Wife has been too lonely for words without you. All day wife was very lonely in bed, and had to hug poor Herbert (the hot water bottle) till he nearly burst, and he is a very bad substitute for the very nicest husband that ever was.

Your wife loves darling husband.—Your own Chris.

On Sunday she wrote:

My Own Darling Old Angel Husband. —I hate Sundays, with no chance of a post and no chance of hearing from the nicest husband in the world.

I have now decided to have six (children) myself. What do you say to three sets of twins. I do wish to see you. I miss you like hell. I wish we could hurry up and live together. I shall have to have my valentine husband made to talk if I can't have you.

Writing on Jan. 31, 1920, from the Villars Palace Hotel, Switzerland, Mrs. Russell stated:—

Darlingest Old Thing.—Wife is so happy she is almost bursting with it. I've never in all my born days had two days like these last two! You'll be

furiously jealous, but I can't help it! We have been able to do no sports, as it has rained the whole time, but the people here are too cheery and priceless for words. I need hardly say your wife has a vast following of adoring young men, who stand and fight as to who shall dance with her, etc.

MRS. RUSSELL.

THE PEOPLE.

THE HON. JOHN HUGO RUSSELL: Son and heir of Lord Ampthill.

THE HON. CHRISTABEL HULME RUSSELL (née Hart), daughter of a colonel.

EDGARD JACQUARD MAYER: Aged about thirty-five. Described as of independent means. Cited as co-respondent.

GEOFFREY: The seventeen-months-old son of Mrs. Russell. Mr. Russell denies that he is the father of the boy. If the husband wins this action the boy is nameless. If the wife is successful Geoffrey is in direct line of succession to the Barony of Ampthill.

all the beauty attributed to sex relationship in married life by ardent husbands and wives is camouflage and self-justification. Everyone must realise that it is the beastliest side of one's nature, but they all try to hide it under some blithering rot or other.

Husband's Evidence.

Several letters written by the husband were read before Sir Edward referred to the "Hunnish scenes" which Mrs. Russell alleged had taken place while she and her husband were living in Curzon-street. Counsel next went over the ground covered so exhaustively during the hearing of the previous case, the sleep-walking allegations, the husband's acceptance of the fact that he was the father when Mrs. Russell first told him that she was going to have a child, his doubts, and finally this letter:—

"If you are going to have a baby, I can't be the father. But I absolutely believe in you, and know that you are as true and honest a person as ever was. You told me yesterday a fact which I for one instant have never doubted—that you have never lived with another man.

"It seems absolutely inexplicable, and last night, summing everything up, I came to the conclusion that a mistake had been made, and that you are not going to have a baby.'

With regard to the unnamed co-respondent, Sir Edward alleged that Mrs. Russell had visited him at his flat.

Petitioner, in the witness-box, gave evidence bearing out counsel's opening statement, and for the time the tension was loosened until Mr. Patrick Hastings rose to cross-examine. Peculiar questions were put eliciting from the husband a statement that he had on many occasions dressed up as a girl, and that he had kept a complete outfit of woman's clothes. He also told the court that he had tramped the streets on many occasions since 1921 looking for work.

That was the last thrill of the day. But there will be many more if, as appears likely, the case goes on for another fortnight. Meantime, three people must endure the mental agony of waiting.

For the baby, its greatest possession at the moment is a brain which is not old enough to understand.

10

'This Awful Business'

I can quite understand your feelings about this awful business.
I have never been more unhappy in my life...
THE HON. JOHN HUGO RUSSELL, LETTER TO MRS ALICE LEIGH PEMBERTON, 9 JULY 1922

Patrick Hastings opened the case for Christabel the next day, 7 March 1923. She entered the witness-box. It would have been easy for her to have claimed that she loved her husband at first but became disenchanted with him. With her usual honesty, however, she gave replies to Hastings's questions that may have impressed the jury less favourably.

'When you married your husband, were you in love with him?' – 'No.'

'After you had been married to him for some time, I want you just to tell me in your own way, for the first month or two, how did your feelings towards him develop?' – 'I got much fonder of him.'

'For how long did that continue?' – 'That continued for some long time until, I think, I came back from Switzerland.'

'After that, what happened then; did they change again?' – 'From the very start there came times when we got on badly, and some times when we got on well; but the times we got on badly became much more frequent after I came back.'

'I only want to ask you one question about these relations that took place between you. How often did they take place?' – 'Practically every time we ever slept together.'

'I must ask you this one question: in fact did your husband ever penetrate you?' – 'No, never.'

Christabel said that, to the best of her memory, there had been no change in August 1920. The relations, such as they were, had continued after that. She danced every evening. Nothing was concealed from John Hugo: her many different partners picked her up from the house. Hastings moved on to December 1920.

'On the 18th, did you sleep in the same bed?' – 'Yes.'

'And again on the 19th?' – 'Yes.'

'On either, or which, of those nights, did anything take place between you?' –'I remember something taking place on one of the nights, but I cannot tell you which. I remember the end of it was that I threatened to kick him out of bed unless he would leave me alone.'

'Before that termination, I want you to tell us exactly what did take place between you?' – 'The same as on former occasions. He attempted penetration but I would not allow him.'

'The same as before?' – 'Yes.'

'I must ask you this. Penetration you would not allow. Was there an emission?' – 'Yes.' 'Was that exactly as it always was?' – 'Yes ...'

'When that emission took place, had you any pyjamas on?' – 'No.' 'Or had he?' – 'No.'

HILL: 'Was it after that that you threatened to kick him out of bed unless he left you alone?' – 'Yes, my Lord.'

Questioned further, Christabel said there had been similar relations after Christmas. She told the story about John Hugo's toe on the trigger of a gun and his threat to blow his brains out. As a result, she had permitted the same kind of relations to continue.

HASTINGS: 'There has been a great deal of discussion or mention here of something that was called "Hunnish scenes". What did you mean by "Hunnish scenes"?' – 'These attempts, which were usually after a threat of shooting himself, or shooting my cat, occasionally it used to be – something rather absurd.'

HILL: 'Do you mean relations of semi-intercourse, submitted to after a threat by him to shoot himself, or to shoot the cat? Is that what you mean?' – 'Yes.'

Hastings asked if the cat used to sleep on her bed. 'Always, yes.' Had she thought what took place between her and her husband could possibly result in the birth of a child? 'No, I thought it was quite impossible.' The first time she had the slightest suspicion that she was going to have a child was on 17 June 1921, when she visited the clairvoyante. She had never committed adultery. She had never had with any other man the kind of relations that took place with her husband.

Would she ever have allowed another man to do it? 'Never. No other man has ever suggested it, even.' Hastings asked her a question about her brother-in-law, Hilton Welford.

'We know that Mr Welford went down to see your husband. When he came back, did you express willingness to meet your husband?' – 'I was furious with him for having been. I thought he was an interfering fool, if I remember rightly.'

'You said you would see him, did you?' – 'Yes, reluctantly.'

'And then nothing ever came of it, as we know?' – 'That is so.'

She told Hastings that since the birth of the baby she had neither seen her husband nor received any contribution from him towards the care of the child or herself. Hastings asked her about Edgar Mayer. She had not met him in Belgium, as Miss Acton had suggested, but in a dining car as she travelled from Paris to Calais on business. Before her dressmaking business started, she had been to tea with him twice and had dined with him once.

'Have you ever danced with him?' – 'I am afraid Mr Mayer was a very bad dancer, so I was not very fond of him.'

She had danced with him at Ciro's the night she dined with him. She knew that as a businessman he could help her set up her shop; John Hugo would have been 'absolutely useless'. She wanted Mayer as a director. She had visited his flat in Half Moon Street very seldom, for business discussions.

'As far as these waiter people are concerned, about your going there often, is there a word of truth in it?' – 'Not a word.'

She denied that she had ever had any kind of sexual relations with Mayer. 'He never even tried to hold my hand.'

'I do not want to disappoint you, but, in point of fact, he did not seem to be particularly attracted by you?' – 'I think he liked me as a friend, but there was certainly no question of him being in the least in love with me ...'

'About the photograph. Did you even know that Mr Mayer had got your photograph?' – 'Not till I was reminded of the fact.'

'Would you have objected to his having your photograph?' – 'Not in the least.'

'How did he get it? How did the photograph arise?' – 'I think it must have been on one occasion when he came to Curzon Street. I had a whole lot of them that had been sent out from one photographer, and he picked out one of them and said might he have it. They were rather flattering. They were rather nice photographs.'

'And you said he might?' – 'Yes.'

'Did you ever consider there was anything at all risqué or indelicate in that?' – 'Not at all. Hundreds of people must have photographs of mine.'

Questioned by Mayer's counsel, Sir Ellis Hume-Williams, she said it was 'totally untrue' that Mayer had fed her sweets as she lay on a sofa. She had never had a bath in his flat. She had never left his flat with him in evening dress. Hastings asked why he called her 'Peggy'. 'I think he said Christabel sounded like a suffragette,[45] and he did not like it.'

Marshall Hall began a brutal cross-examination of Christabel.

'Will you tell me, has an oath any meaning for you?' – 'Yes ...'

'Have you any religious belief?' – 'I have'

'Do you realize that some of the expressions in your letters that have been read would shock the susceptibilities of people who had religious belief?' – 'It depends on their religious belief.'

'In the description of yourself being laughed at like Christ crucified upside down, did you think that would cause great distress to some people?' – 'No, it did not enter my head.'

'In taking an oath you believe in the sanctity of it?' – 'I do.'

'Did you hear Lady Ampthill say that you had told her that you had taken your marital oath with reservations?' – 'She said there were mental reservations. That was untrue, because I went and told the clergyman that I refused to say that I would obey any man, and that if he made me say it I should say it, not meaning that. He said it was necessary in the service that one should say it.'

'Then was the only mental reservation that you had in reference to the obedience to your husband?' – 'Exactly.'

'As you say, you would obey no man?' – 'No man.'

Marshall Hall took her back to her student days in Paris. She had lived in the Latin Quarter. She agreed that the life there was Bohemian. 'Free and easy?' 'Very free and easy.'

'With very few restrictions?' – 'What do you mean by restrictions?'

'Restrictions as to friendship existing with the members of the opposite sex?' – 'One went about with all the students indiscriminately, whether they were men or women ...'

'You thoroughly enjoyed your life?' – 'Yes; I always thoroughly enjoy my life.'

'Do you always take care that others with you should enjoy theirs?' – 'I leave others to look after themselves.'

'In "others" do you include your husband?' – 'I think he ought to be capable of looking after himself.'

'Unless he interested you enough to take care of him?' – 'I think I have taken care of my mother, and I take care of my baby, because I think they are dependent on me rather.'

'Did you ever take the trouble to take an interest in your husband?' –' I took great interest in my husband.'

Goaded by Marshall Hall's questions, Christabel had walked into his trap. That last answer sounded insincere after the admission that she had not been in love with John Hugo when she married him and the offhand remark about his being able to look after himself. (Most or all of the jury in 1923 probably thought it was a wife's duty to minister to her husband – however much that might differ from what many think today.)

She told Marshall Hall, in answer to a new line of questioning, that she had known nothing about sexual relations when she married John Hugo. She had not known how children were procreated. 'As a matter of fact I never thought about sex matters at all. They never interested me and I never discussed them with anyone.'

'Did you realize that young Russell was very much in love with you?' – 'Yes, he and many others.'

'How many men do you suggest have been in love with you as Mr Russell was in love with you?' – 'I do not know; the number is rather difficult to say.'

'I do not mind within a dozen or two!' – 'Every man who has ever told me that he loves me?'

'Yes, just give me some idea.' – 'I do not know, but I should think twenty or thirty.' 'Did you believe them?' – 'Never.'

'Therefore, may I suggest you are not vain?' – 'I am not at all vain; I know my limitations exactly.'

Marshall Hall's questions took on a less teasing tone.

'Did you believe that Mr Russell loved you?' – 'As much as I believe in the love of any man, I think.'

'Have you any form of love except the love of a parent for a child?' – 'I have love for friends, not because they are men, but because they are friends – or women as friends.'

'Do you represent that you have no sexual love at all?' – 'I do not think I can have, or it has not been brought forth yet.'

Christabel's answers may have helped to prejudice the jury against her, as a somehow unnatural being; but – once again – they scarcely suggested an enthusiastic adulteress. Had she indeed told John Hugo that she was not the marrying sort? 'I should think so. I still maintain that idea about myself.' Counsel reminded her of her trip to Scotland to marry Bradley.

'You went up prepared to marry Bradley?' – 'Yes.'

'And if you could have married Bradley the next day that you arrived at Edinburgh, you would have married him?' – 'I went up there for the purpose.'

'You told my learned friend Mr Hastings that you were not in love with your husband when you married him. Were you in love with Bradley?' – 'No; I was perfectly enchanted when I found we could not get married.'

That might have been a piece of repartee by Cecily in *The Importance of Being Earnest*. Christabel was amusing the gallery, and no doubt thought she was scoring off Marshall Hall. But sometimes it is important to be earnest; her pert, flippant replies may well have seemed malapropos to the jury, who had been torn away from their usual occupations and were not – unlike the public gallery, perhaps – in court to enjoy a Punch and Judy show.

Christabel said she could not remember Bradley's kissing her.

'May I suggest to you why you cannot remember? It is one of two reasons; either it did not take place, or it was such a constant occurrence that you would not notice it.' – 'No; because I am not at all fond of kissing.'

'Before you went up to Edinburgh to be married to Bradley, had you kissed any other young man, or had any other young man kissed you?' – 'No, I do not think so. Oh, yes, I remember there was one. I was most upset about that at that time. I thought one had babies if one kissed young men.'

'Did you really?' – 'I did. Dreadful!'

When she married John Hugo, had she still thought that kissing caused babies? No, she had outgrown that belief. When had she outgrown that belief? 'I think when I found I did not have one when a young man once kissed me.' Marshall Hall turned to the wedding night with John Hugo, and drew from Christabel a new piece of information.

'Did your husband kiss you?' – 'No. He came to my room while I was undressing, and I went up to him to kiss him, and he said: "I do hope you will never expect me to kiss you when I am standing up. I am much taller than you, and it is most tiring." That was the first night of my marriage.'

HILL: 'Was that said seriously?' – 'That was said perfectly seriously, my Lord.'

Christabel claimed that when she had woken up in the middle of the night, she had not said to John Hugo: 'Is this all that marriage means?' She had said: 'You seem a curious sort of husband to go off to sleep without ever attempting to kiss me or anything.' She added: 'I was extremely annoyed by that time, and would have nothing to do with him ...' Marshall Hall reminded her that her husband had testified they both went to sleep. Christabel: 'How does he know I went to sleep?' It was another of those smart ripostes which played to the gallery but not necessarily to the jury. Marshall Hall smacked her down: '*Do not ask me questions.*' He continued:

'At any rate, you did not want him to have intercourse with you that night, did you?' – 'I did not know what intercourse was.'

'Did you notice that there was any difference in the formation of a man to the formation of a woman?' – 'I knew they are not constructed the same.'

'Did you notice what is the main difference between a man and a woman on that night when he was in bed with you?' – 'How should I?'

'Did you?' – 'No.'

'Do you mean to tell us that you did not know whether your husband was differently made?' – 'That is a most ridiculous question. I have been an art student in Paris, and I have studied anatomy from about the age of twelve.'

'If you had said no, I was going to put that question to you.' – 'I have saved you the trouble ...'

'So you had seen a nude man?' – 'Constantly.'

'And you imagined your husband was made like other men?' – 'Exactly.'

'Have you never had the smallest curiosity to know what that portion of the man's body was intended by nature for?' – 'I had not the smallest curiosity.'

'Do you know now that in moments of passion that portion of a man's body gets large?' – 'I did not know that.'

'Do you know it now?' – 'You have told me.'

'Never mind about my telling you. Do you know now that that portion of a man's anatomy becomes large and rigid?' – 'No, I did not know until you have just told me.'

'What!' – 'How on earth should I?'

'During this partial intercourse, when you say that your husband had emissions, do you say that you did not realize that his person became rigid?' – 'No, I did not.'

'Has he ever had even this partial intercourse with you that is suggested?' – 'He has told you so.'

'Is it true?' – 'Perfectly true.'

'And yet you noticed no difference?' – 'No difference in what?'

'Between the person in quiescence and the person in excitement. I use the word "person"; you know what I mean?' – 'This is – Oh!'

Once again, there was a plus and a minus to Marshall Hall's questioning. On the credit side (from his point of view), strong doubt was being cast on the idea that John Hugo was the father of Christabel's child. On the debit side – if she was not simply having fun at the barrister's expense – it was difficult to sustain the notion of Christabel as Jezebel. That notion faded still more under Marshall Hall's further questions. He was trying to get her to be explicit about what had happened in bed during her visit to John Hugo's naval base at Harwich at Christmas 1918.

'Would you mind telling me the detail?' – 'He took me in his arms, and then he removed the lower part of my pyjamas, and he attempted penetration.'

'I am afraid we must go into a little detail. Was he on the top of you, or beside you?' – 'Beside me.'

'And he attempted penetration. What did he attempt penetration with?' – 'The point of his person.'

'And what did he attempt penetration into?' – 'I am afraid I do not know the name ...'

'Did you know the purpose for which he wanted to put his person inside yours?' – 'It seemed to me objectless: it seemed to have no object; I could see no satisfaction from it ... I could derive no satisfaction from it.'

Had Christabel been happy on a visit to the Welfords at Craig Hall, soon after the stay at Harwich? 'I think I hunted, so I was probably happy, as far as I remember.' What about the partial intercourse? 'I hated it.' Marshall Hall suggested that it was after one of John Hugo's attempts at penetration that she had said, 'I wish to God I had not married you'. Christabel: 'I was disgusted with my husband's general attitude: he was so frightfully weak.'

'I thought you said you were so fond of him.' – 'One can be fond of a person who is very weak ...'

'Did you expect him to insist upon having complete intercourse with you?' – 'If I had wanted anything as badly as he wanted that, I should have insisted ...'

'Looking back on it as a whole, do you think you ought to have married anybody?' – 'Never.'

Marshall Hall asked her about the time before her marriage, when she was in charge of thousands of girls at Woolwich.

'Had you never heard any of them discuss sex matters?' – 'No, never.'

'All these two thousand girls working together in this great machine shop, and you had never heard them talking of sex matters?' – 'No; I think they were always very careful in my presence. They looked upon me as a being from another world, because I was not of the same class as theirs, and they used to treat me with enormous deference and respect.'

'Everybody treats you with deference and respect?' – 'Yes, they all do.'

Counsel tried to suggest that there had been – as John Hugo recalled it – a happy spell in the marriage, when the couple were in Wemyss. He did not get far with that approach. Christabel: 'I enjoyed myself at Wemyss Bay enormously. He was away all day.' What about the night at Glasgow when, according to John Hugo, she had said 'Go on, go on.' Christabel: 'False.' All she remembered was a dance in Glasgow, and a naval friend of her husband's, Denis Friedberger, coming into her room the next morning to say goodbye before he left for China.[46]

'Still no shadow of a sexual feeling for your husband at this date?' – 'No, none.'

'Never?' – 'No, I have never had any sexual feeling for him.'

Christabel was almost beginning to enjoy herself. Perhaps she could make just as much of a monkey out of Marshall Hall as she had made out of Sir John Simon. Her answers became ever more cheeky. Marshall Hall reminded her of John Hugo's evidence that she had had tears in her eyes when he had parted from her at Craig Hall on Christmas night, 1918.

'He tells us that for once, and the only time in his life, he saw you in tears.' – 'I think he said I had tears in my eyes.'

'That is the usual place where people have them?' – 'But I was not in tears. That denotes sobbing, does it not? I do not sob.'

'You know that tears start from the eyes, usually?' – 'That is a different thing.'

HILL: 'She means that she did not weep.'

MARSHALL HALL:'You restrain your tears as you do your passion?'

HILL: 'Tears may have come into your eyes, but you did not weep?' – 'No.'

MARSHALL HALL:'Did they come genuinely into your eyes?' – 'I do not know that there is any other way, except by smelling onions, that would make them come ungenuinely.'

'Do you think that is a humorous answer?' – 'I do not know.'

'Or do you think it will assist the Court?' – 'How am I to say anything else?'

'Do you think our great actresses smell onions in order to produce tears?' – 'I am not a great actress, and I cannot tell you.'

'Are you not?' – 'No.'

'Are you sure of that?' – 'I have not made a reputation on the stage.'

'I suggest you are an actress, not on the stage, but on a much wider stage, and I suggest you are acting now.' – 'I see.'

'And you have been acting through your married life?' – 'Really!'[47]

He reminded her that when John Hugo asked her how she could have written him such affectionate letters from Switzerland, she replied that she was only acting.

Had Christabel won this duel of wits, or had Marshall Hall? She had given the court some light relief. She was not acting in the sense of dissimulating; she was only acting in the sense of projecting her voice and engaging in some play-like repartee. But once again Marshall Hall was able to plant in the jury's minds the impression of a woman treating a very serious subject facetiously. Christabel's defiant insouciance was being presented as cold-hearted callousness. Counsel read out one of the affectionate letters Christabel had sent John Hugo.

'Wife is sitting on your lap and has both arms round your neck and kisses both your eyes and your hair and your neck.' Is that not sex?' – 'No, it is not.'

'Have you ever wanted to sit on anybody else's lap?' – 'My mother's.'

'And put your arms round her neck?' – 'My mother, constantly. I am afraid I still do.' 'And kiss her eyes and her neck?' – 'I always have; and my baby sits on my lap.'

She continued to try to outsmart her inquisitor. He asked: 'Do you realize that there are women in the world who, not liking sexual intercourse, are prepared to pay that as a part of the price for the admiration of men?' 'It seems a very low motive ... I am prepared to pay no price for the admiration of men.' Marshall Hall jumped on that. 'You want to take everything and give nothing?' 'I give my affection.' He asked why she had bothered to tell her husband, in one letter, about her new knickers with a yellow and blue butterfly in beads on one leg. 'Had not that got an underlying reference to sex?' 'If anybody has got a filthy enough mind to put such an underlying sentiment, let them put it.' He asked her about the quarrel with John Hugo in August 1920 and received a new kind of answer – nothing about 'hanky panky'.

'I quarrelled with my husband and Bradley collectively, not separately.'

'Have you quarrelled with Bradley even now?' – 'I quarrelled with him then. He told my husband – I got this only from my husband – that I was driving a car recklessly and that if a certain motor bus did not move out of the way, I should hit it. I told Bradley he was an interfering fool, that I was perfectly capable of driving the car, and I wished he would not report things to my husband. I was very annoyed with both of them.'

Probably deliberately, Marshall Hall 'misheard' Christabel when she said she would die for her child.

'You would lie for that child?' – 'Die, I said.'

'And you would lie for the child?' – 'Lying for a child is not necessary.'

'You would do everything: you would die for it; you would lie for a child?' – 'No, that I would not.'

'You would die for a child, but you would not lie for a child?' – 'Exactly.'

By now, the jury and everyone else in court were aware that they were witnessing a duel to the death. The 'dead needle' between Christabel and Marshall Hall was seen at its sharpest when he asked her why, when she met John Hugo for lunch on 23 June 1921, she had not immediately told him she was pregnant.

'Why did you not the first thing say to him: "Stilts, I am going to have a baby"?' – 'I think the extraordinary excitement it would have caused the other people who were sitting about there would have been rather upsetting.'

'You did not meet in the restaurant, did you?' – 'I think we met in the restaurant.'

'You may be right; I thought you met downstairs?' – 'Downstairs would be in Dover Street. Do you think I was going to roar out in Dover Street that I was going to have a baby?'

'You need not roar it out.' – 'Well, whisper it.'

'The first thing he came up, why did you not say: "Stilts, dear old thing, I am going to have a baby"?' – 'I am afraid I am not the sentimental type who says: "Stilts, dear old thing, I am going to have a baby." '

'You are not acting now?' – 'Not a bit; I was imitating you.'

'A very poor model. I hope you will get a better one – and I do not think you need any lessons.'

One gathers from this that Christabel possibly took off Marshall Hall's fruity tones when she repeated the 'Stilts, dear old thing ...' sentence. A reasonable answer to Marshall Hall's question would have been: when you have an important and startling piece of news to break, you do not blurt it out straight away, but prepare the ground and choose the best moment. Instead, Christabel offered this cabaret turn – diverting but somehow off-key.

Next he questioned her about Elfrida Shorten.

'Is Mrs Shorten an extremely great friend of yours?' – 'She was.'

'Is she a truthful person?' – 'Am I obliged to answer that?' 'Certainly.' – 'Well, I will answer it: up to a point.'

'She has been your friend?' – 'Yes.'

'And you, as late as November of last year, were writing her letters of great affection?' – 'I was. We had quarrelled in the meantime, but I was trying to make it up.'

'You spoke of the love which you were hoping for as being incomplete unless you had hers?' – 'She was the greatest woman friend I ever had.'

'Do you think that woman would come here and invent the most deliberate untruths with regard to something you are alleged to have said?' – 'I think she is very bitter against me.'

Counsel asked her about John Hugo.

'You heard him say in the witness-box that he does not believe he is the father of your child?' – 'He does not believe he is the father of my child: he knows he is.'

'You have indeed married a bad man?' – 'I have married a fool.'

'In your eyes a fool is worse than a bad man?' –'I think there is nothing worse than a fool.'

Marshall Hall now played a cunning trick on Christabel. He asked her to compare her own son with photographs of John Hugo as a baby. She claimed to notice similarities in the ears and general shape. Marshall Hall then revealed that the photographs were not of John Hugo at all, but of three strange children which had been collected at random. Christabel stuck to her guns: the ears of one of them *were* very similar to Geoffrey's.

Christabel was asked whether the warning by Maud Acton about being overpowered by a man had ever come true.

'Nobody has ever attempted to do it and nobody has ever suggested such a thing.'

'Yet you used to dance cheek to cheek with these men?' – 'Why should dancing cheek to cheek have the least thing to do with anything immoral?'

'Did you take an immense pleasure in dancing?' – 'I am a very keen dancer.'

'But you never looked upon it in any way as a sexual lure?' – 'Good Lord, no, I should think not.'

'It made no difference to you whether you danced with women or men?' – 'If women danced beautifully, it would be just as much pleasure.'

By the end of the long battle of wits between Christabel and Marshall Hall, honours were about even; but she won the final exchange. He was trying to throw doubt on the doctors' evidence that she was still a virgin, and to suggest that 'partial penetration' had taken place.

'Your condition is such that it is quite inconsistent with your ever having gone astray with any man?' – 'I think there might be one man like John Russell, but I should think it would be very unlikely that there are two.'

Under the headline 'GREATEST COURT DUEL IN MEMORY', *Lloyd's Sunday News* described the exchanges between Christabel and Marshall Hall, in the very best journalese.

'In the Bar robing-rooms at the Law Courts they are still talking of that wonderful, thrilling duel between the Hon. Mrs John Russell and Sir Edward Marshall Hall, KC.

'Not within living memory at least, it is agreed, have those sombre buildings, where so many skeletons are dragged from the family cupboard, and where human wits are strained to the uttermost on the rack of cross-examination, furnished a parallel to the questioning of this young, gently-nurtured society woman pitting herself against the trained intellect and forensic arts of one of the keenest intellects of the modern Bar.

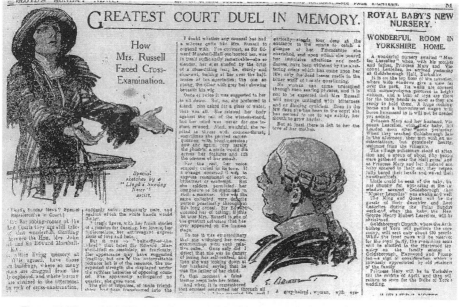

Figure 5. The artist of Lloyd's Sunday News *depicts Christabel Russell and Sir Edward Marshall Hall in their courtroom battle. The 'royal baby' in the column to the right was the Hon. George Lascelles – the future Earl of Harewood, a cousin of the present Queen. By an irony, he was the son of George V's daughter, Princess Mary – the young woman Lady Ampthill had hoped her son, John Hugo, might marry. Instead, she had married Viscount Lascelles. George Lascelles was born in February 1923.*

' "Never heard, never seen anything like it," whispered an elderly barrister to me as Mrs Russell, her four hours of tense verbal battle concluded, stole down from the witness-stand, and the grey-haired King's Counsel sank amongst his documents.

'And certainly those of us packed tightly, even uncomfortably, on the benches had no experience to compare with it. Not until it was all over, indeed, did many realise how deeply, if unconsciously, it had touched even the emotions of the watchers. Then women sighed softly, and men braced themselves, moistening their dry lips – then they knew that they, too, had been living, during those four hours of fierce questioning, through real drama.

'Mrs Russell radiates impressions. She gives you the impression that she is pretty; but, studying her more closely, you discover that her quality is attractiveness, rather than prettiness – the jaw is too long, the nose too prominent, for fastidious tastes. You think she is tall, exceptionally tall, and again you are forced to the conclusion that this is in part the effect of the clothes she wears – dark robes that fold about the figure and enhance its slender lines.

'Her charm, which brought the "twenty or thirty young lovers" (her own phrase) to her feet, may well have been this elusiveness, the enigmatic appeal of a Mona Lisa.

'At times in the witness-box, in the ill-lighted court, against the neutral background of oak panelling, she became merged in the shadows, herself a black shadow, out of which the face would suddenly swim, gleamingly pale, and against which the white hands would flutter.

'A tragic figure, with her frank stories of a passion for dancing, her lovers, her indiscretions, her extravagant expressions of love and hate.

'But it was no "butterfly-on-the-wheel" that faced Sir Edward Marshall Hall so resolutely, so fearlessly. Her appearance may have suggested fragility, but one of the unforgettable pictures left is of the resource, the unexpected strength she displayed under the ruthless batteries of opposing counsel. She apparently anticipated no quarter; she gave none.

'The girl of impulse, of facile friendships, had been transformed into the mother, fighting for her baby's name.

'And it made no difference that she was fighting, not as the primitive animals, but in the social and legal restrictions of a court of law.

'Primitive mother-love burst ever so faintly through the armour of her iron self-control, and at times her fine teeth would be startlingly bared, and you saw, "as in a glass, darkly"[48], the female of the species, snarling defiance over her offspring at all comers.

' "I would die for my child!" – her defiant tones ring yet in my ears.

'So this fashionable designer of dresses revealed herself as one of astonishing capabilities.

'I doubt whether any counsel has had a witness quite like Mrs Russell to contend with. The contrast, as Sir Edward Marshall Hall confronted her, was in itself sufficiently remarkable – she so slender, her eyes shaded by the brim of a close-fitting hat; he, sturdy and clear-cut, looking at her over the half-lenses of his spectacles; the one so young, the other with grey hair showing beneath his wig.

'Once or twice it was suggested to her to sit down. But, no, she preferred to stand. She asked for a glass of water, that was all. She relaxed her body against the rail of the witness-stand, but her mind was never for one instant relaxed. Alert, watchful, she replied to thrust with counter-thrust; sometimes she parried rapier-question with blunt-question; now and again, very rarely, the ghost of a smile would flit across her features and lift the corners of her mouth.

'For the rest, her voice scarcely varied in its tone. If a change occurred it was to express resentment or scorn, bitterness or contempt. But she seldom permitted her composure to be disturbed in such a manner. She was the same collected, very definite person practically throughout this long ordeal. Sir Edward accused her of acting; if this is true Mrs Russell is one of the greatest actresses that has ever appeared on the human stage.

'To me it was extraordinary that she withstood her cross-examination with such relative calm. Once only did I detect that she was in danger of losing her self-control, and then she was looking down at her husband, saying that he was the father of her child. At that moment a faint tremor crept into her tones.

'And when it is remembered that counsel conducted her through all the privacies of her married life, cast doubt upon her girlish beliefs, brought out the broad facts of sex – all before an audience mostly of strangers, and in terms that were not minced or would leave their implication obscure – it will be realised that there were many things which might have shaken the composure of an ordinary woman.

'But if this trial has emphasised any feature it is surely the rarity of such a personality as that of Mrs Russell.

'Today, perhaps, there is no other woman in her equivocal position. She does not love her husband – yet she is striving fiercely to keep him tied to her.

'A gaping world jostles to feed its curiosity – stands four deep at the entrance to the courts to catch a glimpse of her. Friendships she cherished, and upon which she poured her impulsive affections and confidences, have been withered by the shattering crisis which has come upon her life; only the dead leaves rustle in the bitter wind of hostile questioning.

'No woman can come unscathed through such searing phases, and it is not to be expected that Mrs Russell will emerge untinged with bitterness and an abiding cynicism. Even in the few days she has been in the court she has seemed to me to age subtly, her mouth to grow harder.

'But at least there is left to her the love of her mother. A grey-haired woman, with eyeglasses, Mrs Hart has watched over her daughter incessantly in these harrowing times. An uncommon bond of affection exists between the two, and they are often to be seen about the corridors of the courts, walking swiftly, arm locked in arm. They are inseparable.

'Contemplating them together, I think I understand that trait in Mrs Russell – the trait of mother-love upon which she is so insistent. I think I understand what was the impulse which supported her so amazingly through the most searching cross-examination of recent years.

'The cry of her child was in her ears.'

On the sixth day of the hearing (8 March), Edgar Jacquard Mayer was sworn. He was first examined by his counsel, Sir Ellis Hume–Williams. Shown a photograph of Christabel with a dog, he said he had never seen it before. One of her in evening dress he did recognize: he had had it in his flat. He had had other photographs but thought they had been stolen by the Half Moon Street valet, Wilfred Crane. He described how he himself had met Christabel in 1919, in a restaurant-car when both of them were returning from Paris to London. At the end of October 1919 she had come to tea with him at the Carlton Hotel. She told him she had become ill; he recommended a hotel in Switzerland and went with her to Messrs Cook's offices. He had had tea once more with her, at Brown's Hotel, before she went to Switzerland. About May or June 1920 he had met her at Harrington Gardens to advise her on setting up her dressmaking business. He became a director of the company. He received no remuneration as a director.

He was asked about the alleged incident of Christabel's taking a bath in Half Moon Street.

'I was calling in one afternoon at Curzon Street, a few days after they had moved in there, and Mrs Russell remarked – Mr Russell was present, according to my recollection – "Is it not a nuisance? We will not be able to have a bath for a week," and I jokingly said, "Well, you and your husband had better come and have a bath at my place. I am away all day." '

He had not given them a key to his flat; he himself had only one key. He thought Christabel had taken his offer as a joke. He had never thought of the matter again until it had been raised in the 1922 trial. She had never taken a bath in his flat.

What about the photographs of her in his flat? He said he had been at Curzon Street one afternoon when a parcel of press photographs of Christabel arrived. He liked two of them and asked if he might have them. In one she was wearing morning dress, in the other, evening dress. He had cut them to fit them into frames. Those photographs had now been stolen, the frames left behind.

He claimed that Christabel had only been to his flat twice. Several other ladies had been there, sometimes to leave with him, in evening dress, for dinner and the theatre. Christabel had never done that. The evidence of the chambermaid Gower was 'absolutely untrue'. Men visited him too. He thought that one lady who changed in his flat had taken a bath. 'She was there before I arrived.' On another occasion he had seen a hairpin left behind – after a number of men and women guests had changed in his flat. There was 'no impropriety' on any of the ladies' visits. It was again 'absolutely untrue' that he had fed Christabel with sweets when she was lying on a sofa. He had once taken her to a dinner and dance at Ciro's.

'You were launched upon the troubled sea of dancing, and I am afraid you did not make much of a success of it?' – 'She did not think very much of my dancing on that occasion.'

'And as a dancing partner with Mrs Russell, was that your first and last attempt?' – 'Well, not from my choice, but from hers.'

He had resigned as a director of the dressmaking company in January 1921. After that he had seen Christabel only once, passing through Claridge's. 'She nodded to me, and I am afraid that at first I failed to recognize her.'

'At any rate, you did not speak to her?' – 'I did not speak to her at all.'

'Now you are cited as Co-Respondent, in a suit, when you did not speak to the lady when you met her at Claridge's Hotel?' – 'I hardly recognized her first as she passed along; I had not seen her for such a long time.'

Hume-Williams asked Mayer whether there was the least truth in the suggestion that he had committed adultery with Christabel. 'Absolutely none – absolutely none.' Had he ever been guilty of the least familiarity with the lady? 'None whatever.' Asked by Marshall Hall about the Half Moon Street servants' evidence, Mayer said he thought they had 'assisted the detectives'.

'Do you suggest that either Lord or Lady Ampthill or Mr John Russell would be parties to concocting a case against you?' – 'I do not.'

Marshall Hall asked whether Mayer was in the habit of meeting ladies in restaurant-cars and becoming great friends with them without any introduction. 'It is not a habit, and I did not become great friends.' Marshall Hall persisted: 'Would I be using a vulgar expression if I suggested you had picked her up?' Mayer said he had not done that.

Counsel asked him about his divorce from his wife. Had he committed adultery? 'Yes: she could not have got the divorce without it.' But he and his wife had remained on cordial terms for the sake of their daughter. His wife had once visited Christabel's shop, on his recommendation, to buy some clothes. If indeed Christabel had said he was getting too fond of her (and he thought Maud Acton was lying about that) it was quite untrue. Mayer added: 'A man realizes that a woman is of one sort or another, and I think Mrs Russell would impress any man, who had any experience of the world, that she was not a woman of that type.'

Now that the star witnesses had testified, it was time for the minor players, the walk-on parts and the cameo rôles. To contest the evidence that Mayer had only women visitors, Adolph Carol Marks, a stockbroker, of Davies Street, was sworn. He had been to the Half Moon Street flat. Marshall Hall barged in with an apparently racist question:

'Is Mr Mayer a member of the Jewish persuasion?' – 'I could not tell you, Sir.' 'Are you?' – 'No, Sir.'

Next Ethel Hunter (aunt of Christabel's biographer, Eileen Hunter) came to the witness-box. She and her husband Noel had been close friends of Mayer since 1910. She had often been to Half Moon Street, always to the knowledge of her husband, and sometimes with him. She had occasionally changed her clothes there, in the bedroom. Once, she had met Christabel there: the object of the meeting was to introduce to her a woman who wanted to start a dressmaking business, but that woman failed to turn up. In case it was going to be suggested that the servants had mistaken Mrs Hunter for Christabel, Marshall Hall made her agree that there was not the slightest resemblance between them. She had never had a bath in the flat. Her husband gave evidence that he had been to Half Moon Street both on his own and with his wife.

Mary Naismith, once again insistent that she was not a 'fortune-teller', gave almost exactly the same evidence as in the first trial. But Patrick Hastings, seeking to establish that Christabel had remained a virgin after conception, required Dr Stanley Dodd to be a lot more explicit than in 1922.

'Is one of the signs of non-penetration the existence of the hymen?' – 'It is.'

'I think we ought to be quite clear about it ... Is the result of penetration in a normal woman the rupture of the hymen?' – 'That is so.'

'Are there occasionally known to medical science cases where a hymen is not ruptured?' – 'Many cases are seen in married life in which the hymen has never been ruptured, although pregnancy may have occurred or not, as the case may be.'

'Does that depend to some extent, if not wholly, on the character of the hymen itself?' – 'It does to some extent.'

'In the case of this lady, was her hymen a fragile one or not?' – 'I should say it was a very normal one.'

'That is to say – ?' – 'No undue degree of tenderness about it, and not unduly thick.'

'In your opinion, if there had been penetration, would you have expected the hymen to have been ruptured?' – 'I should have.'

'Was there any slightest sign that the hymen had been ruptured? – There was no tear and no notch in it at all.'

MARSHALL HALL:'No tear and no what?' – 'No notch – to show where the tear had been.'

HASTINGS: 'In addition to that are there certain things, if I may use the expression, in the hymen which are known to medical men as rugae?' – 'Yes. Those are inside the hymen; they are in the vagina itself; they are little duplications of the mucous membrane of the vagina which, as a rule, after penetration and repeated connection are straightened out. That is the way they disappear. But in Mrs Russell's case they were still present, showing that the vagina had never been stretched.'

'Is one of the methods of testing what you were looking for the insertion of a finger?' 'Yes.'

'Was it easy or was it difficult to insert your finger?' – 'I was not able to put my finger wholly into the vagina, because the hymen grasped my finger just about short of the second knuckle. The hymen would admit the finger as far as that [indicating], but no further.'

MARSHALL HALL:'About an inch and a half?' – 'Yes, perhaps an inch and a half.'

HASTINGS: 'I suppose there are certain reactions which sometimes prevent the insertion of the finger? There is such a thing as vaginismus,[49] for instance?' – 'Yes.'

Dodd said he had done an experiment with a glass dilator to see whether or not there really was difficulty in opening the vagina. There was: the hymen would not admit anything bigger than his finger. Asked whether, if there had been an emission 'at the orifice of the wife's person', that could have resulted in the birth of a child at any time, he replied, 'Yes, it could have.' And was there anything unusual in a woman's not knowing she was going to have a child for months after pregnancy had occurred? 'No, I think it is acknowledged that we meet quite a number of such cases.'

Marshall Hall was not going to let Dodd leave the witness-box without a gruelling cross-examination. It began: 'Do you say really that there is nothing exceptional in a woman of intelligence, an educated woman, coming to the fifth month of her pregnancy without knowing that she is pregnant?' Dodd answered, 'I think so'; but after more bullying questions he agreed to 'very exceptional', at which Marshall Hall crowed: 'I have got it at last! Sir John Simon got it at once, you know.' Counsel then read out a reply Dodd had given Simon in the first trial – he had then conceded 'very exceptional'. Marshall Hall moved on, with gusto, to the question of rugae. Would Dodd not agree that the greatest authority on the subject, Dr Norman Lockyer, thought the presence of rugae of negligible significance, 'because not only are they present after actual parturition, but even having once disappeared they recur'?

HASTINGS: 'Are you going to call him?'

MARSHALL HALL:'*You* are going to call him.'

HASTINGS: 'Then do not quote him till I call him.'

The main proposition Marshall Hall wanted to put to Dodd was that the condition of Christabel's hymen did not rule out partial penetration. Dodd: 'I do not think that a penis of normal proportions has entered the hymen. If you think of the size of my finger and you think of the erect penis, the difference is enormous.' Marshall Hall suggested that a lover might have done what John Hugo Russell was alleged to have done. Dodd disagreed; and Hastings, re-examining, got him to reinforce that view.

'Have you ever heard of the case of a lover who has been in the position that Sir Edward put to you, and been content with that?' – 'I cannot recollect anything of the kind.'

'I do not know whether you were asked as a doctor or as a man of the world, but can you conceive the possibility of it?' – 'I cannot.'

On the seventh day of the trial (9 March), the jury were shown the baby in the judge's room, though not before they had seen what Mr Justice Hill called 'this great bunch of photographs of Mrs Russell and the child'. When the jury returned to the courtroom, and before another witness was called, Marshall Hall made an embarrassed statement. The *Evening Standard* of the day before, and *The Times* of that morning had both carried a story which the *Times* headlined 'RUSSELL CASE WITNESS SENT TO PRISON'. This was about Fred Archer, who had been a valet at Half Moon Street, but had now been jailed for embezzling just over £1 belonging to a baker for whom he had subsequently worked. Marshall Hall wanted the jury to know 'that this man had never been subpoenaed by us, and was not in attendance for us'. Clearly, if he had been going to call Archer as a witness, the jury might infer that he was relying on some very dubious testimony.

HILL: 'It is very unfortunate that the papers pay so much attention to this or any other case in this Court.'

MARSHALL HALL:'The Jury would probably have seen that, and they might have drawn a wrong inference, and I thought it ought to be explained.'

HILL: 'It is greatly to be regretted. I only wish they would leave us alone. It seems to me that these cases would be fully reported if each paper gave ten lines a day.'

MARSHALL HALL:'I do not think anybody can calculate the mischief that a report of a case of this kind does to the country, and the misery it causes to both parties.'

HILL: 'Of course it does.'

This was the first time, in the Russell case, that dismay had been publicly expressed about the lurid reporting of divorce cases – the feeling that had caused George V to write to the Lord Chancellor on the subject, and which eventually led to an Act to restrain such detailed reporting. [50]

Winifred Murray, secretary to Dr Rowley Bristow of Harley Street, was sworn. She gave evidence that Christabel had frequently come to the surgery to be massaged by herself in late 1920 and early 1921. The last treatment had been on 5 May 1921. Oddly, neither counsel asked whether she had noticed any change in Christabel's figure.

Herbert Spencer, a Harley Street gynaecologist, testified that he had known many cases of women who were ignorant of the fact that they were going to bear a child. Indeed, it had happened to one of his own nurses.

'She knew she had some swelling, but she had not the least idea that she was pregnant. I examined her, and found that she was not only pregnant, but she was pregnant with twins, and the labour pains were beginning. I sent her home in a cab, and she had the twins that same night. She was a very experienced nurse who had been in a home for training.'

Needless to say, Marshall Hall was not going to let Hastings get away with that. He belaboured Spencer.

'You know the history of this [Christabel Russell] case pretty well?' – 'I do not know it very well.'

'A single act of coitus, no penetration, no knowledge of her monthly periods having ceased, no knowledge of her pregnancy, no sickness, no alteration in her figure except that she got a little fat, no discoloration of her breasts, and no penetration at all, external emission: have you ever known a case quite parallel with that in your experience?'

'I have known many cases of all these points.'

'All in the same case?' – 'I cannot say that they were all in the same case.'

'Now, in the case of this nurse of yours, when did that happen?' –'Do you mean the date? Was it lately?' – 'No, it was some years ago.'

'You recorded it, of course, in *The Lancet*?' – 'No, I never recorded it.'

'You thought it was quite a normal thing for a woman to go until the actual labour pains were on her and not know she was pregnant with twins?' – 'It was not normal, but I was not very surprised about it: I have known others.'

'Was it not worthy of record for the benefit of your brother practitioners?' – 'If I were to record all the interesting cases, I should have nothing to do but to write.'

Spencer had proved more than a match for Marshall Hall. Counsel subsided.

Trevor Davies was called, obstetric surgeon at Queen Charlotte's Lying-in Hospital. He had been called to see Christabel's baby on the day of his birth. He said Geoffrey was an exceptionally well-developed child, larger than the average full-term child. He weighed 10½ pounds. The fingernails and toenails had grown beyond the ends of the fingers and toes. He had measured the child, who was 22 inches long.

'In point of fact, did what you found, including the toenails and fingernails, give any indication as to whether it had been carried a long time?' – 'Yes, they did.'

'What was the indication?' – 'Those points told me that the child was at least mature and, in all probability, post-mature.'

Marshall Hall tried to bludgeon him into recanting this view, but he refused to do so.

Christabel's brother-in-law, Hilton Welford, now entered the witness box, a man of thirty-two.

He said he had first heard there was trouble between Christabel and John Hugo on 6 July 1921 and that he had gone to Oakley on the 7th to talk to John Hugo 'and see if I could not square things up between them. I thought it was such a dreadful thing that nothing seemed to be done to try and bring them together again, as far as I could see ...' He found John Hugo was out shooting rabbits. He joined him; then they had lunch and went into the library for a talk. Marshall Hall interrupted Hastings's examination to ask what John Hugo had said. He told Welford that he had many times attempted relations with Christabel. Welford replied: 'You must have been more successful than you thought.' To which John Hugo rejoined: 'You may be correct but I cannot understand it.' They had a walk in the garden and then went into the smoking room where the paper that had already been produced in court was written. Welford said: 'He specially made a note of the 18th December, 1920, when he and his wife had slept together at Oakley.' John Hugo had told Christabel that he wanted to have relations with her but, as he said to Welford (Marshall Hall made him give the exact words): 'You know how difficult it is to do things when people are not willing.' In Welford's recollection, John Hugo had admitted that 'The child may be mine.' Welford had asked him if he honestly thought Christabel had misconducted herself with Gilbert Bradley. When he said 'No,' he persuaded him to cross out that allegation on the paper.

'I then asked him if he could honestly and truthfully name any man as Co-Respondent. He said, "No, I believe Chris to be perfectly 'straight'." I think, my

Plate 18; The Russell family at the Christening of Geoffrey and Susan's youngest child, Vanessa, in 1961.

Plate 19; A family group: *left to right,* Anthony Russell, David Russell, Susan Russell holding Vanessa, Geoffrey Russell, James Russell, *c.* 1962.

Plate 20; Christabel in Ireland, not long before her death in 1976. *Stan Shields.*

Plate 21; Christabel, in characteristically striking dress, at a society wedding.

Plate 22; Geoffrey and Vanessa celebrating his victory in the House of Lords hearing of 1976.

Plate 23; Lord and Lady Ampthill with 'Jack Russell'.

Plate 24; Geoffrey in James Bond mode in the Bahamas in the 1960s.

Plate 25; Evening News, 25 February 1976. Geoffrey had been paid £30,000 to relinquish any right to the Ampthill estates – though not to the title.

Plate 26; The Guardian, 27 February 1976: the juxtaposition of photogtraphs of Geoffrey and John Russell suggests a strong family resemblance, especially comparing the mouths.

Pocket Cartoon

By Osbert Lancaster

"Don't tell me that poor dear Bertie is in trouble again?"

Plate 27; Pocket cartoon by Osbert Lancaster, *Daily Express*, 25 February 1976. The reference is to the womanizing philosopher Bertrand Russell (Earl Russell, 1872-1970).

Pocket Cartoon

By Osbert Lancaster

"Tell me, Cumberbatch, d'ye remember a rather interestin' little wager you made some fifty years ago?"

Plate 28; Pocket cartoon by Osbert Lancaster, *Daily Express*, 13 April 1976.

"Would someone refresh my memory?—I haven't seen a virgin since Poona!"

Plate 29; Cartoon by 'JAK', *Evening Standard*, 25 February 1976.

Plate 30; Victory: Geoffrey Russell in April 1976 after the Lords' Committee for Privileges decided he was the rightful Lord Ampthill.

Lord, that is about all.'

Welford also recalled John Hugo's telling him, 'My father would kill me if he knew I was giving you this.'

'I suppose he did not mean really that he would kill him?' – 'I think he spoke rather jokingly.'

Welford had not been able to persuade Christabel to meet John Hugo. 'She was very angry.' He had no doubt that if the meeting could have taken place, the two would have been reconciled.

Marshall Hall cross-examined in his usual style. He read out a letter Christabel had written to John Hugo from Craig Hall in which she asked him to come and abduct her sister Gwen. 'She is so fed up with Hilton and so detests him ... She does have a damnable time. It is rotten.' Was that true? No. So Mrs Russell is a liar? No, she just uses extravagant language. Did she write irresponsibly, then? 'I do not know that she is irresponsible. I think she wrote things that are not as other people would have written them.' Marshall Hall also suggested that Welford had been browbeating John Hugo into admitting that the as yet unborn baby was his. Welford denied it; but he admitted he had said to John Hugo: 'You *must* be mistaken. This *must* be your child.'

Marshall Hall now introduced something that was new in the case: a letter John Hugo had written on 9 July 1922, just after the beginning of the first trial, to Mrs Alice Leigh Pemberton, who was an aunt both of Christabel and of Hilton Welford. In it, he wrote:

'I can quite understand your feelings about this awful business. I have never been more utterly miserable or unhappy in my life and I fully realise and am truly sorry for the unhappiness it is causing others. I am not taking this step out of spite or hatred for Christabel or because I have not the pluck and strength to make further efforts to turn our marriage into a success. The position between Chris and myself for the past year has been such that a baby, of which I am the father, is out of the question. Details need not be gone into here, sufficient is it to say that during this period Chris would not even kiss me or allow me to kiss her. Under these circumstances, am I likely to have forgotten any occurrence which might have raised my hopes for a change in this uncompromising attitude? You must guess that a baby of my own is the one thing I have longed for all this time as I had hoped it would make things easier for both of us...'

Marshall Hall put it to Welford that John Hugo would have been likely to say just the same kind of things to him at their meeting almost exactly one year before. He was not impugning his honesty, he said, only his memory. But Welford insisted that John Hugo had conceded the child might be his. By contrast, the barrister suggested, John Hugo had a crystal-clear memory of that interview; and here he employed one of his favourite shock tactics throughout the case – getting very explicit about sexual matters.

'I am only putting details to you to show how minute is the boy's memory of what took place ... In your attempt to get some sort of recollection of something that had happened that might make him the father of the child, did he even say this to you: "Well, if you press me, I do remember having two wet dreams"?' – 'No, I honestly cannot remember that.'

'You cannot have forgotten that?' – 'He might have said that, but I cannot remember it' ... 'Just to remind you of it, did he give this description of one of those occasions: He had dreamt that he was on horse-back, the horse was jumping a fence, and seemed to be getting higher and higher, and then he woke up? Surely you could not have forgotten that?' – 'Yes, I am afraid I have.'

'I should have thought that those were things you would not forget?' – 'No, I do not remember those. In fact, I may even go further and say that I do not think that was said.'

Flora Campbell was sworn: she had become nurse to Christabel's baby, at Harrington Gardens, on 1 November 1922. She said Christabel was out from 9.30 each morning until the evening. Occasionally she came back for lunch, but she was always home at night to see the baby go to bed. Marshall Hall asked if Christabel was nursing the child: was she breast-feeding him? The answer was no.

Ada Warnes, a trained nurse, looked after the baby in early January 1922, when he was ill. She said Christabel was always home between six and seven o'clock in the evening. Christabel was not nursing the baby: he was bottle-fed. Marshall Hall drew from the nurse the information that, after Christabel had seen the baby, she generally went out to dinner, getting home 'any time between 10 and 12'.

Florence Daisy Ashwell, who had taken over from Ada Warnes on 17 January 1922, looked after Geoffrey for ten months. She testified that Christabel had come home between 7 and 7.30 p.m., and that she always came 'straight into the nursery'. She had only missed doing so twice, in the early autumn. Marshall Hall asked if she had known Mr Bradley. 'I do not know him.' Pressed further on the point, she said she had only seen him in photographs in the newspapers. Sir Ellis Hume-Williams and Hastings both objected that the case against Bradley had already been dismissed. Marshall Hall said he wanted to read out letters that showed Bradley had been visiting Harrington Gardens while Florence Ashwell was working there.

HILL: 'The lady says she does not remember seeing him. That is all it comes to.'

MARSHALL HALL: 'Did Mrs Russell go out to dances most nights?' –'Mrs Russell went out, but I do not know where she went.'

'Were you awake when she came in?' – 'Not often.'

On the eighth day (13 March 1923) Blanche Hart was questioned by Patrick Hastings. He asked if she had been regular in her monthly periods. She had not; and she said that her daughter Christabel took after her in that respect. Then he turned to Christabel's men friends. She knew Bradley and Cross well.

'Did you ever hear at all of Mr Mayer as a friend of your daughter's?' – 'As a business friend I had heard of him.'

HILL: 'Not otherwise?' – 'No, my Lord. I had heard very little about him at all.'

Hastings asked Blanche about Christabel's sex education. She replied: 'She once asked me what marriage was, and I said that that was the only thing I could not tell her, because I thought it was her husband who would have to tell her that.' That conversation had taken place when Christabel was about seventeen. Marshall Hall cross-examined.

'Your daughter has been working very hard in [her] business?' – 'She has.'

'Can you tell me, has it been more than keeping itself going? Have you had any dividends?' – 'No dividends yet.'

'I think your daughter has been busy on other matters, has she not? She has been writing a good deal lately?' – 'I do not think so.'

'Do you know that she has been writing her reminiscences?' – 'I think there is talk that she might.'

'Is it not completed yet?' – 'No.'[51]

Questioned more, Blanche agreed that terms had been talked about, and thought that Christabel had had one payment on account, from one of the newspapers. Marshall Hall got nastier.

'Have you ever tried to be firm with [your daughter]?' – 'I think I am always firm with her.'

'Might I suggest that your idea of bringing her up and exercising firmness has always been to allow her to do whatever she wanted and in the way she wanted to do it?' – 'No.'

'Have your will and hers ever come into contact?' – 'Yes.'

'Have you ever succeeded in impressing your will upon her as against hers?' –'I think I have many times.'

'Do you think that John Russell ever had the smallest chance of making her do anything that he wanted, that she did not want to do?' – 'As John Russell, I should think not, but as any other man, yes.'

Marshall Hall wrung from Blanche a clearer account than the court had yet heard of the day (29 May 1921) when Christabel, in a rage, had ordered John Hugo out of her mother's flat, calling him 'all sorts of a cad'.

'Did he say that he would not leave the flat as it was your flat?' – 'No. I told him not to leave the flat. I tried to make peace between them.'

'Mr Russell always treated you as a lady, did he not?' – 'Yes.'

'He behaved very well to you?' – 'Yes, always.'

'He was very fond of you?' – 'I believe he was.'

'Is there any justification for saying that he insulted you and was rude to you?' – 'Yes, at that interview, because he lost his temper, and said, "It is enough to make me wish my mother-in-law was in hell"; and that was too much for my daughter; that is why she ordered him out of the room. That is how it happened.'

'You have remembered it always?' – 'Yes, I have remembered it always. I have never heard anybody wishing me in hell before.'

'If I put it to you that Mr Russell never said it or never wished it – ?' – 'He did say it. He may not have wished it. I do not think for a moment that he did.'

The next witness was Henry Chicheley Haldane, a London solicitor. He said that Christabel had asked him to have inquiries made about Edgar Mayer to make sure that he was a fit and proper person to become a director of her company. The report on Mayer had been quite satisfactory.

Now Hastings called a stream of witnesses, all of them either employees or friends of Christabel's. In examining each one of them, he was intent on establishing that Christabel was always on the Curzon Street premises at tea-time – presumably to prove that she could not have been philandering with Mayer in nearby Half Moon Street in the afternoons. First came Henrietta Elsa Fox, whose job with Christabel was as a model, 'showing off dresses'. Next, Anita Mazzini, who was Italian and needed an interpreter. She was a fitter at Curzon Street. Then Ellen Sophia Menzies, head milliner at the shop. She testified how hard-working Christabel was: 'Every dress was designed by her personally; every customer consulted her personally; the travellers were seen by her; she was much the hardest-worked person in the house.'

Hilda Walton had taken over from Elfrida Shorten as secretary of the company. Like all the other staff and friends, she said Christabel never left the premises between 4.0 and 6.0 p.m. Marshall Hall cross-examined sarcastically, implying that all the staff had been suborned to support their boss, and were playing along if they knew what was good for them.

'Mrs Russell is very popular with her staff?' – 'She has every occasion to be.'

'I do not suggest she has not, but the staff get on very well with her?' – 'Yes.' 'They are very fond of her?' – 'Yes.'

'And the whole staff are here to say that she never left the house between half-past four and six?' – 'In January and February 1921, Mrs Russell could not have passed the door without my knowing.'

The payroll witnesses rolled on: Gertrude Giggiotti, housekeeper at Curzon Street, was responsible for sending up tea to Christabel. In response to Marshall Hall she agreed that, no, she did not actually see her drink it.

Ella Milne was a friend of Christabel's, and bought dresses from her – 'I had so many frocks just at the beginning of the year.' She said she had tea with Christabel at least once a week. Marshall Hall: 'I need not trouble you.' Gwendoline Sanders, who had known Christabel since 1919, swore she had never been to see her at Curzon Street and found that she was out. Alice Johnstone, Christabel's maid at Curzon Street, said she would see John Hugo in Christabel's bedroom at breakfast-time, wearing a dressing-gown over pyjamas. The couple had breakfast together – Christabel in bed, her husband perhaps sitting on the end of the bed. She had never heard John Hugo burst into Christabel's room in the night.

Mabel Louisa Scobey was a friend of Christabel's who had met her at a dance some years before. She had helped her with the curtains and furniture for the shop. She knew that Christabel and John Hugo quarrelled occasionally, though they never did so in front of her. In general, they seemed to be on very good terms. Answering Sir Ellis Hume-Williams, she said she only remembered one visit by

Mayer to Curzon Street, on business. It was in the morning. She told Hastings: 'Mrs Russell never worried about anybody's opinion whatever; she did what she knew was quite all right, and she did not care what people said or thought.'

Zara Marcella Laing, of Four Acres, Hartley Wintney, Hampshire, was called, the wife of Lieutenant-Colonel Laing. She said she had known Christabel 'ever since I can remember', certainly since she (Christabel) was three. She very often visited Curzon Street. She had heard of Mayer 'vaguely, as a business friend'. Sometimes the Russells stayed with the Laings in Hampshire; and on 17 February 1921 Mrs Laing had had a birthday party at Claridge's and both the Russells were there – on very good terms, she would say. When Marshall Hall tried to get Mrs Laing to badmouth her friend, she deftly volleyed the shot back.

'Would you like to treat your husband as Mrs Russell treated hers?' – 'I do not think I should ever get the chance.'

Perhaps emboldened by this, Patrick Hastings re-examined Mrs Laing.

'I think I ought to ask you this, as you have known her so long. Have you ever seen any sign of her being an actress?' – 'No, I should have said that it was one of the things she could not do.'

HASTINGS: 'That seems to distress Sir Edward.'

MARSHALL HALL: 'It only astonishes me.'

HASTINGS: 'Why do you say she is not an actress?' – 'She was always much too outspoken, and she never attempted to pretend anything was not what it was; there was no making out that a thing was different or in any way sort of playing a part.'

Evelyn May Geen, of Allen House, Allen Street, Kingston, the wife of Albert Geen, was another old friend of Christabel's. She remembered the Russells being on good terms between October and Christmas 1920. Just before Christmas John Hugo had asked her to design a ring for Christabel. (The ring was handed around the jury.) Marshall Hall cross-examined her.

'Discussing things with Mrs Russell, did you realize that she had any sexual feeling of any sort or shape?' – 'I thought she had very little, because in all the time that she has known me, I think she has only kissed me once.'

'She says in one of her letters that she does not like ladies kissing her, and I presume the converse would also be true. Did she ever convey to you the idea that anything to do with married life – you know what I mean – was distasteful to her?' – 'Not until after the last case, then she told me.'

'After you had heard the evidence in the last case, she told you that married life in that sense had always been distasteful to her?' – 'Yes.'

'And you believed that, of course – you accepted that?' – 'Exactly.'

'And everything to do with sexuality?' – 'Yes.'

Marshall Hall then read out the very affectionate passages from Christabel's letters to John Hugo sent from Switzerland – 'I've got my arms round you and I've kissed you on your eyes and mouth and your head is against my neck and I can kiss your hair. Good-night, my darling angel, I want you ...' Was Christabel sincere when she wrote that, or was she acting? 'Can you imagine a woman writing a letter like that to a man unless she was sexually attracted to him?' he asked. Mrs Laing: 'It is such a difficult thing to say.' Marshall Hall: 'Is there any limit to your believing Mrs Russell? Would you believe her through everything?' 'Yes, I would.'

Benjamin Sumner Hoare, a publisher, was examined by Hastings. He had known Christabel since 1915 and used to dance with her regularly. He often dined with the Russells at Curzon Street. He also used to pick up Christabel and take her out to dine and dance.

'Did you ever at any of those dancing parties either meet Mr Mayer or hear of him?' – 'I met him once at a party at the Savoy on Armistice night, 1920.'

'That was the only time?' – 'I think I have seen him at dances at Curzon Street.'

'Dances given by Mrs Russell?' – 'Yes.'

'At the time of the party at the Savoy ... do you happen to remember whether she danced with Mr Mayer or not that night?' – 'I should say she did not dance with him at all. As far as I remember, she danced with Mr Bradley the whole night.'

Cross-examined by Marshall Hall, Hoare said he had never danced with Christabel 'cheek to cheek'. 'I believe it was the fashion,' he added, 'but I never indulged in it myself ... I did not care for it, but I think a great many people did.' Asked if he had ever discussed sex with John Hugo, he replied: 'Sex in the abstract, but not sex as far as his marriage was concerned.' With Christabel, he had discussed 'general sex subjects'.

MARSHALL HALL: 'Would you go so far as to ask her whether she liked sex acts?' – 'Good gracious, no. I should not think of such a thing ...'

'So far as you could observe, she was not at all attracted by sex questions at all or sex consideration?' – 'No, I should say not.'

John Hugo Russell was recalled. Questioned by Marshall Hall, he remembered that in the interview with Hilton Welford he had said that he might have to resign his right to the Ampthill title in favour of his younger brother (if that were permitted by law) to avoid the possibility that Christabel's child, which he felt sure was by another man, might one day succeed to the title.

Patrick Hastings did not usually interrogate as aggressively as Marshall Hall, but for once he did so in asking John Hugo about Christabel and Mayer.

'Tell us, now. Do you believe now – you – that your wife, knowing in July that you were going to take proceedings for divorce against her, was walking out of her door in Curzon Street, round the corner up to Half Moon Street, in order regularly to commit adultery with Mr Mayer?' – 'Yes, I do.'

'You really do?' – 'Yes.'

'With the shop, as you know, occupied by dozens of people who knew her well?' – 'Yes.'

John Hugo admitted that his solicitors had had Christabel watched by detectives from July 1921 for some weeks.

'And if those detectives had ever seen her going into Half Moon Street, you have no doubt they would be here, have you?' – 'I should think they would; but you see she was out of London a lot at that time.'

Sir Ellis Hume-Williams asked similarly pointed questions on behalf of Mayer, once again making great play with the failed charges against Bradley and Cross in the first trial. Marshall Hall re-questioned John Hugo.

'Are you in any way acting here merely as a puppet directed by your parents?' –'Good Lord! No.'

Hastings was not so sure. He drew from John Hugo the admission that he had shown his mother his letter to Alice Leigh Pemberton before he sent it off on 11 July 1921.

On the tenth day of the hearings, Mr Justice Hill summed up. Maurice Hill, who was sixty-one, was a man of cerebral antecedents. His father, Sir George Birkbeck Hill, was a literary scholar and edited Boswell and Johnson; Maurice's great-uncle was Sir Rowland Hill, inventor of the penny post. Maurice Hill had taken a double first in classics at Balliol College, Oxford. He was at home with Admiralty cases – just before the Great War he had drafted a scheme of state insurance to cover merchant shipping against war risks. It might be said that he was all at sea with divorce; at any rate his *Times* obituary said 'he hated divorce cases', and he made the heartfelt and much repeated quip that in his court he had 'one foot on sea and one in a sewer'. In court he could be informal, discarding his wig and listening 'with his gown half-way down his back, seated sideways in his chair'; but this was a man with a much more old-fashioned cast of mind than Sir Henry Duke who had heard the first trial. Hill expected ladies to behave like ladies and not to treat marriage with flippancy. If one takes Duke's summing-up as a whole, it is broadly pro-Christabel. If one takes Hill's, it is tilted the other way, pro-John Hugo and anti-Christabel.

Hill's charge to the jury began: 'We have now reached nearly the end of this long, difficult and anxious case.' He had noticed that they had given the evidence their closest attention. He said the things that judges usually say to juries: that it was for the jurors to judge, not for him; he could indicate how things struck him, but they were not bound by his view on any question of fact. He said they had listened to able and eloquent speeches – 'the case for each side has been presented with marked ability'. The jury were to weigh what counsel had said; but it was for them to decide.

A number of topics had been introduced which, in his view, did not assist them to determine what they had to determine: had the Respondent (Christabel) been shown to be guilty of adultery? Patrick Hastings had suggested Christabel was being 'persecuted' by her husband. The judge did not agree. 'Can anyone doubt that the Petitioner honestly believes in his case, or that Lord and Lady Ampthill, in supporting him, are not doing what they believe to be right?'

The jury were not to reach their verdict through either sympathy or resentment. Whether they approved or disapproved of the conduct of either party, their character and conduct were only of moment in so far as they threw light on the question: did the Respondent commit adultery?

Hill thought it of no assistance to ask, had John Hugo failed in virility, or 'Should he have done more?' Neither was it helpful to ask, 'Should he have restrained himself from the partial intercourse in which he did indulge?' 'Again, on the matter whether a man is acting in an unbeseeming manner if he goes to a fancy dress dance dressed in woman's clothes, I cannot conceive how it helps us to determine the question of whether the Respondent committed adultery or not.' Whether John Hugo should have given his wife more money, or whether she was grasping in persuading him to take the lump sum from the Navy, were also irrelevancies. 'We know that this marriage was one of those rather hasty war marriages, in which there is little thought of how the home is to be carried on when the war is over.'

Then came Hill's first sideswipe against Christabel:

'In the spring of 1921 there is the suggestion of setting the young people up in a cottage. Lord Ampthill offered to increase the allowance if the wife would live with the husband in the normal way. That offer is rejected with scorn by the wife ...'

Hill could have said 'rejected by the wife' or 'firmly rejected by the wife' but he chose to add 'with scorn', an emotive and a pejorative term.

Hill exonerated the Ampthills of unkindness towards Christabel: she had been welcome at Oakley and if she did not choose to go there more often, 'it was obviously her own doing'. He added:

'Her treatment of her husband, which is not really disputed by anybody, is open, no doubt, to grave censure. I do not mean merely the refusal of ordinary marital intercourse, but her foolish, self-willed and selfish conduct, bent on her own ambitions and her own pleasures and sacrificing to them the ordinary domestic life with her husband. It may be open to censure, but that does not really help us in the consideration of whether she was guilty of adultery ...'

Here, under the guise of being strictly fair to Christabel, Hill is saying a great deal more against her than for her. His severe words are likely to have reinforced any 'anti' feeling towards her by the jury.

Hill advised that the jury were not to be swayed, either, by sympathy for the child, Geoffrey.

'The child is not a party to this suit. Your verdict, if it be for the Petitioner, will, of course, put upon the child a grave imputation – stronger than an imputation; it will put the gravest possible reflection in the matter of legitimacy; but the issue you have to try is the issue between the husband and the wife. If your verdict is against the Respondent, well, it must indirectly brand the child with bastardy; but as against the child, that is not final or conclusive.'

The legitimacy or otherwise of the child, Hill said, could be determined in another court – the child represented by a guardian. He presciently added: 'It might be that in the future a question might arise in respect of the title to the Barony of Ampthill, and it might arise in Proceedings before the Committee for Privileges of the House of Lords.' Over half a century later, this prophecy was dramatically fulfilled.[52]

Hill admitted that the conduct of the two parties had a bearing on the question to be decided. He thought John Hugo 'perhaps rather young for his years'. Christabel was not only older, she had done amazing war work. 'Ask yourselves: Who do you think was the stronger character of the two?' It was clear what answer the judge expected. 'It is not disputed that, bent upon her own way, she generally got it.' It was Christabel who had made the stipulation about 'no children'; she who had demanded John Hugo take the Navy's lump sum; she who insisted on separate rooms at Lincoln Street and Curzon Street. 'The offer of life in a cottage was scorned by her.' (There was that slur again.)

Hill then showed Christabel contradicting herself – could this woman's word be relied on? On the one hand she had said that at the time of her marriage she did not love her husband. 'She does herself an injustice, I should think you will think,' said Hill, reminding the jury of the almost passionate letters she sent John Hugo from Switzerland. But, Hill very fairly stated, there was no evidence that she was 'a woman who was given to what I may describe as lewdness in her behaviour', though (again the sideswipe) 'she was reckless to a degree'. He was referring to her escapades with Bradley and Cross – men already found to be innocent in the first trial.

'She was represented by Mr Hastings as a woman altogether devoid of sexual appetite and always revolted by the sort of semi-intercourse that her husband had with her. Upon that, you will bear in mind the letters from Craig Hall and Switzerland and ask yourselves: Is this a woman totally incapable of pleasure in the embraces of a man? I need not amplify this.'

But Hill could not resist amplifying it quite a lot – and in this part of his speech he made his most withering comments about Christabel.

'These are matters which you will weigh. You will consider whether this is a woman to whom adultery presents itself as a horrible thing, as something morally revolting from which she would start back. In that connection I think you will bear in mind the letter which she wrote to Miss Acton on the 4th July, 1921, in which, while declaring that the child was the husband's, she speaks of herself as longing for the fray, and Miss Acton taking a box for the *Russell* v. *Russell* case with rows of co-respondents. That is a letter which, to my mind, is a very distressing letter. Shocking written by a woman who is not innocent, it would be more shocking written by a woman who is innocent. You have to judge. But it shows the levity in regard to so shocking a charge as that of adultery.'

One gets a real sense, here, that Hill is gunning for Christabel. He cannot see that in the letter to Miss Acton – who she knows is now hostile to her – Christabel is probably being defiantly facetious, to keep up her spirits. (She may also have been hoping that Maud Acton would report her feisty attitude to John Hugo.) Marriage, to Hill, was a sacrament, with a sacred vow; so to make jokes about divorce was to laugh in the face of God. He tempered his harsh criticism with a possible let-out clause for Christabel.

'On the other hand, this woman at the time was pregnant, and people who are pregnant may sometimes say things when they are not always so fully in control of their nerves, and it may be right to say that it was written under the sting of what she thought and what she believed was an unjust accusation.'

Once again, what Mr Justice Hill had said in Christabel's favour was outweighed by what he said against her.

The jury also had to decide, Hill told them, on the relative truthfulness of the two parties. They had to ask themselves: 'How far is he or she prone to tell the truth?' and 'How far can his or her memory be relied upon?' He thought John Hugo's desire to tell the truth had not been impugned, though his memory was sometimes in question. 'With regard to the Respondent, her truthfulness is gravely impugned in this case.' Was that quite a fair summary? After all, Christabel had accused John Hugo of lying; he had said the same about her. It was a case of whose word one accepted.

The two main questions the jury had to decide were: had Christabel committed adultery with a man unknown?, and had she done so with Edgar Mayer? Hill dealt with the man unknown first – a slightly insensitive proceeding, as it must have left Mayer sweating, whereas there was no 'man unknown' to sweat. John Hugo, the judge pointed out, was trying to prove that there was no sexual intercourse of any kind between him and Christabel at any time during which Geoffrey could have been begotten. If the jury believed that, they must find Christabel guilty. If they were in any doubt on the matter, they must find Christabel not guilty. The burden was on John Hugo, to prove her guilty. 'He who affirms it, must prove it.'

Hill did not intend to deal with the medical evidence at any great length. As his 'sewer' remark suggested, he had less of a stomach for such matters than Marshall Hall, of whom it was said: 'He has a one-track mind – a dirt-track.' Hill felt there was no serious discrepancy between the extremely experienced surgeons and physicians who had testified on both sides. Ten months' gestation was quite possible. Conception could arise from an emission of semen in semi-intercourse. He regretted that John Hugo's advisers had not been given the chance, by Christabel's, to have her examined by their own independent expert; but Christabel's were within their rights not to do so.

Hill now made an important point in Christabel' s favour: if indeed the semen were from some man other than John Hugo, then the condition of Christabel's hymen, the rugae and so on, meant that that man must have had the same kind of relations with her as her husband had had. In well-phrased prose, Hill spelt out the corollaries:

'If the Respondent gave herself up to another man, would not she give herself up utterly? If another man was permitted to come in contact with her at all, would he have stopped short of complete satisfaction? You must carefully consider that.'

The second of these questions might be paraphrased: if another man had had sexual relations with Christabel, wouldn't he, so to speak, have made a better job of it than John Hugo had done? Hill emphasized that if Christabel had allowed another man semi-intercourse that would count as adultery. 'Complete penetration by another man is not necessary to constitute adultery.'

As reference had been made to it, Hill addressed the subject of proceedings for nullity. The people who had talked of bringing such proceedings were mistaken. Such a decree was not granted to people who wilfully and wrongfully refused marital intercourse (there was another sharp rebuke to Christabel): it was only granted when one or other of the couple was impotent to consummate the marriage.

At about this point, Hill told the jury he would need about one hour more to speak on a few other topics and deal with the Mayer case. Would they prefer to sit on, or return the next day? Everybody was getting tired and the foreman of the jury at once opted for an adjournment.

On the final, eleventh day of the trial (16 March), Hill discussed Welford's visit to John Hugo and read out some of the notes he had made – among them one in which he hoped John Hugo 'would meet C.R. and make it up with her'. The rather unalert foreman interrupted: 'May I ask, my Lord, what "C.R." meant in that?' Hill gave the obvious answer: '"C.R." is Christabel Russell.' That the foreman could ask such a question after more than ten days of evidence does not suggest that Christabel was being judged by the brightest in the land.

Hill now passed to the charge that Christabel had committed adultery with Edgar Mayer. He was dubious about the servants' evidence as to Christabel's visiting Mayer in Half Moon Street; in particular, he thought that 'Crane is a man whom I should think you would not rely upon unless he is corroborated ... In cross-examination he appeared to be a man who in other matters had no regard either for decency or truth.' He thought it quite likely that the servants had mistaken some other woman for Christabel. There was no evidence of behaviour by either Christabel or Mayer that 'would raise a suspicion outside that they were in any way lovers'. Could the jury be satisfied beyond reasonable doubt that Christabel had committed adultery with Mayer? It was clear that the judge thought they could not. The jury retired at 11.34 a.m. At 1.22 p.m. they asked for 'substantial further time' and were sent in sandwiches and coffee. They returned to the court at 3.15 p.m., with their unanimous verdicts: Mrs Russell was not guilty of adultery with Mayer, nor he of adultery with her; but she was guilty of adultery with a man unknown. John Hugo was accordingly granted a decree nisi.

Marshall Hall was triumphant. Many thought that what had clinched the verdict was his impassioned closing speech to the jury, in which he begged them to free John Hugo Russell 'from the tie which he once hoped would be a tie of love but which is now a rusty chain that burns into his soul'. Was Mr Justice Hill happy with the verdict? Of course he could not say so. But when the foreman of the jury asked if Hill would absolve them from attending as jurors 'for some little time', the judge said:

'I want to thank you very much for the very great pains you have taken in this case. I never knew a Jury to give more steady attention to a case. I can do this. I can absolve you for five years, but my power only extends to this Division: I cannot control any other Divisions. As far as this Division is concerned, you are exempted for five years.'

The *Daily Express* reported what happened after the verdict.

'A few rushed to the doors to give quick news to the waiting crowd in the corridors and in the courtyard beyond. Lawyers were on their feet. Ushers exerted themselves to stay the tumult of comment.

'There were questions of Mr Mayer's costs to be paid by the Hon. John Russell, and the actual granting of the decree nisi, at the normal request of Sir Edward Marshall Hall.

'And what of the great actors in this closing scene of the drama that had held the stage for eleven days?

'As the jury returned Mrs Russell's solicitor whispered, "Seize your lucky charm!"

' "I have it in my hat," she replied. "I hope it will stand by me..." '

'I watched the face. She looked neither to the right nor to the left. Her eyes were fixed on the judge. She was a sphinx. What was passing through that clever brain of hers? Who could say?

'Not a mutter from her lips. Not a word to her mother, who sat on her right, and who bore herself with the same air of detachment that has characterised her attitude throughout. Not a glance at her sister, Mrs Welford, whose impassive features have surely never relaxed once during the whole trial.

'Mrs Russell's brain was working. She was going over matters in her mind.

'Then suddenly, with a whimsical smile, her lips parted. She was herself again. Or was she the consummate actress Sir Edward Marshall Hall declared she was?

'Anyway, from now on for the few moments the formalities lingered, she kept the fascinating smile, one of her chief characteristics.

'All the witnesses for and against her testified to the fearlessness of Mrs Russell, a woman who holds a pilot's certificate, and has flown an aeroplane alone.

'And Mr Russell? All through the eleven days this young man, six feet five inches tall, has sat with bowed shoulders looking steadily at the ground. He entered court to hear the verdict and sat in exactly the same attitude. The return of the jury did not rouse him. The verdict had apparently no interest for him.

'Was it that, win or lose, the matter was sorrowful to him? For this woman in the case was, as he has insisted all through, a woman whom he dearly loved.

'It was no triumph to him to hear that she had been found guilty. He sat, as he listened to the verdict, heeding no one, looking at no one, apparently as dejected as ever.

'Not so Lord Ampthill, who sat next to his son. There was anxious interest writ all over his face. His head was craned to see the jury over Lady Ampthill's hat. He followed every word, and when the verdict was pronounced his features bore a great expression of relief.

'Lady Ampthill quietly inclined her head. Her brother was in court. They exchanged a glance; that was all.

'Then suddenly father and mother remembered the boy at their side. With a gesture that could hardly be noticed, Lady Ampthill slipped her hand across her husband and squeezed that of her son. Lord Ampthill followed her example...

'There were congratulations on one side of the court, commiserations on the other. The Russell family crowded round Sir Edward Marshall Hall, shaking his hand earnestly, and pouring out gratitude for his wonderful conduct of the case...

'Not a glance did Mr Russell give to his wife, leaving her with her condoling friends at the opposite exit. She never turned her head in his direction. They appeared separate in spirit as the poles.

'In the courtyard they almost met. Two closed motor-cars were waiting. Mrs Russell, her mother, and her sister stepped into one. A matter only of seconds, and Lord and Lady Ampthill, with their son, took the other.

BOOS AND CHEERS

'In the quadrangle of the Law Courts a vast crowd assembled. Men and women of all ages and all classes pushed, swayed and surged, in order to see the boyish man and beautiful woman about whose lives has raged one of the greatest legal battles in the world.

'The two closed motor-cars appeared almost simultaneously. A burst of cheering greeted Lord Ampthill's car, but the Hon. John Russell did not look triumphant.

'Mrs Russell's car passed almost in silence. A few cheers and a few boos rose from the crowd as the motor-car forced its way through the densely packed square.

'Mrs Russell sat back in her seat, calm, self-possessed, and smiling.'

Some members of the English aristocracy felt that their whole class was being besmirched by the Russell Baby case. On 2 March 1923 – the day after the second trial opened, when the newspapers were full of the scandal – Dorothea Ponsonby, wife of the politician Arthur Ponsonby (later Lord Ponsonby of Shulbrede)[53] wrote to him from a Brighton hotel.

'I am saying aloud in a letter to Girly [their daughter Elizabeth][54] about the Russell Case. I couldn't sleep last night and it became a nightmare, when I thought of what nice young men could really think of her – not to mention Ria,[55] and Maggie[56] and all the rest. Anyhow perhaps I can prevent her from talking about it.'[57]

11

The Appeal

A trial judge should be quick, courteous and wrong. That is not to say the
Court of Appeal should be slow, rude and right, for that would be
usurping the function of the House of Lords.
LORD ASQUITH OF BISHOPSTONE, A LAW LORD

On 18 April 1923, Christabel Russell appealed against the decision in the High
Court, on five main grounds:
1. That the verdict was against the weight of evidence;
2. That there was no evidence on which the Jury could find that the Respondent
   had been guilty of adultery as alleged;
3. That the learned Judge was wrong in law in admitting such evidence of the
   Petitioner as purported to show that intercourse did not take place between
   him and the Respondent when they were occupying the same bed and/or when
   they were occupying adjoining rooms in the same house;
4. That the learned Judge failed to direct the Jury on six points [which were listed];
5. That the learned Judge misdirected the Jury on five other points [also listed].

The appeal opened on 24 July 1923 before the Master of the Rolls Lord Sterndale,
Lord Scrutton and Lord Warrington. Each, in his own way, was a remarkable man.
When Sterndale suddenly died, of a cerebral haemorrhage, four months later, his
Times obituary described him in the purplest of passages:

'He was to many the embodiment of splendid manhood, the physical type of
Englishman that we all take delight in – broad-shouldered, mighty in sinew, calm in
manner, and with an unruffled serenity; he diffused a golden feeling of sunshine,
not languorous but with something of the bite of those Alpine sunrisings and
downsettings which he loved, or of those high dales in which he lived.' [Sterndale
had been a keen mountaineer.]

Very different from this paragon was Lord Justice Scrutton (1856-1934). In a
period when obituarists usually adopted the principle *De mortuis nil nisi bonum,* his
Times obituary did not mince words:

'His brusqueness of manner, irritability and petulance impaired the dispatch of
business in his Court, and at last an active protest was made on behalf of the

solicitors ... against the rudeness with which they were treated in chambers.'

His entry in the *Dictionary of National Biography* – clearly written by somebody who disliked him (F.D. Mackinnon) – is even harsher. Mackinnon concedes that Scrutton was very clever: he gained a double first and several prizes at Cambridge. But even at university he was 'rather uncouth and was thought to have been the only Englishman of his time who never shaved in his life'. Already, as President of the Cambridge Union, he had a downy beard; by the time of the Russell appeal, he had a bushy one, carved in an Elizabethan style. At Cambridge he was lanky and wobbled about on a penny-farthing bicycle.

He became a KC in 1901. Mackinnon conveys an unappealing eccentric.

'Scrutton got through an immense amount of work, spending his time either in the courts, or in the hideous room which he occupied in the hideous block called Temple Gardens, and in which a Spartan rigour reigned. Scrutton sat on a windsor chair, without a cushion, at a battered writing-table, to the side of which was a table, loaded with papers, that had come out of one of his father's ships; a rough piece of wood filled the hole that had enclosed the mast. [Scrutton's father was a prosperous shipowner.] When darkness set in the only source of light was a Victorian chandelier with fishtail gas burners. The other two rooms were filled with 'devils' and pupils. [Mackinnon, later a lord justice, was among these.] At 4.15 p.m., the group met together for some repulsive tea and dry Bath Oliver biscuits. Scrutton, silently absorbed in thinking about his work, would stride about the room until, almost daily, the top of his head crashed into the knob of the chandelier ...'

Scrutton was appointed a judge in 1910.

'[He] soon proved himself a very efficient judge, though not a popular one [MacKinnon writes]. He had never had good manners and he indulged in petulant rudeness to solicitors' clerks on summonses. Eventually all the chief City solicitors, his former clients, gave a joint retainer to Alfred Chaytor, then a leading junior who took silk in 1914, to make a protest to the judge in court. Chaytor discharged his task with firmness.'

Scrutton listened without comment. For a while he mended his ways; but later he responded with such brutal rudeness to an appeal from H.A. McCardie ('whom he probably despised intellectually') that McCardie refused to submit his case notes to the Court of Appeal unless he could be assured that Scrutton was not sitting on it. The most famous case over which Scrutton presided was the trial for murder of George Joseph Smith in the sensational 'brides in the bath' affair (1915).

Lord Warrington, whose father was a partner in the royal jewellers, Garrard & Co, was less clever (he took a second at Cambridge), less high profile and less nasty than Scrutton. He was a Chancery judge before being raised to the Court of Appeal in 1915. His *Times* obituary of 1937 described him as 'never profound'; but the *Dictionary of National Biography* suggests that 'the higher he went the better he got'. He had one particular qualification for judging the *Russell* v. *Russell* appeal: in 1916 he had been one of the lords justice of appeal who reversed the judgment of Mr Justice Bargrave Deane in the *Slingsby Baby* case[58], It was not, perhaps, a good omen that he and his fellow judges had unanimously decided that that baby was not legitimate.

Patrick Hastings presented Christabel's appeal to the three judges. He succinctly reviewed the story of the marriage and the course the two cases had taken in the courts below. 'It would be practically impossible', he said, 'to find a jury who would not strain the evidence in favour of Mr Russell, for Mrs Russell had treated him' (here counsel must have deliberated over the nice choice of an adverb that would not shed too unbecoming a light on his client) 'very exceptionally'. His main contention was that it was legally not permissible for a husband or wife to give evidence of non-intercourse so as to prove that a child born when they were cohabiting was not the child of either one of them. He supported this argument with a string of cases, so long that he had not come to the end of it when the court adjourned for the day.

The next day, he cited more legal precedents, and claimed: 'Mr Justice Hill's statement that "if the husband had satisfied that jury that there was no intercourse at the crucial time" they might find in his favour, was a wholly inadequate interpretation of the law on this point.' Striking back, Sir Edward Marshall Hall maintained that Hill's direction was 'simply sufficient'. To buttress his contention, he cited several cases to prove that 'intercourse is not a necessary presumption from the parties' having slept together', and that there might be evidence to show either that it had taken place or that it had not.

After the three judges had conferred together, Lord Sterndale gave the judgment. He made it clear that the whole case was distasteful to him.

'I am glad to say that it is not necessary for me to go into the story of these two young persons' marriage (it is not a pleasant story in any way) nor is it necessary for me to go into what passed between them when the husband wished to have connection with his wife as a husband has with his wife: that is not a pleasant story either. I am very glad to be relieved from having to go into any part of it.'

He dealt with the criticisms Hastings had made of Hill's summing-up. Sterndale had come to the conclusion that there had been no misdirection and that no valid complaint could be made against the summing-up. 'The sole and only question that we have to decide is this: Was the evidence that the husband gave, that on a certain occasion (I think there were two nights in question) he had no connection with his wife, admissible or not admissible?' It certainly appeared to Sterndale that, without John Hugo's evidence, the decree would not stand. Assuming the husband's evidence to be admissible, it was not a valid complaint that Mr Justice Hill had not dealt correctly with it in the court below, because the judge had distinctly stated that the burden of proof was upon the petitioner (the husband). The question remained – was that evidence admissible? If the husband was right in saying there was no connection, then the adultery was proved and the inference was irresistible that the child was the child of another. To see whether that evidence was admissible it was necessary to look at the legal history of the matter. He referred to the judgment of Lord Mansfield in the case of *Goodright* v. *Moss*

(1777): 'The law of England is clear that the declaration of a father or mother cannot be admitted to bastardize the issue born after marriage. It is a rule founded in decency, morality and policy that they shall not be permitted to say after marriage that they have had no connection and therefore the offspring is spurious.'

The Master of the Rolls then quoted from the Evidence Amendment Act 1869 allowing husbands and wives to give evidence in 'proceedings instituted in consequence of adultery' – as had not previously been the case. Sterndale said that this did not mean that husbands and wives could give *any* sort of evidence. For example, they could not give hearsay evidence. Their testimony must be upon matters within the issue and relevant to the issues of the trial. The evidence of John Hugo Russell was clearly relevant to the issues of the trial. It was urged that the husband's evidence was excluded by Lord Mansfield's ruling. Sterndale could see no reason why such evidence should be excluded. It was most certainly relevant. (True – but what about Christabel's evidence?)

Sterndale said he would not refer to the several cases cited for the appellant, Mrs Russell, for they were all cases in which the *legitimacy* of a child was the direct issue, whereas whether or not the child was affected was not the direct issue here. Hastings had cleverly argued that, if John Hugo's evidence were admitted, any husband might repudiate a wife who had a child by denying he had had intercourse with her. Sterndale thought that 'men like that are rare'. Displaying once again his puritanical, if not prudish nature, he added:

'Morality and decency, in Lord Mansfield's judgment, seem to me to come to the same thing. Now decency is very difficult to apply in the Divorce Court, and for this reason, that from the very nature of proceedings there, evidence must constantly be given, perfectly admissible evidence, that is perfectly loathsome to the ordinary man or ordinary woman's mind. Take, for instance (I do not say that the analogy is complete at all, it is not), what happens in nullity proceedings. Probably no more disgusting details are ever given than in some nullity cases. There is no doubt of their admissibility.'

On the whole, Sterndale concluded, the authorities cited did not seem to establish that the evidence was inadmissible in cases arising in consequence of an accusation of adultery; and if the doctrine were established in cases dealing with legitimacy of children, it was not an exception that ought to be extended. It seemed to him that admitting such evidence in a case like the present one was right. The appeal therefore failed and must be dismissed with costs. Scrutton and Warrington concurred.

By now, Christabel was a marked woman. Heads were turned and voices lowered wherever she appeared. Eileen Hunter records:

'Even in that era of formality, of conventional good manners and white tie and tails, she was the cause of a breakdown in the whole structure when she appeared one night at the Berkeley Hotel, which was then one of society's favourite haunts for dining and dancing, and several members of the conventionally attired company actually climbed on to chairs to stare at her once her arrival had been noticed.'

London taxi-drivers had taken to referring to the Hotel Russell as 'the Half Way Inn'.

Figure 6; Advertisement in Modern British Architecture and Decoration, *edited by Charles Holme, The Studio, London 1901.*

If Christabel were not to be for ever regarded as a loose woman, and her son a bastard, there was only one course left open to her: an appeal to England's Supreme Court, the House of Lords. In the spring of 1924, she took that step.

12

Triumph in the Lords

As I came out of the House of Lords after the case a flower seller rushed up to a newspaper boy who was dashing along from one of the distributing cars.

'Who's won, mate?' she asked.

'The gel!'

'Thank God!' she cried, and hurried along to try to catch a glimpse of the victor as she came out. I think she expresses the feelings of many women today.

LEONORA KYLES, 'THE HOUSE OF LORDS AND A WOMAN: WHAT THE RUSSELL DECISION MEANS TO WIVES', *THE PEOPLE*, 1 JUNE 1924.

Christabel's appeal in the House of Lords opened on 20 March 1924, before five law lords whose combined age was almost 350 years. The oldest and the youngest of them, Lords Finlay and Birkenhead (born 1842 and 1872 respectively) had both been lord chancellor. The other three – Lords Dunedin, Carson and Sumner – were all lawyers of distinction, though not all well loved.

Finlay, a Scot, had been more admired as an advocate than as a judge. He had been involved in some famous cases, including divorce cases. In 1886 he had represented Lord Colin Campbell, fifth son of the eighth Duke of Argyll, in a notorious divorce, action brought by his wife, Lady Colin Campbell. In 1901 he had defended Geoffrey Ampthill's kinsman, Earl Russell (the elder brother of Bertrand Russell), at the peer's House of Lords trial for bigamy: Russell was sent to Holloway Gaol for three months. In 1912 Finlay represented the White Star Line at the Board of Trade inquiry into the loss of the *Titanic*.

He became increasingly reactionary. In the year of Christabel's House of Lords appeal, he was involved in a libel action brought by Marie Stopes over statements made about her books advocating birth control – as we have seen, John Hugo had sent Christabel one of her books. Finlay declared that her views were 'revolting to the healthy instincts of human nature'.

Lord Dunedin (born 1849) was also Scottish, but educated at Harrow and Cambridge where he acquired 'an English veneer which never wholly rubbed off'. He was an early friend of Robert Louis Stevenson, who was called to the Scottish Bar on the same day in 1874. (Stevenson consulted him about his last, unfinished, posthumously published novel, *Weir of Hermiston*.) Dunedin was an enthusiastic sportsman. Like Christabel, he liked dancing – 'hard and late' – and had generally a taste for the good life. He married a baronet's daughter and became successively Conservative MP for Bute, lord advocate and in 1903 secretary for Scotland.

Lord Carson was an 'Anglo-Irish' Protestant, born in Dublin in 1854. He was renowned for three main reasons: his demolition of Oscar Wilde in the playwright's libel action against Lord Queensberry in 1895; his successful defence in 1910 of George Archer-Shee, the naval cadet expelled from the Royal Naval College, Osborne, for alleged theft; and his campaign against Home Rule for Ireland. In 1895 his aggressive cross-examination tempted Wilde into damagingly flippant answers of the sort Christabel later gave to Marshall Hall. Questioning Wilde about an Oxford servant, Carson demanded:

'Did you ever kiss him?' – 'Oh, dear, no. He was a peculiarly plain boy. He was, unfortunately, extremely ugly. I pitied him for it.'

'Was that the reason why you did not kiss him?' – 'Oh, Mr Carson, you are pertinently insolent.'[59] 'Why, sir, did you mention that this boy was extremely ugly?' – 'For this reason. If I were asked why I did not kiss a door-mat, I should say because I do not like to kiss door-mats. I do not know why I mentioned that he was ugly, except that I was stung by the insolent question you put to me ...'

Carson secured Archer-Shee's acquittal on the theft charge. Terence Rattigan dramatized the episode in his play *The Winslow Boy*, in which the barrister based on Carson puts the boy through a ruthless, bullying interrogation in private before deciding he is innocent and taking on the case. Carson's violent opposition to Irish Home Rule culminated in a display of raking invective in December 1921 as he attacked the treaty establishing the Irish Free State.

Carson's was a powerful and brooding presence. 'His features were perpetually set in a scowl.' His second wife, Ruby, whom he met while watching a tennis game, was thirty years younger than he: 'This provoked ribald jokes by his contemporaries about the reasons for his fatigue during the day.'[60]

Figure 7 Lord Carson by Harry Furniss
National Portrait Gallery

Lord Sumner (born in Lancashire in 1859) had gained a double first and the Newdigate Prize for verse at Balliol, Oxford, and become President of the Union in 1882. His early work at the Bar was mainly commercial; he was in regular competition with T.E. (later Lord Justice) Scrutton. Like Scrutton, he was a curmudgeon, particularly after he was raised to the Bench in 1909. Most reports of him give the same unengaging impression. He was 'frigid, aloof and intimidating, set off by his heavy-jowled, tight-lipped physiognomy and cold stare'. 'His judicial reasoning ... dominated by an iron logic, was seldom tinged by human sympathies, which he dismissed as legally irrelevant ... Lord Robert Cecil noted of him that "some very able lawyers can be very cruel men".' He had 'a volcanic temper'. Lord Buckmaster wrote: 'He certainly did not wear his heart upon his sleeve, but fastened it in a burglar-proof safe; and woe betide the man who fumbled at the lock.' He was a disappointed man. Asquith had considered him for the Woolsack on Haldane's resignation in 1915. He was again considered and rejected in 1922. In 1928 Baldwin replaced Cave with Douglas Hogg, saying, 'I will not have Sumner in the Cabinet.'

But Sumner had a powerful understanding of the law. Not one of his rulings was overturned on appeal. You knew where you were with him. 'A judge', he said, 'must bring down his fist with a thump.' In the case of *Bowmam* v. *Secular Society* (1917), he boldly rejected the time-honoured dictum that 'Christianity is part of the law of England.' His judgment in that case was so finely framed that Quiller-Couch included it in *The Oxford Book of English Prose*. Somebody else who admired Sumner was his last pupil, John Buchan, who recalled how eloquently he talked of men and politics in private.

F.E. Smith, Lord Birkenhead, was the star of the hearings. In an age of outstanding lawyers – Marshall Hall and Carson among them – he outshone them all. His rise had been meteoric. At Oxford he had been President of the Union: his verbal duels with Hilaire Belloc were legendary. He was a friend there of the cricketer C.B. Fry. (It was unkindly said: 'While C.B. made runs, F.E. made history.') He led a wild social life, but still took a first. Passing his Bar finals with distinction, he set up practice on the northern circuit, in Liverpool. He was super-confident and sometimes made cheeky replies to judges. ('What do you suppose I am on the Bench for, Mr Smith?' 'It is not for me, your Honour, to attempt to fathom the inscrutable workings of Providence.' 'Mr Smith, having listened to your case, I am no wiser.' 'Possibly not, m'lud, but much better informed.') In 1906 he became Unionist MP for Liverpool. His maiden speech in the Commons was considered the best ever, 'a masterpiece of raillery'. Birkenhead's son later wrote: '[Joseph] Chamberlain's austere mouth melted into a broad grin, and Carson was so happy as to look "almost human".'

Smith's legal career continued in parallel with his political one. In 1910 he defended Crippen's mistress, Ethel Le Neve, and got her off. In 1913 he successfully defended the young Arthur Ransome's biography of Oscar Wilde against a vindictive libel suit by Lord Alfred Douglas. In 1915 he was appointed attorney-general. In 1916 he prosecuted in the trial of Sir Roger Casement for high treason. It used to be maintained that he conspired to blacken Casement's name by circulating his homosexual diaries. This canard has been discredited: in fact, he described the Foreign Office's suggestion that this should be done as 'a ghoulish proposal' and offered the defence the diaries to support a plea of insanity. Smith was made Lord Chancellor (and Earl of Birkenhead) in 1918 – at forty-six, the youngest since Judge Jeffreys. There was much doubt as to whether the high-living lawyer would be up to the job, and the King asked Lloyd George to think again; but the appointment went ahead.

As Lord Chancellor, Birkenhead campaigned for reform of the divorce law. 'Citing heartbreaking cases of women trapped in long-dead marriages, he argued that once divorce was admitted on any grounds it was nonsense to allow it only for adultery, as if the sexual relationship was the most important part of marriage. Cruelty, desertion, drunkenness and insanity should equally be allowed as grounds to end a marriage.'[61]

Figure 8 Lord Birkenhead by Robert Stewart Sheriffs
National Portrait Gallery

Judges are meant to be independent and impartial, and no doubt most of them try to be; but there was old history and there were tensions and bad blood between some of the five men whose decisions were going to be Christabel's last chance. They had things in common (as a superficial example, both Carson and Birkenhead had been involved in cases relating to Wilde); but they had also had fierce disagreements. Early on, Birkenhead had supported Ulster's resistance to Irish Home Rule and had been Carson's 'galloper' in the torchlight processions and parades of volunteers which culminated in the Ulster Convention of 1912; but Carson was furious when Birkenhead signed the Irish Free State treaty in 1921, and he was not a forgiving man. Birkenhead had condemned the imperialist Tories who made a hero of General Dyer, the officer responsible for the Amritsar massacre of 1919 in India; but Sumner and Finlay had both championed Dyer after his censure by the Commons in 1920.

The *News of the World* described the 1924 scene:

'The House of Lords presented the deserted appearance usual on such occasions. The stained glass windows gave an ecclesiastical atmosphere to the proceedings, and the Throne on which the King and Queen sit in state under the golden canopy was emblematic of the power and majesty of the law. The long tiers of red benches occupied by the peers for legislative purposes were empty, except for the presence of the four law lords who had taken part in the case, with Lord Birkenhead on the Woolsack in the far distance presenting a somewhat stranded appearance.'

To represent Christabel in the House of Lords appeal, her solicitors had briefed

Stuart Bevan. He was an impressive KC for whom great things were predicted; but he died comparatively young in 1935, after becoming recorder of Bristol. His *Times* obituary expressed surprise that it had taken him an unusually long time to find success at the Bar, considering that he had 'such natural gifts and such aptitude for the law'. He had a 'distinguished appearance' and 'an attractive, persuasive voice'.

'Many juniors gave up free time to profit by listening to him conducting a case. His careful choice of words and unruffled demeanour no less than the care with which he chose one from a great variety of spectacles and the nervous questioning grunts after he had put a question were as enjoyable to the spectator as they must have been alarming to the witness. He was always effective, whether he appeared before judges or juries. He did not indulge in "fireworks", but relied on his skill and force of character.'

Bevan was married to the sister of George Grossmith, the co-author of *The Diary of a Nobody*. He was noted as a connoisseur of antique furniture, silver and etchings. The great and the good who attended his memorial service at the Temple Church in 1935 included the Hon. Victor Russell – John Hugo's uncle – who was one of the opposing counsel at the 1924 House of Lords appeal.

Bevan opened the case for Christabel on 20 March. He said that the appeal was rested on three grounds:

1. that the verdict was against the weight of evidence;
2. misdirection; and
3. the wrongful admission of evidence.

As to the first point, Sir Douglas Hogg for the respondent (John Hugo Russell) submitted that it was not open to the appellant in the House of Lords hearing, as it had been abandoned by her counsel in the Court of Appeal, and was so treated by the court. Bevan contended that the point had not been abandoned – 'but, if I am wrong in that contention, I apply for leave to raise the point before your Lordships'. Birkenhead said their Lordships were of the opinion that the point that the verdict was against the weight of evidence *had* in fact been abandoned by the appellant's counsel in the Court of Appeal.

The law lords also held that there had been no misdirection; so Bevan was obliged to rest his case solely on his third point – that John Hugo's evidence of non-access was inadmissible. Bevan immediately cited the judgment of Lord Mansfield in the case of *Goodright* v. *Moss* (1777) – that it was not open to the husband or wife to give evidence of non-access, to bastardize a child born in wedlock. But, said Bevan, the authorities went far beyond that. *Rex* v. *Sourton* (1836) had shown that neither husband nor wife could be examined as to non-access, where the legitimacy of a child born after marriage was in issue. That case related to the settlement of a pauper infant – the question of which of two parishes should be responsible for the maintenance of the child, depending on whether the child were legitimate or not. In *Rex* v. *Kea* (1809) it was held that a wife could not give evidence to bastardize her child though her husband was dead. Bevan cited several more old cases in support of his contention.

Anybody who trawls through the *Russell* v. *Russell* trials and appeals will find that barristers on both sides frequently argued that 'There is only one question to be decided.' In the hearing before the lords, Bevan said that in the second trial 'The only issue before the jury was, Who was the father of the child? and they had found that an unknown man was. The effect of the husband's evidence was to bastardize the issue exactly in the same sense as in *Goodright* v. *Moss*.' Further, in the appeal, the Master of the Rolls (Lord Sterndale) had misunderstood the meaning of the word 'decency' as used by Lord Mansfield.

Douglas Hogg, for John Hugo, also used the tactic of 'There is only one question ...' He argued that 'The only question is whether or not there is a rule of English law which prevents evidence being given by the parties who were best able to give evidence that there was no intercourse between them when the child was conceived.' He added:

'For a great number of years, the law was believed to be that if a child was born in wedlock, and the husband was within the four seas at any time between the possible period of conception and the birth of the child, the child was presumed to be legitimate ... That rule depended on the feudal law and was designed to secure certainty as to the person to perform the feudal services, and it is now exploded. The *Banbury Peerage* case and *Morris* v. *Davies* show that the illegitimacy of a child born in wedlock may be proved, just as any other fact may be proved, except that there is a presumption in favour of legitimacy.'

Hogg proceeded to cite many more cases which he thought bore out his argument. He pointed out that in *Synge* v. *Synge* (1900), in which a wife was suing her husband for desertion, evidence of the wife's refusal of marital intercourse was admitted. And in *Hetherington* v. *Hetherington* (1887), Sir J. Hannen had drawn a distinction between cases where the issue was bastardy and where it was adultery. It was conceded that there was nothing in the *Russell* case which could be used against the child Geoffrey in proceedings to establish his succession.

Here Lord Dunedin interrupted:

'But the only reason for the decree nisi is based on the fact that the husband was not the father of the child. Then this extraordinary result must follow that for the purpose of his succession the child will be held to be legitimate, though all the world would believe him to be illegitimate.'

Hogg retorted that it was no more extraordinary than finding that the wife has committed adultery with the co-respondent, but that the co-respondent has not committed adultery with her. Where the issue was adultery, 'the birth of a child is a mere accident. The important fact is that the child was conceived at a time when the wife was having no relations with her husband. Suppose a miscarriage. Is the evidence to be excluded then? The application of the rule cannot depend on such accidents as that.'

The lords adjourned the proceedings on 25 March to consider the evidence and the arguments. They did not reconvene to give their judgments until 30 May. In the meantime, the British Empire Exhibition had begun at Wembley. George V opened it on 23 April (St George's Day) by sending a telegram to himself – routed from London to London via the British Empire. The electric message passed through Canada, New Zealand, Australia, South Africa, India, Aden, Egypt and Gibraltar, taking one minute and twenty seconds to go round the world before being returned to the King 'in good order' by a young telegram boy in front of 50,000 people in the Wembley Stadium. Like the 1951 Festival of Britain which opened six years after the end of the Second World War to show that Britain had recovered, the 1924 Exhibition opened six years after the end of the First World War with a similar message. Both had funfairs: in 1924 even George V and Queen Mary unbent so far as to be filmed riding round Wembley on a miniature railway. By May 1924 the show was in full swing. The whole nation was on the razzle. The issue of the *Daily Mirror* which carried the Lords' judgment in *Russell* v. *Russell* also contained this cartoon.

Figure 9 The Daily Mirror, *31 May 1924*

In its report of the final dénouement of the Russell Baby case, The *News of the World* recorded:

'When delivering judgement the Law Lords do not wear their wigs and gowns. Counsel, solicitors and the public are herded together in the fenced-off enclosure at the end of the House, the fence being the famous historic "Bar" at which so many distinguished people have been arraigned. The judgements are printed beforehand, and the Law Lords rise in their places and read their judgements in turn. The conditions do not lend themselves to oratorical displays, and the obvious desire of most of the legal peers is to get the task completed as soon as possible. There were no outward signs that the Law Lords were dealing with a case which had occasioned so much public interest, but those who understand such matters appreciated that a rule of law of far-reaching importance was being laid down by these five quiet-voiced, intellectual-looking legal luminaries. Several MPs were in one of the side galleries, and they remained while each of the judges read his lengthy conclusions in the case...

'Mrs Russell herself, dressed in a black costume and white blouse, and wearing a black hat with white stripe, was an early arrival, with a friend who has been at her side since the first day of the first High Court hearing – her mother. Still as a statue, her face turned towards the Law Lord pronouncing judgement at the moment, her hands clasped on her lap, this woman who has fought so long and so tenaciously for her honour and the name of her little son betrayed nothing of the fire within her. Amid the sombre severity of her attire, her wedding-ring gave forth a solitary gleam. One by one the Law Lords uttered their judgements.'

Lord Birkenhead gave his opinion first, 'in his customary and rapid tones'.

'My Lords, this long drawn-out litigation has been so much reduced in the course of its passage through the Courts that only one main issue, and that of law, survives.

'There are, it is true, matters, relatively of less importance, which are still material and upon which a conclusion must be recorded. But these do not involve much research or difficulty when a decision has been reached upon the question which is fundamental.

'The appellant appeals here against the decision of the Court of Appeal declining interference with the finding of the jury that the appellant had committed adultery with a man unknown. I ignore the changing details and recriminations which the two long hearings disclosed. For, in my opinion, these no longer possess any relevance.

'My own impression may be stated at once, that unless the evidence given by the husband, the petitioner, was in law receivable there was no evidence of adultery proper to go to the jury at all. But I am willing to hear argument on the point. The question, therefore, if I am right, which your Lordships have to decide is whether or not by the law of England evidence of non-access may, in proceedings for divorce, be tendered by a spouse and received by a Court with the object or possible result of bastardizing a child of the marriage.

'I have formed the clear opinion that such evidence is not receivable; that it ought not to have been allowed to go to the jury; and that therefore, unless there was other evidence proper to go to them, the verdict cannot stand.'

Birkenhead rested his decision mainly on the Mansfield ruling in *Goodright* v. *Moss*, and he gave his opinion as to what Mansfield had meant by 'decency'.

'Lord Mansfield was not concerned with the grossness or indecency of the subject-matter which the reception of such evidence might involve. Nor indeed ought any judge, who understands his business, to trouble his head as to the indecency of evidence if its examination be required for the elucidation of truth. No Court is contaminated by examining any facts, or reviewing any language, which the administration of justice requires. Judges must do their duty, sacrificing if necessary their delicacy in the process. What Lord Mansfield meant was that a deeply seated domestic and social policy rendered it unbecoming and indecorous that evidence should be received from such a source; upon such an issue; and with such a possible result.'

Birkenhead added:

'Nor ought we to shut our eyes to the glaring absurdity in which a different decision would involve the administration of this branch of the law. This evidence, we are told, is admissible in Divorce; being therefore so received it bastardizes the child. But if and when the child, as in this case he certainly will do, becoming of age, applies for his writ in this House, and proceedings follow, the evidence will not be admissible and he will be pronounced legitimate. Equally, of course, if the child instituted proceedings tomorrow for a declaration of legitimacy we should be afforded the agreeable prospect of holding judicially in 1924 that the infant was illegitimate; and in 1925 that he was legitimate. Nothing but absolute necessity, founded upon decisions binding upon me, would drive me to a conclusion so ludicrous and incongruous. I find here no such necessity.'

Next, the octogenarian Viscount Finlay gave his judgment. 'This is purely a question of law,' he said. He was in agreement with Birkenhead: the husband's evidence should not have been admitted. Then, Lord Dunedin. He was prepared to be 'indelicate' in exactly the sort of way Birkenhead had said judges should be, when necessary.

'My Lords, I am sorry to have to go into details which may shock listeners, and I regret wholeheartedly that, according to a recent decision of this House, cases such as the present may not be tried *in camera*; but, as it stands, if justice to my thinking is to be done one must mention these things.

'*Fecundatio ab extra* is admittedly, by the medical testimony, as vouched by the learned judge in his summing-up, a rare, but not impossible, occurrence; but its accomplishment will depend, not only or exclusively on the proximity of the organs, but on certain other potential qualities of the particular man. A comparison in this matter between the unknown man and the husband is obviously an impossibility. The crucial evidence therefore comes to be this, the testimony of the husband, that on particular nights he did not indulge in what had been a usual practice.

'I may here leave the particular facts, and put the question as general: Is a husband to be allowed to go into the witness box and say, "Though I am not impotent, though I had connection with my wife on other occasions, though I was in bed with her on certain nights, yet I say on those nights I did not have connection, and if, accordingly, her conception must be referable to that period she has been guilty of adultery?"

'My Lords, so stated, the proposition, I confess, to my thinking, is outrageous ...'

Dunedin agreed with Birkenhead that in the Court of Appeal Lord Sterndale had been wrong in his interpretation of what Lord Mansfield had meant, in 1777, by 'decency'.

'My Lords, decency, as Lord Mansfield used the term, I venture to think had nothing to do with the feelings of judges. Judges are bound to do their duty. How far they may become case-hardened to all they are called on to hear. will depend on individual attributes. But, whether it pains them or not, I am sure they will do their duty. The decency that Lord Mansfield referred to was the decency before all the world of laying bare the most secret, and, at the same time, the most sacred, of the legitimate relations of man and woman as husband and wife. I do not think I need emphasize the natural repugnance which such a proposal excites.'

Dunedin wondered whether the admittance of a husband's evidence might result in a husband's claiming that he had used contraceptives and that therefore a child could not be his. Was a jury going to have to consider whether that statement satisfied them? Then again, 'If this evidence is rightly admitted it puts a weapon in the hands of a husband tired of his wife and anxious for a new start (for be it remembered this method of proving adultery is unavailable to the wife).' Dunedin was of the opinion that the words of Lord Mansfield were directly applicable to the *Russell* case. 'I am, therefore, unhesitatingly of opinion that the evidence ought not to have been admitted, and that the verdict cannot stand.'

As she heard those words, Christabel knew that she had won. But it was only by the narrowest of majority decisions. Lords Sumner and Carson – the two judges renowned as merciless inquisitors – entered judgments dissenting from the previous three. Sumner said:

'My Lords, the only question upon which I shall trouble your Lordships, is the admissibility of the petitioner's evidence to the effect that at no material times were his relations with his wife such as could have resulted in the birth of the child ...

'It is, of course, impossible not to be very fully alive to the fact that this case excites and will continue to excite warm feelings of sympathy, commiseration and chivalry. Some will be on the side of the husband, more of the wife, most of the child. I recognize that such sensibilities are respectable and deep, but they do not concern the law. The questions raised in this appeal come before your Lordships on a basis of fact, which is settled by the verdict of the jury, and as, in my view, they are pure questions of law, difficult but dry, on which it is impossible to dogmatize and useless to be perturbed, I am constrained, to my regret, to submit to your Lordships a longer examination of the law than I should have wished, or perhaps than is proper in a mere dissentient opinion.'

Sumner was as good as his word, referring to an almost interminable succession of old cases. But the central import of his opinion can be easily summarized: that Mansfield's words of 1777 applied only to cases strictly relating to legitimacy, not to cases of alleged adultery. To support his views, Sumner – with a lubricious ingenuity – invented two imaginary cases.

1. A married woman bears a child, congenitally afflicted with a venereal disease, and then it is stated of her husband that he is responsible. To clear his character he brings an action of slander, and, to meet a plea of justification and proof that he was in fact infected with this disease, he desires to say, as the fact is, that though he lived in the same house as his wife, yet, knowing himself to be infected, he was scrupulous to keep away from her at all times material to the child's conception. If this evidence is admitted and believed his character is at least cleared from the worst imputation. If it is not admitted, his case is gone. Does this evidence bastardize the issue any more than the present respondent's did? On the other hand, does anyone say that in such a case the plaintiff s mouth would be closed?

2. Again, a man is indicted for incest with a young woman alleged to be his daughter. His one defence is that, though born of his wife during their marriage and brought up as his child to avoid scandal, he had not begotten her; she was a bastard of his wife's. If he can give this evidence, he has a defence to go to the jury; if, on the other hand, the rule applies, then, in a case where no evidence of non-access but his own is available, he will go to prison.

As Christabel listened to these weirdly fanciful hypotheses, she had the comfort of knowing that nothing Sumner said could negate her victory. Later in his long speech he turned to the argument that husbands would be able to rid themselves of wives of whom they were tired. He said he thought the suggestion was 'rather one for melodrama than for the disillusioned minds of those who know the Divorce court', but, in any case, 'the risk, great or small, must be run'. Sumner felt that 'in the administration of justice nothing is of higher importance than that all relevant evidence should be admissible ...' He therefore thought that the opinions of the judges in both courts below were right, that the evidence was properly admitted, and that the appeal should be dismissed.

Lord Carson agreed with Sumner: 'The only question which this House is now called upon to decide' was whether 'the evidence of the respondent [John Hugo Russell] was admissible on the issue of adultery to prove non-access or non-connection with his wife, the appellant'. He, Carson, declined 'to be any party to throwing any doubt upon the verdict of the jury or to being influenced by the fact either that the charges against certain named co-respondents have failed or that there was no confession which could be used against the appellant'. The question to be decided was purely one of law. In his peroration – which everybody at the hearing knew was going to have no effect whatever – Carson said:

'Here is a husband who knows, and who has proved to the satisfaction of a jury, that he has not had access or connection with his wife, and that his wife therefore must be guilty of adultery, and he is to be informed that the law of England gives him no relief, and binds him to his adulterous wife, because he is not allowed to give evidence which he alone is capable of giving!'

The order of the Court of Appeal was reversed. John Hugo was to pay the costs in the Court of Appeal and also the costs in the House of Lords as regarded the question of the admissibility of the evidence; Christabel was to pay the costs in the Lords as regarded the questions of misdirection and verdict against the weight of evidence, which the law lords had thrown out.

The next morning, the broadsheet newspapers reported the lords' speeches at some length. The tabloids also gave a surprising amount of space to the judgments; but, unlike the quality papers, they described Christabel's dress and demeanour in court; her reaction on grasping the majority decision; her triumphal return to Curzon Street and her mother's joy. The *Daily Mirror*'s 'Through the Mirror' gossip columnist wrote:

'As the five law lords delivered their judgments ... I was impressed by the extraordinary contrasts of the scene. Down in the high-vaulted Gothic Chamber, the apparently impassive law lords, coolly, impersonally, often almost inaudibly, read their several findings. And there, in the Serjeants' box, was Mrs Russell, strangely self-contained, listening to every word, forgetting her surroundings, and keeping her eyes on each Judge as he read.

'In the space beneath the galleries a few scores of spectators – chiefly women – endured the discomfort of being wedged closely together while they listened breathlessly to the slow drone of solemn voices. And in a side gallery a number of MPs followed the proceedings closely. For the onlookers there were two moments of crisis. The first as Mrs Russell heard Lord Birkenhead's last word, when she seemed to heave a sigh of relief. And then, again, as Lord Dunedin, the third to deliver judgment, concluded in her favour and so assured her of a majority verdict.'

The columnist broke the good news to Christabel's mother.

'Mrs Hart, with whom Mrs Russell lives, was overjoyed when I acquainted her with the nature of the verdict. She has been ill for some weeks with influenza, and said the news was a tonic which would soon get her well. Mrs Russell also has been ill – with measles – but the boy Geoffrey has luckily escaped.'

The *Mirror* reporter added:

'Mrs Russell is a very modern product. You are struck with this the first moment you meet her. She is clever and original, and always 'in advance', for which reason she has become, entirely by her own efforts, one of the smartest West End dressmakers. She was, I believe, the first Englishwoman to go in for shingled hair, and that was four years ago, when people regarded it as madness for a girl to cut her hair short like a boy.'[62]

Under the headline 'MRS RUSSELL'S HOUR OF GREAT TRIUMPH', the *Daily Sketch* reported:

'Mrs Russell and her aunt, Miss Erskine, sat throughout the last stage of their long-drawn-out ordeal in Black Rod's box, just inside the doorway of the House of Lords and beside the bar.

'Both were in black, with furs, but Mrs Russell threw off her cloak as soon as she was seated and sat looking steadily in front of her. Her small hat of shiny black had a brightly polished long feather and a thin pale ribbon for relief.

'She looked more worn than at the trial, but was as unmoved and composed, as though the proceedings mattered less to her than to the many women crowding with the men into the spaces reserved for the public and counsel.

'It was a long time after the first three speeches had made it plain that the majority was in her favour that she even gave a smile. Mr Withers, her solicitor, went up to whisper to her, "You know you've won!" and she nodded, "Yes, I know." '

A cross-head to this story read: 'Mrs Russell and Lord Carson in Silent Encounter'.

'Lord Carson's was almost a fighting argument, and when he spoke of the hardship of a husband tied to a misconducting wife, because he was unable to give the evidence which no one else could, he looked hard across at Mrs Russell, who met his eyes steadily.'

The *News of the World* report gave further detail about the verdict and its aftermath.

[After her solicitor had told her she had won] 'Mrs Russell turned at once to listen, with unrelaxed intentness, to the judgements which followed. Lords Sumner and Carson were against her, but she heard them throughout without a sign of impatience or restlessness. Mrs Russell was no longer a divorced woman. With head erect and the bright colour in her cheeks undimmed, she left the House and was shepherded by friends to a car outside. Then only did her iron nerve give way. When the car reached her house in Curzon-street she had to be lifted from the cushions and carried inside. Friends and employees crowded round her, congratulating her, kissing her, shaking her hands, some of them laughing and some in tears.'

Under the crosshead 'Mrs Russell Vanishes', the *Daily Sketch* reporter amplified the *News of the World*'s story. 'Friends crowded towards Black Rod's box to congratulate Mrs Russell at the rising of the House, but she vanished up the peers' corridor.' The *Mirror*'s main report gave more detail about her return to Curzon Street.

'Mrs Russell's return from the House of Lords was eagerly awaited by her sales girls and secretaries, who had clubbed together and bought a beautiful bunch of hothouse roses – 'so that it shall be the first thing she sees when she comes home,' they explained.

'The waiting was relieved by streams of callers, a shoal of telegrams and endless telephone calls.

'A maid who had been sent out with a long list of things to buy forgot them all in her excitement on learning the news while out, and returned 'mad with joy' with only two pink roses for her mistress.

'It is the most wonderful thing that ever happened.

'We hardly dared expect it.

'These were some of the comments by Mrs Russell's waiting friends.

'Just before teatime a taxi drew up at the door containing Mrs Russell and her solicitor. There was a wild rush, and she was half-carried into the house.

'She was very calm, with the forced calmness of pent-up emotion and relief, but her eyes were radiant.

'In her short black suit, that had the appearance of a riding-habit, and her cloche hat with its red varnished quill, Mrs Russell looked scarcely older than her youngest apprentice. She is a very beautiful woman.

'Smiling with tired but happy relief, she turned to *The Daily Mirror* and said: "My lawyers have forbidden me to say a word – not even how pleased I am – but, of course, that's easily seen."

' "It's an enormous relief, and I'm going for a rest in the country tomorrow." '

While all this jubilation was taking place in Mayfair, a despondent trio was photographed leaving the Law Courts –

Figure 10
John Hugo Russell, Lord Ampthill and Lady Margaret Ampthill

Dr Stephen Cretney has written that 'the Russell divorce seems to have been one of those few *causes célèbres* which directly prompted an important change in the law.' But the change only remained in force for twenty-five years. Cretney adds:

'The so-called rule in *Russell* v. *Russell* (i.e. that neither spouse could give evidence tending to show that he or she did not have marital intercourse if such evidence would tend to bastardize a child prima facie born in wedlock) caused expense, particularly in many wartime divorce cases where the birth of a child of whom the husband could not be the father had to be proved by reference to military records or other third-party evidence of his absence beyond the seas. It was strongly criticized by the (Denning) Committee on Procedure in Matrimonial Causes (Final Report, Cmd. 7024, 1947) and was abolished by the Law Reform (Miscellaneous Provisions) Act 1949.

'Subsequently, the Civil Evidence Act 1968 made spouses compellable witnesses on the question whether or not marital intercourse had taken place between them; and provided that witnesses in proceedings instituted in consequence of adultery were no longer excused from answering questions which tended to show that they had been guilty of adultery.'

Figure 11 The Daily Mirror, *31 May 1924*

13

Afraid of Love

I think your daughter has been busy on other matters, has she not?
She has been writing a good deal lately?
Sir Edward Marshall Hall, cross-examining Blanche Hart in 1923

In 1924 Christabel Russell was the most famous woman in Britain. The year before, that position had been held by Lady Elizabeth Bowes-Lyon when she married the Duke of York (later King George VI). In 1926 it was taken by Agatha Christie when the crime novelist did her 'disappearing act', probably to spite her unfaithful husband; in 1932, by Amy Johnson when she made her solo flight from London to Australia in seventeen days; in 1936, by Wallis Simpson at the time of the Abdication.

Christabel was 'hot'. It was natural that publishers should approach her with a view to a bestseller by or about her, or both. We have seen that Marshall Hall, cross-examining her mother in 1923, was under the impression that Christabel was already writing her memoirs, and Blanche Hart thought she had received an advance from a newspaper. In the end, Christabel did not write an autobiography; but she did write a novel with unmistakable echoes of her own life-story. *Afraid of Love* was published in 1925 by Hurst & Blackett of Paternoster Row, London. We know that the Christabel Russell who wrote *Afraid of Love* was our Christabel, because at the back of all the books in Hurst & Blackett's list that season was an advertisement for the novel:

'*Afraid of Love*, By Christabel Russell (The Hon. Mrs John Russell)

'Meryl Gould, a charming young widow with an only child, sets out to fight the world alone. Disillusioned through an unhappy marriage, she bravely faces enormous odds, determining never again to fall prey to love or to be dependent on any man. What the world taught this young woman, Christabel Russell tells in her own characteristic and forcible style. *Afraid of Love* is a masterly piece of writing and also a brilliant defence of the modern girl which will appeal to all readers who are interested in the trend of present-day thought.'

Even in this brief summary of the plot, one can discern something of Christabel. As it develops, one soon sees far more. The narrative opens in Johannesburg – 'The room in its perfect stillness and repose was like a painting by one or other of the Dutch School ...' The heroine, Meryl, is not yet a widow. Her husband is away hunting lions.

'She did not miss her husband. All that was smashed up between them. The little sigh which had escaped her was the only sign she gave of remembering what she had hoped of her marriage, the airy castles she had built on the day when she and Tony Gould came down the aisle of St Peter's, Eaton Square, with Mendelssohn's "Wedding March" pealing above them, she with Madonna lilies nervously clutched to her breast, he morning-coated, top-hat in hand ...'

Meryl had been 'a girl fresh from school in the haphazard days of the war'.

'She had wanted to help, of course. Everyone was doing war work ... To drive a car loaded with wounded – that was not quite "nice". To sleep on the floor of a garage, fagged out, wrapped up in an overcoat – the idea was fantastic. So Meryl had become a VAD,[63] and scrubbed the floors of wards, and met Captain Anthony Gould, DSO. He had seemed very splendid to her then, just recovered from his wound. His good looks, his unimpeachable record, the interest he had taken in the young probationer whose auburn curls escaped from beneath her neat uniform cap, all combined to throw that same auburn-haired probationer head-over-heels in love with him.'

Meryl reflects: 'None of her relations had been in the church on the misty November morning when she was married ... She hadn't minded that much.' (Of course, it had been the bridegroom's parents who absented themselves from Christabel's wedding.) Meryl's husband works for the Blanfontein Diamond Co. at their mine in Johannesburg. Their son – also Tony – is three (just the age Geoffrey Russell would have been if, as seems likely, Christabel was writing her novel in 1924).

'Perhaps the coming of the child had removed the last possibility of happiness with his father. [True of Christabel and John Hugo.] Dreaming what it would be like to have a child of her own, she had always pictured the growth of some new understanding between Tony and herself – a mutual pride in bringing to birth something so much a part of themselves. When she first knew that she was going to be a mother, she had not funked the issue, nor hid with blushes and secret smiles what to her simplicity was the loveliest and most natural happening in the world.'

Not 'funking' things is a prime trait of Meryl throughout the book. She even despises a flighty girl who goes to Paris to be with an old businessman who has proposed marriage. Meryl despises her, not for her mercenary lack of scruples, but because, when the old man wants the girl to sleep with him in Paris, she 'funks' it.

' "I am going to have a baby," [Meryl] told Tony, straight out, and looked for response in his sombre eyes.'

What a fool she had been to imagine those words would be a magic talisman to turn the dull metal of their married life to gold again ...

All Tony is interested in is drink, poker and other women.

'Rebounding from the indifference of the father, she had come to centre all her thoughts and hopes in the child, and what chance would young Tony have of growing up the fine, straightforward man she planned him to be with that other older Tony lurking always in the background, hating the child who had lost him a mistress and given him, instead, a wife? To grow up in the same house with a man who, night after night, came home unsteady with drink, who cursed and swore regardless of who might hear, and who would even stand over the cradle and say to his own son: "I hate you! Why the hell did you come?" – that was no future for him.

'The child was absurdly like his mother, with the same close auburn curls, the same level grey eyes and pale colouring.'

As we, who know Christabel's history, read on, we cannot help anticipating that, in one way or another, Meryl will be rid of her husband. Sure enough, he is killed by a lion. She goes back to London with her son. The husband had run into debt, so she is left without much money. The solicitor who tells her this thinks: 'There was something disturbing about the girl – about her coldness, her determination, disillusion she had suffered.' Her son, now five, is 'slim and straight as a young birch-tree'.

In a restaurant she sees an attractive man with a girl, Doria, who is leaving the handsome boyfriend to marry a wealthy old industrialist, Sir Marcus Crane. (The same surname as that of the discreditable Half Moon Street valet who had testified against Christabel in court.) Doria is about to join him at the Hôtel Meurice, Paris. Meryl has at first been staying at the Savoy, but considers three guineas a night too expensive and moves to a cheaper hotel in Bloomsbury. She appeals to Tony's former employers in Blanfontein for capital to start a business, but they refuse.

She bumps into the handsome young man – Paul Masterman – whom Doria has left. He falls in love with her but she rejects him: 'Friendship, yes; but I'm finished with love.' Christabel describes what happens to Doria in Paris. Here Christabel exploits all the knowledge of Paris gained in her youth – the Troika and Caveau Caucasien nightclubs, the Cabaret restaurant just off the Champs Elysées; the Café Miramas; and the Pavillon des Deux Lacs ('in pre-war days, the *Pavillon Tyrolien*').

Masterman asks Meryl to help him furnish his new flat in Jermyn Street. (Christabel, too, went in for interior decoration as a sideline: one is reminded of Mrs Beaver in Evelyn Waugh's *A Handful of Dust*). She gets a French woman assistant, Mademoiselle Pigou. Masterman is 'frank and open, fond of his own society'. In Christabel's book, 'secretive' is no good; 'straight' is high praise. Masterman says of Meryl, 'She has the pluck of the pluckiest man alive' – words that could accurately have been applied to Christabel.

A mystery backer sends £5,000 to Meryl's solicitors to enable her to open a dress shop in Dover Street (near Curzon Street and, we recall, the street where Christabel broke the news of her pregnancy to John Hugo). The backer is, of course, Paul Masterman. Meryl celebrates with a Bronx cocktail at the Berkeley, in those days in Piccadilly – we know that was a favourite haunt of Christabel. Meryl emphasizes to Masterman her independence: 'I have to answer for what I do to no one in the world'; and again, 'I love my son, but then he depends on me for love, I depend on no one.'

'Only a pretty doll' and 'a featherbrain' are the novel's descriptions the kind of woman Meryl/Christabel despises. They are the descriptions of Doria, who returns to London from Paris, disgusted with Sir Marcus Crane, and leaps to the conclusion that Meryl – who encouraged her to go out to Paris – has 'got off with' her own former boyfriend, Paul Masterman. Doria is not the only person who thinks that: it is the gossip in the cheaper hotel to which Meryl has moved from the Savoy.

'One morning in the hotel the twittering, Catholic Miss Candler drew her aside and archly remarked: "We're all so pleased that you're going to be happy."

' "But I don't understand," Meryl replied.

' "He's such a charming man, Mr Masterman."

'So that's what they thought and gossiped about! Meryl felt a quick surge of anger. "I'm not in love with Mr Masterman," she returned coldly. "I'm not in love with anyone, Miss Candler – nor do I want to be." And she left the unfortunate lady gasping.

'Ever after that Miss Candler regarded her from a distance, curiously, and Meryl knew that it wasn't that she didn't love Paul Masterman that made her so remarkable a phenomenon, but the fact that she didn't want to love anyone at all.'

From interest, not attraction, Meryl takes up with a rich connoisseur and womanizer, Graham Vayne. He gets very short shrift when he tries to seduce her.

' "What are we going to do now?" her host asked as the big restaurant began to empty. "It's rather too late for a show, even a music-hall. Shall we dance, or would you like to come back with me and look at my pictures?"

'She had never been to his big house on the west side of Berkeley Square. It would be rather fun to go back to the lair of "The Hunter after Wild Beasts" ...'

At his house, Vayne inevitably makes his move on her.

' "My library," he said, closing the door behind him.

' "Please don't close that door," she begged. Then added: "Did you ask me to dine with you, Mr Vayne, so that you could bring me back here and insult me? Am I just a new victim for your cynicism – or what?"

' "Don't jeer at me, you cold, level-headed little thing! I asked you here because I wanted to tell you that I love you. I love you, d'you hear? Ever since I met you, since Paul told me about you, I've loved you more and more."

' "Love! You?" ...

' "Do you hate me, Meryl?" He put the question so simply, and in so passionate a tone, that she was surprised out of her anger.

' "I didn't hate you, Mr Vayne – but each minute you're making me wonder why I admired you for your repression, your self-control, the way in which you didn't spend yourself uselessly. Don't you see that I don't want any of – this?" '

From John Hugo's testimony in court, we know that Christabel said something similar to this to him – though 'spending' himself uselessly (in the sense that word was used by the Victorian roué Frank Harris) was precisely what John Hugo had done – except on one occasion in December 1920.

When Meryl tells Vayne 'I don't want any of – this,' he challenges:

' "Not even with Masterman?"

' "Not even with him."

' "He's in love with you."

' "Perhaps. But he doesn't force his love on me. I don't want love. Why must you spoil our friendship in this way?"

' "Why? Because you're made for love. Every fibre of you calls to love."

' "Every fibre of me calls me to work," she corrected, "to live life to the full with my eyes open, not in that sort of romantic half-sleep which schoolgirls call love." '

As far as we can judge from the trials, these were very much the sentiments of Christabel; but in her new rôle of novelist she was canny enough to realize that so unsusceptible a heroine was not going to appeal to a popular readership, and that she must let some love in and begin steering the narrative towards a happy ending.

Masterman invents an engine that is bought for a large sum by none other than Sir Marcus Crane, the unscrupulous businessman whose advances Doria spurned at the Hôtel Meurice. Masterman's success takes him abroad a lot. His absence stirs unexpected feelings in Meryl, but 'She would not allow herself to believe that she missed him.'

At the time Christabel was writing her novel, her main relationship was with her young son, Geoffrey. She makes good use of her knowledge of the way a child speaks; and no doubt some of the things that happen to young 'Tony' in the book were based on Geoffrey's experiences. At the beginning of Chapter XIII, Meryl and Tony are returning from a visit to the zoo, and he questions her about the missing Paul Masterman.

' "Mummy dear, where's Mr Paul?"

' "He's gone away, darling."

' "Is that why he never comes to see us, mum?"

' "I expect so, boy."

' "He used to play such lovely games!"

'The boy clutched her hand tightly in ecstatic memory of those wild games in the Hotel Normandy which used to bring [the proprietress] Madame Parisot upstairs in terror lest her ceilings gave way...'

Paul Masterman is packing up his belongings in Jermyn Street and planning to move. London, with no chance of his winning Meryl, is depressing.

'Somehow, by going into business she had escaped him. He had once thought it wise and plucky of her.

'He saw his mistake now. No woman should waste herself on that sort of thing. It hardened them, and killed sympathy in them, and taught them the philosophy of "each for himself" '.

'He began to take down the photographs which decorated the mantelpiece and the top of his tall bookcase.'

'Meryl's portrait in a silver frame! She in a white frock, with her fair hair waved in shining splendour about her grave little face. With her was the child with whom he had once delighted to play, because he seemed to him just another Meryl, so like his mother was Tony ...'

We remember the photographs of Christabel that Edgar Mayer had in his flat; also the photograph of Christabel with Geoffrey by Madame Yevonde (Jacket photograph), mother and child almost rubbing noses like Eskimos.

The workings of the dress shop are described. When a theatrical manager brings in a chorus-girl, a mannequin languidly shows off a dress, while Meryl's assistant, Mademoiselle Pigou, makes her sales pitch – 'Madame has just ze figure for a sheaz frock – ze long legs, ze pretty shoulders.'

Meryl is 'sickened' by these words. 'Always that appeal! She did not sell a dress for the sake of the dress, as Meryl found herself doing, but for the body underneath it. It was the French way of persuading the man with the cheque-book ...' Here again, one senses Christabel's distaste for anything sexual.

Sir Marcus Crane is taking an ever greater interest in Meryl. He urges her to expand her business, but she tells him she would really like to give it up.

' "You know why I started this shop, don't you?"

' "Because you're a capable, practical woman, Mrs Gould."

' "Because I have a son, Sir Marcus. You've never met him, have you?"

'He shook his head.

' "He's rather a darling. Someone once told me," she went on, "that he thought it must be very wonderful to see oneself mirrored in someone else. It is wonderful – but rather terrible, too! One is so utterly and completely responsible for the child one has given life to. My boy has no one in the world but me. He's a baby now, but time goes quickly, and he'll grow into a big boy and want all the things which boys ought to have – good schooling, jolly holidays, tuck boxes, and books. And, even if I didn't feel so strongly that he relies entirely on me for those things, I should feel that because I love him with every fibre of me he has a right to everything that I can win for him."

' "And so you'll go on?"

' "And so I'll go on," she repeated.'

Meryl seriously thinks of marrying Crane or Vayne, to give her and her son security, but the reader is not cheated of a happy ending. Christabel has taken a risk in making Meryl so cold and intransigent; but it is the same kind of risk that Jane Austen took when she portrayed Mr Darcy as so proud and Mr Knightley as so reproving: the breaking down of that resistance makes the reconciliation all the more startling and enjoyable. It has to be said that Christabel's dénouement is more Mills & Boon than Jane Austen.

' "Meryl, can you forget all our misunderstandings?"

' "Of course. Oh, I'm so glad you're back. Tony has missed you dreadfully. He remembered all the time what a wonderful dragon you used to be!"

' "And you?' he asked. 'Didn't you miss me?"

'She hesitated a moment before replying. Then she smiled at him, and with a little beseeching gesture held out her hands.

' "Oh, my dear, my dear, never go away again."

'Half-dazed, half-incredulous, he took her hands and drew her to him. At the touch of her lips the difficulties of the past months vanished like mist in the sun. This was the magic moment towards which all his life had been drifting.

'And she! She had felt the exultation of surrender, no longer afraid of love, but finding it a friend.'

Afraid of Love is the nearest Christabel ever got to a self-portrait, though identifying the 'Meryl' figure with her cannot be carried too far: one doubts that 'the exultation of surrender' was one of Christabel's more prominent traits. The novel, taken together with her ultra-candid answers in court, enables us to make some speculation – it cannot be more – as to what Christabel really felt about love and sex. Was she 'afraid of love'?

The trials and the novel all strongly suggest that – at least, up to 1925 – Christabel did not experience love, other than the filial and maternal kinds, and that she positively disliked almost any kind of sexual relation with a man. Her behaviour in this respect diverged so much from the norm that one inevitably asks 'Why?' – however difficult it may be to arrive at an answer.

If a woman does not want sexual attentions from men, it may be because she has been 'interfered with' when young, an experience that has put her off sex with men for life. That was the case with Virginia Woolf, although, like Christabel, she married. She had been sexually molested by a half-brother when a girl. There is no evidence that anything of the sort ever happened to Christabel. If it did happen, her father might be the first suspect. It seems unfair to voice any suspicion against Colonel Hart, who may have been a man of irreproachable conduct; but Christabel's great-niece, Philippa Enderby, the granddaughter of Gwen Welford, says: 'There was some dark mystery about the Colonel. Nobody *ever* spoke about him, in the family – either in Christabel's family, or in mine.'

When a woman 'hates' (as Christabel, in court, freely admitted she did) sexual relations with a man, another possibility has to be considered: that she is a lesbian. (Virginia Woolf, again.) If somebody were going to make that suggestion about Christabel, they might point to her beseeching letters to Elfrida Shorten ('the best woman friend I ever had'), more passionate than the jokily tender letters she sent John Hugo from Switzerland; to her being as happy to dance with a woman as with a man; to her being known by the ambiguous name 'Chris' (like Georgina/George, the tomboy in Enid Blyton's 'Famous Five' books); and the description of Meryl in *Afraid of Love* – 'She looked like a handsome boy.' Those who would categorize her as a butch horsewoman need to take into account her delight in, and appearance in, fashionable Art Deco dresses – though of course there are *femme* lesbians too. But I do not think that Christabel was a lesbian. There is her evident delight in the company of men and, in later years, her companionship (to put it no higher) with two men.[64] Besides, in the society she moved in, a rumour would have spread – and none did. Also, Christabel being as wilful and forthright as she was, if she had been lesbian she would not have hesitated to take women lovers, nor cared much who knew about it. She would have been 'straight' about being gay.

One is left with a third and perhaps rarer possibility: that here was a woman almost devoid of the sexual instinct. Some people lack sight, others hearing; and some human beings are almost sexless. Elizabeth I, the Virgin Queen, may have been one such. Her dalliances with Leicester and Essex sound very like Christabel's with her swains: witty banter, gourmet food and dancing. Benjamin Jowett, the Victorian Master of Balliol, may have been another: his biographer Geoffrey Faber writes: 'It was easy enough for him to lay down moral laws, as he himself had no inclination to break them.' Time and again in the trials Christabel expresses her antipathy towards sexual relations, even kisses. When she drew male nudes in her Paris days she took them home *to draw clothes on them*. She was 'perfectly enchanted' when, on the trip to Edinburgh, she found she could not marry Bradley after all. She was supremely uninterested in the functions or even the names of the sexual organs. It may seem impertinent and muck-raking to attempt to pry into Christabel's sexuality; but in investigating the 1920s scandal these questions can hardly be avoided. At best, one might conclude, Christabel was undersexed, perhaps frigid. Describing his youth in his memoirs, the cartoonist Sir Osbert Lancaster wrote: 'And then sex reared its beautiful head.' Who can doubt that Christabel would have favoured the cliché version of that saying, in which the word 'ugly' replaces 'beautiful'?

There is one tantalizing coda to the publication of Christabel's novel in 1925. When she died in Ireland in 1976, on the very eve of the battle between her son and his half-brother Johnnie as to which of them should succeed to the Ampthill barony, *The Observer* (22 February 1976) stated, in an obituary article: 'Christabel would deserve a footnote in history even without the famous case. She wrote a novel, *Afraid of Love*, and then signed on to star in a film of it, for the then princely salary of £100 a week.'

The British Film Institute has a record of the film, but no copy of it. Details are to be found in *The British Film Catalogue 1895-1970* by Denis Gifford (1973) which states that the story is by the Hon. Mrs John Russell and summarizes the plot as 'Woman leaves faithless husband to manage lover's dress shop'.

Most of the cast were professional actors. Juliette Compton and Leslie Faber were both well known; Moore Marriott specialized in playing hoary rustics and was in a number of films with the comedian Will Hay; Adeline Hayden Coffin (born 1863) had been taking part in films since *Manxman* (1916); Jameson Thomas had appeared as 'Omar, the Desert Lover', in the screen version of *Chu Chin Chow (1923)* and later broke into mainstream Hollywood cinema, with rôles in two important films of 1934, *Scarlet Empress* and *It Happened One Night*, the Frank Capra masterpiece.

The première of Christabel's film was at the New Scala Theatre in Charlotte Street, London, on 15 March 1925.

The film, which was directed by Reginald West and produced by F.J. Nettlefold, was given a damning review in the trade paper *The Bioscope*. It is clear from the plot summary that the story had been much changed from the one Christabel told in her novel – mainly, no doubt, because of the difficulty there would have been in filming lion-hunting in South Africa on a low budget:

'Piqued by the friendship of his wife, Rosamund, with Philip Brymer, Anthony Bond, a wealthy stockbroker, invites his mistress, Ruth, to a gay party at his house in Grosvenor Square. Outraged by her husband's open infidelity, Rosamund determines that she will become self-supporting and, with the help of money borrowed from Brymer, opens a dress shop. Anthony further insults her by taking Ruth to the shop, with the result that Rosamund goes away with her small son to the country, where she earns a living by her pen. Five years later Anthony, now tired of Ruth and of his life of debauchery, calls upon Rosamund with a view to taking their child away from her. Moved by the child's faith in its father (whom it has been taught to believe dead), Anthony relents and, returning alone to Grosvenor Square, shoots himself as Ruth, now an outcast, arrives to beg charity. Rosamund and Brymer determine that they will devote their lives to the care of Anthony's son.'

The Bioscope offers a terse assessment: 'Indifferent production of a dull and disjointed story of the penny novelette type. Mrs Russell's personality and the mannequin parade are the main features of appeal. The film could be improved by considerable compression ... Apart from its curiosity value, the picture makes poor entertainment.' Christabel's acting is judged no less severely: 'Of the Hon. Mrs John Russell one can only say that she walks through the part of Rosamund with more apparent concern for her many elaborate gowns than for the emotional demands of the character. To be candid, her performance is that of an untrained and unpromising amateur.'

It is unlikely that Christabel had serious ambitions to become a film star or a screenwriter. She may have seen the movie as one big advertisement for her shop. And just possibly there was a subsidiary motive: it may not have been displeasing to her further to embarrass the Russell family, at a time when 'going on the stage' was only a little more respectable than prostitution, and films were one step more daring than the theatre.

Whatever her motive, and however substandard the result, how one would like to be able to fix on to a projector a flickering, monochrome, silent film of Christabel as she was in the mid-1920s – wearing dresses she had designed, acting the story she had at least partly written and perhaps even shedding the odd tear without benefit of sliced onions.

14

Swift to Bless

It was at [Liverpool] Cathedral ... that Swift once arrived for the Assize service to find that the judicial entry coincided with the singing by the choir of '... slow to chide and *swift* to bless ...' This *may* have been a coincidence, but those familiar with Dean Dwelly's skill in stage management at his cathedral will doubt this.

E.S. FAY, THE LIFE OF MR JUSTICE SWIFT, LONDON 1939

The ruling of the House of Lords was clear enough; but John Hugo Russell still refused to accept that Geoffrey was his son and heir. So on 25 November 1925 Blanche Hart, as Geoffrey's guardian, petitioned that the boy should be declared unchallengeably legitimate under the Legitimacy Declaration Act of 1858. Two of the clauses of Blanche's petition stated part of the reason for making it:

'7. DURING the course of such [divorce] proceedings the said Honourable John Hugo Russell persistently denied that the said child was his son and has since refused to acknowledge him in any way notwithstanding the failure of his Petition. His allegations obtained considerable publicity and his attitude towards the child is widely known.

'8. IT is impossible to make proper arrangements for the child's education until it is known what his future status is to be. My daughter and I have endeavoured to have the said child entered at Eton College, Windsor but owing, as I am informed and verily believe, to doubts as to his legitimacy arising from statements made by the said Honourable John Hugo Russell in the course of the above Trial we have not hitherto succeeded in entering the child for Eton or elsewhere.'

Early in 1926 it was ordered that Lord Ampthill should be invited to see the proceedings; also, his sons, John Hugo, Guy, Edward and Leopold, all of Oakley House, Bedfordshire. On 8 February, Samuel Holmes, managing clerk of Blanche's and Christabel's solicitors, Messrs Withers & Co., swore an affidavit as to what had happened when he tried to serve the petition and citation on John Hugo, on 26 January.

'On arrival at Oakley station I saw the Honourable John Hugo Russell one of the above mentioned parties and I approached him for the purpose of serving him with the Petition and Citation. I informed the Honourable John Hugo Russell that

I wanted to serve him with the Petition and Citation and I handed the same to him but he refused to take them. I accordingly served him but he allowed them to drop on the Railway Station. I left the papers there. The Honourable John Hugo Russell then left on his bicycle for his home, Oakley House ...'

Holmes had no better luck when he arrived at Oakley House and tried to serve Lord Ampthill with the documents. Ampthill sent his chauffeur round to say that he was not able to see him and would not accept any correspondence. The documents were posted instead.

The case finally came to the High Court in July. The Russell case had already conscripted the talents of some of the most celebrated English lawyers – Sir Henry Duke, Sir John Simon, Patrick Hastings, Sir Edward Marshall Hall, the curmudgeonly T.S. Scrutton, Lord Birkenhead and Lord Carson. Mr Justice Rigby Swift, who presided over the Declaration of Legitimacy hearing, was another such 'character', a picturesque figure around whom stories accreted. Some of his views were notably liberal, for their time; for example, he thought there was 'some good in every criminal'. He was also known as a *bon vivant:* Lord Denning, writing more than half a century later, in *The Family Story* (1981), recalled·'He always had a good lunch, did Mr Justice Swift! He liked one or two tots of whisky.'

Born, like Churchill, in 1874, Swift was a Lancastrian who stayed 'true to his northern roots'. Barristers referred to him as '*Rig-ba*' in imitation of his accent. When James Sexton ousted him as MP for St Helens in the General Election of 1918, Swift put an arm round his shoulder and said, 'Well, Jimmy, 'owd lad, tha's done it gradely.' Swift had not gone to university but had trained in his father's chambers in Liverpool. His biographer writes that 'legal onlookers delighted to hear father and son referring patronizingly to one another as "m'learned friend"'.

In 1902 Swift married a shipowner's daughter, Martha Walmsley. That they never had children was 'the great tragedy of his life'. In the same year he defended a man on a murder charge and won. In 1909 his fees topped 5,000 guineas. That was as much as the Liverpool Bar could offer; Pickford advised him, 'Go to London.' He did so. 'F.E.' spoke for him at the St Helens election of 1910, but Swift (for the Unionists) lost to the Labour candidate. Eleven months later he won the seat. He took silk in 1912.

In 1920 he was appointed – by Birkenhead – a High Court judge. At forty-six, he was then the youngest Justice on the Bench. He was known as a 'strong' judge, a 'without fear or favour' man; but what got him talked about among lawyers was his engaging sense of humour. He was not as irrepressibly jokey as Mr Justice Darling, whom Max Beerbohm depicted donning a black cap hung with bells, but he made good jokes and had particular fun summing up the 'Mongoose Case'. That was an action for slander: Sir Cecil Levita, a former chairman of the London County Council (and a great-uncle of David Cameron, MP) had suggested to a friend at the Carlton Club that Richard Lambert, editor of *The Listener,* was unfit for that post. Levita alleged that Lambert had been bamboozled by a Manx farmer who claimed to be in touch with a ghostly mongoose which was eighty-six years old, could say nursery rhymes and had a working knowledge of Russian, Manx, Hebrew, Welsh, Hindustani and Arabic. (Lambert received £7,500 damages and kept his job.)

Another example of Swift's sense of humour was recalled by Kenneth Rose after the death, in 1971, of Lord Goddard, the former Lord Chief Justice of England, who was a friend of John Hugo's uncle, Victor Russell. Next to crimes of violence, Goddard 'detested homosexual practices, particularly buggery'.

'He enjoyed telling the tale of how he once sentenced a man for a crime of violence. The prisoner had picked up a warder's cap and hurled it at Goddard with the words, "Take that, you old bugger!"

'Later the prisoner appealed. The appeal was heard by Mr Justice Swift, rather a wag, and dismissed. But Swift added: "I see from the record of the court below that the prisoner also passed certain reflections on the habits of my brother Goddard. On consideration, I believe them to be without foundation." '

In spite of his taste for levity, Swift had deep religious convictions and would hammer anyone he considered immoral. When the black magician Aleister Crowley appeared before him, suing the painter Nina Hamnett and her publishers, Constable, for what she had said about him in her book *Laughing Torso*, the necromancer was dealt with severely. Hamnett had claimed that in Crowley's 'temple' on Sicily a baby had mysteriously disappeared. She never proved that, but her counsel read out a number of Crowley's poems, adding that some of them were 'too indescribably filthy to be read in public'. The excerpts that were read had a visible effect on Swift, who summed up:

'I have been for over forty years engaged in the administration of the law. I thought that I knew every conceivable form of wickedness. I thought that everything that was vicious and bad had been produced, at one time or another, before me. I have learned in this case that we can always learn something more if we live long enough. Never have I heard such dreadful, horrible, blasphemous, abominable stuff as that which has been produced by the man who describes himself to you as the greatest living poet.'

The jury found for Hamnett and Constable.

Swift's first famous case was the trial of Mrs Thelma Bamberger on a charge of perjury. This beautiful young woman had petitioned for divorce and a decree *nisi* had been granted. However, the King's Proctor had intervened, asking that the decree be rescinded. Then Mrs Bamberger, like Christabel, appeared before Sir Henry Duke. The King's Proctor's case was that she had not disclosed the fact that she herself had committed misconduct. He alleged adultery with four men. She denied it, and added that the marriage with Bamberger had not been consummated and that she was in fact *virgo intacta*. (The parallels with Christabel become stronger.) Sir Henry Duke found that she had been guilty of adultery with two of the named men, and rescinded the decree *nisi*. He also called her 'a willing perjurer'. She was arrested on that charge. After an operation for appendicitis she appeared before Swift. Her counsel, Sir Richard Muir, made an impassioned speech on her behalf.

'He began slowly, carefully choosing his words ...

' "A new idea has come into the minds of those conducting the criminal administration of England – that perjury in the Divorce Court is a thing that must be punished, and that punishment must be begun."

'He paused. Then his words took on a new urgency as he pointed to his client sobbing in the dock and went on, "Who has been chosen to make an example – carefully chosen? This little woman! A woman of no consequence, with no friends, with no one to offend ... She does not matter! She is neither a peeress nor a Cabinet Minister. They can begin to clean their Augean stables with her!" '

Muir then made a vitriolic attack on the divorce laws themselves.

' "In other countries these people might have gone and got their divorce, followed their own separate stars, been happy. Instead of that they are, by the King's Proctor's decree, doomed and damned in this world that they may never marry anyone. They must either sin or remain united in misery for ever!" '

Swift, in his summing-up, poured cold water on this eloquence. 'According to the law of this country it is as much perjury to say that which is false in the Divorce Court as it is to say it in any other court.' The jury found Mrs Bamberger guilty. But Muir was on his feet again – to tell Swift that, two days before her appearance in the Divorce Court, she had gone through a form of marriage at Gretna Green with a man of twenty-six. Swift listened intently; then addressing the dock he said, 'Thelma Bamberger, the sentence of the court upon you is that you be imprisoned for nine calendar months.' The *Bamberger* case set many people wondering whether the public interest could not be better served by enlarging the grounds for divorce, and so releasing the Divorce Court from its preoccupation with adultery. It was that feeling which was to force A.P. Herbert's Marriage Bill through Parliament – passed into law as the Matrimonial Causes Act 1937. (It was by that Act that Christabel and John Hugo were eventually divorced.) Swift was also the judge at the trial of Madame Fahmy for murder, already referred to.[65] He sentenced Sinn Feiners to fifteen years in jail for setting fires in Manchester – the charge being 'treason felony'. He ordered a violent robber to receive eighteen lashes of the cat o' nine tails, 'so you can feel some of the pain you caused'.

His biographer, E.S. Fay, writes:

'His frequent excursions to the Divorce Court ... have left their mark, and it is noteworthy that his judgment in *Warren* v. *Warren* in 1925 was the first of the now lengthy line of cases in which judges have been enthusiastically whittling away the unfairness of the House of Lords decision in the famous Russell divorce case of the previous year.[66] It is noteworthy because the quirks of our divorce law greatly troubled the judge ... Sometimes, as in *Warren* v. *Warren*, he could find a loophole within the four corners of the judicial oath, and whenever the way was thus open for him to extend the law along the paths of natural justice, he did so with evident pleasure.'

In legal textbooks, the rule in *Warren* v. *Warren* is summarized thus:

'A wife's admission that she had committed adultery, even if accompanied by a statement of her belief that a child, subsequently born, was the result of the adultery, cannot bastardize the child without evidence of the non-access of the husband.

'The confession of the wife, therefore, that she has committed adultery is admissible as evidence in a suit for divorce so long as she does not assert that the husband could have had no access at the time of conception.

'*Russell* v. *Russell* (1924) distinguished.'

In later years – perhaps influenced by Muir's speech in the *Bamberger* case – Swift said (and was much criticized for saying):

'To my mind the divorce laws of this country are wicked and cruel. These people ought not to be subjected to the dreadful indignities to which they are, and I wish some of those learned ecclesiastics who have so much concern for the well-being of society could come and sit there [pointing to the public gallery] where they would be mere spectators, or here, where they would have to deal with matters ...'

These humane views, and Swift's friendship with and respect for Birkenhead, who had raised him to the Bench, may have predisposed him in favour of the ruling that Blanche and Christabel were seeking. The legitimization of Geoffrey was almost a formality. It would have been difficult and sensational for Swift to oppose the decision of the House of Lords. But it was still a relief to the two women when, with his customary rap-rap-rap of his pencil on his desk, Swift made the declaration.

'29 July 1926, Russell G.D.E. (by the *Guardian* v. *the Attorney-General*)

I decree and declare that the petitioner Geoffrey Denis Erskine Russell is the lawful child of his parents, the Hon. John Russell and Christabel Hulme Russell.'

Henceforward, it would not be open, even to the monarch or to Geoffrey himself, to dispute that Geoffrey was John Hugo's son, and second in line to succeed to the Barony of Ampthill.

By 1926, Christabel was so rehabilitated in Society and society that a photograph of her could appear in Hugh Cecil's *A Book of Beauty*, alongside images of Viscountess Curzon, Lady Diana Cooper, Lady Lettice Lygon, Gladys Cooper, Mrs Dudley Coats and La Marquise de Casa Maury.

15

Whatever Happened to Baby Geoffrey?

[Geoffrey] has behaved so very well all the way along ...
NOËL COWARD, *DIARY*, 8 NOVEMBER 1964

Over the years, the late Lord Ampthill was often asked: 'What was it like, being the Russell baby?' His answer: 'Exactly like any other baby because there I was in a perambulator at the time of the trials; and how many persons do you see reading the *Times* law reports, or indeed the tabloids, in their prams?' Because his contemporaries were also in their prams, he did not get teased about the scandal at school; but some of their parents were fascinated by it, so Christabel was reluctant to attend such school functions as Sports Day and Speech Day. 'In any case, I don't think she would particularly have enjoyed the mothers' egg-and-spoon race,' Geoffrey Ampthill added.

As we have seen, his name was put down for Eton soon after his birth, but Eton declined to have him because he was the Russell baby. Geoffrey thought the college did him a favour. 'I'm absolutely delighted I didn't go there because I had the great pleasure of going to Stowe instead.'

At first, Christabel and Geoffrey lived with her mother, Mrs Hart, in Harrington Gardens, South Kensington. Geoffrey was looked after by his grandmother when Christabel went out dining and dancing. He only just remembered Mrs Hart, as he was five when she died. 'She was a little bit austere but she was a good-looking old lady and a great personality in her own right, which is perhaps why she brought up Chris and Chris's elder sister in a way which caused both of them to be rather well educated, one in art, the other in music.' As Geoffrey was Christabel's only child, and she had had to fight so hard for his rights, it might have been natural for her to dote on him too much, be over-protective; but that did not happen. 'She was not a doter. She wasn't a particularly *tactile* person. I think that may explain a bit of why she didn't want to carry through with full sexual activity.' There was no rôle for him in most of her London life – the dress shop, the dining and dancing – so he was often sent to stay with his great-aunt Caroline Carew-Erskine, who had a cottage in Over Stowey, a pretty village just at the foot of the Quantocks in Somerset.

The cottage had a walled garden and an orchard. 'Callie' – as Geoffrey's great-aunt was known – kept chickens, and put the eggs in waterglass. She lived with a very good-looking writer named Constance Bloomfield. They had been friends in the First World War and had lived together ever since. (It was possibly a lesbian relationship.) Geoffrey loved Callie, who became a kind of surrogate mother.

Figure 12 Over Stowey, Somerset
Woodcut by Jack Hillier, 1936.

'She was a welcome change from Chris, in that she was energetic enough to do what had to be done, but Chris had this *unbounded* energy, she was very rarely still. I maintain I was worn out by the age of eighteen when I went off to the war. I have never encountered such a superabundance of energy in anybody else. Callie was the most stable influence in my life in my childhood.'

Much of Geoffrey's childhood was spent in the flat above Christabel's dress shop in Curzon Street. The furthest afield they went was to a Queen Anne house on Ham Common. After a year at a school on the other side of Richmond Park, Geoffrey was sent to board at Cheam, which was still *in* Cheam, in the suburbs of London near Sutton. There were about eighty boys at the school. Among them was Prince Philip. He, Geoffrey and 'the school fat boy' shared a dormitory for three in the last year the school was at Cheam, before it moved to near Newbury. Philip was about to leave for Gordonstoun and later to pursue his career as a naval officer.

'We had great fun [Geoffrey recalled] but unfortunately the small room we were in was not far distant from the headmaster's study. He had to pass through our room from there when there was a pillow fight or some other riot going on in the bigger dormitory beyond us, so occasionally we got implicated in the general misbehaviour and were beaten – not often or severely. Philip was very nice. He was good at work and excellent at games. But I don't think he was terribly happy: I believe there were terrible money troubles.'

Also at the school was Philip's cousin David, Earl of Medina, son of the Marquess of Milford Haven. (He was later best man at Philip's wedding to Princess Elizabeth, but fell into disfavour with the royal family by trading on his friendship with the prince to advance his business career.)

Prince Philip has written to me that he well remembers Geoffrey at Cheam, adding:

'I imagine that Cheam was a fairly standard Prep School of those days. Precious few "Mod Cons", certainly no running water in the dormitories; communal baths once a week; fishcakes for breakfast on Tuesdays; peculiar games such as "dibbs" using sheep's knuckle bones. We used to be mustered along the main road to cheer King George V and Queen Mary on their way to the Derby in their gigantic Daimler.'

The headmaster, Harold Taylor – known by the boys as 'HMS T' – was a cheerful clergyman who had been a chaplain in the First World War. Prince Philip's biographer, Philip Eade, writes:

'For all his bonhomie, Taylor was a staunch disciplinarian, declaring sloth, dirtiness and untruth to be deadly sins, and resorting to corporal punishment at least as often as his peers, using a cane for daytime offences and a sawn-off cricket bat for those caught pillow-fighting after lights out. It was generally conceded that he beat "without rancour"; though some boys thought that he joked on the subject a little too readily. It was indicative of his reputation that when, shortly after Taylor retired, his one-time charge became engaged to the future Queen of England, the former headmaster was sent a rough rhyme:

'Whoever of his friends then thought,
When venturing, Cheam School he bought,
He'd lay his cane athwart
The bottom of a Prince Consort!'

'His first taste of this punishment as a new boy prompted Philip to ask the headmaster's wife, "Do you like Mr Taylor?" The experienced Mrs Taylor countered expertly. "Do you, Philip?" she asked. "No," said the young boy unequivocally, "I do not." '

Jimmy Taylor, the headmaster's son, was at school with Geoffrey.

'His nickname was "Chinny" [he recalls] because, like his mother, he had a rather prominent chin. He was a nice, kind, gentle boy. The only trouble was, he was no good at games. He couldn't catch a ball, couldn't *see* a ball. And as sport was the number one area of interest there – my father played for the MCC – that was a drawback. Geoffrey was never in any kind of team. Most people would have been bullied for that. He wasn't bullied: I think we felt sorry for him.

'My mother became a friend of Christabel Ampthill. She only told me about the Russell Baby case on her deathbed. We weren't told about it at school – and if we had been told, we wouldn't have understood.'

Another contemporary of Geoffrey's at the school – he was in the same form as he – was John Wynne.

'Many of the boys [he remembers] had a service background or a colonial background – Rhodesia and so on. My own father was a mining engineer. Geoffrey was a kind boy. Once, my mother was visiting Cheam the same day as his mother, and HMS T and his wife invited the two women to supper with their sons. Christabel was very beautiful, very striking and elegant. I didn't know about the Russell Baby case at the time, though when I was an adult my mother mentioned it to me.

'When Geoffrey and I were in the second-to-bottom form, the Earl of Medina, Prince Philip's cousin, was a prefect – there was a big gulf between us. We had to show him our hands before meals so he could see whether we had washed them. It was a pity how he turned out later in life.'

In 1933, while Geoffrey was at Cheam, the school was visited by J.F. Roxburgh, who had founded Stowe ten years earlier with one hundred boys. He was recruiting new young people to come to Stowe. He preached, one Sunday, in the Cheam chapel – 'and that, as far as I was concerned, was the highlight of my childhood experiences, because he made an absolutely marvellous speech for boys between the ages of ten and thirteen and caused all of us to fall about laughing'.

It happened that the day Roxburgh came to Cheam, Christabel was also visiting the school to take Geoffrey out to lunch. He was summoned to see her in the headmaster's drawing-room.

'I said to Chris immediately, "Stowe is the place for me to go. Anybody who can make jokes as good as that deserves my support" – or words to that effect. I was introduced to the great man and he said, "How do you do?" in the most gracious manner, adding, "We'd absolutely, I'm sure, love to have you at Stowe, but do you think you can pass the exam?"

'And I said, "I think so, sir; but the person to ask is the headmaster of *this* establishment, who will tell you in a flash." And Roxburgh said, "Well, if you can pass the exam then you can consider yourself most welcome." '

Lord Annan has written: 'Stowe stands in the most sublime setting of any school in England.' The Oxford classics don C.E. Stevens described it as 'that other Eton, demi-paradise'. Formerly the seat of the Dukes of Buckingham, it has architecture by Vanbrugh and Robert Adam and grounds laid out by Capability Brown, littered with Palladian bridges, temples and grottoes. Geoffrey was happy there, and retained much admiration and liking for Roxburgh. 'He had immense presence. He had impeccable manners of a slightly flamboyant sort, but they were a delight. He knew all the six hundred and thirty boys in the school by their Christian names and he remembered what their parents had said the last time he had talked to them.'[67] Geoffrey's most direct experience of the headmaster was 'when he summoned me at the age of fifteen and I wondered which of my misdemeanours he required to see me about.'

'I duly paraded at six o'clock one evening and he said, "Oh my dear Geoffrey, how good of you to come and see me." He said: "Two things. One is congratulations." (I'd passed whatever those exams were that enabled one to get straight into Oxford or Cambridge or anywhere else you wanted to go – at the age of fifteen instead of sixteen, which was the normal age; I had got six credits which meant you wrote to whatever college you'd decided upon and they wrote back and said, "Which train shall we meet?") And then he went into a pantomime and said, "The other matter ... I don't know whether I can bring myself to ask you ... because it is the most enormous favour that you'd be doing for me, if you would be so kind as to do what I'm about to ask you." He went on in that vein for a while and I said: "Sir, anything in the world I can do, naturally I shall be only too pleased to do." So he said, "Oh, you are kind. Would you mind stopping playing cricket?" at which I said, "Sir, I'm sorry you had such anguish asking that question. Of course I shall be *delighted* to stop playing cricket." It was because I was so bad at it, it was fouling up the game for everybody else and therefore neither my colleagues on the field nor myself were having a good time. He said, "Oh goodness gracious, that's a relief. That's lovely. You've made my day. Now there's some theory going around that one's supposed to take exercise. Would you mind thinking of something to do instead?" And I promised to do so; and I do occasionally give it thought to this day.'

The novelist T.H. White was a master at the school then. He taught English. He had written *England Have My Bones* and *The Sword in the Stone* by the time Geoffrey left, among other works; and Geoffrey recalled he was writing a book on *How to Fly an Aeroplane* – 'which he had somehow an eccentric idea he wished to learn how to do'[68]. He lived in a gamekeeper's hut in the middle of a wood, a couple of miles away from the school. Geoffrey did not see a great deal of him, but gratefully remembered that he urged the boys to read P.G. Wodehouse. 'That was huge fun. I became addicted and have been ever since. White said: "This is not part of your official reading; but this is something that you can do with my blessing, because he writes so economically and so clearly. And so hilariously, of course."'

Geoffrey's main subject was history, which he studied under W.L. McElwee, master of the History Sixth – 'the most enchanting man'. He and his novelist wife Patience lived in Vancouver Lodge, a converted farmhouse on the Stowe estate. They used to entertain the historians to tea on Sundays. 'It was a sort of "working tea", inasmuch as you were expected to make an intellectual contribution.' Sir Peregrine Worsthorne, who was at Stowe with Geoffrey, recalls Bill McElwee in his memoirs. At Oxford, Auden had loved McElwee, without having his love returned, and had written many of his early poems for him. A.J.P. Taylor was a close friend of his, as was Lewis Namier, whose pupil he had been. Under him, the History Sixth was 'not only the school's intellectual powerhouse but also its most exclusive social club'. At the Sunday teas he and Patience encouraged 'sophisticated gossip'. McElwee became a friend of the Russell family. He went fox-hunting with Christabel; and as late as the 1960s he came to Leeds Castle to give some tuition to Anthony Russell, Geoffrey's youngest son.

Apart from Worsthorne, who was two years his junior, Geoffrey knew no future celebrities at Stowe. David Niven was there before him; George Melly arrived after him. His best friend there was called Lionel Buxton. 'He was killed at Anzio. He went into the Coldstream Guards and I went into the Irish Guards so we didn't soldier together, and I must say I still remember the heartbreak when he was killed.'

In the school holidays he often went riding with Christabel. In his early childhood he had been put on Shetland ponies, even though he and his mother thought them 'horrid animals – no manners and ill-humoured'. From the age of twelve he was usually mounted on one of Christabel's horses. He had some falls. Twice he broke his nose hunting. 'At the age of fifteen I had a deviated septum – septum is the bone down the middle of the nose. That was painfully removed at the Royal Free Hospital. It was the beginning of sinusitis which has been my main ailment all my life.' When he stayed with Callie in Somerset, he enjoyed stag-hunting, when there were no foxes.

Geoffrey left Stowe a little earlier than most of his contemporaries, because he was feeling restless and wanted to get on with doing something. As an interim it was suggested that he should learn to speak French fluently. He already had some French, because when he was twelve Christabel had sent him to stay with a family in Blois. Now he was despatched for six months to the University of Neuchâtel in Switzerland. Early in 1939 he returned to London. War was obviously looming, but he was still too young to participate, so he became an articled clerk to the president of the Institute of Chartered Accountants, Sir Harold Barton of Barton & Mayhew. At that time he was living in Down Street, off Piccadilly. While based there and studying accountancy he was, for a couple of months, a member of the Home Guard. Piccadilly was his beat; he carried a truncheon to stop people looting from shops when they were blown in. It only lasted for two months because the shopkeepers did not bother to replace the glass to have it blown in again; they boarded up their shop fronts, and the Home Guard were relieved of their duties. 'It was pretty scary,' Geoffrey recalled. 'I'm not sure it wasn't the scariest time of my army or sub-army life.'

Geoffrey was about to take the intermediate accountancy examination when he was called up. He became Guardsman Recruit Russell in the Irish Guards at the Guards' depot at Caterham. He was relieved not to have to take the accountancy exam. 'I think I might have failed it. But the training was valuable experience which I've made use of ever since.' The capacity to understand accounts and balance sheets stayed with him. He learned the trick of being able to add up three columns of figures in one go. Drawing on this kind of know-how he set up a company, just before he joined the army, with his old schoolfriend Lionel Buxton. It was based around a Hungarian inventor who was making weapons of war 'and needed a little help'.

'Lionel and I set up a company called Defence Equipment Ltd. The Hungarian was called Nicholas Straussler. He was a very nice but slightly mad person, but he was the most extraordinarily inventive chap. He invented a way of making tanks amphibious ... and an improved gas-mask which could be manufactured for 6d instead of 9d. The military respected his creative mind. His designs were patented and he made a lot of money from the royalties; where I came in, was that because of my accountancy training I was aware that there was no tax on such royalties. Lionel Buxton and I did not make vast sums, but £10,000 then was something like £100,000 now, and we were both able to live it up a bit.'

Before going off to twelve weeks' training at Caterham Barracks, Geoffrey prepared himself for the ordeal by moving into the Berkeley Hotel (always a favourite of his mother's) for five weeks. After this luxurious interval, he went to Caterham, 'where they put the clippers through one's hair'.

As an Honourable, he was assigned to the Brigade squad, destined to become an officer provided he went through the routine of being an ordinary soldier first. 'And the Brigade squad was pushed a bit harder than the rest – it was quite strenuous. It was the winter of 1940, which was pretty parky; and Caterham is not the pleasantest place in the world. After the first six weeks of the twelve – I suppose you were thought by then to know how to behave as a soldier – you were allowed out for the first time, so I booked my room back at the Berkeley Hotel'.

During the week he stayed there, he went up in the lift with General Sir John Dill, who was the senior serving army officer. With Dill was a lady, who spoke to the General in French: 'What do you think this young man is suffering from? Has he got a disease of the scalp?' Thanks to his spell at Neuchâtel, Geoffrey could understand French and could speak it passably. So he replied, in French: 'No, it is entirely the fault of the general who is accompanying you. My hair has all been removed on his orders.' Dill and his companion 'had hysterics'; and the general said, 'Come and have a glass.'

After six more weeks at Caterham, Geoffrey was sent on to Sandhurst – 'a piece of cake after the Caterham depot' – for a four-months' course. Then he was posted to the training battalion of the Irish Guards at Hobbs Barracks, on the road from East Grinstead to Lingfield. He was now an officer.

'There was one jolly encounter [he recalled]. After a little while, three of us who'd joined at the same time were marched to "Commanding Officer's Orders" at noon. The commanding officer was Hugo Gough – Colonel Lord Gough, a veteran of the previous war in which, Nelson-like, he had lost both an eye and an arm. He was not a believer in aspirin but did believe in repairing to the officers' mess after the nine o'clock morning parade to drink sherry in fairly large quantities before giving his orders at noon.

'We were marched in and stood smartly to attention in front of him, and he asked a question. And, being mildly less dopey than the other two, I took a smart pace forward and said "SIR" in a loud voice, which was the routine I'd learned; and he said, in an expansive way (sloshed, I mean), "Oh, thank you very much." Afterwards the adjutant came out and I said, "I'm dreadfully sorry, but I didn't really hear exactly what the commanding officer had to say – what the question was that he asked." And he said, "Oh, the question was: 'Do any of you understand the internal combustion engine?' " – to which I had indicated my reply in the affirmative. So I decided to keep my mouth shut, because the internal combustion engine was something I did not understand; but it resulted in my becoming the transport officer, and that suited me beautifully.'

Whilst at Hobbs Barracks, Geoffrey 'learned the tricks of the trade'.

'The main trick was to ignore Army Council instructions. They used to provide you with an enormous amount of bumf which told you, for example, that if you were in transport you had every week to remove the sparking plugs from the engine, clean them and reset the points. This invariably resulted in the engine no longer working properly, because untrained mechanics (but good soldiers) don't necessarily do that sort of thing very well; so I instituted the system of throwing Army Council instructions straight into the waste-paper basket and telling the guardsmen to do the elementary things such as keeping the vehicle – whatever it was – clean, which they were extremely good at; driving carefully, which they may or may not have been inclined to do; and noting the three orifices into which you poured the correct liquids – petrol, oil and water. Other than that, "If anything goes wrong, let us know and we will get somebody who knows what to do." I built up stocks of spare parts and used to drive the Ordnance frequently up the wall. When I got into technical difficulties, I called in REME – the Royal Electrical and Mechanical Engineers. They used to love fixing things and telling us how half-witted we were, not knowing how to do it ourselves.'

In the spring of 1944 the Division came to the south and waited for the invasion of Normandy. They were not required to go on D-Day, 'because you don't need an armoured division until there's some space for it to operate on'. They went on D-Day plus eight. 'A lot of extremely brave people had gone ahead of us and had had a beastly time, obviously, on the beaches.' Much of the resistance had been pushed back towards Caen. Enough space had been cleared, though 'a lot of fireworks were still going on'. In the last week of August 1944 the Division received orders from Montgomery to proceed to Brussels. It encountered little German resistance – 'It was looking like being the end of the war.' In each French village they passed through, women who were known or thought to have been collaborators were having their heads shaved in the village square, 'and in the woods behind the village very much more dreadful things were happening to the men – the people being judge, jury and everything else'. Geoffrey was incensed by the attitude of the French during the five days in which the Division drove through France. 'The attitude was: "*What took you so long?*" '

Figure 13 Souvenir card given to the liberators of Belgium.

The Division entered Brussels on 3 September[69]. 'The Belgians were infinitely more pleased to see us than the French were.'

The Germans had left behind a lot of good bottles of wine, and the men got through them. Three days later they were told they could move on, but Geoffrey was involved in a bad accident.

'I got squashed by a three-ton lorry. I was put into the hospital at Brussels – run by the Germans practically at the point of a revolver – as our hospital was still back in Normandy and my pelvis had been broken in about six places. After a few days I was flown back to England in a workhorse aeroplane of the day, a Dakota; and then I and others were shoved into various hospitals. Mine was in Warrington. It was not really a hospital at all, it had been a loony bin, but was now for casualties who did not require too much in the way of surgery. Pelvises are things you can't get at much to mend the bones, so you lie for between three and four months with sandbags from your knees to your chest so that you can't move, and then it mends itself – especially at that age, when bones mend more easily. Then that was over: back to hobbling round on sticks for a while. And it was in that period, as a semi-invalid, that I met my future wife.'

She was Susan Winn, daughter of the Hon. Charles Winn, brother of Lord St Oswald of Nostell Priory, West Yorkshire. Her mother was now Lady Baillie, who owned Leeds Castle in Kent, once a royal palace. Geoffrey was first taken to the castle, shortly after leaving hospital, by Susan's elder sister, Pauline, known as Popsy. Olive and her sister Dorothy Paget were the daughters of Almeric Paget, first and last Lord Queenborough. He was a grandson of the Earl of Uxbridge who commanded the British cavalry against the French at the Battle of Waterloo in 1815. ('By God, sir, I've lost my leg!' – Wellington: 'By God, sir, so you have!') Olive's and Dorothy's mother, Pauline Whitney, was the sister of William C. Whitney, United States Navy Secretary in President Cleveland's first administration and a fabulously wealthy member of the east coast Whitney clan. Geoffrey recalled: 'Almeric Queenborough remained an extremely dirty old man right through to his dying day. He was mad keen, at the age of eighty-something, about my mother, to the extent that she was chased round the drawing-room after the rest of us had retired to bed.'

Olive had come to live at Leeds in 1926. It became a famous centre for high society. The Windsors stayed; so did such Hollywood stars as Douglas Fairbanks Senior and Junior, Frederic March, Charlie Chaplin, Errol Flynn and his wife, Lili Damita, James Stewart and Gertrude Lawrence. Cole Porter entertained the company with *risqué* songs. The Austrian tenor Richard Tauber was a particular friend of Olive's and had his piano brought to the castle. High-level political figures also gathered at Leeds. It was the Camelot of the 1930s, a sophisticated milieu. The chief members of Olive's 'court' were David (later Lord) Margesson, who had been a successful Tory Chief Whip, and Geoffrey Lloyd (later Lord Geoffrey-Lloyd), a future Minister of Education. Geoffrey Russell was very fond of Margesson, who became a sort of surrogate father to him. He was much less keen on Lloyd.

During the Second World War, some economies were made, but the castle was still a centre of political intrigue. David Niven, a guest in 1940, met Olive's 'courtiers'. He wrote: 'As a group they depressed me. I had the feeling that they had no right to eat and drink and dress for dinner, make small talk and gossip like ordinary people. I was quite unreasonably shocked that they were not locked in their offices for the weekend, working tirelessly to find ways to finish the war before it got properly started.' Social life at Leeds Castle was once again in full swing when Geoffrey met his future mother-in-law for the first time just after the war.

Olive had had three husbands. The first – the father of Pauline and Susan – was Charlie Winn, second son of Lord St Oswald. Her second husband was Arthur Wilson Filmer, a big-game hunter and a collector of art and antiques. The third was Sir Adrian Baillie, Bart., who came from the border country between Edinburgh and Glasgow and had coal money. They had a son, (Sir) Gawaine Baillie,[70] who was eleven in 1945.

That year Olive Baillie took Geoffrey for a walk and tried to persuade him to marry Pauline.

'That was on the edge of my deciding I really wanted to marry Suzy. I was never going to want to marry Popsy, she was not such an easy proposition. Olive was trying to get Popsy married off to somebody of whom she approved, and she did approve of me. She was right in what she said on that walk: 'Suzy's not bright enough for you.' She was not in the least foolish, but she was uneducated, as girls were then. Both of the girls had a governess and they went to school for a while, but Olive was not a good mother in that sort of way.'[71]

Geoffrey proposed marriage to Susan, and was accepted. But before they could be married, he had to complete his army service.

'You were not necessarily demobbed immediately the war ended. They couldn't let everybody loose at the same time. It worked on a points system, depending on when you had joined. And as I hadn't joined, because of age, until late in the war, I was released later.

'The war had ended – with a minor omission. They'd forgotten that there were still 350,000 Germans sitting in Norway. So they made a composite battalion of six hundred guards in England who'd been knocked about a bit and we were sent off to Oslo to see what could be done about these Germans. This was about July of '45, soon after the treaty had been signed. The Germans behaved impeccably. They were not prisoners exactly, they were soldiers sitting there wondering what to do next, but they kept themselves to themselves, in their barracks.'

There was one German on the quayside, when the Guards arrived, and he had a bunch of keys. Geoffrey had been appointed transport officer, as usual, but also president of the officers' mess 'because the commanding officer got the idea that I'd been a bit posh'. One key was for a warehouse full of alcoholic drinks. The other was to the compound where all the German vehicles were held. Geoffrey took charge of both keys and dealt with the transport first. He found the best car he could for the C.O. and a jeep for himself He also found the personal bus of Admiral

Raeder, who had been in command in Norway. It was fitted up with a sitting-room, a kitchen and two bedrooms. 'I kept that for weekends.' Then the drinks warehouse was unlocked.

'There was some quite good champagne – 1934 and '37, which were good years; and some decent claret too. All the bottles had "WEHRMACHT" stamped over the French label We sampled a lot of bottles and then we decided we'd better save a few, otherwise we'd all be permanently sloshed; so when our tour of duty was over – it lasted four or five months – we left the ammunition behind, because we did not think it would last long enough to be effective in any future war, and we filled the lorries with as much of the good wine as we could lay our hands on. We distributed it among the guardsmen as well as the officers – I think we might have done slightly better than the men. It was a happy time.'

Back in England, Geoffrey was married to Susan at Leeds Castle. The first three nights of their honeymoon were spent at the Ritz, Paris. Then they moved on to Monte Carlo. Because Lady Baillie was a very keen gambler, and had lost a lot of money in Monte Carlo before the war, the red carpet was laid out for her daughter and new son-in-law. They had a suite in the Hôtel de Paris which cost £7 a night, including meals, for the two of them.

On their return, Olive Baillie's sister, Dorothy Paget, sent them a message. She was a top racehorse breeder, who had won the Grand National with Golden Miller in 1934 and a wartime Derby with Straight Deal. She was to give a party on her birthday after an evening at a musical starring Jack Hulbert and Cicely Courtneidge and she wanted the Russells to come.

'[At the end of the musical] we applauded vigorously and went on to dine in a house which Dorothy had hired for the occasion in Belgravia. We all assembled at eleven o'clock at night and had a glass or two. Eventually dinner began and it was quite good, done by outside caterers. The other guests were principally her two trainers, one for the jumpers and one for the flat, and their hangers-on. We got through the meal. I was put in the place of honour next to her and we had a nice time – she was extremely intelligent, but mixed up beyond belief. And then, at the end of each course, we had to sit back while she had the same course over again. Because she had an eccentric way of organizing her life and she paid no attention to the clock as far as meals, or anything else for that matter, were concerned; and she needed a big meal so we sat there while she gobbled her way through another first course, and then a second second course. So dinner took about three hours, at which time the doorbell rang and there was a postman, bringing her vast quantities of telegrams to celebrate her birthday. This had obviously been organized by her ladies-in-waiting, who were all Russian refugees. One of the Russian ladies was authorized to open the telegrams, and they were all from her horses, having been sent by the Russian ladies on behalf of each one of her horses. As she had two hundred and forty horses when she died, this meant a fairly big volume of trade for the Post Office.'[72]

After their marriage, Geoffrey and Suzy bought a house in Montpelier Street,

London. Then they moved to Egerton Terrace, a cul-de-sac in Chelsea. Smith's Charity, which owned it, leased it to them for twenty years for £3,750. (After the couple were divorced in 1971, the Charity woke up to what the property was really worth. It is now worth about three and a half million pounds.)

Leaving the army, Geoffrey needed a job. At the age of twenty-six he was appointed general manager of Fortnum & Mason.

'My mother knew a nice old boy called Walter Thornton-Smith, who lived in a big, rambling house near Maidenhead called Shoppenhangers Manor. We stayed with him. He ran an antiques business and was a bit of an old rogue. He had a sort of shooting-range, in which pellets were fired at pieces of furniture to give the "ageing" appearance of woodworm. But I couldn't help liking him and he apparently liked me, too. He knew about my accountancy training and he recommended me to his brother, Ernest Thornton-Smith, who was a director of Fortnum's[73] Ernest asked me to make a report on the store. I took some time to do it, and it was very critical of the management. As a result, I was appointed general manager. The previous manager, Mr Rand, was demoted to be co-manager alongside me.'

Geoffrey did not make the typical young man's mistake of coming in like a white tornado and changing everything at once. He just did what the directors asked him to do – to make more money than they had been making up to then. That was not easy, because rationing was still in force; it was not lifted until after he left the store in 1951 – lifted when the Labour government fell in 1952. Also, the Labour government rationed foreign exchange. 'There was a complete absence of foreign exchange,' Geoffrey recalled. 'Whereas everybody had behaved with absolute integrity about rationing in the war, once the war was over people wanted the things they had been missing.'

He saw that the whole point of Fortnum's was that it had things that other shops did not have. It had to sell cornflakes, like other stores, and it had to charge the same amount for cornflakes. It made no money from that, because so many of Fortnum's customers wanted things delivered, and the delivery charges were borne by the store. A few luxury specialities had survived the war. Mr Floris still made chocolates for Fortnum's in the building, though eventually he wanted more freedom to supply other people. Geoffrey expanded the store's business in a way that made it more rational. 'There had been no proper management up to then. We did what we could to get back into our stride – again, with goods you could not easily buy elsewhere.' His two biggest coups were with Ferragamo (who had sold his shoes at Fortnum's before the war) and Emilio Pucci.

After Geoffrey had been at Fortnum's for five years, he resigned over a scandal for which he was in no way responsible. In 1951 Ernest Thornton-Smith, the brother of Geoffrey's friend Walter, was caught by the firm of Seager Evans, which made gin and other products, dealing heavily in the shares of Seager Evans the day before they announced 'a walloping issue' which was going to push the share price up by a very large amount. This leaked. In those days, insider dealing, as it has now been known for decades, was not actually a crime in law; but it was certainly a crime as far as the City was concerned. The board of Seager Evans learned of Thornton-Smith's misconduct and asked for his resignation, which he duly gave, as was reported in the newspapers.

'At the next meeting of Fortnum's [Geoffrey recalled] we said: "Ernest, we were sorry to hear of your misfortune with Seager Evans, but as we, Fortnum's, are a respectable company, we're very sorry, you must resign from us, too." And he said, "Sorry, but I won't." So then we had to set in motion having an extraordinary general meeting to remove him, under the law. We had given him every opportunity to think about it and to realise that Fortnum's – above all firms – really couldn't have somebody on their board who behaved like that. So we started the process going.'

However, Ernest Thornton-Smith was cunning. He somehow learned that the person who wanted to own Fortnum's more than anybody else was Garfield Weston, founder and chairman of the firm that makes bread, biscuits and Ryvita. Weston was very rich. He had made most of his money by selling Canadian wheat to the United Kingdom and then turning it into medium-quality bread; and he had briefly been a member of the United Kingdom Parliament. Thornton-Smith went to see Weston, who confirmed that he did desperately want Fortnum's. The two of them went into the market and bought shares. Geoffrey got wind of this alliance and resigned in order to oppose it. He flew to Richmond, Virginia, in an attempt to persuade Weston to abandon his pursuit, and succeeded only in prompting Weston to beg him to stay on. He declined.

So the extraordinary general meeting took place, attended by six hundred shareholders. Five hundred and ninety-eight of them voted to remove Thornton-Smith from the board; but two voted for him to stay – Thornton-Smith himself and Garfield Weston, who had by then become a substantial shareholder. Those two won by three-quarters of 1 per cent. Not only did Geoffrey's resignation stand firm; all the rest of the board resigned, except Thornton-Smith and the deputy chairman, who stayed on to effect the handover. That was the end of Geoffrey's enjoyable career there.

He was not long out of a job. The chairman of Fortnum's, Ian Anderson, who was essentially a stockbroker, was also chairman of the Piccadilly Theatre. He invited Geoffrey to run its board. It was the beginning of a new career. Geoffrey brought in a good general manager, who played a large part in his subsequent life in the theatre. But in the meantime some quite different work came his way, through Olive Baillie.

'Whilst I'd been at Fortnum's, shopkeepers (especially those who didn't have a Sale – which is beneath the dignity of Fortnum's) took their holidays in January; and I'd had an urge for the sunshine and had been going to the Bahamas ever since 1946, and I had rather an affection for the place. Dry land: it's dull, inasmuch as the highest mountain is about eight inches high – there is no soil and therefore things don't grow over there. But it has the best sea water, I think, in the world, for clarity and for the colour, which changes all the time according to the angle of the sun. I decided to investigate further. My mother-in-law needed somewhere to go for the sun, and I said, "I've found a house which I think you will like on something called Hog Island." She said, "That doesn't sound very attractive, but never mind." It was actually a very very nice house, the bones of it. She went out the next year to case the whole island and came to the conclusion that I was right: this was the best house for her. The only problem was that there was no bridge to Hog Island; you had to have your own boat to get you and your guests backwards and forwards.'

Hog Island had formerly been inhabited mainly by semi-wild pigs. In 1959 the lush, tropical habitat was bought by a rich American called Huntingdon Hartford ('Hunt' to his friends), co-heir to the A&P supermarket fortune. He renamed Hog Island Paradise Island and brought over from France, packed in foam, a fourteenth-century cloister, which was reconstructed as part of the 'Versailles Gardens' of his Ocean Club. Apart from the lack of a bridge, the island had all the advantages. Before Hartford acquired it, it was almost totally undeveloped. Olive Baillie's house ('Harbourside'), the one next to it and the Porcupine Club on the other side were the only buildings. In winter the club was full of eastern seaboard people escaping the eastern seaboard climate. Lady Baillie, too, was only there in the winter. Geoffrey went out there for his January holiday. At Christmas he had to be in England for his young family. He and Susan had four children: David, born in 1947; James, born eighteen months later; Anthony, born 1952, and Vanessa, born 1960.

Anthony has kindly allowed me to quote from his remarkable memoir. Originally entitled *The Castle Way* – an allusion to the ceremonious manner in which life was led at Leeds Castle where he spent large parts of his childhood – it is being published as *Outrageous Fortune*. He observed that his two grandmothers – Granny A and Granny B (Lady Ampthill and Lady Baillie) – were very different from each other, as were their respective castles. So were his two brothers. As a young child, he noted:

'David is the mild-mannered one with the brains and James is the mischievously disruptive one with the looks ... When we are together, [they] are generally solicitous towards me. By way of contrast, they are at battle stations with each other a great deal of the time ... Regrettably, they appear to work overtime to find the other's weak spots which, of course, they do unerringly, and often ... [James] focuses his swashbuckling demeanour on David whose temperament is wholly unsuited to such aggressiveness. And so they go at it, hammer and tongs, brains v. brawn, usually for no other reason than James feeling slighted, probably wrongly, by David's supposedly greater knowledge or intelligence. Very seldom do fists fly but, naturally, when they do it all ends in tears (including my own, the neutral observer's, who would like it all to stop...)'

Having never had a father himself, Geoffrey did not quite know how to behave like one. Sometimes he would address one of the boys with jocose formality: 'My dear sir, I trust your lamb chops are to your satisfaction?' At other times he could be frighteningly severe. Anthony recalls a day in the 1950s when, in the nursery,

James was 'dancing around the breakfast table like a madman, laughing and loudly exclaiming how funny our nursery assistant, Anne's varicose veins looked'. Anne, a tall Canadian girl, about twenty, was crying. The boys' nanny was imploring James to stop, but he wouldn't. Nanny left the nursery, telling him, 'I'm going to have to tell your father.' Anthony remembers what happened next.

'Hearing the familiar floorboard squeak from just outside the bathroom on the half-landing, I turn to see our father coming up the stairs, an aura of dread emanating .from his three-piece, navy blue pin-stripe suit, and a stern, frighteningly stern, expression on his face. James is suddenly quiet, as if struck dumb, and the only sound in the nursery is an intermittent, gentle sob from Anne. Climbing the last few stairs, his left hand on the banister, our father enters the nursery and without so much as a by-your-leave (or a sympathetic offer of a hanky to Anne) he quietly instructs James to bend over the armchair adjacent to the storage cupboard, by the left window, and starts whacking away at my brother's bottom with his right hand, very hard. I watch this whole affair in a state of extreme shock. I do not know how many whacks James receives but when it's all over he too is crying ... He goes off to school in a sorry state.'

For quite long stretches, Geoffrey was away, supervising the decoration of Lady Baillie's house on Hog Island. It was executed by Stéphane Boudin of the French firm Jansen, who had done a lot of work at Leeds Castle. Geoffrey bought his mother-in-law a boat which could ferry eight to ten people to and from the island, with a cabin in case it rained. 'She was happy as a sandgirl. She brought out Lord Margesson, Geoffrey Lloyd and many other friends. It was a happy time. It was the year of Canasta – that was the game she liked playing.' After the Fortnum's affair came to a head, Geoffrey negotiated with the Bahamian government that a Bill should be passed in his favour, giving him freedom from taxation and the right to bring in the people he wanted. He then built a new hotel. There had not been a new one since long before the war. He bought from the government a stretch of the best beach, Emerald Beach, four miles outside Nassau on New Providence Island. 'This was years before the famous Lyford Cay was developed by a Canadian called Thompson – that is now *the* fashionable place, where you pay $1 million to buy a small two-up and two-down.' It was a swamp before Geoffrey began building. 'Nobody dared to go there after four o'clock in the afternoon, because you were eaten alive by mosquitoes twenty-four hours a day, but by sandflies after four o'clock. They can drive you potty.' It cost a lot of money to drain the swamps. Then the Emerald Beach Hotel was built, with 350 rooms. The Bahamian government insisted it be built in 'colonial' style.

The hotel no longer exists. 'It occupied a great stretch of prime beach. They tactfully arranged to burn it down after it had been around for about thirty years. The government appropriated the land and now there are three or four hotels on the site; one of them has six hundred rooms, and they are all absolutely hideous. They forgot all about "colonial" picturesqueness and the casino has now moved into the biggest of the hotels.' Geoffrey was invited to run the gambling in the

Bahamas, but the Mafia's involvement was enough to put him off.

Back in London, his career as a theatre impresario began to take off. He worked for a firm called Linnit and Dunfee, and when Bill Linnit died Jack Dunfee asked Geoffrey if he would like to take his place. 'So I said, Yes, all right. I didn't know anything about the theatre; but then I didn't know anything about transport when I became transport officer in the army; and I didn't know anything about groceries when I became general manager of Fortnum's, so that was nothing new.' At first he was just landlord of the Piccadilly Theatre. All he needed to do was to choose what to put on next.

'When the play that you'd got in the theatre was obviously on the slope, you tried to find out what would be ready when that collapsed; or of course you could break the contract if it slipped below a certain level. If you thought the thing had a chance, you *gave* it a chance: it's a difficult business and you want to help each other like mad. You don't want to push a play out. Nobody knows until the damn thing opens and even then you don't know. The first play I had anything to do with was called *Salad Days*. It had been an end-of-term romp at the Bristol Old Vic in the early Fifties. It got some of the worst notices I think I've ever read for anything. Milton Shulman [in the *Evening Standard*] said it was without doubt the most dreadful evening he had ever spent in his life, with knobs on. It ran for seven years. As the impresario – not a word I specially care for – it used to drive me absolutely crazy. I mean, it had tunes in it which were fun tunes, but the whole thing was an acute embarrassment. It made £750,000 by the time we closed it in London. It only cost £2,000 to put on.'

Salad Days brought Geoffrey money, but he was far more proud of his production of *Candide*, although the adaptation of Voltaire's fable was not a commercial success. Lillian Hellman wrote the translation; Leonard Bernstein composed the music; the clothes and sets were by Osbert Lancaster; and Antony Armstrong-Jones, before he married Princess Margaret and became Lord Snowdon, took the still pictures of the actors on the sets.

Geoffrey also put on a version of Noël Coward's *Blithe Spirit*, retitled *High Spirits*. At first a well-known actress was cast in it; but Coward came to a rehearsal and told Geoffrey: 'She moves like a pregnant camel with piles. You must sack her.' He did so. Asked if the actress had cried, he replied: '*Did* she? My coat shoulder was sopping wet; and on it, after she had left, I found one large false eyelash.' Geoffrey won favourable mention in Coward's diary.

'*8 November 1964. High Spirits* opened on Tuesday to a wildly enthusiastic audience, much more so than ever hoped for. The show went wonderfully and the next morning, as I anticipated, disaster ... The main burden of the notices is that the beautiful play [*Blithe Spirit*] has been mucked about with. Timmy [Gray] and Hugh [Martin] have properly bought it ... Cis [Cicely Courtneidge] also got some well-deserved cracks for vulgarizing Madame Arcati, and serve her bloody well right ... The one I am really sorry for is Geoffrey [Russell]. He has behaved so very well all the way along and I am afraid, unless a miracle happens, that he will lose a packet. The miracle just *might* happen, but I fear it is unlikely.'

The miracle did not happen.

After *Salad Days*, for which Geoffrey gave Bill Linnit, not himself, the initial credit, none of the plays he put on made a fortune. 'Let us not kid ourselves: I did not have a record of a series of successes.' Michael Codron, director of the Aldwych Theatre, who had dealings with Geoffrey, said:

'He was a novelty in our profession: a gent. At one time he could have insisted that I should fulfil a particular clause in a contract and pay him a lot of money. He let me off; I'd have been ruined if he hadn't. You could call the plays that he put on in the theatres of which he was managing director, "estimable", but they weren't commercial, after *Salad Days*. And the theatres he ran were not well sited in the West End.'

In August, Lady Baillie's 'court', as Anthony calls her circle, tended to be at her Castèu Cansoun de la Mar on Cap Ferrat in the south of France. Geoffrey and Suzy would join the court for two or three weeks, and sometimes the children were invited too. Anthony remembers 'a well established timetable of breakfast in bed, morning swims, sunbathing, cocktails, luncheon (sometimes taken with friends on the Cap, Beaulieu or Eze), afternoon rests, shopping, cards, evening drinks, changing for dinner, dinner on the terrace or dinner with friends on theirs – then Granny goes gambling in Monte Carlo, or to the casino in Beaulieu, accompanied by a small, devoted côterie ...'

Granny B's friends included Mary Lasker, widow of the American advertising mogul Albert Lasker, who made a fortune by finding a delicate way of advertising sanitary towels. She lived in the Villa Leopolda, the grandest palace on Cap Ferrat. Anthony thought she looked 'like a big bird but with bigger hair and very expensive jewellery'. Lobsters and Grand Marnier soufflés were served at her dinner-parties.

Other holidays were spent in the Bahamas. Lady Baillie extended her empire there by buying first the Porcupine Club and then Greyleath, a magnificent eleven-acre property next to Harbourside, which she gave to her two daughters, Suzy and Pauline (Anthony's 'Auntie Pops'). Greyleath had a fine garden and an Olympic-sized swimming pool.

Among the friends the Russells made when staying there were Ivar Bryce and his wife Josephine, who was a sister of Huntingdon Hartford and shared his A&P fortune. Ivar had been at Eton with Ian Fleming, author of the James Bond novels, and was his best friend. Andrew Lycett describes him in his biography of Fleming.

'He and Ian discovered they both enjoyed the kind of laddish escapades frowned upon by school authorities, like playing truant and meeting girls. Ivar brought a touch of exoticism to Ian's life. He was the scion of an Anglo-Peruvian family which had made a fortune trading guano, the phosphate-rich deposit of fish-eating seabirds which had been widely used as a natural fertilizer. With his thick, sensuous lips, Bryce was distinguished by satyr-like good looks which he owed to his part-Aztec Indian origins.'

Josephine Bryce owned a house in Market Street in the centre of Nassau.

'After their wedding [Lycett writes], as a thank-you present for Moyns [Ivar's childhood home in Essex, which 'Jo' had acquired for him a couple of years earlier], Ivar built her a "love-nest" in a secluded spot beside the sea on the main [Bahamian] island of New Providence. Xanadu, as it was called after Coleridge's pleasure palace, had all mod cons, yet it was exotically finished in shell, ivory and mother of pearl. Its crescent beach of golden sand was protected at either end by a sculpted sphinx.'

The Russells were often with the Bryces, either at Greyleath or at Xanadu, and saw quite a lot of Ian Fleming and his wife Ann, too, though Geoffrey was mystified as to why the couple 'enjoyed beating each other – something I had had quite enough of at school, thank you very much'.[74] Fleming found Nassau unexciting: his feelings about the place were similar to those of Bond in his short story 'Quantum of Solace': 'The winter visitors and the residents who had houses on the island talked of nothing but their money, their diseases and their servant problems. They didn't even gossip well. There was nothing to gossip about. The winter crowd were all too old to have love affairs and, like most rich people, too cautious to say anything malicious about their neighbours.' But, like Lady Baillie, Fleming enjoyed gambling. He patronized the Nassau casino. In the Bond novel *Thunderball* (1961, based on a screen treatment with Kevin McClory and Jack Whittingham), Largo rents his luxury beachside villa, Palmyra – a thinly disguised Xanadu – from an Englishman named Bryce.

In 1967 the journalist Ann (now Dame Ann) Leslie was at Lyford Cay researching an article for *Queen* magazine, 'A Month in the Life of the Bahamas'. While there, she had an amusing encounter with Lady Baillie, which showed something of the character of Geoffrey's mother-in-law.

'One day I got a call from her, inviting me to a "luncheon party". I innocently asked whether I could bring with me the photographer I was working with. "A *photographer?*" she expostulated in the tones of Lady Bracknell's "A *handbag?*" I was to explain to her ladyship, tactfully, that Patrick was not some common-or-garden snapper, but the Earl of Lichfield no less. "Don't tell the snobbish old bat!" hissed Patrick. So I didn't. "She'll find out soon enough!" he grinned. And she did: from then on I was bombarded with panic-stricken messages from Hog Island telling me that Lady Baillie would be *delighted* if I brought along my photographer. But Patrick refused to go. "I'm afraid Lord Lichfield is *much* too busy," I'd regretfully inform her minions.'

Anthony Russell was at Greyleath for the Easter holiday of 1966. There he and James experienced a tongue-lashing from their father, almost as painful as the physical punishment James had suffered. Anthony, now fourteen, had been dragooned by James into roaring round Paradise Island in a rented speedboat. They managed to ram it on to a beach, causing considerable damage to the craft. Anthony writes:

'At lunch, as usual, on the terrace overlooking the pool, Pa plays the rôle of the hanging judge as only he knows how, silently deliberating as to whether the usual punishment fits the crime, whilst Ma, David, Nanny and Vanessa make valiant efforts not to give off the unseemly air of onlookers at a public execution.

'James and I sit side by side and stare sullenly at our plates; Ma makes half-hearted attempts at polite conversation but there is nothing, apparently, to talk about. Not until the end or the meal does Pa commence his summation and it is a real corker, laced with vitriol, stupefying anger and withering condemnation. The tone of delivery is measured and calm but, like his mother, Pa has always been able to be devastatingly forceful without ever raising his voice. My insides turn to jelly and I imagine my face turning puce. Stealing a look at James, whose Ray-Ban sunglasses provide him with a smattering of cover, I notice that he, too, uncharacteristically, finds himself floundering in the eye of the storm. The nursery incident, when I was still in the high chair, returns from out of the blue to stymie and dislocate my thoughts, and perhaps my brother cannot stop himself having unpleasant recollections of the same morning.'

In London, Geoffrey's career as a theatre impresario was coming to an end. The London theatre was changing. Costs trebled in the space of two years after the National Theatre, the Royal Shakespeare Company and the Royal Court Theatre started being given huge sums of money by the Arts Council. Stage hands, who had previously been moonlighting as Covent Garden porters, were now full-time and unionized. Geoffrey called it a day.

By then personal tragedy had struck him and his family: in 1969 his second-born son, James, was killed in a car crash.

'That was a dreadful day [Geoffrey recalled]. He died on the 17th of October – two days after my birthday – aged twenty-one. He did it on his way to work on the A1. He had a motor-car which – a silly thing to have done – had a powerful engine inside the chassis which was not intended for it. He was bumbling along – the police made a very thorough investigation of how this happened. On the dual carriageway there was a barrier in-between which was, unlike the barriers today, quite high. There was no evidence at all that he was going too fast; but the car decided to go its own way, instead of the way he was going, and he went through the barrier. Fortunately he caused nobody any harm.

'Suzy was very good. We were both ... there's no word for it. It was the worst thing that ever happened to us.'

Anthony Russell writes about his brother, recalling both how glamorous a figure James seemed to him and how the news of his death was broken to him. While Anthony was at Stowe, James and his girlfriend Charlotte[75] had promised to take him out to lunch. They were very late. At five to three, while Anthony was unenthusiastically watching a rugby match, they arrived.

'Mid-way through the first half [of the match], I looked over for the umpteenth time towards the main drive and there, miraculously, it was. The best-looking sports car in the world with the best-looking couple I knew seated within, ambling gently past the pavilion, heading, as I had suggested, for the slip road adjacent to my study block.

'I felt a surge of excitement combined with immense relief. Everyone around me had turned to look, some asking if I knew who it was! I informed them proudly as James and Charlotte, both wearing leather jackets and jeans, got out of the car and took in their surroundings.

'They saw me heading towards them and came to meet me.

' "I'm really sorry," James said. "We were a little late setting off." I kissed Charlotte and she apologised too.

' "Look, we've cancelled our dinner so we can take you out for supper instead, is that all right?" she asked.'

The terrible news came only two weeks later.

'I was in my study working on a history essay. Trevorrow [a fellow pupil] was also busy at his desk – when someone knocked on the door. I couldn't imagine who'd be paying us a visit at eight-thirty in the evening. The door opened and a junior boy informed me that Mr Vinan, my housemaster, wished to see me in his study. Not, to my knowledge, having transgressed significantly in the recent past I had no idea as to why my presence might be required. I put on my jacket, went up the stairs, turned left into the main thoroughfare between our house and the North Front entrance hall, and after a few paces, wheeled left to face Mr Vinan's study door. It was ajar. I knocked and immediately heard him say, "Come in."

'Mr Vinan was seated at his desk, an expression of rigid blankness on his face, holding the telephone to his ear but not speaking. Without looking directly at me, he stood up, came round the desk, holding the telephone out towards me. "It's your father," he said. As I took the phone from his hand, he immediately strode out of the room, closing the door behind him. Mystified, but with a creeping wariness, I spoke tentatively into the mouthpiece.

' "Hello."

'Something was wrong. My father sounded strange. Then he said he had bad news. "It's pretty rough. You'd better brace yourself."

'My mind raced. What could have happened? There was a desperate quality m my father's voice which I had never heard before.

' "It's James," he said. "He's had a motor accident ... It happened this morning ... he was killed ..."

'A physical force hit me in the chest. It felt like a boxer had just punched me with all his might. I gripped the telephone harder and gulped a few times, as if something had become wedged in my throat. Suddenly, the room felt claustrophobic. My father was still talking but his words had become a blur. My mother came on the line. When I heard her voice, I could control myself no longer. I burst into tears. She tried so hard to be strong and to comfort me. But I could not be comforted. Nor could I speak. After a few minutes, we agreed to hang up and call again in the morning.'

There was a cremation at Golders Green, which only Geoffrey attended. It was followed by a memorial service in Leeds parish church, Kent. 'We did not put up a stone, there was no point,' Geoffrey said. 'He is buried anonymously. Two days after my birthday I have a quiet day if I can, and think about him an awful lot.'

Geoffrey Ampthill broke down as he told me that. A phrase from an Edith Piaf song of my youth sprang into my mind – 'Ne pleurez pas, milord.' I wondered whether to put a consoling arm round him, but decided against: he belonged to a less demonstrative, less touchy-feely generation than mine. He wanted to play me Mahler's 'Resurrection Symphony', which had been played at the memorial service, but could not find the record. 'James was such a bright hope,' he said. 'He had *drive*. And the girls loved him.' Naturally David Russell, the steady son, of strong integrity, was also grief-stricken; but not all his memories are tender of the brother he so often fought. He had grown rather tired of having him held up as a paragon. 'He got two per cent in theology in the entrance exam to Stowe, so he was sent to a Dublin school instead,' he recalled. 'Before leaving for Ireland, he filled a suitcase with condoms to sell.'

David – now Lord Ampthill – was in publishing for some years and became Master of Sackville College, a Tudor almshouse in East Grinstead. Anthony, the third son, has had a 'more adventurous career' as a pop singer and impresario in America. His friend Mick Jagger told him: 'You're pretty good. But you're never going to make it – you've just had it too cushy.' (Lady Baillie had set up large trust funds for each of the children.) By his first marriage to the New Yorker April McKenzie Arbon, David had two daughters, Christabel and Daisy. The marriage was dissolved in 1998 and in 2002 David married Christia (Tia), the widow of Prince Rostislav Romanoff. It is Anthony's son, William, who has been brought up in America, who is likely to succeed to the Ampthill barony one far-off day. Geoffrey's daughter Vanessa married twice.

Geoffrey's own marriage to Susan ended in divorce in 1971. 'It had reached the stage where I was saying cutting things to her in front of the children,' he recalled. That is confirmed by part of a letter that Anthony wrote his grandmother, Lady Baillie, as early as 1961, when he was nine (but never sent her).

'... I probably shouldn't be saying this but now that I have had lunch and dinner a few times with Mummy and Daddy in London, sometimes with David and James, sometimes not, I have noticed that Daddy often says very unkind things to Mummy. He thinks he's being funny but I don't think he's being funny at all. He thinks we're laughing with him but I'm not laughing with him; in fact, I'm angry with him. He puts Mummy down, tells her she's foolish, makes fun of her. It makes me feel horrible. I want to stand up for her but don't know what to do. I can't say anything because I feel tongue-tied around him, incapable of standing up even for myself. I don't know why. Does he do things like this to Mummy in front of you and the court? I hope not because she does not deserve it. I think she's clever and kind, just like Nanny. Do tell Daddy to behave properly if you see him being nasty to Mummy because someone has to. You wouldn't believe how awful the atmosphere can be in the dining room on these occasions.'

Anthony remembers his father's snapping at his wife, in front of the family: 'Oh, Suzy, do pipe down, you don't know what you're going on about.' Anthony adds:

'My parents were so far apart in their likes and dislikes, habits and personalities that sometimes their charm, good looks and fondness for a stiff drink seemed to be all that they had in common... My father always seemed on much better form when guests were present... He worked harder on being witty and worldly-wise, elements of his social armoury he particularly prized but which were on display less frequently when only the family was present.'

Geoffrey remarried. 'Suzy remarried as soon as I did,' he said. 'Almost anybody would do, and she chose Colonel Remington Hobbs, who would *not* do, but she married him nonetheless. He died ahead of her. He was so mean. Sometimes I had to visit them, for the children. I used to bring a case of wine, half red, half white – nothing grand, but goodish. He used to keep my bottles and decant the house plonk into them. He was *that* sort of man.'[76]

Ian Fleming was wrong when he stated, in 'Quantum of Solace', that there were no love affairs to gossip about in the Bahamas. Geoffrey met Elisabeth Mallon, who was to be his second wife, at the Bryces' Xanadu. She gave her account of that first meeting, in *Woman* magazine (4 September 1976):

'It was a glorious day in 1970 and I was lying in my bikini soaking up the sun on a raft that floated on the clear blue waters of Nassau Bay.

'Suddenly a sleek, dark head appeared at the side of my raft and a man hauled himself out of the sea to sit dripping beside me.

' "Hello," he said, "I'm Geoffrey Russell, who are you?"

'Now I know this sounds ridiculous but at that instant I fell in love – boom, just like that.

'We lay side by side on that raft and talked for the next two hours, there was so much we wanted to say to each other.

'As we swam reluctantly back to shore together I was certain I had found the man I wanted to marry.

'Geoffrey had told me that his marriage was breaking up, that he had four children[77] and was a theatrical impresario in London. I had told him about my life, about my brief unhappy marriage that had ended in divorce, about my family at home in Paris, and how worried my mother had been when I decided to leave France to work in public relations in the United States.

'I certainly didn't know then that Geoffrey was the heir to a famous English title or that his birth had caused a scandal that rocked English high society even in the cynical 1920s. But that forgotten "scandal" was to bring anguish to Geoffrey, his mother and me three years later – after I had become his wife ...'

Geoffrey and Elisabeth were married in 1972. Georgina Howell interviewed Elisabeth for *Tatler*.

'She is a ravishing Parisienne with green eyes and an hourglass figure, the kind of beauty who would be accompanied by crowds of paparazzi in other countries but passes almost unnoticed in the British press. Both twice married, wealthy and well travelled, they live in the smartest modem house in Chelsea. Built in steel and glass by architect John Guest, it has vinyl slats instead of curtains and Ultrasuede instead of wallpaper. The garden is entirely covered with black industrial rubber.'

Elisabeth, Howell recorded, had reached a stage where she could spend the day arranging flowers and going to the hairdresser; instead, she chose to work from 6.30 in the morning until ten or eleven at night at her catering firm in Battersea, cooking, supervising and delivering special lunches and dinners to a large circle of clients. The company was called Mallon, her maiden name and nickname. She had picked up some of her skill as a cook at La Pyramide in Vienne, where she was taught by the inventor of nouvelle cuisine, Fernand Point, the man who taught Paul Bocuse.

Geoffrey and Elisabeth spent fifteen happy years together. They were divorced in 1987. According to Geoffrey, the main reason for the break-up was the arrival in London of Elisabeth's mother and the mother's partner, a French lawyer. The mother and the *maître* moved into the house that Geoffrey and Elisabeth had by now in Cathcart Road, London – ostensibly for a week or two until they could find a London base themselves. They were still in Cathcart Road three months later. Geoffrey politely asked how long they were thinking of staying and whether there was anything he could do to help. This led to a big row. 'Everybody began to fall out,' Geoffrey said. By that time, in any case, Elisabeth's cuisine business in Battersea was flourishing; and Geoffrey was 'well stuck into the House of Lords': their agendas were different.

But in the 1970s, when Geoffrey faced the toughest battle of his life, Elisabeth was right beside him, literally and metaphorically.

16

The Young Pretender

'Peer's sons in title "feud"'
HEADLINE IN *THE SUN*, 13 JUNE 1973

On 3 June 1973, John Hugo, third Lord Ampthill, died in London. He had been suffering from cancer for some time. The newspaper obituaries paid tribute to his service in the Navy and in the House of Lords, but the main focus of the articles was the Russell Baby case. The *Times* obituarist wrote: 'The death of Lord Ampthill inevitably recalls the prolonged litigation of some 50 years ago in which he was intimately involved and which produced what *The Times,* in a leader of 1924, called a memorable judgment.' The *Daily Telegraph* commented:

'Lord Ampthill succeeded to the peerage in 1935 and the same year [actually, in 1937] his matrimonial litigation ended when his wife was awarded a divorce. Their son now succeeds to the peerage ... The heir, Mr Geoffrey Russell, 51, is a theatrical impresario, who at one time was general manager of Fortnum and Mason's.'

Geoffrey, too, thought that all he had to do now was to go through the formalities that would lead to his taking his seat in the House of Lords. He telephoned Lord Buckhurst, with whom his sons David and Anthony were staying at Buckhurst Park in Sussex – the park described by A.A. Milne in *Winnie-the-Pooh.* (Lady Buckhurst was Anthony's godmother). He actually spoke to the Buckhursts' son William – the future Earl De La Warr – and said, 'Pray tell the boys that they have suffered a minor elevation.' (In other words, each of them would now be styled 'the Honourable'.) But he was in for a shock. His father had married twice after the divorce from Christabel. By his second wife, Sibell Faithfull Lumley, he had no children; but by his third wife, Adeline Hone (daughter of Canon H.E. Hone of Godalming) he had a son, John, in 1950, and a daughter, Georgiana, in 1953. Geoffrey wrote a letter of sympathy to Adeline, Lady Ampthill. Instead of receiving a reply from her, he had one from his father's youngest brother Leopold:

Dear Mr Russell,
As an Executor of my brother, the late Lord Ampthill, I am replying to your letter of 4 June to his widow, my sister-in-law, who is of course very distressed.

I would first like to thank you for your kind letter of sympathy at what is a very sad moment for us all. At the same time I think it is only fair to let you know that, as my brother's conviction in regard to yourself never changed throughout his lifetime, it is possible that the succession may be a matter of dispute. I can assure you that there are no feelings of ill-will towards you personally but I am most anxious that you should be spared any possibility of embarrassment. In the circumstances, you may feel that it would perhaps be better if you were to refrain from attempting to establish contact with members of my brother's family at the present time.

Yours sincerely, Leo Russell

Oddly, Leo Russell addressed this letter to 'The Hon. Geoffrey Russell' – a form of address which could be correct only if Geoffrey were a peer's legitimate son.

In 1973 Leopold Russell was sixty-six and a director of the Cement and Concrete Association. At the time of the first Russell divorce hearing in 1922, he was at Eton, and in Geoffrey's view 'he was so unmercifully ragged about it that it left a huge chip on his shoulder, never filled in'. Geoffrey was convinced that it was his uncle Leo who put John Russell up to challenging his half-brother for the peerage. That was also the view of a *Daily Express* article (25 February 1976) headed 'We're sorry for Geoffrey, says uncle': 'It is the 59-year-old [*sic*] Leopold above all in the family who persuaded his diffident Old Etonian accountant nephew John, 25, to press his claim to the title. Uncle Leopold has given his nephew both moral and financial support in the pursuit of the claim.'

The *Daily Mail* of four days earlier had contained a more detailed account of how the Russells had conspired to mount a challenge to Geoffrey. It read like a scene from *Kind Hearts and Coronets*.

'On the day of the third Lord Ampthill's funeral, in June 1973, the uncles and aunt of young John Russell told him they would back him if he decided to claim his father's title.

'Yesterday the eldest uncle, the Hon. Edward Russell, 75, former managing editor of the *Morning Post,* said at his home in Washington DC: "We are completely behind John and we are helping him in this struggle."

'Financial backing is also coming from Admiral Sir Guy Russell, 69, chairman of the East Anglian Hospital Authority, and their sister, the Hon. Mrs Phyllis Thorold, an Extra Lady-in-Waiting to the Queen.

'Lord Ampthill never met Geoffrey Russell and the two claimants to the title face each other for the first time in the House of Lords on Monday.'

The correct procedure when a peer dies is that his heir writes a letter to the Clerk of the Crown in Chancery to petition him to ask the Lord Chancellor to request the Crown Office to issue a writ of summons to the House of Lords. Geoffrey had waited a few days before writing to the Clerk. ('It is normally thought to be good manners to wait for a while after your predecessor has died.') The Clerk replied on 8 June 1973.

'Sir,

I have laid your letter of the 7th June before the Lord Chancellor, who directs me to say that he is unable to authorize the issue of a Writ of Summons to enable you to take your seat in the House of Lords. Your proper course in these circumstances is to petition the Crown praying that you may be declared entitled to the Barony of Ampthill and that a Writ of Summons may issue to you. Such a petition requires to be presented to the Home Secretary, who would refer it to the Attorney General for a report on the claim. In the light of the Attorney General's report, and following the usual practices, the petition is referred to the Committee for Privileges to examine all matters relating to the claim and to report accordingly.

'You should be aware that a claim has been made on behalf of the Hon. John Hugo Trenchard Russell, praying that a Writ of Summons may issue to him, and his advisers are likewise being informed that the Lord Chancellor is unable to agree to the issue of the Writ and that their client should proceed in the manner described above.

'I have the honour to be, Sir, Your obedient Servant,
Denis W. Dobson, Clerk of the Crown in Chancery.'

Christabel was travelling across Australia. On 13 June 1973 Geoffrey wrote to her, care of the Manager of the National Bank of Australia:

'You will be astonished to hear that we have trouble on our hands from a small section of my late lamented father's remaining family. The plot is apparently being master-minded by his youngest brother, Leo, and it takes the form of my half-brother John (the 25 year old son of Jack and Adeline, his widow) applying to take his seat in the House of Lords.

'Needless to say, I do not intend to allow your valiant fight of fifty years ago to have been in vain, and I have lined up the best legal advice obtainable. They are most confident that the other side have not got a leg to stand on, but we may need your help.

'We both have dreadful memories, but I do have a very clear recollection that around the time that my father asked you to give him a divorce in 1937 you told me that he had apologised to you for his appalling behaviour throughout the case and admitted that I must be his son. Do you remember this happening and, if so, did he communicate these tidings in writing or verbally?

'It would be enormously helpful if you could cable me urgently with your reply. Please do not fret about the situation for I intend to fight just as hard as you did all those years ago. Every single person who knows either of us is wholeheartedly behind us and feels totally revolted that the issue should once again be raised.

'I do hope all goes well with you. Continue to enjoy yourself hugely, and do not contemplate an earlier return on account of this situation. If it ever does reach the stage of legal proceedings (and we are very confident it will not) that would not be for months.'

'Christabel replied, by aerogramme from Sydney, on 21 June. In the letter scribbled in agitation and blue ink on blue airmail paper, she came as close as she ever did to describing what happened at Oakley House in December 1920.

'My dearest Geoffrey,
All my horror at your letter is beyond all. It is midnight when I write and I came too late for post offices so will rush in the morning and send the cable. Alas I remember nothing about [the questions you ask] not even how I knew (written I am sure as I don't ever remember talking to him). It is the sort of thing ought to stick but I am so hopeless.

'One important [thing] that I never told anyone, being absolutely unable to talk of any of such things and could not get that far on that kind of talk.

'We were (Pa and me, I mean) in a double bed at his family a week or so before Christmas of the year before you were born. Pa for the first time really tried to get at me and managed after a long time to give me what I thought [a] very pleasant sensation. He stopped in what I assumed mid-way and I was disappointed and said "Go on, go on" and he said "It is now, I can't do it again." Why I shall never know. Anyway it was just 9 months from your birth [sic]. How was I not (or did I?) sensible [enough] to tell lawyers, I don't know but all I remember is thinking I could not tell anyone. Probably I did?? If not it is a useful bit perhaps tho' now I'm more ashamed at not having been able to say it than I would have been to do so. How awful being this ghastly thing starting again. I will let you know my get-at-able addresses so I can be all quickly able to come.

'I think I ought to come now. Can you telegraph yes or no as I was about to start arrangements for my long trek by land and I can start at the nearest point of the nice long bit near Australia and get that bit to get to India so hardly any shipping. It will take all a month so this address will get me and I can telephone quite often.

'Oh goodness me. I am in a misery over it. It is too ghastly to think one has to start again.

'Leo was always [a] bad horrid creature. I am too wretched to write sense, but you know I am on the spot if wanted. Get me a room out [at] Wimbledon or any cheap place. I have a feeling that Pa has to pay me all my life.[78] Who would know? I don't even know who my solicitor is.

'Oh hell it is awful for you. All love and to Elisabeth.
    C'

On the advice of his solicitor, Derek Clogg of Theodore Goddard and Company (the firm that had obtained Wallis Simpson's divorce for her in 1936), Geoffrey now wrote to various of his mother's old friends to ask if they had any evidence that the third Lord Ampthill had ever acknowledged that he was his son. On 16 June 1973 Janet Austin, who in 1918 had been Commandant of the British Red Cross Society in Staffordshire, wrote to him from Lichfield:

'I could not stand in a court of law, & declare that I had a recollection of the

l Russell Lᵈ Privy Seale.   with one Eye

Colour plate 1; Hans Holbein the Younger, *John Russell, 1st Earl of Bedford.*
By gracious permission of Her Majesty the Queen.

Colour plate 2; 'Spy' cartoon of the 1st Lord Ampthill, *Vanity Fair*, 28 July 1877.

Colour plate 3; 'Spy' cartoon of the 2nd Lord Ampthill, *Vanity Fair*, 21 March 1891.

Left and above: Colour plates 4, 5 and 6; The 2nd Lord Ampthill claimed he was 'almost ruined' by the costs of the *Russell* v. *Russell* divorce trials; but he still had enough money left over to institute a silver cup and medals for the London Rowing Club in 1930.

Colour plate 7; Sir William Orpen, *Sir Henry Duke (Lord Merrivale)* – who presided over the first *Russell* v. *Russell* divorce trial. *The Benchers of Gray's Inn.*

Colour plate 8; Lady Margaret Ampthill with two of her sons, John Hugo Russell, later 3rd Lord Ampthill (*right*) and Guy Russell.

Colour plate 9; Oakley House, Bedfordshire, where it is assumed the Russell baby was conceived in December 1920.

Colour plate 10; Sir John Lavery's portrait of the 1st Earl of Birkenhead, whose judgement was so critical in winning Christabel her case. *National Portrait Gallery.*

Colour plate 11; Etienne Drian, *Lady Baillie* (centre) *and her two daughters, Susan* (left) *and Pauline, at Leeds Castle, Kent.* The portrait was painted in 1948, two years after Susan's marriage to Geoffrey Russell. *Leeds Castle Foundation.*

Colour plate 12; Leeds Castle, Kent.

Colour plate 13; Christabel's Dunguaire Castle, Kinvarra, Co. Galway, Ireland.

Colour plate 14; Geoffrey's second wife, Elisabeth (*née* Mallon).

Colour plate 15; Geoffrey Ampthill as Lord Chairman of Committees at the House of Lords.

communication to which you refer, but I remember very clearly your mother saying to me on one occasion something – if not exactly – like this: "Everything is settled amicably now & Geoffrey's parenthood established beyond doubt by all concerned." I also understood from what she said, that your father had apologised to her sometime before the Second World War years.'

On 26 June Muriel Malcolm (née Laing) wrote from Duntrune Castle, Lochgilphead, Argyll:

'I well remember your mother saying that she had met your father, when he was wanting a divorce, and he retracted all his accusations, and was friendly. At my age I fear that I cannot give a date, or place of meeting.

'I feel that it is ridiculous to question your birth, this was proved to everyone's satisfaction except your grandmother [Lady Margaret Ampthill], who was at the bottom of all the trouble.'

Geoffrey was also in touch with Eileen Petrovitch (Eileen Hunter), whose book about Christabel was now at the proof stage. On 26 June he wrote to Derek Clogg:

'The two-thirds of the book devoted to the case were culled from the *Times* law reports, so she cannot help us with the official transcript of the evidence. However, she has some photographs of my father which she is bringing to me on Thursday, together with a proof copy of the book. One of the photographs appearing in the book is of my father dressed as a woman, not exactly what we are looking for but it will presumably give the other side a twinge as well!

'She clearly remembers my mother telling her that my father had spoken to her around the time of the divorce [and] ... had apologised and admitted I must be his son.[79] She is willing to swear an affidavit to this effect, but at my mother's request this statement made by my mother is not included in the book. A pity.'

As hearsay evidence, none of the three recollections – Austin's, Malcolm's or Hunter's – would have been admissible in court. One that might have been came in a letter to Geoffrey from Evelyn Whiteside, who had been a buyer at Fortnum & Mason during his years as general manager: 'Your father came into my office at Fortnum's on several occasions and barked at me – "Where is my son?" & I always directed him to your office on the 5th [floor]!' But John Hugo Ampthill had never spoken to his son.

On 27 June, sending Derek Clogg a photostat of his mother's revelatory letter ('together with a transcript to save you going mad trying to decipher her appalling handwriting'), Geoffrey added that he was baffled by something: had not Mr Justice Swift declared, in 1926, that under the Legitimacy Declaration Act he, Geoffrey, was the lawful child of his parents? Was not that declaration binding on the monarch and all persons whatsoever? 'Does this not eliminate Johnny, Leo et al, or am I reading it upside down?' Thus early did Geoffrey identify the most telling objection to John Russell's claim.

On 3 July 1973, Geoffrey wrote to Christabel, who was still in Australia:

'There is not an enormous amount to report to you, for as always when lawyers get their hands on a situation, everything takes an age.

'The procedure seems to be this. Both I and Johnnie the half-brother have to prepare a Petition which goes via the Home Secretary and Attorney General to a body of ageing peers called the Committee for Privileges of the House of Lords. They decide who wins the contest.

'It will take months to prepare the Petition, for Counsel has to wade through every word of the two divorce cases, Court of Appeal and House of Lords of 1921 to 1924, plus the short case in 1926 where the Order was made establishing my legitimacy. It seems that my father and his brothers were prevented by that last 1926 case from ever disputing the matter, but it does not bind Johnnie for he was of course not then born.

'From their reading of the case so far, the lawyers are absolutely astonished that the jury in the second case found you had been up to no good with a gent unknown. Everyone remains completely confident we shall win, and the whole thing is therefore just a tiresome and expensive bore.

'One of the things which will help is the apparently strong resemblance of myself to the gent, plus what is said to be the even stronger resemblance of David. (We are both trying our best not to feel insulted!) We need photographs of the fellow at all possible ages and have raised a few but could do with more. Do you have any ideas? Eileen Petrovitch coughed up a couple (one of dear Pa looking sweet as a female!) ...

'Once again, I urge you not to fret about it and to carry on with your little drive home...'

Geoffrey wrote to Derek Clogg on 10 July: 'I think we have struck oil!' He had been in touch with his first cousin Pauline, a daughter of Christabel's sister Gwen. Pauline was now married to (Sir) John Curle, who had been ambassador to Liberia, Guinea and the Philippines – 'This presumably makes her respectable.' She remembered a meeting between Christabel and the third Lord Ampthill at the time of their divorce. 'She saw and spoke with my father who was being both charming and friendly.' Geoffrey added:

'A further item: Elisabeth sat next to Lord Shackleton at a dinner at the American Embassy last week. We had never met, but he picked me out of forty other men present, without prompting and without difficulty, on the similarity of looks to my father. He asks that we bring in our Petition with all speed so the matter can be resolved before the opening of Parliament so that their Lordships can have something better to stare at on the peeresses' benches whilst awaiting the arrival of the Queen! He is, of course, on the Committee for Privileges.'[80]

On 16 July, Elisabeth was examined by the eminent obstetrician and gynaecologist George Wynn-Williams at his Wimpole Street consulting rooms. Geoffrey wrote to Wynn-Williams that day:

'I was very glad to hear from Elisabeth that you found her in good order when you saw her this morning ...

'She has reported your kind interest in the hoary old problem regarding myself which has once again arisen. It may come to pass that my Counsel, James Miskin,[81] will need the best medical opinion on some of the evidence given nearly fifty years ago: would it be a dreadful imposition to look to you? ...

'The verbatim report of the case runs to over five hundred pages, but about eighty-eight would be relevant. It is not disputed that my parents occupied the same bed on the 18th and 19th of December 1920 and that I emerged on the 15th of October 1921 (300 or 301 days later) weighing $10^1/_2$ lbs., and described as "post-mature", which has not been much said since! What passes way over most of our laymen's heads is the chat about annular distensible hymens, and it is on this aspect we may need help. You may recollect my mother was "intact" when examined five months pregnant, which throws some light on the mythical un-named suitors (the three named co-respondents were dismissed), not to mention the sad state of affairs which existed between my mother and father.

'I do apologise for troubling you with all this, and knowing how grossly overworked you are, I shall fully understand if you want no part of it.'

Wynn-Williams was away on holiday, but after some weeks he replied to Geoffrey:

'Reading through the case that you have sent me, and having had experience of women who have had babies while still remaining a virgin, I do not feel that the circumstances surrounding your birth were impossible, as pregnancy can occur if the semen is deposited around the entrance to the vagina.'

John Russell's petition to the Crown was sent to the Home Secretary (Robert Carr) on 6 August 1973, Geoffrey's on 6 August. By 9 August Geoffrey had seen a copy of John's petition, and wrote an angry letter about it to Derek Clogg, commenting:

'It was not access or non-access that was in question (for it was common ground that my parents slept together on the 18th and 19th of December 1920 when I was conceived), but whether my father's attempts at sexual intercourse could have resulted in my birth. Medical evidence at the time would seem to have proved this conclusively in my mother's favour, whilst that of today would have caused my father to withdraw his Petition.

'I take the greatest possible exception to the allegation that the granting of the Declaration of Legitimacy was obtained by fraud and/or collusion: if there had been such, my father would have been in no way disbarred from an action to upset the High Court's Declaration during his lifetime. Why did he not do so?

'Is it not a principle of English law that it is not retrospective? In any event by the time of the amending legislation of 1949, 1965 and 1973 advances in medical knowledge would, I suggest, have removed all doubt from a jury's mind, and the law regarding legitimacy has not altered anyway, except in phraseology.'

Geoffrey added that his father had acknowledged his paternity on many occasions:

'(i) at the meeting with my mother in 1936, of which we have evidence;

'(ii) to me through his solicitors, Messrs. Taylor and Humbert, in 1952 and 1953 (subsequent to the birth of my half-brother) when he requested, and I acquiesced to, the alteration to the Oakley Settlement [Geoffrey had then agreed to renounce any right to the Oakley properties – but not his inalienable right to the Ampthill title – in exchange for a payment to him of £30,000];

'(iii) on countless separate occasions during his life when he approved the publication by *Debrett, Burke's Peerage, Who's Who, Whitaker, Dod's Parliamentary Companion,* etc. of the statement that I am his son and heir.

'While it may be true that my father did not acknowledge his paternity to his immediate family to avoid the admission of having perjured himself in 1922-26, all other branches of the family have always accepted me as the heir to the barony and will come forward to say so.[82]

'As you observe, I feel deeply incensed that we are being put to this vast amount of trouble and expense due to the vindictive pursuit of a long-ago settled dispute, even though my half-brother and Uncle Leo may be inspired by a misguided sense of loyalty to a dishonest cause ...

'Would you consider the moment opportune to let the other side know that now we are aware of the half-baked nature of their case, we are no longer willing to exercise the restraint we have hitherto shown?'

On the same day, Geoffrey sent Clogg a second letter, containing a titbit of gossip: 'Adeline [Lady Ampthill] is so distressed by and opposed to John's action that there is a break between them.' Clogg replied to both letters on 10 August. He thought that everything Geoffrey had written in the longer letter was perfectly valid. He was very optimistic about the position generally. He began the letter 'Dear Geoffrey' but styled him 'Lord Ampthill' in the formal typed address at the end.

Meanwhile, Geoffrey had written to three of his mother's doctors in Ireland asking whether, in their opinion, she would be capable of giving evidence in court. They all reported that, because of worsening arteriosclerosis, it would be wrong for her to appear. Early in September, at the request of Derek Clogg, he sent six Polyphotos of himself and photographs of his father and his father's brother, Guy Russell, to Jacques Penry, a 'facial topographer', of Pembury, near Tunbridge Wells. Penry sent his report to Messrs Theodore Goddard and Company. He conceded that facial topography was not a subject yet taught in schools or universities, but claimed that his own professional skill had been acquired by a practical, direct and very detailed study of hundreds of thousands of photographs. As a result, he was able to make 'facial links' between generations. He accepted that it might be difficult to prove the validity of his conclusions, but asserted:

'I am confident ... on the basis of a very close scrutiny of all the photographs and newspaper clipping photographs provided me, that the Hon. Geoffrey Russell is, in fact, the son of his father, the late Lord Ampthill ... and, of course, his mother, the Hon. Mrs John Russell.

'The most apparent evidence is:

'(a) The close similarity of the *overall* shapes of the heads of father and son, even if there is an absence of photographs of the father during certain extended periods. There is, however, a good range of photographs of the son from infancy until recent weeks.

'(b) The same type of prominent (protruding) chin; the same approximate height and slope of forehead from brows to normal hairline and the type of hairline (at top and top-sides of forehead); the same definition of the central part of the upper lip which in both subjects is particularly revealed when smiling.

'(c) *Important:* the very close overall resemblance between the son and his uncle, Mr Guy Russell (obvious in the clipping-photograph of the latter with Field-Marshal Lord Gort) ... This resemblance is more marked than that of father and son and shows the lineage continuity ...

'(d) *More important:* the apparent defect in the left eye of both father and son ... It would seem that under emotional or other stimulus the father's left eye was subject to squinting. In the case of your client, I first noticed this same defect when I met him in your office recently ... Your client's right eye seems to "wander" occasionally, and in my estimation this is undoubtedly an hereditary eye-peculiarity.

'(e) *Equally important:* the ear configuration of both subjects. The shape of the ear remains constant throughout life, having assumed its permanent pattern before birth. It is unique to every individual and, like the fingerprint, does not repeat itself in every particularity. However, a *general* pattern of ear can constitute part of a family's facial "imprint". I have made several sketches highlighting points of your client's and his father's ears for your scrutiny, and you will note the similarity of overall pattern ...'

Derek Clogg warned Geoffrey that John Russell and his advisers were probably going to demand blood tests: they had secured a sample of the late Lord Ampthill's blood before he died. Ideally, samples of Geoffrey's blood and of Christabel's should be obtained. Geoffrey, though angered by this development, was quite prepared to supply a sample of his own blood. Christabel was still on her travels, and a game of Hunt the Baroness began. On 27 September 1973 Geoffrey wrote to Clogg:

'Her ladyship proceeds at a furious pace: our man in Lahore was unable to do much more than wave as she sped through, but has reported to the Foreign Office that she is in excellent health and spirits ...

'She is due in Kabul tonight and the Consul there is going to try and induce her to call me. But that does not sound like a very good place for blood-letting, so I fear we will have to wait and intercept her in Tehran 1,500 miles on.'

On 10 October Geoffrey wrote to Sir Peter Ramsbotham, the British ambassador in Tehran:

'I hate to trouble you with a personal problem at this anxious time, but I urgently need to communicate with my eccentric mother, Christabel, who is due any day in Tehran.

'The old lady is driving herself alone back to London from Australia, and cabled yesterday from Herat in Afghanistan asking for mail to be sent to your embassy. She has so far eluded the traps we laid for her in Madras, Delhi, Lahore and Kabul, and it has become vital to contact her in connection with litigation following the death of my father in June.

'Could you be very kind and instruct your staff to watch out for her and ask her to telephone me? ...'

The letter Geoffrey sent for Christabel to collect in Tehran asked if she would be willing to 'shed a small test tube' of blood in a Tehran hospital.

'The only other item is that Eileen [Hunter]'s book is out. It is just as dreadful as we all expected it would be, for the lady really cannot write to save her life. I will bung off a copy to you ... Meanwhile I enclose an amusing notice of it by Michael Foot – much too good for the book, but great fun about you!'

In his *Evening Standard* review of 20 September, Foot had joshingly suggested 'the British aristocracy is not what it was', since it no longer provided spicy cases like the Russell Baby affair to entertain the lower orders. Christabel, he wrote, 'was a woman of tremendous spirit and independence. She was not to be done down by the spiteful, effete Russells ...' Frank Giles, in *The Sunday Times*, wrote that the book had 'all the ingredients of a goings-on-in-high-places story'. In the *Sunday Telegraph*, John Foster (who was to become Geoffrey's counsel in the battle with John Russell) said the book was written with good taste, but that Eileen Hunter was no lawyer. The Earl of Arran ('Boofy') had a column in the *Evening News* headed 'LORD ARRAN WRITES'. (*'Mirabile dictu!'* somebody once scrawled across a Garrick Club copy.) He said:

'The "Russell Baby" case was the scandal of my youth. Little else was talked about.

'Of course times have changed. Now, although it hits the headlines, we regard it as a period piece.

'But in the twenties things were different. Then there was a clear difference between what was acceptable and what was not. Now, no longer.

'For instance, divorce was looked on with a jaundiced eye. Illegitimacy was seldom or never referred to, though rumours were rife.

'One knew, or was to believe, that so-and-so was not his father's child. My great-grandmother, Lady Palmerston, had five children by her first husband, Lord Cowper. It was said that only one of them was legitimate.

'It was customary, when a wife had a lover, for her to go to bed with her husband as well, so no one could say with certainty that a child was not the husband's.

'(Those, of course, were the days before the Pill was invented.)'

In the agenda for a conference between Geoffrey and his solicitors on 4 December 1973, it was noted that 'The blood sample for genetic analysis was taken from the late Lord A without his knowledge or consent.' Derek Clogg returned to the charge on this in a letter to John Russell's solicitors, Warmington & Hasties: 'If you had conducted the blood tests properly, this would of course have been an admirable way to short-cut proceedings; but you did not.' Clogg also pointed out that at the time the sample was taken from Lord Arnpthill, he had received blood transfusions, which could have adulterated the sample.

In March 1974, national politics had an effect on Geoffrey's case. The previous December Edward Heath had introduced the 'three-day week' to deal with what Anthony Barber, the Chancellor of the Exchequer, called 'the gravest situation by far since the end of the war'. Heath was waging a battle with the miners, which he lost. He was forced to call a General Election, which he also lost. On 6 March Labour was back in government, with Harold Wilson in his third term as prime minister. Geoffrey Ampthill recalled how the change of government affected him.

'In 1973 the Home Office referred my Petition to the Attorney General, who was Peter Rawlinson, now Lord Rawlinson, who happened to have been in my regiment during the war. And he was willing to carry that on, but he approached "the other side" to come clean that we had been in the same regiment, though we had not actually served in the same battalion for more than a momentary period. It was all right: Johnnie's side agreed that he could do whatever the Attorney General does. He was poised to get on with that and to reach his view of the matter when the Tory Government fell. He was replaced by a Labour Attorney General, Mr [Samuel] Silkin. Mr Silkin was in *no* way interested in dealing with an age-old peerage case. He therefore did nothing about it at all. I think a year passed before the Solicitor General, Peter Archer – now Lord Archer (not to be confused with anybody else of that name) – said, "You can't leave this fellow swinging in the wind like this for ever. Would you like me to take it over instead?" And Silkin said, "Yes, by all means!" And so Peter Archer got on with it – he received the petitions from both parties and then summoned both parties – separately – to a hearing. And in due course he wrote a report, which concluded with words to this effect: "Without doubt, Geoffrey should be the next Lord Ampthill." But he also concluded that, as the original case had been finally resolved in the House of Lords, it was probably right that the matter should be left to them, to make the final decision. It would be heard by the Committee for Privileges, which consisted of four law lords and five lay peers.'

In April 1974 Philip Howard of *The Times* wrote to both Geoffrey's solicitors and to John's, saying that he was preparing an article about the disputed succession to the Ampthill barony, and asking for their help. 'I am aware that the matter is *sub judice*,' he wrote. 'I therefore do not want to discuss the merits of the case, solely the law and the facts.' The two solicitors consulted each other about the approach. For once they were agreed: they would not assist Howard in any way. He still wrote an article. It appeared on the front page of *The Times* on 27 April 1974. He was (and still is) one of the paper's star writers. While perhaps his forte is humorous writing, he was the reporter chosen to cover Sir Winston Churchill's funeral in 1965, and was later literary editor. The headline to his piece was 'Succession to Ampthill barony revives sensational legal case of 1920s'. Howard rehearsed the history of the 1920s cases, which he had scrupulously researched. His piece ended: 'If the Attorney General decides to refer the Ampthill affair to the Committee for Privileges, the hearing is not expected to take place much before the end of the year.'

Geoffrey was indignant, not so much at the content of the article as at its timing. Howard (as journalists do, to scoop their rivals) had jumped the gun. On 29 April Geoffrey wrote a pained letter to the Editor.

'Dear Mr Rees-Mogg,
I assume that someone else was minding the store on Friday evening, for a certain imbalance was apparent on Saturday. Relegated to page 5 was the coup d'état in Portugal, to page 6 the Presidential election in France and the turmoil in the Middle East, whilst on the front page, to compete with the greatest robbery of works of art in history,[83]was an untimely piece on that ageing Russell Baby.

'Over the weekend, between visits and telephone calls from your contemporaries, I have contemplated trying to get you a wigging from the Press Council, or instructing my solicitors to issue a writ. But Fleet Street is presently clogged with the latter, and I gather from the chap from the *Sunday Express* that his editor positively revels in such admonitions, even when delivered at the Bar of the House.

'I say your report was untimely because last June it had been fully reported that my half-brother, for reasons still totally obscure, was proposing to dispute my succession. Whilst a great deal has transpired since then in the nature of Petitions to the Queen, memoranda to the Attorney General and a stupefying quantity of correspondence between our respective solicitors and with the Treasury Solicitor, no particular event has occurred which warrants Mr Philip Howard's report of last Saturday. It seems to me that there was no justifiable occasion for dragging up all that lurid but ancient history.

'Mr Howard makes the good point that some general benefit arose from this saga in that thereafter the reporting of evidence in divorce cases was forbidden. I hate to raise the cry of "unfair" but, having made that contribution, it does seem to me that an element of restraint might be exercised in reporting any present events which qualify as of interest to the public. Inevitably, even when the admirable Mr Howard attempts to pot into a couple of paragraphs the essence of the four cases in 1922 and 1923 (of which the verbatim reports run to nearly two thousand pages), a wrong impression can be given. What causes unnecessary distress (to my mother in particular, bothered enough to have to rehash the events of fifty years ago at the age of seventy-eight, and to my children, one of them still at school with all that that implies) is the endless repetition of the unhappy sexual relationship between my parents. Could you not call a halt, at least on that aspect?'

Philip Howard's sources were optimistic in suggesting that the Committee for Privileges hearings would begin by the end of 1974. They did not begin until 23 February 1976. Exactly a week before that day, Christabel died in a Galway hospital. In April 1975 Geoffrey had written to Derek Clogg that the strain of the long-drawn-out proceedings was 'unquestionably hastening my mother's complete mental breakdown'. He now received a letter of sympathy from his father's third wife. Adeline: 'From all accounts I have read in the newspapers she must have been a splendid mother to you and I am sure you were a splendid son to her. I feel so sorry for you in your grief.'

Geoffrey replied: 'I was very touched by your kind letter of sympathy on my mother's death. It was generous of you to write, and I appreciate it very much.

'She was a most remarkable lady who gave much joy to everyone, except of course my father in their pathetically unhappy marriage. From the time I was a child when speaking of him she always shouldered the burden of having caused him so much unhappiness and she was greatly relieved when much of the bitterness was dispelled at their meetings in the thirties.

'You will understand how deeply upset I am that she did not live to see the outcome of this ridiculous re-opening of the saga which Johnnie has been misguided enough to embark upon. I like to think it was not really his idea that has caused such infinite distress to my mother, my wife and my children.'

17

The Life of Christabel

I think it might be a good thing for the world to know that I have not one
backward look that saddens or distresses me – I've loved every hour from one
day old to seventy-eight.

CHRISTABEL, LADY AMPTHILL TO EILEEN HUNTER, 1973

Trying her hand as a novelist and a film star after the brouhaha of the trials,
Christabel had realized that neither activity was going to make her fortune. So she
continued with the dress shop, taking time off to dance, hunt and socialize. When
John Hugo's father died, in 1935, she became Lady Ampthill. In 1933 – eleven
years after her husband had petitioned for divorce – she had petitioned for
Restitution of Conjugal Rights.[84] Dr Stephen Cretney writes: 'It seems improbable
that she actually wished him to return to her, but had the husband refused to do so
the court would have had power to make enhanced financial orders.' In fact, the
Restitution petition was withdrawn after Christabel and John Hugo had agreed
terms for a separation agreement. In 1935 Christabel petitioned for divorce on the
ground of her husband's adultery, committed with a woman named Doris Jones at
a London hotel four years earlier. However, she did not apply for that decree to be
made absolute (thereby freeing John Hugo to remarry) until January 1937.[85] Dr
Cretney suggests that Christabel may have been playing her cards cleverly.

'One explanation for the delay on the wife's part (both in petitioning and then
in applying for the decree to be made absolute) could be that he was anxious to
remarry whereas wife refused to allow him to do so unless and until he had made
the financial arrangements which she regarded as appropriate. But there is no
evidence that this is what actually happened.'

In the 1930s, Christabel and Geoffrey went on some holidays together.

'In 1936, when I was fifteen [Geoffrey recalled], we travelled to Marrakesh in
Morocco – the country was still governed by the French. We met the ADC to the
Governor, and Chris asked him, "How can we get over the Atlas Mountains?" He
said we would need half a dozen mules and five chaps. I had a revolver – there were
brigands up there. It was April, but at the very top, on the last day, we found snow.
A mule broke its leg. I handed the revolver to one of the men, who finished it off.
On some of the narrow pathways there was a drop of two thousand feet.

'Two years running, Chris and I stayed with people in Hungary. We shot partridges and coursed hares on horses.'

The London shop was doing well. In 1942 Elizabeth Jane Howard married the naturalist-artist Peter Scott (*Plate 16*). She writes: 'My mother concerned herself with my clothes and took me to Curzon Street, where Chris Ampthill designed and made my wedding-dress of off-ration white lace, a soft turquoise dress and short-sleeved jacket to match, and two pinafore dresses, one of blue linen and the other of a pretty flecked tweed. Underclothes had to be made of parachute silk and curtain netting.'

By the late 1940s, Christabel had made enough money to buy a house in the country, Chelsbourne, near the village of Brook in Sussex. Somebody who knew her then was the future debutante Anne Hopkinson (now Mrs Minoprio). Her parents, the barrister Francis Hopkinson and his wife Ursula, lived in Cheyne Gardens, London, after having spent the war in Denham.

'Christabel used to come to dinner, arriving on her bicycle, carrying her sidesaddle on the handlebars because she'd been hunting with the Beaufort one day and was hunting in Leicestershire the next day. She wore specially designed clothes made by her own company, which were Bermuda shorts with a skirt over the top – a flap in front and a flap behind – so that she could bicycle and equally go out to dinner wearing the same clothes.

'She said to my parents one evening in London, "I've found the perfect house for you. It's only a few miles from Brook and it's a ruin up on the North Downs." My mother was not frightfully keen on the whole idea; but off they went and they were taken to this ruin called Dundas Farm, which had twenty acres. They paid less than £1,100 for it. Christabel said: "That's the perfect house for you." She didn't do it up for them. They didn't like her taste. I remember the taste of her house at Brook vividly. I loved her house there, it had this charming little stream running past it; but it was very "Ye Olde Worlde Beamy Housey". She'd done quite clever things. There were funny cupboards that looked like rabbit hutches. I remember my mother being rather dismissive of them. But anyway, my parents moved into Dundas Farm once it was renovated. And my father became an apple farmer.'

Born in 1936, Anne had been a wartime child in Denham – 'and nothing much ever happened, except that John Mills once climbed trees with us'. With Christabel as a near neighbour, life brightened up.

'She said, "I will teach you to ride sidesaddle on one of my horses." Her horses were pretty serious stuff. She had uncontrollable horses that various quite grand gentlemen couldn't handle – she told them, "I'll deal with your horses." I was a child who couldn't really ride, I merely had a romantic idea about riding sidesaddle, like the heroine of a Georgette Heyer novel. I've never been more terrified in my life. I was plonked on her sidesaddle and the very powerful horse would take off – petrifying! But the great thing about Christabel was that she had total control over men and horses. You know, she said "Do this" and the horse did that or the man did that, and that was that.'

When Christabel and Anne came back to Chelsbourne after riding, they would swim in the pool in her garden. 'And for Christabel there was only one way to swim, and that was nude. I can remember it being a great shock to me because I wasn't used to swimming at all, let alone nude. And one wasn't used to seeing somebody of that age in the nude. The local bus was a double-decker and one of the entertainments was to drive past her house and see her ladyship swimming starkers.'

One day Anne and her mother were invited to lunch at Chelsbourne. Christabel asked them to arrive early, at eleven o'clock.

'She said, "Oh, Ursula, I've got to go and exercise my hunter. Could you look after my Jewish tailor who's coming down from the East End to lunch?" Then she suddenly turned round and said, "Her Grace hasn't come down yet." A duchess was upstairs, it may have been the Duchess of Newcastle. So my poor mother was landed with the situation of two people she had never met – the tailor and the duchess – who had to be entertained until Christabel came back at lunchtime. That was absolutely typical.'

Christabel's great-niece, Philippa Roberts (now Mrs Enderby), also remembers visits to Chelsbourne.

'She was wonderful with us children. She used to make up games for us and we used to have blue or orange plastic (or whatever the equivalent was then) fish, which we used to race down the stream. Also, she had a sort of jumping-ring for her horses and we used to run round and do the jumping instead of the horses. My memory is of sun and lots of fun for the children. She would take us out on the Downs and put us on tin trays, and down we'd go, bumping down on the trays. And she had the most lovely car, a Lee-Francis, which she called "the Whizzer". We all used to crowd into that and go to the top of a hill and rush down the other side. She did everything of which parents would say, "Oh, no, you mustn't do that" – everything that would be castigated as dangerous, playing by water, going fast in the car, all the things children love doing.'

Philippa's father was drowned in a sailing accident in 1947. In 1948 her mother was remarried to the diplomat (Sir) John Curle.

'Chris came to stay at their home, Appletree House in Northamptonshire. There was great excitement at her tremendously lavish arrival; and she handed out to each of us a fiver – an enormous amount of money to a child then. In the early 1950s she came to hunt with the Bicester, and I hunted with the Bicester as a child. I mean, as a nine-year-old I went out every Saturday; and I remember being immensely embarrassed by her because she went like the devil, but she also fell in water like the devil. People would say, "What is your aunt doing *today*?" Like all children I was a conformist, and I hoped she wouldn't be anywhere near me.'

Christabel's grandchildren – Geoffrey's children – saw most of her at Egerton Terrace in the 1950s when she took a flat at Carrington House, off Curzon Street. David recalls:

'One day she came to lunch – we boys were sort of eight, nine, ten – and we were going to Battersea Funfair that afternoon. We had lunch and then she said, "Excuse me, you go on in the other car; I've just got to go back home, I forgot to put my knickers on." And so she went back to Carrington House and duly equipped herself and then enjoyed Battersea Park – of course, she *immediately* got us all on to the Big Dipper.'

When the children were at their home, she kept them amused with the aid of a telephone directory.

'This is when we were sub-teenagers [David recalls]. She had a particular line in infuriating people. She'd ring somebody up – name picked at random – and announce that it was the Campden Hill Pet Shop and that the pair of gorillas which they had ordered would be coming round later that afternoon – or it might be an anaconda, anything that anybody would not want. To the delight of us children.'

In the Fifties, Christabel was still in demand on the social scene. Anne Minoprio remembers:

'I was at Rona McCorquodale's coming-out dance at Badminton in 1954. I was sitting at the same table as Christabel and two men. One was Peter Whiteley, who married [the Earl of] Guilford's sister. I forget who the other was – but both men agreed that if Christabel said, "Jump out of that window," they would jump.'

Colin Alexander, who was a pupil at Stowe in the 1950s (today he is an esteemed Canadian poet) met Christabel at a tea-party held by Bill and Patience McElwee. He thought her stunningly beautiful. His mother was fascinated to learn that he had met the Russell Baby's mother and asked him how old he thought she was.

'Oh, about forty.'

'She's well over sixty!'

In 1957 Christabel emigrated to Ireland. She thought the hunting there would be more exhilarating and the living cheaper. At first she lived in County Meath and was briefly Master of the Ballymacaid Hunt. The she moved westward to Dunguaire Castle (pronounced 'Dungora') in County Galway, a romantic tower near Kinvarra on Aughnish Bay, an inlet of Galway Bay. Built by the Hynes clan in 1520, the castle stands on the site of the palace of King Guaire Aidhne the Hospitable, who ruled Connaught in the seventh century. Like most historic places in Ireland, it has a preposterous legend attached to it – in this case, that of the Road of the Dishes, which tells of the magical transportation of dishes laden with food from the King's table to the hermit St Colman macDuagh, the Irish monk who became bishop of Lindisfarne. During the seventeenth century the castle passed to Richard Martyn, Mayor of Galway. In 1912, Edward Martyn, a founder of the Irish Literary Renaissance Society and the Abbey Theatre, sold the castle to his friend and fellow writer Oliver St John Gogarty. The literary revivalists – among them W.B. Yeats, Lady Gregory of Coole Park, George Bernard Shaw and J.M. Synge – often met there. Christabel bought it from St John Gogarty, who died in 1957. He had begun restoration work. She completed it in a way that somehow married harmoniously near-medievalism and the 'Contemp'ry' style of the 1950s.

David, who was a good rider, was her favourite visitor. He recalls:

'Several times she met me in Dublin, where she must have been on business of some sort; and more than once I remember driving the car for her, at the age of fourteen or fifteen, across Ireland. In those days she had an old Volkswagen which she thought was the best thing for pulling horse boxes.

'She would sit in the driving seat and put the machine into gear; and I would sit on a cushion on top of the brake between the seats. She would start the car off and get it into third or fourth gear and then go to sleep, and I would steer the thing from Dublin to Galway. We'd potter across at a steady forty-five miles an hour. There were only about two corners between Dublin and Galway, and you'd probably meet no more than three or four other vehicles. The greatest hazard would be wandering cattle or sheep on the road. It was the best part of a hundred miles. I used to love doing that – steering it while she slept.'

The boys would usually stay for about eight days. They came home 'wrung out': life with Christabel was something of a commando course.

'We would get up at eight and have breakfast. Then she would put us in our hunting stocks – tie the damn things properly with about eight large safety-pins. Very constricting: it had to be tied tightly to stop you breaking your neck. And then, off we'd go; and whereas they meet in England at quarter to eleven or something, it was rather later there – they didn't hunt for so long. She could be critical of one's riding. If you didn't make a horse walk out she'd give you a rap on the shoulder with her stick. She always rode on a very long rein that made every horse immediately behave itself.'

David confirms what Anne Minoprio said. 'Always in England', he recalled, 'she would get free hunting because people would put her on the most difficult horses and she would teach them manners. Not by beating them about, but by telling them not to be so silly.'

Not far from Dunguaire was the medieval walled town of Athenry (pronounced 'Athen-*rye*'), founded by Melier de Bermingham who built his castle by the Clareen River in 1235. In Athenry Willie Leahy had his stables: Christabel hired horses for the boys from him, or from Commandant Lundun in Kilcolgan, County Galway, though he used to retire to bed for the winter, only getting up for funerals. The packs the Russell family turned out with were the Galway Blazers, the Stonehall Harriers down in Limerick, and the County Clare. 'The County Clare was a harrier pack,' David says. 'They didn't mind what they chased – it could be a fox or could be a cat – all round the "runaways" as they called the runways of Shannon Airport (rather as the Irish say "fillum" for film).' Lady Cusack Smith had her own private pack, the Bermingham and North Galway, which hunted on Sundays, making it possible for Christabel to hunt seven days a week. At that stage Lady Cusack Smith did not go out herself. Among those who did ride with Christabel and the Russells was the American-born Lady Hemphill (the subject of John Betjeman's poem 'Ireland with Emily').

Anthony Russell, five years younger than James, came to Dungaire in the

Sixties and wrote an account of the visit, headed 'Terror at the Gallop'.

'David, James and I were going hunting and I was deeply troubled. Almost everything about the trip displeased me ... For a whole week it would be just Granny A, the boys and me. Nanny wasn't coming. Granny said she didn't need Nanny and what Granny said Granny got.

'I had mixed feelings about Granny A. We hardly ever saw her because she was always travelling or hunting or both. But when she did enter our lives, she blew in like a hurricane and engulfed the household for however long she was around in a Blitzkrieg of non-stop activity. Walks, games, come here, go there, do this, do that. It took everyone at least a week to recover after she left ...

'Granny A was a terror but she loved us and this was her way of expressing it. "After all, my darlings," she would say, "you don't get to see me that often."

'I hadn't been to Ireland before, so that and staying in Granny's castle seemed like fun, but I was yet to be convinced about the hunting. David and James had gone the year before and said it was great, but they were much older than me.

'To bring my riding up to a standard where I'd be capable of handling a day or two out with the Galway Blazers – just the thought of it made my head spin – I attended Colonel Hislop's riding school near us in Kent once a week all summer. By the end, the Colonel, a large, friendly man with a huge moustache and a firm manner, had me clearing jumps which looked as high as my pony's head and cruising round the cross-country course with confidence and, dare I say it, just a hint of style. He told me I'd be fine, especially if I kept myself at a sensible distance from the gentlemen who drank more than one glass of port before the off.'

Suzy drove the boys to London Airport in her new Jaguar on a cold, rainy January day. After she had kissed them goodbye, they flew to Shannon in a Viscount plane, a comfortable craft whose four large propellers made a tremendous din. (James flirted with the air hostesses and got their telephone numbers.) Christabel was at the airport to meet them.

' "Over here, boys, over here," her melodious yet firm voice rang out across the reception area.

'She need not have spoken. Granny stood out wherever she was ... [She was] dressed in a long flowing gabardine skirt, dress shirt, waistcoat, tweed jacket, hat, veil and shiny black boots. The crowd waiting to meet their friends and family parted like the Red Sea for Moses as she strode towards us with a huge smile on her face.

' "How are you?" she enquired (strong emphasis on the "are"), ignoring the formality of kissing but hugging us all powerfully from a great height and pounding on our backs with enthusiasm.

'The greeting over, she summoned porters with a wave of her riding crop as she sailed off towards the luggage conveyor belt, assuming, quite rightly, that we'd follow.

'It was just a few moments before our suitcases appeared, one after the other. Granny instructed our bemused porter how to load his trolley and then, as we headed for the car, exhorted the poor fellow to walk quicker, walk slower and heaven knows what else. Conversation was sparse because Granny seemed intent on conducting our exit from the airport as if it were a military exercise.

' "Left here, right here, mind that dog, follow me, catch up!"

Christabel's Volkswagen Beetle was outside. 'I wondered if the four of us plus the luggage could fit in. David and James thought so. Granny knew so.' The journey to Dunguaire Castle took just over an hour. The battlements reminded James of the crossbow shoot-outs in his favourite television programme, *William Tell*. After carrying his suitcase up the stairs to the top of the castle, he felt 'like I'd just conquered the leaning Tower of Pisa – straightened'. His grandmother said, 'Oh, there you are. What took you so long?' She then left the boys upstairs while she went down to prepare high tea. Anthony wondered why she, 'a massive devotee of the great outdoors if ever I knew one, should wish to have her castle sealed up like an Egyptian tomb'. He adds:

'I was having a quick puff of James's cigarette when Granny's voice echoed from below.'

' "I can smell that."

'Seconds later she marched into the room. "How dare you smoke in my house." I'd never seen anyone look so angry and talk so quietly at the same time. She took the cigarette from James, walked into the bathroom and flushed it down the loo. "Don't ever let me catch you smoking again," she said and left, leaving the three of us speechless and staring at our feet.'

Downstairs, later, they were given a slap-up meal. Christabel's anger had evaporated. 'Granny could be as funny as anybody I knew and this night she was in full flow. By nine-thirty I could stay awake no longer and was allowed to skip clear-up duties and go to bed. Tomorrow we were getting to know our horses, and the day after was the hunt.'

At the meet, he found he was improperly dressed and that his pony and he were half the size of everybody else. Fifty or sixty ladies and gentlemen were on horseback and perhaps fifty more on foot. Most of them were knocking back glasses of port: Anthony thought it would be hard to follow Colonel Hislop's advice to stay clear of the heavy drinkers. He felt he needed some port, but 'with Granny on patrol' there was no chance of that.

' "Never overtake the Master; it simply isn't done," Granny reminded me.

' "Stay close to me," she went on, "and don't forget, give your pony his head."

'This sounded like, "If in doubt take your hands off the wheel.", but I nodded and promised to heed her advice as best I could.

'If I had been a soldier in the trenches during World War I, I imagined this is how I would have felt right before "going over the top". And I was meant to be having fun ....

'As we clop-clopped our way down a narrow country lane lined by hedgerow, I noticed my pony's behaviour had taken on a rather authoritarian air, completely absent up till now. I wasn't sure if this was a good thing or not. His whole demeanour seemed more alert, aggressive even ...'

A mighty howl went up from the hounds. The Master's horn sounded. The riders began to gallop. Anthony cleared two walls and a stream. Nearing the front of the field, he rode close to his grandmother. 'She looked stunning galloping sidesaddle with breathtaking skill, her face beneath her veil and black top hat a vision of unbridled joy and determination.' Then Anthony fell – over his pony's head and hard on to the grass. Horses thundered by. He felt battered but not in pain. Somebody retrieved his pony. He caught up with the hunt an hour and a half later; but when a pub came into view, the chance of having an iced Coca-Cola was irresistible. He does not record whether Christabel later commented on his performance; but his account is the most vivid vignette we have of her, doing what she did best and enjoyed most. Geoffrey's experience of fox-hunting with his mother, thirty years earlier, must have been very similar.

Anthony wrote, and in 2003 recorded, a roistering pop song about fox-hunting with Granny A – 'The Ultimate Ride'. Part of the lyric, in which Colonel Hislop is demoted to a Major, runs:

'This is the ultimate ride
We rock the Irish countryside
The fox is running for his life
And Granny A is out-a-site!
This is my one and only plan
Stay on the pony if you can
Soak up the beauty of the land
And pray the Lord's a hunting man!
Hunt yearning now unfurling right before my eyes
Under dark and threatening skies
The meet gets high
Mid-morning gets me thinking what's my line?
Will I end up ditched and dying before my time?
I'm just eleven; from seven the Major taught me well
I'm gonna jump those walls and maybe if I fall
Someone'll prise me from my shell
Squeeze me please me let me be a man
If I should need a hand I'm sure an Irishman will be glad...
This is the ultimate ride
This is the ultimate ride
This is the ultimate ride.'

Christabel organised paperchases for Kinvarra children; but otherwise 'there wasn't much interface with the locals', David remembers. But Christabel did take him to dinner with the film director John Huston and his daughter Anjelica, at St Clerans, a Georgian mansion near Galway. Anjelica was a year older than Anthony Russell.

'I was born in 1951 [she recalls] when my father was making *African Queen* in the Belgian Congo. Then he went to France to work on *Moulin Rouge*. While he was in France, he was invited to Ireland to go fox-hunting. He fell in love with it and decided it was where he wanted to live and bring up his family. For two years we lived in County Kildare: that was his base while he and my mother searched the counties. They found St Clerans about 1953-4. My father became an avid member of the Galway Blazers and became Joint Master of it with Paddy Pickersgill.'

Anjelica Huston rode and hunted with Christabel. She recalls her with affection.

'Her presence in my memory is of an individual so brilliantly composed as to make me feel sometimes that she is almost a figment of my imagination. I first saw her at a meet, riding to hounds with the Galway Blazers. I must have been five or six at the time, and she must have been in her sixties. An imposing figure, she was the only woman in the Blazers to ride sidesaddle. And she was immaculately turned out with the white collar of the hunt members and beautifully pinned stock, the gleaming ebony toe of one Maxwell boot with shining silver spur at the heel peeping from the hem of her blue serge habit.

'She wore a tall beaver top hat, over an impeccably coiffed bun. Two white stripes of hair ran from her temples to the nape of her neck pinned under a hairnet. She spoke in fine imperial tones. And everyone was respectful to her almost to the point of seeming fearful. She was serenely intrepid and galloped over five-foot double stone walls with the ease of someone on a yachting holiday. Later on, I became the second woman to hunt with the Blazers wearing a riding habit, entirely because of her influence on me, though I never reached the pinnacle of elegance that she alone could project on a hunting field.

'I never saw her fall. And as that is a particularly dangerous thing to do when riding sidesaddle, the hunt members were terrified about the inevitable. One day it happened that she did come loose – after taking a ditch, her foot caught in the stirrup, her habit tangled in the saddle, her long hair came loose and was whipping about her thoroughbred's hocks, when, some few yards before taking off over a gruesome wall that undoubtedly would have killed her, her passage was narrowly intercepted. From her dangling position under the horse's belly, she proclaimed to her rescuer: "*I suppose I should thank you, but oh, what a wonderful way to die!*" '

Christabel befriended Anjelica, inviting her to tea at Dunguaire.

'It stood alone surrounded by swans gliding through the water. It was the most romantic setting I have ever seen. Lady Ampthill saved many old foxhounds from being destroyed and there were always several around. Smelly, aged beasts that she doctored up and doted upon.

'I think one reason she liked children (well, most of us) is that they didn't hold her in reverence; they answered her back, tit for tat. One's initial impression of her might be: very imperious and rather frightening. She spoke in the slow, emphatic English of the Anglo upper class. Her stature, the way she held herself, was something from the eighteenth century. It led to the idea that she was aloof; but she wasn't, she was *sweet*. She was very welcoming. I remember that when she asked if

I'd like to come over, it was very one-on-one – she didn't say, "Could so-and-so bring you over?"

'She was my inspiration to ride sidesaddle. My relationship with my father was very difficult, but I *almost* regained his respect with my sidesaddle riding. And when I was in the film of Evelyn Waugh's *A Handful of Dust*, I based my character on Christabel.'

The best friends of both Anjelica and the Russells in Galway were the King family, then living at The Cottage, Oranmore. 'Commander Bill King was a wonderful man,' Anjelica says. 'He had been a hero in the war, a submarine commander – a very small, bird-like man. His wife was the writer Anita Leslie, daughter of Sir Shane Leslie, who was a cousin of Winston Churchill. She was fabulous, too. Their children, Leonie and Tarka, were my sort of age. Leonie married Alec Finn and they live at Oranmore Castle.' Leonie remembers:

'My mother loved Christabel, but my father hated her, as she usually required some long-drawn-out errand to be performed. And – for no reason that anybody could ever work out – Christabel took a great dislike to me. She came to the house and said (I was about six): "You nasty nasty nasty girl, where is that delightful brother of yours?" She used to take him camping, but never took me.'

Tarka King confirms that.

'For some unknown reason she hated Leonie and would sometimes give me money in front of her, saying: "Here is half-a-crown for you (pressing the silver into my hand) but nothing for *you*" – looking directly at her. To this day I don't know why!

'It must have been around 1957 when Christabel appeared in the west of Ireland driving a Dormobile camper van. It had two bunk beds and a roof that folded upwards. She would sometimes pick me up after school on a Friday and we would drive off into the wilds of County Clare for the next two days. None of the roads was tarmacked then and the going could be quite rough. She was looking for a property to buy and restore and we spent a lot of time fighting brambles and jungle surrounding fifteenth-century Norman keeps along the coast. Once she fell down a well and, in the struggle to get her out – we were entirely alone – suffered quite bad grazing from briars and stone to her knees, arms and face. That night she had a cramp in her neck and I had to massage it for a long time. It was the first session of many but I never went below her rib cage and it was all entirely innocent ... I think the gear lever was difficult for her to move, which is why she suffered the neck cramps.'

Christabel needed Tarka to communicate with the locals as they were mostly very much off the beaten track and she could not understand a word anybody said. He was attending the local national school at the time and was being taught Irish, and also spoke with a strong brogue.

'Once the van became bogged near an old castle along the north Clare coast from Ballyvaughan and I had to go for help. An old boy with two horses was ploughing nearby and came to the rescue. He took a strong shine to Christabel (she was still a very handsome woman then) and hung around until late when we made camp further along the track. It was the week after the well incident and her face was still quite scratched. The next morning, when Christabel and I were still in pyjamas, the man's wife turned up in a storm and accused Christabel of bewitching her husband – putting a "hex" on him. Through her five teeth, sticking out in different directions, she said he had come home the previous evening in an altered state of mind and was not the same man – I was having to translate all this for Christabel. Later a priest turned up and grilled me as to who we were and what we were doing. There was a gap in the camping expeditions after that.'

Tarka's last contact with Christabel was out fox-hunting some years later.

'Hounds were hunting and there was a check amongst the rocky ruins of an old demesne. A late arrival, a Frenchman on a grey hireling, was galloping to catch us up and could not stop his horse when it reached us, a group of stationary riders, one of whom was Christabel riding sidesaddle. His horse piled into the group at high speed and Christabel was knocked off her mount on the off-side, landing headfirst on a flat boulder. Her veil and top hat had come off and her skull had made direct contact with the stone – shattering.

'I dismounted with a couple of others and we picked her up and carried her across the fields to a road. At one point we had to pass her unconscious body through a hole in the old demesne wall and shards of broken skull could be clearly seen sticking out of her blood-soaked hair. I ran ahead to the road and waved down a passing car that fortunately turned out to be an estate. She was bundled into the back and the driver roared off to Galway Hospital. I missed it, but apparently she appeared out hunting eight weeks later wearing a motorbike helmet. My father said that, from then on, whenever she jumped into or entered a field of riders, everyone left immediately.'

Two people who became friends of Christabel in the 1960s were Martin Lutyens, a great-nephew of the architect Sir Edwin Lutyens, and his Spanish wife Beatriz. Martin's mother, who used to stay in Somerset with a cousin called Dirom Crawford, had got to know Christabel in the days when the latter visited 'Callie' Carew-Erskine in that county. Christabel had given Martin's sister Priscilla (Scilla) a dress as a wedding-present. Martin recalls:

'I remember Chris's visits to Spain. She stayed with us twice in the mountains in Spain, near the French border – the nearest town was Boadella. My father-in-law, Eugenio Pinedo, was a civil engineer. He was building a big dam at government expense and he had a beautiful house where we used to take the children for their summer holidays.

'Chris stayed with us there. Once I fetched her in person at Serena Airport, at four in the morning. The other time she arrived in a taxi at about six a.m. We were all still in bed; the taxi-man was obviously instructed to hoot loudly. That woke us up. Chris came in, having been up all night. She was deposited in her room and re-emerged about twenty minutes later in a bikini saying, "Right! What are we going to do now?" '

Beatriz Lutyens remembers:

'A woman called Gambica was the best-known flamenco dancer in the gipsy style. She had a canvas made and she danced on top of it. We were staying very near Gambica's place, at my parents' home, and my father got us good seats in the front. Chris was thrilled. And then a newspaper paparazzo stood right in front of her, just as the dance was beginning. So she kicked him and he went rolling on the ground while Gambica was dancing. He was furious. My father had to pick up the pieces.

'Another time, when my father was building this big dam in the Pyrenees, Chris wanted to go and see how it was done. My father said she could go, but that she must dress very simply – no jewellery. Well, that was impossible for Chris. Not that she wore very expensive jewellery, but she always had accessories. And I can still see her coming down the stairs with this lovely floaty summer dress and *festooned* with necklaces. But anyway, down we went, and she caused a sensation with the workers. One of them said to another one, in a strong Andalusian accent: "*¡Jesus. Que sardina!*" (Jesus! What a sardine!) – because she was as thin as a rake, and in Spanish a very thin person is a sardine.'

Martin and Beatriz stayed with Christabel in Ireland.

'She had this lovely castle by the sea [he recalls]. And she was very naughty, because the moment we arrived the castle was open to the public and some people were visiting – was it Mark Girouard with three or four friends? And Chris told us we had to show them round – it was the first time we had ever set foot in the place! Knowing more of life now, I would say: "Look, I'm terribly sorry, but I'm new to this place"; instead of which, I tried to bluff my way through, and of course it turned out that at least one of the party knew all about Irish castles and bowled me out middle stump – very embarrassing.

'Another day, she said: "I've got a terrible headache, I'm going to bed. Would you mind looking after some people for dinner?" So we found ourselves being Mr and Mrs Host to a bunch of people she'd got from the Irish Tourist Board. And after dinner, having said she had this awful headache, she summoned us all to her bedroom, one by one. There she was, sitting regally and looking marvellous till God knows when. The next morning I said, "Look, honestly, you shouldn't have done that to us – lumbered us with those people."

'You know she was totally anti-smoking. Well, her daughter-in-law – Geoffrey Ampthill's first wife, Suzy – smoked a cigarette and stubbed it out bang in front of Chris, and I thought: ."Suzy is a strong girl!" But the funny thing was that Chris's cook used to smoke as she cooked. She had this lady called Mrs Bugg who did for her and cooked a bit, and she always had a cigarette drooping out of her mouth as she was making the soup. The ash would get longer and longer and finally it would drop into the soup – Chris must have known what was going on, but I suppose it wouldn't have been easy to get another Mrs Bugg.

'Another story about Chris. We had some cousins who lived in Australia, and one of them, Lydia, was a very high-profile Australian wine-grower. She knew all about Australian wine and people tended to have to sit back while they got a lecture on the excellence of Aussie wine. And Chris was at dinner with my parents and Lydia was going on and on and on, and she eventually turned to Chris and asked, "Now, what do you think of Australian wines?" She said: "*I only drink my bathwater.*"

'She looked after a lot of superannuated, mangy hounds. She brought one of them, an old bitch hound called Potent, to stay with my sister Scilla and her husband, Richard Chester-Master. And Richard, who also liked to push people around a bit, said: "Chris, that hound of yours absolutely *stinks.*" She looked at him and said, "Well, Potent thinks *you* stink, too – but she's much too polite to say so."

'There was a horse show at Olympia; and, according to my parents, Chris borrowed a cavalry charger from some male admirer and went in for showjumping. And she went right round the arena and knocked down every single jump. She got off her horse at the end of it and wasn't embarrassed or put out or anything – she'd had a go. She was somebody who would always have a go.'

Lutyens's mention of 'some male admirer' touches on the delicate and probably unresolvable question of Christabel's relations with men from the 1930s onwards. Two men were regarded by her near relations and circle as having been her 'boyfriends', possibly lovers, in those years. In the Thirties she was attached to Charles de Beaumont (*Plate 12*), a dashing, D'Artagnan-like figure who was a champion fencer. In 1929 he had reached the semi-final in the individual sabre competition in the Ostend Tournament. He was the first international fencer to win the Miller-Hallett International Epée Competition in three successive years – 1930, 1931 and 1932. (He also won it in 1934, 1935 and 1938.) He was one of the British team in the British-American match in New York in 1934, and captained the British Olympic fencing team at Berlin in 1936 and again in London in 1948. In later years he kept a photograph of Christabel by Madame Yevonde (*Plate 2*) in a brown envelope which he inscribed 'Chris Ampthill, my great girlfriend in the 1930's'; and his son, the antiquarian book-dealer Robin de Beaumont, does not think his father would have been satisfied with a platonic relationship. Geoffrey Russell (as he then was) liked de Beaumont, though he remembered he had to be told to put out his cigarette before attending a service, with Christabel, in the chapel at Stowe.

The other man, who was later regarded as at least Christabel's 'protector', was very rich: Sir Cyril Kleinwort (1905-80). In 1961 the family bank, Kleinwort & Son, merged with Benson Lonsdale to form Kleinwort, Benson, Lonsdale, the holding company whose main subsidy then became Kleinwort, Benson Ltd., the merchant bank. The first chairman of the group was Cyril's brother Ernest. In 1966 Cyril Kleinwort became chairman of the bank. His *Times* obituary claimed that 'He was the main force who took Kleinwort, Benson ... from fairly modest size to become the City's largest merchant bank with assets which at his death totalled over £2,000m.' For much of the time Christabel knew him, he lived at Sezincote, Gloucestershire, a fantasy palace in Indianate style which had been designed for a 'nabob', Sir Charles Cockerell, in about 1805, by his brother, the architect Samuel Pepys Cockerell. John Betjeman, who had stayed there as an Oxford undergraduate in the 1920s, described it in his autobiographical poem *Summoned by Bells* (1960) –

The bridge, the waterfall, the Temple Pool –
And there they burst on us, the onion domes,
Chajjahs and chattris made of amber stone:
'Home of the Oaks', exotic Sezincote!
Stately and strange it stood, the Nabob's house,
Indian without and coolest Greek within ...

Christabel did not visit the house too often, since Kleinwort was married, with three daughters. Whether she became his mistress is not certain; Anne Minoprio thinks that the main attraction of the friendship, for Christabel, was that Kleinwort provided her with mettlesome horses to ride. She recalls that the initials 'C.K.' were engraved on a brass disc attached to the head-straps of the horse on which Christabel tried to teach her to ride sidesaddle.

Anthony Russell was becoming more and more keen on pop music, especially that of the Beatles. In 1964 Christabel took him to a Beatles concert at the Odeon, Hammersmith. A girl in front of them was screaming throughout. Anthony recalls:

'Granny A gave her a gentle prod with her umbrella and spoke to her in an angelic tone of voice. "You know, my dear, it's only the plain girls who scream." '

David Russell has kept several letters of the Sixties from Christabel to him and his mother Suzy. In them we catch her authentic voice for the first time since the trials of the Twenties. In April 1966 she visited England to see *The Match Girls,* a play produced by Geoffrey.[86] On 18 April she wrote:

'My dearest Sue – [It] was all too lovely & marvellous for words & so lovely to be spoilt & cosetted after my tough life here. I adored every minute & the culminating bliss was The Match Girls loved equally by me & Teddy Wolfe.[87] It is a truly lovely entertainment & so beautifully done – my only criticism is that I'd put the best actress in London on to do Mrs Besant – it could be made a superb part – I can't believe that I can have produced such a very intelligent son. How could *anyone* ever have thought it out? The set (how short it looks, has it two t's perhaps)[88] was genius & so *beautiful.* We were all mad about it & so lovely to see a musical not depending *wholly* on clothes – How is my angelic granddaughter [Vanessa Russell]? I do hope better – I don't know anyone I like being with as much as I do her ...

'All my love & all my thanks for giving a huge slice of real bliss.

'Love, C.'

In an undated letter, she wrote to David: 'Thank you for your super letter – It made me curl up in a ball of delight – Such bliss that you follow in my footsteps with the horse ...' In 1969, when he was a junior editor with the publishers Hodder & Stoughton, she wrote to ask his advice about the approach Eileen Hunter had made to her to write her biography. 'Not a *word* to the family,' she urged. Was £500 a big enough advance?

'Mrs Petrovitch [Hunter's married name] thinks I am an unusual sort of creature & not built in the normal way & thinks my outlook might be a useful asset to many who spend their lives grumbling & complaining! Anyway, if I get £500 or more I could do another trip like my last one & get a *terrific* dashing young two year old or two & have the fun of making them into lots of lolly & perhaps breaking a bone or two I may have missed in the past!'

She told David that Eileen Hunter was 'a delightful creature without a nasty thought anywhere – *rolling* in money but in no way spoilt by it'. She wanted David to have lunch with Hunter and hoped that Hodder might publish the book; but Hunter was bound by an 'option clause' with her last publisher.

In October 1969 Christabel came to England again for James's memorial service at Leeds Castle. On October 29, back in Ireland, she wrote to David:

'I can't seem to get back to normal yet – all these last 10 days have been such a slice out of hell. The only thing that really gave me heart was your reading the Lesson – It was superbly done & made one think there must be some meaning in this extraordinary universe – I was indeed proud of you.'

He stayed with her in November. On the 23rd she wrote to him: 'Never have enjoyed a visit more – I actually cried all the way home when leaving you. You did me a power of good after many weeks of being so very down & low.'

Christabel and her sister Gwen had fallen out and did not speak to each other for fifteen years (about 1950 to 1965). But in the mid-Sixties there was a reconciliation and Gwen and her granddaughter Philippa came to stay at Dunguaire. Philippa Enderby recalls:

'Gwen and Chris were complete opposites, but they were absolutely iron-willed, both of them. Especially Gwen. When her husband, Hilton Welford, died in 1926, my mother and her two older brothers were asked, "You must be very sad that your father has died?" and one of the boys answered, "Wish it had been mother." She was like iron. My mother used to say, "She treated us like servants." '

'Gwen and Chris clashed head-on. My grandmother was anti-hunting; she was part of the RSPCA – Christabel had no time for them. They were on a complete collision course all the time. For a while, in the Fifties, Chris rented a house in Crowcombe, Somerset, from a man named Trollope-Bellew. That was the time when my grandmother and she weren't speaking. We drove through Crowcombe one weekend. My mother said, "Oh, I can't see Chris", and got on the floor of my Mini in case she appeared.'

'Once they had been reconciled, Christabel invited Gwen and Philippa to Galway.

'*That* was an experience! We arrived, and that was absolutely fine. Then we went up to the drawing-room and the whole drawing-room was full of peat smoke. So we said, "Can we have a window open?" "*No!*" I was spluttering and coughing and she said, "You'll just have to go and sit in the other room." The next morning we got up and she called out, "You can't come down! You can't come down!" She was entertaining. She had all the hunt people there, and we weren't allowed down – out of our turret – until they had gone. This was not the best of starts to the reconciliation process.'

Philippa also remembered: 'Chris fell out with people over there. She said the Irish were totally incompetent, and naturally they didn't like it. She had stand-up rows with some of them, and a blinding row with one Master of Foxhounds. A blazing row with the Galway Blazers!' Even people who were inclined to be well disposed to Christabel were disconcerted by some of her law-unto herself eccentricities. Ulick O'Connor, the writer, actor, champion boxer, pole-vaulter and rugby player, wrote in his diary on 1 August 1970:

'Tennis with Desmond [Guinness] in the morning, at Castletown House, Cellbridge ... The pock of the ball on the strings of the racket is the only sound. We play with studied precision like dancers under a ballet master. Nothing so common as rushing to the net. We lob the ball from the base line. Like the scene at the end of Antonioni's *Blow-Up* where the actors mime a game in Hyde Park at dawn. This of course enables Desmond to chat away as he plays, like Christabel Ampthill across the drawing-room at music recitals.'

By the early 1970s, Christabel was tired of Ireland. She was ready for one last adventure. She sold Dunguaire Castle to the Irish Tourist Board and prepared for a riding trip across Australia. Her most recent travels – equally intrepid – had been to Afghanistan and the Himalayas. In 1969 she had arrived at Eileen Hunter's house in Surrey wearing a striped tweed skirt and matching poncho, a swathed turban and large flower earrings and carrying two small canvas bags. She was off on her exotic journey in two days' time. 'All the way there and back for only £300,' she crowed. 'Mostly *young* people.' Hunter wrote: 'I could imagine them only too clearly and felt a pang of commiseration as I considered their present blithe ignorance of what might be in store for them when her ladyship came amongst them.' (She was right: Christabel was appalled when some of the hippies smoked cannabis on the bus, and she left the party.) She had bathed in the nude in Iran, 'in the pools left by a great river fed by mountain snows'; had been asked by a taxi-driver in Kabul if he might sleep with her; and had stayed on a house-boat in Kashmir.

Christabel's great-niece Philippa was a travel agent. In 1970 she had a telephone call from Christabel, who said, 'Philippa, I want to go to Perth. Not Scotland – Australia.'

'So I said, "All right." I told David, "Your grandmother wants to go to Australia"' He said, "I'll sort her out." She went to Perth and she rode across Australia. A kangaroo hopped out of the bush and her horse shied and she fell off and smashed her front teeth. She got a matchbox, put her teeth in it, went to the nearest dentist and said, "Stick 'em in!" Which he did. It's so Chris.'

On 5 June 1970, Eileen Hunter had a letter-card from Christabel, beginning, 'I cannot describe the delight I am getting from this fantastic journey. The country entrances me – its enormous rolling plains – white trunked gum trees and lovely bunchy-topped sort of fir trees and a horizon too far away to be a reliable affair ...' She added:

'In [the bush] ... there are lovely parrots of every shape and colour, small flaming birds whose names I don't know, and jackdaws quite unlike ours with beautiful bubbling liquid song.

'Once in a leafless tree with fawn smooth trunk and branches, I saw a conclave of nine grey and pink parrots who when they saw me left their perch and came swirling round me in a feathery cloud as though they wished to examine me more closely before returning to their tree ...'

The stages of her journey were described on the Australian BBC, and she was interviewed by the *Daily News*. The *News* reporter wrote: 'Her ladyship only lies long abed while waiting for her trousers to dry, she shows no fatigue on the journey that would daunt many people years her junior.' He noted that 'All she carries with her is another pair of trousers, jerseys, some rainproof things and two toothbrushes – as she hates to use one that is wet.' The newspaper failed to get her to push her riding-hat to the back of her head, so as to get a good photograph: nothing would persuade her to be incorrectly dressed for riding.

Three weeks later, Eileen Hunter had a brief note from Singapore: Christabel was going on to the Philippines, where Philippa's stepfather, John Curle, was British ambassador. 'I have suddenly got £100 of tickets for £25! *Who* could resist such bliss and luck. A nice gentleman friend stepped up. Oh, goodness, what a lucky creature I am. After Australia, seven weeks of *utter* bliss, now I get more...' The 'nice gentleman' asked her to marry him, an offer she graciously refused. Why, Hunter asked, was Christabel constantly showered with marriage proposals? Her looks and outstanding individuality, she thought, were only part of the answer: the real lure was 'the attraction of the unattainable'.

Christabel next took a banana boat to India, bought an old Dormobile, and drove it back to England with no licence or insurance. It was while she was on her way back in the van that Geoffrey contacted her about collecting blood samples. She returned to Ireland and bought a little thatched house at Craughwell, Country Galway. The Galway Blazers had their kennels there, though by that stage she was barely going out with the hunt. She was suffering from arteriosclerosis and from a muscle-weakening illness called Simmonds' Disease. ('I have been in bed for over a week,' she wrote to Eileen Hunter, 'with *horrid* Mr Simmonds.')

She was interviewed at Craughwell by Catherine Stott for a profile which appeared in *Harpers & Queen* in September 1976. (By then, Christabel had died.) Stott wrote:

'After months of waiting for her to return from an extraordinary solitary journey across half the world by motor-caravan, I tracked her down to a caravan in the rubble-filled "garden" of a cottage she is renovating in deepest, stoniest Co. Galway ...

'Physically, she is still superb. Tall, reed-slim, cypress-straight. Her hair is still a silky dark blonde, her make-up expert, her complexion bronzed and barely lined; her jaw-line firm, thrusting and determined. Even in the harsh Galway light she appears to be a woman in her fifties ... Her figure has remained a trim eight stone all her life.'

Stott thought Christabel had adapted well to the 1970s.

'In only two ways has she failed to enter the decade. She still uses the "Mayfair Cockney" drawl redolent of the Twenties where every vowel stretches elastically into four syllables. Equally, her attitude towards servants is frankly despotic, and rather unnerving to those she stays with who have to act as liaison officers between her and the staff. She has her own rigid set of standards which she insists others conform to. Like Sir John Gielgud she thinks aloud – social hypocrisy is beyond her. If she thinks you are wrong, she is quick to tell you so. If you are three minutes late, she will have left without you. (I was held up at a filling station and consequently had to find my way alone through fourteen miles of identical lanes in the Western Ireland outback, to her cottage. God and the Garda Siocana were on my side. Together we found it.) If you drive too closely behind her, she will stop her van, get out and loudly admonish you. If you fail to hoot at a passing peasant wobbling on a bicycle, she will slap you on the knee and admonish you for being "a foolish gel!" ... And yet she is lavish with her praise, her admiration and her friendship. She can give like nobody else, and two minutes after an admonition which has left you feeling like a whipped cur, the legendary Christabel charm will fall on you like the sudden hot rays of sun on your back on a dull day.'

Stott soon experienced Christabel's talent for getting other people to do what she wanted. The cottage was being rethatched. The thatcher was running out of straw. Stott was persuaded to drive him and Christabel from croft to ever more distant croft in search of some – after Christabel had given her indolent builders 'their statutory fifteen minutes of hell'.

'Together we clock up sixty miles of rough-track driving. At each croft she alights, drives a hard bargain with the crofter down to the last penny, gets a firm delivery date for each bale, cuts them down and emerges from the three-hour experience tireless, immaculate and ready for a good dinner. By contrast, I am hot, exhausted and longing for a cigarette and a stiff drink. But knowing her disapproval of both these weaknesses I content myself with a tomato juice and a Polo mint.'

Stott thought Christabel spoke of hunting 'with the same passionate glow that another woman might speak of a lover'.

' "Hunting," she says, closing her eyes in blissful contemplation, "has been the most important thing in my life. More important than people, I suppose. The most exciting thing. Oh I loved dancing, too, and I was very good, but I wouldn't have given up half an hour's hunting for all the dancing in the world. It is the thrill of having an animal in your hands, of 'making' a horse, of getting him to do things he probably wouldn't do for anybody else. It's all so utterly satisfying. Even when I was working in Curzon Street I managed to hunt four times a week. Yet I never owned a horse until I came to Ireland. I was very good on a horse, good *for* the horse, so everybody lent me theirs." '

In 1975 Geoffrey arranged for Christabel to be admitted to St Thomas's Hospital in London. 'The arteriosclerosis was making her a much less jolly person,' he recalled. Christabel checked herself out of the hospital after twenty-four hours, but the consultant who had examined her told Geoffrey: 'There is nothing we can do for her. She will die in a year or eighteen months.' In January 1976 a doctor in the Galway Hospital telephoned Geoffrey to say that his mother had had a massive stroke. 'Come as quickly as you can,' he said. 'We'll talk about it. We are all very fond of her and respect her.' Geoffrey took the earliest aeroplane to 'the wrong side of Galway' and went to the hospital by taxi. He met the doctor, who said:

'Lady Ampthill is so well known in this part of Ireland, not only because she was brilliant on top of a horse, but also because she was such *fun*. In my opinion (and another doctor has had a look at her) she is not ever going to be happy again. She has two drips into her arms. One is providing water; the other is providing the equivalent of food. What I want to suggest to you is that we should withdraw the food but leave in the water one – because if people get dehydrated, they are uncomfortable.'

Geoffrey went in to see her. 'She was beyond recognizing me. From time to time she twitched, made jerky movements. She was mentally dead, obviously, but not quite dead. I said my goodbyes and then went back to the doctor. I told him, "I'm absolutely in agreement with what you said before. To keep her alive as a cabbage, as they say, would just be cruel." It was a Catholic hospital; the nurses were nuns.' The food tube was withdrawn.

'If there is a heaven,' Christabel had told Catherine Stott, 'I hope I can ride in it.' She died on 16 February 1976. Stan Shields, the Galway photographer who had taken the pictures to accompany Stott's profile (*Plate 20*) had become her friend.

'The first time I met her, she took the fucking nose off me [he says]. She was just back from Australia, she'd driven back. She was a bit domineering, she could bully. But I stood up to her and after that we had respect for each other – I was no longer the little boy.

'Of all the people I have photographed, the two who have made the greatest impression on me were Watson of Crick and Watson, the discoverers of DNA (he was so modest), and Lady Ampthill.

'I was so taken with her that, when she died, I went to the morgue to pay my respects – I felt I had to. She died in what used to be called Galvia Hospital, Galway – later Galway Hospital and now known as Bon Secours Hospital. A dead person looks dead, but it was a kind of "healthy corpse" – it's an expression we have here. Jesus, she looked better dead than when she was alive! She was one tough cookie. There was not much flesh but, by God, there was *bone*.'

Christabel had died just two months too early to see the final act of her drama played out. Her *Times* obituary concentrated almost exclusively on the trials of the 1920s. Geoffrey wrote a pained letter to the newspaper, signed 'G', listing her other achievements. Perhaps the most fitting tribute to her came in a letter to David Russell from Mary Deane, an old family friend.

'*You* – David – were your Grandmama's Pride & Joy – how she loved your visits to her in Ireland – & her visits to you in London. – There will never be another like her, she had all the rare qualities, unfashionable these dull, dirty days – Elegance, wit, charm, courage & inspired taste in everything she touched – & how we shall all miss her – & how we all loved her ...'

18

The Title Fight

The two rival claimants have never met.
Alan Whittaker, 'Lords Rule on Lady C's Love Tangle'
NEWS OF THE WORLD, 30 NOVEMBER 1975

The sensational 'Russell Baby' court case will be fought all over again in the House
of Lords on Monday – fifty-four years after it first rocked fashionable London.
Malcolm Stuart, 'Did the "so naughty" society beauty lie about her baby?'
DAILY MAIL, 21 FEBRUARY 1976

Mr Geoffrey Russell said yesterday that he had taken 'a Trappist vow of silence'
and had absolutely no comment to make on the case.
Nigel Hawkes, 'The last word on "virgin birth"',
THE OBSERVER, 22 FEBRUARY 1976

The 1970s 'title fight' before the House of Lords Committee for Privileges caused
almost as much of a stir as the 1920s proceedings in the Law Courts; it would have
been theoretically possible for somebody to have attended both. The hearings
began on 23 February 1976 in Committee Room No. 4 of the Lords. Its neo-
Gothic windows overlooked the Thames, with pleasure boats chugging past. The
room was dominated by a large portrait of a stern-faced Queen Victoria.

Everyone attending – the law lords, the lay lords, the claimants with their
supporters and counsel, the officials, the press and 'visitors' – was handed a plan of
the room indicating where the parties were to sit.

The clerk to the Committee, seated in a corner of the room, was (Sir) John
Sainty, a distinguished historian of Parliament. He recalled:

'John, the third Baron Ampthill, was a long-standing friend of my father. He
was a familiar figure from my childhood and I saw him frequently after I entered
the service of the House of Lords [as Clerk to the Parliament Office] in 1959 ...

'It so happened that I was selected to serve as clerk, or secretary, to the
committee for privileges of the House for the hearing of the Ampthill case in
[1976]. I remember being in the committee room supervising its setting up for the
hearing when I caught sight of a man whom I had not seen before. On enquiry I

was told that he was Geoffrey Russell, one of the claimants. I was struck by his resemblance to the third baron, particularly in his colouring, and formed the opinion that, if the case were to be decided on visual evidence alone, he was in with a chance. Naturally, in view of my official position, it was an opinion that I tended to keep to myself!'

At the hearings, the two claimants, with their families and other supporters, sat alongside each other (though with some distance between them), so that they could not easily glower at each other. In *The Sunday Times*, Mark Boxer ('Marc') squashed their heads together in his deft caricature – from left to right, the

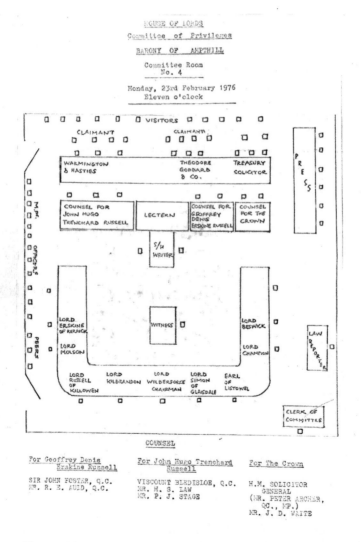

Figure 14 Seating plan, House of Lords, Committee for Privileges, 23 February 1976

bespectacled John Russell; his sister Georgiana; his aunt Mrs Thorold; Geoffrey Russell's secretary 'acting as a buffer state'; Geoffrey's wife Elisabeth; and finally Geoffrey himself, with the jutting chin remarked on by the 'facial topographer'. (David Russell, also present, was disappointed to be left out of the cartoon.)

THE AMPTHILL QUESTION:
How frank was Christabel?

Figure 15 Cartoon by 'Marc' (Mark Boxer), The Sunday Times, 29 February 1976.

The hearings were a gift to the caricaturists. Osbert Lancaster who, born in 1908, was old enough to remember the 1920s brouhaha, drew two pocket cartoons for the *Daily Express.* In one, Maudie Littlehampton, holding a newspaper headlined 'RUSSELL BABY', is saying to her husband, 'There you are, dear – nothing but repeats!' (*Plate 28*). In the other, an old lady is whispering to a friend: 'Don't tell me that poor dear Bertie is in trouble again?' (*Plate 27*). This, of course, was a reference to Geoffrey Russell's kinsman Bertrand Russell (Earl Russell), the philosopher, a notorious womanizer. *(Private Eye* parodied his 1967 autobiography: 'At a party I met Lady Utterly Immorell. We decided to become intimate on the following Thursday.') Once, both Bertrand Russell and Geoffrey were at Woburn Abbey with John, Duke of Bedford, when a coach disgorged a bevy of swimsuited Miss World contestants, who joined them for lunch in the Canaletto Room. Geoffrey Russell recalled: 'I feared the old goat was about to put into practice the CND motto – "Make love, not war."'

'JAK', in the *Evening Standard,* chose to depict the peers sitting in judgment. One of them is saying, 'Would someone refresh my memory? – I haven't seen a virgin since Poona!' (*Plate 29*).

The lords on the Committee were a more formidable group than the bleary old buffers drawn by JAK; though they included Lord Molson, who had been at school and Oxford with Evelyn Waugh, and was rather a figure of fun to Waugh and his circle: they called him 'Hot Lunch Molson' because he had stated at Oxford that it was imperative always to have a *hot* lunch; or they called him 'Preters' because he had pompously claimed, 'I am preternaturally interested in politics.' During his career in the Commons he had been known as 'Mumpy'. But Molson had taken a first in Jurisprudence and was a man of principle: he had not been afraid to risk his future in the Conservative Party by an outspoken attack on Neville Chamberlain's deal with Hitler at Munich, and had voted against the Conservative government in 1940.

The chairman of the Committee was Lord Wilberforce, one of the pre-eminent lawyers of his generation. He was a great-great-grandson of William Wilberforce, the anti-slavery campaigner, for whom Wedgwood had made medallions showing a black man in chains with the legend 'Am I not a man and a brother?' – much the question that Geoffrey Russell was asking John Russell in the committee room. After the Second World War, Wilberforce had developed a programme for the eradication of Nazism from German law. As a QC he had appeared in several notable cases, such as the one that established the right of the Prince of Hanover to be a British subject, pursuant to an Act passed in the reign of Queen Anne; and *J. Bollinger* v. *Costa Brava Wine Co.* which stopped Spanish vintners using the description 'Spanish champagne'. He went to the House of Lords in 1964 and, as his *Times* obituary put it almost forty years later, 'bestrode the world of the highest judiciary'. He was not an ivory-tower lawyer. *The Times* recalled: 'He was a keen follower of the turf, with a considerable knowledge of the Stud Book. Unusually for a judge, he could be seen, after a day's sitting in the High Court, in the local tea-shop off the Strand studying the form in *Sporting Life*.'

During the war, Wilberforce was commissioned in the Royal Artillery and saw active service in Norway before being transferred to the Army legal staff. Others of the lords in Committee Room No. 4 had also had a 'good war'. The Labour peer Lord Beswick had been a Royal Air Force pilot. (During the 1976 hearings he was designated chairman of British Aerospace – an appointment which drew satirical comment from the Conservative Spokesman on industry, Michael Heseltine: 'The French could fight for our aircraft markets, the Americans were out there selling by every means at their disposal. But the leadership of the British aerospace industry was incarcerated in a committee room in the Houses of Parliament rewriting some bedroom farce of almost indescribable irrelevance to this nation. This is a dilettante approach, nauseating humbug.') Lord Simon of Glaisdale had been in the Burma campaign. Lord Russell of Killowen (no relation of Geoffrey) had been parachuted into Normandy and won the French Croix de Guerre; Lord Molson had been a captain in an anti-aircraft unit. These men had been trained to kill; checking uppity counsel was nothing to them.

Among the lords, the mix of political parties and classes was well balanced. Some were the sons of peers: Listowel was the fifth Earl. Others were of the people: Lord Champion a former railway signalman, Lord Beswick a miner's son. The cumulative experience of these men was impressive. Lord Erskine had been governor of Northern Ireland in the 1960s. (His wife Henrietta had suffered a heart attack on being screamed at by Protestant extremists.) Lord Kilbrandon, a Scottish lord of appeal, had been chairman of the Royal Commission on the Constitution. In spite of a limp from an old skiing injury, he would walk to the hearings from Gray's Inn in his Inverness cape. He was renowned for 'cutting any arguments to fundamentals' and for 'complete impartiality, patience and courtesy'. As a law lord, Russell of Killowen was considered 'logical and ingenious on a point of law; formidable and sardonic in his cross-examination of witnesses; full of persuasive charm in his handling of the court'. His *Times* obituary (1986) credited him with 'wit, not always kindly' and 'devastating repartee'. Lord Simon of Glaisdale was President of the Probate, Divorce and Admiralty Division of the High Court from 1962 to 1971; Lord Kilbrandon, a Scottish Lord of Appeal.

Lord Listowel – at his death in 1997 one of the last figures to survive from the postwar Attlee government – was perhaps especially well qualified to sit on the panel, as in 1934 he had secured an Act to enable warring couples to avoid divorce. Not exactly a practiser of what he preached, 'Billy' Listowel had himself been married three times: first to the political activist Judith de Marffy Mantuano; secondly to the former blues singer Stephanie Wise; and thirdly to a former hairdresser, Pamela Read. (He was divorced from two of them and had children by all three.) In 1957 Harold Macmillan had appointed him governor-general of Ghana, where he worked closely with Kwame Nkrumah.

As we have seen, James Miskin QC had originally been going to represent Geoffrey Russell, but had had to stand down in 1975 on being appointed Recorder of London. Sir John Foster QC was chosen to replace him. Foster kept his date of birth out of the 1976 edition of *Who's Who*. He was in fact seventy-two that year – 'a bit long in the tooth', Geoffrey thought, though Foster's adroitness in responding to Wilberforce's acute interventions showed that he was still quick on the draw. He had another qualification for debating what had and had not happened in the 1920s: like Bertrand Russell, he was a famous womanizer. Sir Isaiah Berlin, who knew him well – both were Fellows of All Souls and both had worked for the British Government in the United States during the war – gave this opinion of him to Michael Ignatieff:

'John Foster ... [was] a legal adviser [to the British Embassy] who had been a Fellow of my College; he was a very agreeable, remarkable, very odd man ... he was a very free spirit, lacked certain human qualities, benevolent, amusing, not exactly an adventurer, but full of vitality and fun, couldn't understand why poetry was written, why words were put in this funny way together, had never read a novel in his life because he didn't want to read false statements about reality when you could read history and newspapers, and he couldn't imagine living in a world that didn't have telephones, for example. He didn't smoke, didn't drink; he went to bed with more ladies than anybody in the twentieth century. His promiscuity was total. He didn't know the meaning of the word 'love', I think. He was like a very nice dog, a very frisky dog who didn't happen to have a human soul. He had a heart, a nervous system and a very good quick brain. Terribly benevolent. He was a pure Benthamite Utilitarian. He believed in maximizing human pleasure. He was altruistic. But pleasure to him meant physical pleasure. Therefore medicine he was prepared to back because that minimized pain. But ... research into, I don't know what, crusaders of Malta, seemed to him to be mad, absolute rubbish. But since people enjoyed it, he didn't want to stop them, because pleasure was all right and they took their pleasure in these funny ways. His natural friends were the slightly dubious Jewish lawyers in Brooklyn ... '[89]

Isaiah Berlin hated A.L. Rowse – also a Fellow of All Souls – and is said to have prevented his receiving any Government honour until an eleventh-hour CH, just before his death. But Rowse in his diaries gives a view of John Foster similar to Berlin's, and perhaps slightly more penetrating. In October 1960 Rowse was visiting the press baron Lord Beaverbrook in New Brunswick, Canada. At dinner he was placed next to Lady Jeanne Campbell, *Daily Express* correspondent of the United Nations. (She was Beaverbrook's granddaughter, daughter of the Duke of Argyll and, at the time, the wife of the novelist Norman Mailer.) The usually misogynistic Rowse found her engaging, spontaneous and vivacious. He wrote in his diary:

'We had some gossip about John Foster, whom she had been consulting – "my family has been much before the courts lately," she said a little ashamedly. So she was the Argyll daughter? She was wearing a prehistoric gold bangle, grave-good from Inverary, which she had not returned to the Museum. I gave her my clue to John's sensual utilitarianism – the early rejection by his mother and his devotion to the old maid he calls his aunt; no aunt at all, but she had looked after him from a child when his mother rejected him. "That fits in with the fact that he really hates women," Lady Jean said. That had never occurred to me, for he is a tremendous performer with them.[90] But no love, no ties, no emotion; just mutual pleasure. It gives him pleasure to meet his girl's lover coming to see her as he is leaving. Is he getting his own back – not vindictively, it makes him laugh so much. In the nineteenth century he'd be the victim of a *crime passionel*. Our society cares too little for that.'

At seventy-seven, Lord Bledisloe, whom John Russell had chosen to be his counsel, was even older than Foster. A big landowner at Lydney in Gloucestershire, he had served in the First World War as an officer in the Royal Artillery, and in the Second World War as a squadron-leader in the RAF. 'The other side made a great mistake in choosing him,' Geoffrey Ampthill thought. 'He was primarily a tax lawyer. He didn't know the first thing about divorce or legitimacy cases.'

The first day of the hearings, Peter Archer, the Solicitor General, outlined his understanding of the matters to be resolved in the legitimacy battle. He told the Committee that he was not concerned to support or oppose either claimant's petition, but to assist the lords. As lawyers sometimes need to do, he stated the obvious.

'The position is if Geoffrey is to be regarded as legitimate that would establish the claim in his Petition, and John's Petition would be dismissed. If Geoffrey were to be regarded as illegitimate then the claim in his Petition is not established and then his Petition would be dismissed, and presumably John's claim would be established. That appears to be the essential issue, my Lord.'

Archer proceeded to summarize all the 1920s hearings, quoting Lord Dunedin's speech in the House of Lords.

'The appellant conceived and had a child without penetration having ever been effected by any man; she was fecundated *ab extra*; she had denied intercourse of any sort with any man not her husband; she had admitted that her husband had never effected penetration, but she had said, and he had admitted, that he had been in use to lie between her legs with the male organ in more or less proximity to the orifice of the vagina, and to proceed to emission; but he asserted that, in his opinion, all he had done could not have caused conception, and he specially denied that there had been these practices during the relevant period, though he admitted that he was in bed with her on at least two nights during the same.'

Archer further pointed out that, in the House of Lords' decision of 1924, 'it was accepted ... by all concerned that the evidence in question, the evidence of non-access, would not have been admissible in any event in legitimacy proceedings [because of the Lord Mansfield judgment] and that that was already the established rule'. Lord Wilberforce beadily interjected: 'That acceptance, as I understand it, was not confined to those learned Lords who thought the evidence was not acceptable in divorce proceedings?' Archer: 'That is my understanding, my Lord, that everyone accepted that.' Archer also reminded the lords that the court legitimization of Geoffrey in 1926 was binding ... on Her Majesty and all Persons whomsoever' unless it could be proved that it had been obtained by fraud and/or collusion. He also told them that John Russell's side was demanding blood tests, but that in his (Archer's) opinion, the sample of the late Lord Ampthill' s blood, taken on 29 April 1971, was 'probably now ... too old for helpful analysis'. Wilberforce again interrupted:

'It is really your suggestion, is it, Mr Solicitor, that the Committee should take as a preliminary point, as it were, the question whether the Declaration of Legitimacy is or is not binding on the basis that if the Committee finds that it is binding that is an end of it; only if it is held not to be binding do questions of evidence, including perhaps questions of blood tests and so on, really arise for consideration: is that your suggestion?'

Mr PETER ARCHER: 'My Lord, yes.'

Wilberforce then asked the claimants' lawyers to address the Committee. Sir John Foster said he was happy with the Solicitor General's submissions as to procedure. One of the points Bledisloe wanted to make on John Russell's behalf was that the late Lord Ampthill's brother Leopold had not received a summons to the legitimization proceedings of 1926 in which, potentially, he had an interest. Foster forestalled this objection: in the first place, Leo had been a minor at the time; secondly, 'the father, grandfather and the uncles were all evading service, rather, if I might characterize it, an undignified kind of procedure – the issue-server turns up, the chauffeur says they are not there ...'

During one pause in Foster's submission, Lord Russell of Killowen commented: 'Much of what is said here would be more nearly relevant if the lady had had ordinary complete intercourse with anybody at all.' Foster: 'Exactly, my Lord.'

There were a few light-hearted exchanges to relieve the tension in Committee Room No. 4. For example:

Lord KILBRANDON: 'I am not sure that the last passage of Lord Dunedin which you read this morning, Sir John, is acceptable nowadays, that fecundation *ab extra* is adultery. That has been questioned in connection with artificial insemination.'

Sir JOHN FOSTER: 'I think not, it does not apply to adultery.'

KILBRANDON: 'I doubt whether it is accepted, fecundation *ab extra* which includes artificial insemination is adultery.'

FOSTER: 'I would have thought, my Lord, fecundation by a man *ab extra* is adultery but not by, as they say, the man in the bowler hat.'

KILBRANDON: 'I would hope not.'

Aware that Bledisloe was going to claim that Christabel had obtained the legitimacy declaration by fraud – because, in his submission, she had taken a lover or lovers and knew that John Hugo Russell was not the baby's father – Foster countered with the logical argument: 'If there had been a lover, he would have been the person who had practised abnormal sexual intercourse in the sense in which my friend used it, in other words that he would have fecundated Christabel from *extra* as well. So ... there is nothing in that point at all. It does not prove that she was aware her husband was not the father because the only sexual intercourse she had had, as proved by the fact that her hymen was not penetrated, was that.' To the suggestion that in 1926 Leopold Russell, as a minor, should have had a guardian appointed to protect his interests, but had not, Foster had a brusque rejoinder: 'If I may say so colloquially, "So what?"'

That first day, the *Evening News* painted in some journalistic colour.

'Geoffrey Russell is accompanied by his wife, the beauty of the occasion, superbly turned out in navy blue silk ...

'Sadly the true heroine of the occasion is missing. Christabel was the brightest of bright young things whose alleged relationship with "four young men in the Oxford and Bucks Light Infantry" figured in the original divorce case ...'

The morning papers the next day also covered the hearing at length. 'The rival claimants to the Barony of Ampthill studiously ignored each other,' the *Daily Mail* reported. 'Only Mrs Phyllis Thorold, sister of the late third Lord Ampthill, stole a long glance at Geoffrey Russell ... She was the first member of the family knowingly to set eyes on Geoffrey Russell since he was born.' (If Evelyn Whiteside's account of Lord Ampthill's surreptitious visits to Fortnum's was true, this was not quite accurate.)

In *The Guardian*, under the headline 'Splitting heirs on the ermine', Simon Hoggart wrote:

'The sad gaiety of the roaring twenties crept back like a wraith to the House of

Lords yesterday, as nine ageing peers began to consider the Russell baby case – perhaps the most famous paternity suit of them all.

'The Russell baby himself, who smiles wide-eyed and angelically from the newspaper clippings of the day, is now 54, a prosperous theatrical impresario with gold-rimmed halfmoon glasses and a remarkably beautiful wife.'

Hoggart thought John Russell looked 'slightly nervous' and, like the *Mail*, noted that he and Geoffrey 'contrived to avoid each other throughout the session with that easy blend of politeness and cutting rudeness which only the British aristocracy can carry off.' Sir John. Foster 'stood over his lectern like an amiable vulture, muttering at times in a voice so low that only their lordships directly in front of him could have heard'. The two Russell factions sat in silence for most of the time, though there was 'a tiny whispered cheer' from Geoffrey's side when Sir John made a point that everyone could follow – the point that any lover must have had intercourse *ab extra*. 'WHICH BABY IS THE BARON?' demanded *The Sun*. Its reporter, Brian Woosey, noted: 'One lawyer estimated that five million words of evidence had already been committed to the records. A team of stenographers started tapping out the latest evidence at the rate of thousands of words an hour. The whole hearing is being tape-recorded.'

Back in 1974, Geoffrey Russell had had a spat with the *Daily Express*, when the paper's 'William Hickey' gossip-column editor, Ross Benson (always referred to by his *Daily Mail* rival, Nigel Dempster, as 'the pomaded Pompadour'), had written about what was in store at the Committee for Privileges. After speaking with Geoffrey on the telephone, Benson had led with an inflammatory paragraph headed 'Oh Lord, will this scandal end soon?' Geoffrey had written to his friend Jocelyn Stevens, then deputy chairman and managing director of Beaverbrook Newspapers, whom he knew from the Bahamas, to complain that Benson had not checked back with him, as he had promised to do. Both Stevens and Benson had sent mollifying letters, but the damage was done. Now Stevens made amends. On 24 February 1976 the front-page headline of the *Express* read, in Stonehenge lettering, 'MY MOTHER'S HONOUR', with the sub-heading, 'Why I'm fighting so hard, by the man in a battle over his peerage and his parents'

Accompanied by a large photograph of Geoffrey and the glamorous Elisabeth, the article began:

'A lady's honour – a term straight from the 1920s world of *Upstairs*[91] – was considered at the House of Lords yesterday in the strange case of the Russell baby.

'For the central figure, Geoffrey Russell, now a greying 54, has told friends: "I am fighting this case as hard as I can for the honour of my mother. It is her good name and reputation that are at stake." His mother Christabel, who was the key to the Ampthill peerage, died in Ireland only last week at the age of 80 ...'

Clearly, the *Express* was rooting for Geoffrey.

On the day that article appeared – the second day of the hearings – Foster made the case against Bledisloe's demand for blood tests, under pressure from the lay peer Lord Beswick, who was insistent that the tests should be made. Foster retorted that none of the safeguards stipulated by the law on blood tests had been met. For example, the late Lord Ampthill had not, as required by the law, given a certificate that he had not had a blood transfusion within three months – and in fact he *had* had transfusions. Once again – as with his 'man in the bowler hat' sally – Foster showed his talent for introducing a picturesque and vivid phrase into his argument, when he added that blood tests 'would be putting the petitioner, Geoffrey, in what I would call an Agatha Christie position. Somebody could have substituted the blood samples. I cannot prove it but I am saying that my petitioner should not run the risk of somebody having substituted the blood samples or got it wrong or mixed them up at the laboratory. All these things could have occurred.' He also scotched an allegation that Christabel had refused to provide a blood sample: she had provided one. It was at his, Foster's, urging that she and Geoffrey had decided not to agree to blood tests.

Lord BESWICK: 'Would that not be a matter to be decided by the Committee?'

FOSTER: 'I think with respect not, because the first point of course is to get rid of the legitimacy decree. If I am right about that the question does not arise.'

Foster added that the blood samples from the third Lord Ampthill had been taken without his knowledge; also, that his medical records, except for a few odd documents, had mysteriously been destroyed, on the orders of the doctor who had arranged for the blood test to be taken. And 'the verification required by the statute in the forms is a long way from being satisfied'. Foster also pointed out that the third baron was alive for thirteen months after the Blood Test Act came into force in 1973. It would have been open to him to give a 'regularized' blood sample in that period: why had he not done so?

Now it was the turn of Lord Bledisloe to make his case in his own words – not as unappealingly paraphrased by Foster. As he rose to speak, he had already conceded that his charge of 'collusion' could not be sustained, and, chivvied by Wilberforce, had formally abandoned it. In his opening address, he said:

'The preliminary point is said to be the effect of the Declaration of Legitimacy. As I understand it, I say the normal way to try a case is to find the facts and then apply the law ... Now, the only question of fact to be determined in this case is whether or not Geoffrey Russell is the son of the late Lord Ampthill; there is no other question of fact. The determination of that fact would take a very short time. So I would submit to your Lordships the right way to deal with this case is the normal way: find the facts first, then look at the law.'

The second point he wanted to make was that, in his view, 'this Committee has a complete discretion as to what it will do. It is not bound by any judgment of the court. It is not bound even by its own previous decisions in peerage cases.' Perhaps Bledisloe thought that this suggestion of their unique all-powerful status would flatter the Committee into setting aside the legitimacy decree of 1926.

CHAIRMAN: 'I take leave to doubt a good deal of that, Lord Bledisloe, but please go on. This case has been referred to the House of Lords by the Crown so I do not think we need consider whether there is any jurisdiction apart from the reference, and I should very much doubt whether there is.'

Viscount BLEDISLOE: 'What they are saying ... is that the House of Lords has inherent jurisdiction in determining who are its members.'

CHAIRMAN: 'I very much doubt that unless you very much qualify it.'

BLEDISLOE: 'I shall refer your Lordship to a number of peerage cases on that point ...'

Here, as so often during the hearings, one gets the strong impression that Wilberforce has already all but made up his mind that Geoffrey's case is unassailable. In his exchanges with Bledisloe he frequently seems impatient or frankly hostile. Here are some examples.

CHAIRMAN [to Bledisloe]: 'I doubt if you are going to get much out of this book. By all means give us any passages, but they seem to be on a very different point.'

CHAIRMAN [to Bledisloe]: 'You need not re-read that paragraph, which anyway is obsolete ...'

CHAIRMAN: 'Where is this leading us, Lord Bledisloe? You are reading a great deal of material which seems to have very little value.'

Occasionally Bledisloe gets ratty and hits back.

CHAIRMAN: 'Page 285 is all you want, is it not?'

BLEDISLOE: 'Your Lordship continues to try to hurry me. It is very difficult in cases of this kind.'

CHAIRMAN: 'One is trying to extract a proposition which we can apply.'

BLEDISLOE: 'So am I. This is an important case.'

At the core of Bledisloe's submission was the idea that the Committee should apply good old British common sense to the case. He took them back to basics: the honour of Baron Ampthill of Ampthill had been granted to Lord Odo Russell in 1881 and to 'the heirs male of his body lawfully begotten and to be begotten'.

'The task your Lordship is set [he continued] is to decide what individual fills that description. It is the heirs male of Odo's body lawfully begotten and to be begotten. Your Lordship has to decide who was the eldest son of the late Lord Ampthill, not who as a result of some Act of Parliament is deemed to be the son of Russell ... No Act of Parliament can say that a boy is my child when in point of fact he is not. It is a matter of fact.'

In the passage of his address which followed, Bledisloe showed that he was as capable as Foster of decorating his argument with an entertaining allusion.

'My learned friend went so far as to say ... that if the decision of the House of Lords had been the other way, that they had upheld the Court of Appeal and the jury, the child by its next friend could have gone along and got a declaration of legitimacy.

'Supposing that were the situation, and supposing Geoffrey had applied to the court for a declaration of legitimacy, and the evidence had been the evidence of blood tests, that he was not the child of the late Lord Ampthill – Russell as he then was – and that he had not a drop of Russell blood in his veins, is it really to be said that he has a right to a declaration of legitimacy? The answer must be no. This has nothing to do with the present case, but supposing a hereditary peer married an English girl and she gave birth to a child within the period in which she could conceive it, and suppose the child turned out to be black and there was evidence of blood tests which showed perfectly clearly that it was the child of General Amin of Uganda.[92] This is cloud cuckoo land. We do not live in the land of make-believe ...

'This is not a court of law, and this is a committee which is going to use common sense. I will show your Lordship it is not bound ...'

Bledisloe told the Committee that he wanted to refer them to the *Banbury Peerage* case, but unfortunately their Lordships had not been provided with copies of the relevant pages. This statement drew another tart interruption from Wilberforce.

CHAIRMAN: 'What we understand we want [the *Banbury Peerage* case] for, is authority for the proposition that illegitimacy of a child born during wedlock can be proved. Is that right?'

BLEDISLOE: 'Yes, and also the proposition that the Committee for Privileges is not bound by any decision of the Courts.'

CHAIRMAN: 'Of course it is not. We know that.'

'Hot Lunch' Molson also had a swipe at Bledisloe, asking him whether what was decided in the *Banbury Peerage* case (which originated in the seventeenth century) could be binding now and was not affected by the Legitimacy Act.

BLEDISLOE: 'What happened in the end was – and this case was a long time before the Legitimacy Act –'

MOLSON: 'Exactly. Are we to understand that the decision that was given in the 17th century is binding upon us now and has not been altered by the wording of the Legitimacy Act which says that it is to be binding on the Queen and on whomsoever?'

Bledisloe replied: 'Yes.'

Ordering an adjournment for lunch, Wilberforce pointedly advised Bledisloe that in the afternoon he should concentrate on 'the real point' – which was why, in Bledisloe's view, the Declaration of Legitimacy should be set aside. He added:

'I do not think their Lordships will be much assisted unless you can persuade them that this [Legitimacy] statute does not apply to this particular case, to Her Majesty, to the House of Lords and the parties ... Unless you can satisfy us as to that, references to other authorities are not going to be illuminating to us.'

In the afternoon session, nothing abashed by the Chairman's directive, Bledisloe explained why he wanted to cite some early cases which, in his opinion, had a bearing on the present case. What the old cases suggested was 'that you can take all the surrounding circumstances into consideration and decide whether a man is or is not the father of his child'. What Bledisloe seemed to be implying was that, as the third Lord Ampthill had never acknowledged Geoffrey as his son (this, Geoffrey's side vehemently disputed), Geoffrey could not succeed to the barony.

Bledisloe returned to his plea for blood tests.

'I ask your Lordships rhetorically and hypothetically to say that if – and it would be possible in this case – it could be proved without a shadow of doubt by blood tests that – we have the jury's verdict – Geoffrey was not in fact the son of the late Lord Ampthill, with not a drop of Russell blood in his veins ... If it could be proved ...'

CHAIRMAN: 'But it cannot be inquired into. How can it be proved if it cannot be inquired into?'

BLEDISLOE: ... 'If your Lordships feel so disposed to direct this evidence, it is not a question of taking blood tests but of making available the results of the blood tests that have been taken. I take a risk. I do not know what the results would be. But if that were done and your Lordships were satisfied by the doctors' evidence that Geoffrey could not possibly be the son of the late Lord Ampthill ... would your Lordships because of the Declaration of Legitimacy ... think you were bound to advise that the writ of summons should be issued in his favour? I would have submitted to your Lordships obviously not. It is cloud cuckoo land if you know somebody is not *de facto* the son of his father.'

CHAIRMAN: 'But we do not know, that is the whole point, and we are not allowed to know beyond what the Act has said. You are putting an impossible hypothesis. Your hypothesis is impossible in law.'

Lord Molson again intervened: surely it was difficult to imagine any wider terms than that the legitimacy decree should be binding on Her Majesty and all persons whomsoever. If Parliament had intended to make an exception in the case of the peerage, would it not have said so? Bledisloe replied, 'I do not imagine Parliament was thinking of the peerage,' and supported this assertion by reference to a case which had been mischievously instigated by Sir Alan Herbert. Herbert, a barrister who was on the staff of *Punch* (as 'A.P.H.'), liked to test the limits of the law by dreaming up amusing stunts. On one occasion, for example, he decided to find out if a bank could be required to honour a cheque written and signed on the flank of a cow. (It could.) In the case Bledisloe was citing, *Rex* v. *Sir R.F. Graham Campbell ex parte Herbert,* members of the Kitchen Committee of the House of Commons were summoned to a police court on the ground that they had sold by retail intoxicating liquor for the sale of which they did not hold a justices' licence as required by section 65 of the Licensing (Consolidation) Act of 1910. The magistrate held that the matter fell within the scope of the internal affairs of the House of Commons and therefore within the privileges of the House so that no court of law had jurisdiction to interfere. It was on the basis of this flimsy and frivolous case that Bledisloe was ingeniously trying to suggest that the Lords were not bound by the Legitimacy Act. He conceded that the Herbert jape was 'a very long way from peerage cases' but emphasized that 'it was decided that [the Licensing statute] did not apply to the House of Commons'. Bledisloe buttressed the frail edifice of this argument with the resounding words of Chief Justice Denman in the case of *Stockdale* v. *Hansard:*

'The Commons of England are not invested with more of power and dignity by their legislative character than by that which they bear as the grand inquest of the nation. All the privileges that can be required for the energetic discharge of their duties inherent in that high trust are conceded without a murmur of a doubt.'

No one interrupted to point out that hereditary peers were not chosen by the people. But neither was Bledisloe allowed to get away scot-free with his suggestion that Parliamentary privilege was paramount. A lively interchange followed, in which Wilberforce, with his cutting, forensic mind, delivered the *coup de grâce.*

BLEDISLOE: ... 'The House of Commons were not subject to the provisions of the [Licensing] Act, [which] presumably applied to everybody.'

KILBRANDON: 'Not subject to the jurisdiction of the law. They might have been breaking the law but they could not interfere.'

CHAIRMAN: 'You cannot send a policeman in: that is the difference. The difference here is that this Act especially mentions Her Majesty ...'

Disregarding Wilberforce's pre-lunch injunction, Bledisloe drew to the Committee's attention a juicy case of the late nineteenth century involving aristocratic families, the *Aylesford Peerage* case. In 1875, Edith Lady Aylesford, wife of the seventh Earl, committed adultery with the Marquis of Blandford (later Duke of Marlborough) and went to live with him. Six years later she gave birth to a son, Guy Bertrand. When the seventh Earl died in 1885 and the Hon. Charles Wightwick Finch came forward to argue his claim to the earldom before the Committee for Privileges, his counsel proposed to read out as evidence of adultery letters written by Edith Lady Aylesford.

BLEDISLOE: 'Then the letters were put in and I suppose I had better read them quickly and see the sort –'

CHAIRMAN: 'Need we spend much time on this? This might be relevant if we got to a later stage and we began investigating letters written by the late Lady Ampthill. It might become material then.'

Soon Wilberforce was reiterating his contention: 'None of this helps you to get over the Declaration of Legitimacy. It arises afterwards ... You are quite right to refer these cases to us but I do not think we want to spend much time on them at this stage when we are preoccupied with the apparently binding effect of the Declaration of Legitimacy.' In return, Bledisloe rather despairingly repeated his contention that what mattered was common sense and getting at the truth. Once again there was an interchange in which Wilberforce delivered a withering and dismissive retort.

BLEDISLOE: 'As your Lordships will remember – I am not sure that my Lord Lord Wilberforce accepted it – what Palmer[93] says is that the House of Lords 'has an inherent jurisdiction, as guardian of its own privileges, to determine who are its members and what is their precedence *inter se.*'

KILBRANDON: 'It is a very interesting point because that means that the House of Lords is not then bound by Her Majesty in Parliament.'

CHAIRMAN: 'It is totally heretical. The orthodox view is that this House can only act in peerage cases referred by the Crown. It can deal with false precedence in its own privileges. Of course you cannot decide on a peerage case unless there is reference by the Crown.'

Lord Champion, perhaps feeling that Bledisloe was getting unfairly besieged, tried to help him out:

'Is it your case that this Committee would be committing a nonsense if they recommended, contrary to proof that Geoffrey was not the son of the third Baron, to the Queen, that Geoffrey should receive the writ of summons to the House? Is that what we are trying to establish?'

BLEDISLOE: 'What I said, possibly rather rudely, although it was not intended to be rude, was that your Lordships are not rubber stamps ...'

CHAMPION: 'Therefore evidence as to the circumstance of the birth of Geoffrey is admissible before this Committee?'

BLEDISLOE: 'Yes, and I would say this, on the footing of the *Aylesford Peerage* case, that we know that what I call the surrounding circumstances are admissible, that the blood tests themselves are surrounding circumstances, or would be if we had them ... Mind you, if we have the blood tests they may operate against me. I am taking that risk because my client is perfectly straightforward about this. He said: "I do not want to be Lord Ampthill if Geoffrey can show conclusively that he is my father's son." ...'

Lord RUSSELL OF KILLOWEN: 'The blood tests would not show conclusively that Geoffrey was his son; they might show conclusively that he was not. That is right, is it not?'

BLEDISLOE: 'Yes, that is technically right. They could show conclusively that he was not. They could, because we have taken a lot of blood ... We have blood tests of John's uncle, the two brothers and one sister of the late Lord Ampthill, and his own blood test ...'

Bledisloe aggrievedly added, accepting that Sir John Foster had secured blood samples from Christabel and Geoffrey: 'He has got them, but he refuses to let us see them.' He added:

'I am told that if we had the blood test from Christabel and Geoffrey, the experts – and they are all distinguished people and there is no question of cooking anything – in a short time could tell us certainly whether he was a son of the late Lord Ampthill, or to a very large extent what the probabilities are.'

The day's session was nearly at an end. Wilberforce said that he did not want to rush things. Sir John Foster might wish to answer some of Bledisloe's arguments. 'We face very serious constitutional questions here.' Wilberforce adjourned the sitting.

The evening newspapers that day and the morning papers the next day (25 February) went to town on what some of them, with journalistic verve, called 'DEMAND FOR BLUE BLOOD TEST'. In the *Daily Express*, the reporter Geoffrey Levy described the committee-room scene as Lord Bledisloe – 'a portly, peering figure' – rose to speak.

'It was heady, legal stuff. Hard for laymen to follow ... Gnarled and well–thumbed law books appeared. ... And there is so much more to come. The long table in front of the solicitors almost sagging under the weight of at least 60 bulky law books.

'Under the table are as many again, waiting to be called, silent witnesses. No one has yet sat in the witness's chair in front of the lectern and in the middle of the peers' semi-circle.

'It is an elegant room but much too small. All the Russells – on both sides of the dispute – are 6ft.-plus people, including the ladies, and their knees are knocking the chairs of the solicitors in front.

'The single exception is the petite Mrs Geoffrey Russell who has added a Continental dash to the dry proceedings by draping her jacket over the back of her chair.

'Sometimes she rocks it back on its legs, hand on husband's shoulder. She alone is sparkling in that grim row of protagonists. It is the light of battle in her eyes ...'

In a separate article, the *Express* interviewed Leopold Russell, who said: 'I feel no ill-will, no enmity, against Geoffrey, and neither does John. We feel quite sorry for him. It is not unreasonable for him to defend his mother's honour and his claim to the title ... We just feel a great family need to settle the question once and for all and to put an end to the doubts about the succession to the title.' The same piece noted that John Russell was 'so camera-shy that last night he refused to return to his home in Ovington Street, Chelsea, where pressmen were waiting. Later a man left the house carrying a suitcase into a car. Before driving off he said: "Mr Russell does not live here any more."' The *Daily Mail* and the *Daily Mirror* both reported that Willie Hamilton, the Labour MP for Fife Central, was to question the Attorney General over the cost of the Lords hearings. Hamilton was best known as a strident anti-monarchist. He told the *Mirror*: 'It all looks like a beanfeast for the legal profession.'

On the third day, it was obvious that Wilberforce's patience with Bledisloe was running out. At the beginning of the session, he delivered a magisterial admonition.

BLEDISLOE: 'If your Lordship pleases, I was dealing with the *Aylesford Peerage* case. Your Lordship may remember that my friend wanted –'

CHAIRMAN: 'Their Lordships are very anxious not to spend more time than they have to on these authorities because they are firmly of the opinion that the real point of the case is whether it is possible for the Petitioner you represent to attack the Declaration of Legitimacy ...'

But Bledisloe was not to be quelled. Instead of addressing the Declaration of Legitimacy, as directed, he immediately segued into a summary of the *Wensleydale Peerage* case. The monarch had issued letters patent purporting to create Sir James Parke a baron for life. The House of Lords ruled that the letters patent did not entitle him to vote in Parliament. 'This', Bledisloe said, 'was a case in which the Sovereign purported to create a life peerage and the House said that they could not.'

Bledisloe's final point on the issue of blood tests was that, 'over and above all the interests of the child, there is one overriding interest which must be considered. It is the interests of justice.' He quoted Lord Sumner's minority opinion in the 1920s *Russell* v. *Russell* case:

'My own view is that in the administration of justice nothing is of higher importance than that all relevant evidence should be admissible and should be heard by the tribunal that is charged with deciding according to the truth ... It is best that truth should out and that truth should prevail.'

Shortly afterwards, Lord Russell of Killowen got under Bledisloe's guard with a telling thrust, reminding him of 'the well-known point that the law thinks that after a bit one has had enough, it is time to call a halt'. Bledisloe moved swiftly on to the allegation that Christabel had been guilty of 'fraud' in the 1920s. Wilberforce asked him to define the term. Bledisloe replied: 'What is going to be enough is this: if it is shown that [Christabel] has not been frank with the court.' Bledisloe asked: 'Why were the legitimacy proceedings [of 1926] launched?' Answer: 'To stifle ... any further claims by a legitimate son of the third Baron Ampthill'. Foster had suggested two other reasons: first, that without a declaration of legitimacy, Christabel might have difficulty in getting Geoffrey into Eton; secondly, that she wanted to claim maintenance.

In an intervention fascinating to the press, Lord Simon of Glaisdale suggested a further reason.

'Looking through the papers I came across a family settlement. You will correct me if I have got it wrong, but there was a disentailing agreement subsequently under which Geoffrey got £30,000. That would have been a powerful motive in establishing him as a tenant in tail under that settlement, or potential tenant entail, would it not?'

Bledisloe had the answer to that one. Whether there had been a declaration of legitimacy or not, Geoffrey was presumed by law after the House of Lords decision in 1924 to be legitimate. The Russell family had never recognized Geoffrey and they wanted to remove any interest he might have in the Ampthill properties. So they bought him out.

One ill-tempered piece of theatre by Lord Wilberforce does not appear in the official report of the proceedings, but Geoffrey Ampthill remembered it. At the beginning of the afternoon session, Wilberforce asked Bledisloe to resume his argument. Bledisloe replied that he proposed to ask his learned junior, Mr [H.S.] Law, to address the Committee on the question of fraud. At this (Geoffrey Ampthill recalled), Wilberforce picked up a heavy book and slammed it down on the floor in anger, with a terrific thud. He acidly told Bledisloe that normally the Committee heard only one counsel, but as a special concession they would hear Bledisloe's junior on the matter of fraud. Law worried away again at the question of blood tests. Lord Russell of Killowen satirically paraphrased Law's submission.

'Your purpose, Mr Law, as I understand it, is this: that if the other side, having had an opportunity of comparing their analyses of Geoffrey's blood and Christabel's blood with your reports do not say "Snap" to your present offer of to withdraw, you will invite the Committee to say that that shows that the comparison of the results shows that Geoffrey could not have been the son of Lord Ampthill. This is the end of this particular movement, is it not?'

Mr H.S. LAW: 'It is one possible result.'

Lord Russell commented that even if blood tests could show Geoffrey was not the son of the third Lord Ampthill, that would not prove that Christabel knew he was not.

LAW: 'My Lord, I would respectfully submit that is stretching incredulity to its utmost. She was the mother of the child, she must know if she had had any sexual commerce with any other man apart from her husband.'

RUSSELL OF KILLOWEN: 'Supposing that to be so, I hope I do not display any particular expertise in this field if I suggest that not every woman who has had sexual relations with more than one man substantially at the same time knows for certain which it was. They may find out later because the child has a beak nose or something like that.'

Law's insistence that Leopold Russell, as a minor, should have been represented by a guardian in the 1926 case led to more banter with Lord Russell.

RUSSELL OF KILLOWEN: 'Would you agree that there was no obligation on the Petitioner to cite Leopold? It is a trap. You are quite right to look at me like that!'

LAW: 'My Lord, I was thinking before answering your Lordship, knowing what bunkers can do on a golf course ...'

When Law tried to raise a case of 1888 in support of his argument, he was firmly smacked down by Wilberforce: 'This is another "Leopold" case and Leopold has not taken any steps to have it set aside. These cases are totally unhelpful. We must bring it to an end.' Wilberforce adjourned the second day's hearings, suggesting that on the next day Sir John Foster should answer the arguments of Bledisloe and Law.

The *Evening News* that day led with the headline '£30,000 TO BE RID OF GEOFFREY'. The sub-heading, 'Pay-off claim in the battle for the Baron's title' wrongly gave the impression that Geoffrey had sold off his claim to the Ampthill barony. Half the morning papers the next day were obsessed with this aspect of the hearings *(Daily Express:* 'Geoffrey's secret deal with the old baron'), while the rest continued to harp on the demand for blood tests: editors knew that if the tests took place, the revelations would make a great 'story' for them – whatever they proved. In the *Daily Telegraph*, Ann Morrow described the committee-room scene, under the headline 'FASHION AND A PRIDE OF LEGAL LIONS'.

'Yesterday Mr Geoffrey Russell, in pin-stripe suit, with silver hair parted at the side and flattened with oil, sat through the hearing, smiling and looking out across the Thames towards Lambeth Palace.

'His raised eyebrows and curvy mouth are exactly the same in childhood photographs taken with his mother Christabel.

'His exceedingly decorative French wife Elisabeth in a different outfit each day gets more than a fair share of attention. The law lords with their tiny spectacles perched on fine noses, quite often appeared to be looking in her direction.

'Once a public relations girl with Pucci and Revlon ... she looked outstandingly glamorous with her Edwardian hairdo and pink Chanel suit among the pin-stripes ...

'Her beads jangled noisily as she flirtatiously tried to cheer up her husband, if discussion was dragging.

'Mr John Russell, a chartered accountant also in pin-stripe with fair hair unevenly cut, bit his nails throughout the hearing, while his sister Georgiana with porcelain complexion, idly fingered her nails and looked bored and unsmiling.

'Their aunt, Mrs Phyllis Thorold, 75-year-old Extra Lady-in-Waiting to the Queen, looked icily at Geoffrey Russell, remembering perhaps the madcap activities of his elegant and wayward mother ...

'Bushy eyebrows quivering, Sir John Foster QC, for Mr Geoffrey Russell, occasionally gleefully nudged junior counsel in the ribs as a point was scored for his client ...'

On the third and final day of the hearings, Sir John Foster began his reply to Bledisloe, and his summing-up, with a relentless reminder of the Declaration of Legitimacy of 1926.

'The statute says quite clearly, and your Lordships have seen it several times, that it is binding on the Crown. Your Lordships are sitting here by reference from the Crown and it is binding on all persons whatsoever ... unless a fraud or collusion is proved.'

Foster quickly demolished Bledisloe's suggestion that the Committee was 'entirely above any statute'. As for the allegation that Christabel had been guilty of fraud, that was based on the merest speculation. Wilberforce agreed with him: '[The charge of fraud] must be made with particularity and you must be prepared to give proof at the time you make the charge.' Implicitly, this statement ruled out blood tests. Lord Kilbrandon chipped in:

'I do not think it is possible to say on the evidence [Christabel] knew he was illegitimate, whatever the blood tests show.'

CHAIRMAN: 'Let us spell this out, Sir John, it is very important. Lawyers are liable to talk to each other in shorthand, but the point is, is it not – which I think my noble and learned Friend has very clearly brought out – that the most the blood tests could show is this: they might show that Geoffrey was the son of adulterous intercourse. Assuming that the blood tests showed as much as that, what bearing has that got upon an allegation of fraud as affecting 1926? It might still be the case that Geoffrey was the son of adulterous intercourse but that she honestly believed that he was the son of non-normal intercourse with her husband. I want to be quite sure I have got this because it is extremely important, whether that is the chain of argument, which I think is the only chain of argument that is supportable ..'

The tenacious Lord Beswick continued to press for blood tests – 'evidence which is now available and was not then [in the 1920s] available'. He added: 'I thought when one took the oath one swore to tell the truth, the whole truth and nothing but the truth, and she probably gave the truth but not the whole truth?'

Once again Wilberforce administered a smart put-down: 'John cannot go around fishing among a lot of facts not yet established in order to make good his case.' On this, Foster immediately cited the 1930 case of *Jonesco* v. *Beard*, in which the Court of Appeal had held: 'You cannot say, "I will bring an action to try to find fraud and when I do I will prove fraud."' He irritably observed that 'certainly my Lord Lord Beswick is clearly very exercised by this problem'.

As it happens, we know exactly what was exercising – and confusing – Lord Beswick. By a curious chain of circumstances, all his papers relating to the 1976 hearings have come into the possession of David Ampthill. They contain not only a large amount of printed-out cases that the two sides intended to cite; also among them is a single sheet of paper, embossed at the top with the House of Lords' lion and unicorn emblem. On the sheet are Beswick's pencil notes to himself about the case. This is not a formal summing-up, couched in carefully honed phrases; it is more a kind of thinking aloud, high-speed reactions to a moving target. The notes read:

'Once advice tendered *must* it be accepted Essential issue – legitimacy – but was this not settled?

'Upheld because, said Lords, the evidence was not admissable [*sic*].

'See Act 1858 Section 8 that facts other than those relevant to 4 points in para 16 p 31 could these lie?

'Blood samples from Christobel [*sic*] said to be available but is it not also said that she refused?

'Geoffrey living with Grandmother – why?

'Lords reversed the appeal on grounds that evidence had been improperly admitted.

'Not binding on a minor – but many things were decided before my birth but are binding upon me.'

Yet again Wilberforce asked the Committee to consider the incontrovertible character of a declaration of legitimacy. An Act of 1858 (the one mentioned in Beswick's memo) had brought down a very severe 'portcullis' to stave off any attack on such declarations 'except on absolutely limited grounds'. Peter Archer, the Solicitor General, told the Committee he had been unable to discover any case since the 1858 Act in which anybody had sought to set aside a decree of legitimacy on the ground of fraud.

The Committee's hearings were adjourned *sine die* for the lords to consider what they had heard and to reach their conclusions. Some of the events of that final day did not get into the official report, but were covered by Simon Hoggart in his *Guardian* article the next day.

'The submissions in the Ampthill virgin birth case ended yesterday amid more splendid outbreaks of cool upper-class bitterness. Shortly after it finished one of Geoffrey Russell's side remarked about John Russell's blood test reports, on which the case might turn in the end, that they were "useless, ridiculous, we are not even going to do them the honour of looking at them".

'Then from their end of the corridor (the two sides maintain a discreet apartheid before and after hearings) one of John's relatives was asked if it would not be a good idea for the two claimants to shake hands. "I don't see why," he said. 'This isn't a game of cricket, you know." ...

'Yesterday, Sir John Foster, for Geoffrey, launched into a long slow argument to show that [blood] tests were worthless, inaccurate and inadmissible. Just when a cynic might have thought that his scepticism had some ulterior motive, he announced dramatically that John's side had not, after all, handed them over in the first place. Lord Bledisloe, for John, was aghast. "We haven't been given them," Geoffrey shouted from the back of the room.

'There was a frantic rustling of papers and the reports were practically thrown at Sir John. "I don't want them," he said with the disdain of a man handed a half-chewed sweet by a child, and the reports were hurriedly stuffed into the bag of a nearby solicitor, in whose safe they are to reside like some plague-infested rat ...'

The *Daily Express* had spoken to Elisabeth, who said: 'I do not care about being Lady Ampthill. That is just a title, and titles do not matter. We do not change because of them. But if you bastardize a man at the age of 54, it is a question of morality, a question of honour.' Mrs Thorold was also interviewed. 'I do hope we've won,' she said. 'We all care very much for our family tradition – do you know, every member of my family is a member [has an honour] of the British Empire, and then my mother was once the only double-dame in the land until Edwina Mountbatten.' Geoffrey Russell said: 'I don't believe a horse has won until it's past the post. We've had a fair hearing and now we must wait for their verdict. Why shouldn't we wait a bit longer? It's only been 50-odd years, after all.' John Russell's sister Georgiana ('pronounced Georgina but spelled in the old English way') told the *Daily Mail:* 'The marvellous thing was that [my father] at last found happiness when he met my mother (his third wife) and the final 25 years of his life were quite blissful.'

Newspaper and magazine columnists aired their views on the hearings. John Junor, the editor of the *Sunday Express,* wrote that the lawyers in the case would be able to give their wives diamond necklaces from their proceeds.

'But isn't it bloody to see a family tearing itself into pieces? Isn't it soul-searing to see the continuing misery of Geoffrey Russell who for 54 years has had to endure sneers for having had the bad luck to be born the "Russell Baby"? And all for what? There is no great inheritance, no vast estate at stake. All for a miserable title that wouldn't be worth £500 a year director's fees on a fringe bank's headed notepaper.'

The *Economist,* wittily describing Stilts and Christabel as 'not-so-bright young things', also talked money: 'The most the successful claimant will get out of it, financially, is an entitlement to the £13.50 a day (tax-free) allowance for attending the House of Lords.'

The hearings were covered in the *New York Times* and the *Los Angeles Times.* The French paper *L'Aurore,* under the heading 'L'IMACULEE LADY', asked, 'Geoffrey Russell est-il bien le fils pirate de lord Ampthill, conçu par surprise?' and recorded that the 'frères enemis' had never met each other. In London, the *News of the World,* which had feasted on lubricious details, poured scorn on the whole case in an editorial headed 'Panto peers'.

'The ludicrous pantomime over who is entitled to call himself Baron Ampthill is not likely to do much for anything except lawyers' wallets.

'But what is a bit thick is that, as usual, taxpayers' money is helping to keep the nonsense going.

'For who else but you pays the wages of Solicitor-General Peter Archer, QC?

'Heaven alone knows what important Government work has been put on one side so that he can "guard the rights of the Crown and the peerage".

'The joke is that Labour's Mr Archer refused to take the customary knighthood when he got his job, because of the contempt in which he holds titles.

'Anyway, legitimacy can't really bother the House of Lords all that much.

'The Duke of Grafton and the Duke of St Albans sit there today solely because their ancestors were illegitimate sons of Charles the Second.

'Why not give BOTH the Ampthill gentlemen a peerage, and save us from any more of the nonsense?'

The Committee for Privileges was reconvened on 12 April 1976. Its members had unanimously decided that Geoffrey, not John, was the rightful Lord Ampthill. Wilberforce summed up with his usual clarity and concision. John's case, he said, was that the 1926 Declaration of Legitimacy was not binding for three reasons: first, that the declaration was not binding in a peerage case; secondly, that it was vitiated by procedural irregularity; and thirdly, that it was obtained by fraud or collusion. The terms of the Legitimacy Declaration Act of 1858 were, Wilberforce asserted, 'firm and trenchant'. It was vitally important that doubts as to legitimacy should be resolved once for all. 'How otherwise could a man's life be planned?' English law provided that limits should be placed on the right of citizens to open or to reopen disputes. Sometimes justice must even be preferred to truth: 'these values cannot always coincide'. (Wilberforce emphasized that he was not saying this was such a case.) Lord Bledisloe had tried to minimize the effect of the Declaration by calling it 'a paper title', 'a deeming provision' and 'the produce of ten minutes' legal mumbo-jumbo'. Wilberforce, while sympathetic to the position and feelings of John Russell, had to reject this approach. He added: 'If ever there was a case for closing the chapter in a family's history, the case for closing this in 1976, after the distressing revelations and divisions over so many years, must be one.' No court could enquire into the legitimacy or otherwise of Geoffrey. 'To inherit the Barony under the Patent, Geoffrey must show he is the lawful heir: and that is just what the Declaration states him to be.'

Wilberforce proceeded to dispose of Bledisloe's objections. The objection that Leopold Russell had had no guardian appointed was 'multifariously refutable' – 'at most (and doubtfully) it was an irregularity'. Wilberforce added: 'It was a comfort to find that a comparable, if even weaker, argument that the proceedings were invalid because the grandmother [Mrs Hart] was made [Geoffrey's] guardian instead of the mother, and that there was "collusion" between these ladies, was, by the wisdom of Leading Counsel, ultimately withdrawn.' Had Christabel shown 'lack of frankness'? Even if she had, Wilberforce could not accept 'so anaemic an impediment'. There would need to have been conscious or deliberate dishonesty in obtaining the Declaration. Quoting Bledisloe's argument as to fraud, Wilberforce said: 'My Lords, within the limits of moderate comment, it is impossible to do justice to this production. It is exposed to absurdity and irrelevance at every point.' There was no evidence to show that either Mrs Hart or Christabel was 'stifling' anything. Wilberforce also rehearsed all the arguments Foster had raised against blood tests, and agreed with them.

Lord Simon of Glaisdale concurred, mentioning the long-drawn-out and ruinous case of *Jarndyce* v. *Jarndyce* in Dickens's *Bleak House*. In 1828, he said, the great American judge, Justice Joseph Story, had called the first Act of Limitation 'a statute of repose'. Aside from truly exceptional cases, the judgment must be allowed to conclude the matter: that was one of society's purposes in substituting the lawsuit for the vendetta. 'Sometimes it is the parties to the litigation and those who claim through them who are bound by the judgment; but sometimes it is the whole world which must accept the decision.' The judgment creates an 'estoppel' – that which has been decided must be taken to be established as a fact. 'The clamouring voices must be stilled.'

Simon contemptuously killed two birds with one stone: the allegation of fraud and the demand for blood tests.

'A person cannot merely say: "I allege that you obtained your judgment by fraud: let me rummage through your papers and I will be able to turn up something there which will enable me to prove it." He cannot do that because it would be unjust. Nor, by the same token, can he say: "I allege that you obtained your judgment by fraud: let me have a sample of your blood and I will be able to prove it." '

Simon's language was less crisp, more orotund, than Wilberforce's. In his peroration he declared that an end to litigation should not be stayed by undesirable exceptions: 'The bitter waters would never ebb.' Lord Kilbrandon thought the objections raised by John's side that there had been irregularities (over the guardianship of Leopold, for example) were 'frivolous'. As for the idea of blood tests, even if Geoffrey were to discover from tests that he could not be the son of the third Lord Ampthill, he would not be entitled to disclaim the peerage, since 'One of the persons upon whom the declaration of legitimacy is binding is Geoffrey himself. Any attempt by him to throw doubt upon that declaration would therefore be wrong.'

'VIRGIN-BIRTH BOY WINS HIS TITLE' was the *Daily Mirror's* headline the next morning (13 April 1976). More restrained, the *Daily Telegraph* proclaimed: 'Geoffrey Russell Ampthill heir, Lords decide'. Ann Morrow, who wrote the article under that heading, had talked with Geoffrey after the hearing closed.

'He said that the case had made the last two years of his mother's life absolutely miserable and would cost him in the region of £40,000.

' "But I am delighted and I feel my mother's name has been vindicated." ...

'Outside, against a background of traffic and the stares of tourists, Mr Geoffrey Russell told disappointed photographers that his French-born wife Elisabeth was in America for the holiday they had promised themselves at the end of the case.

'At their home in Egerton Terrace, Knightsbridge, he told his 15-year-old daughter Vanessa – by his first marriage – about the Lords' recommendation.

'Relaxing in the garden, which is filled with camellias and overhanging magnolias, he said: "I have told my children everything. Vanessa has read all the documents and understands."

' "I just feel sad that this case ever had to happen. Why? My parents were not bitter towards each other. They met several times after the divorce and were the greatest friends. So why should young John do this? He does not look a bitter sort of chap ..." '

The *Daily Express*'s New York correspondent, Paul Dacre (later editor of the *Daily Mail),* talked to Elisabeth Russell, who asked: 'How do you tell a 15-year-old daughter what something like this is all about when she comes home from school in tears because friends have been teasing her?' Elisabeth told the *Mail* reporter, Philip Finn: 'I will never speak to that man [John Russell] again' – but then, she had never spoken to him before, either. As already noted, Osbert Lancaster produced another pocket cartoon: one elderly London clubman is saying to another, 'Tell me, Cumberbatch, d'ye remember a rather interestin' little wager you made some fifty years ago?' *(Plate 28).*

It seemed possible, however, that the Lords' ruling might not be the end of the matter. 'Already', Simon Hoggart wrote in *The Guardian,* 'there are rumblings from supporters of ... John Russell ... that they will fight on through the Lords debate fixed for 27 April' – the debate to decide whether the Committee for Privileges' recommendation should be accepted. The press eagerly chased this new hare. On 13 April the *Mail* ran a story under the headline 'Hailsham battles for losing brother in "virgin birth" case'. A former lord chancellor, Lord Hailsham – son of that Douglas Hogg who had opposed Christabel in the 1922 divorce case – was a clever man but not a wise one. In 1963 he was thought to have dished his chances of becoming Conservative leader and Prime Minister by paddling in the sea at Brighton and, in the conference hall, ringing a large hand-bell in comic self-advertisement. Sir John Sainty thinks Hailsham was in cahoots with Leo Russell, who had been a friend of his at Eton. The *Mail* piece suggested that 'Lord Hailsham may advise the House of Lords to refer the Ampthill report back to the committee with instructions to demand to see results of blood tests taken from Geoffrey Russell and his mother.' But on the following day the *Mail* had to retract its story: Hailsham had told the paper that John Russell's supporters were mistaken in thinking he wanted the dispute to continue. On the same day the *Daily Mirror* printed a comment:

'The Ampthill case has been a marvellous sideshow from the nobility.

'What would the great British public do without the occasional aristocratic sex scandal? How can anyone even consider doing away with such a fertile source of entertainment? Far be it from the *Daily Mirror* to take a hypocritical stance. This newspaper has been intrigued by the Ampthill case as much as anyone ...

'All in all it's been a case not so much of "Noblesse oblige" as "Much obliged, your Lordships, for a rollicking good show."

'It was worth every penny of the estimated £10,000 cost to the public purse.

'But enough is enough. After half a century of litigation, it's time for the Ampthills to give each other – and us – a rest.

'One side of the family is threatening to continue the feud.

'With a tug of our forelock we humbly beseech: CHUCK IT, CHAPS.'

In a dignified letter published in *The Times* on 14 April, John Russell showed that he was going to do just that. It began:

'Sir, I am grateful for your full and objective report of the findings of the House of Lords Committee for Privileges relating to the affairs of my family. There is only one point which I would ask you to let me correct and that is the suggestion that I intend to circularize members of the House of Lords in an attempt to get them to reject the Committee's decision when the report comes before them later this month. I would like to make it clear that I have no such intention and I accept that I must leave the matter to their Lordships' wisdom ...'

He added: 'Perhaps, however, I may be permitted to say a final word on the constitutional and ethical issues involved.' He went on to quote 'certain illuminating passages' from the opinions of two of the law lords – mainly relating to the issue of blood tests. Citing Lord Kilbrandon's view that, even if blood tests proved Geoffrey illegitimate, he would not be at liberty to disclaim the peerage, John wrote:

'This implies that somebody who knows that he is illegitimate is legally bound to tell an untruth, even if this means deceiving the Crown. Many people will, I think, find this a most unethical doctrine.

'I do not propose to make any further public statement on the affair.'

The letter was sent from 57 Ovington Street; so presumably John had not moved out after all.

The House of Lords met on 27 April to consider the Committee for Privileges' recommendation. Geoffrey was not present: he had joined Elisabeth in New York. His son David stood in for him. Lord Wilberforce moved that the Committee's report be agreed. Immediately Viscount Boyd of Merton rose to speak, and it was soon clear that the report was not going to slide through smoothly. Boyd, who was seventy-two, was an industrialist who had married a Guinness heiress. He had been a scholar of Christ Church, Oxford, and President of the Oxford Union. In the 1950s he had been Secretary of State for the Colonies. A redoubtable adversary. He said: 'I have grave anxiety about the motion. I am not happy that the House should advise the Queen to issue a writ of summons in a case where serious doubts exist and where there is a readily available method.'

From New York, Geoffrey and Elisabeth flew to Los Angeles, to be fêted by the Hollywood set. One person who was not impressed by the newest members of the nobility was the English novelist and screenwriter Frederic Raphael, who had won an Oscar for his 1965 screenplay for *Darling* and was 'hot' once more in 1976 after the television showing of his play sequence about an aspiring Cambridge undergraduate, *The Glittering Prizes*. In April 1976 he and his wife Sylvia were staying in the house of the director Tony Richardson, a block up from Sunset Strip. On 24 April he encountered Geoffrey and Elisabeth at the home of the screenwriter George Axelrod and his wife Joan. Raphael wrote in his diary:

'The Axelrods had fancy company ... Lord and Lady A. He, Geoffrey, a rather long-nosed, pin-striped smoothie, was smug with the title with which he had just been fitted, after a long law-suit which proved, if you accept the judgment, that his virgin mother was impregnated by the contents of a sponge ... Her ladyship is French and worked at 666, Fifth Avenue when she did PR for Worth ... With eyes that knew all the exchange rates, she is descended (by a winding stair) from the Mellons, who were first respected millionaire swindlers, then philanthropists.'[94]

Raphael noted that Elisabeth had been in New York, waiting at the '21' Club[95] for the legal decision. Now that Geoffrey had joined her in Los Angeles, they had been lent a chauffeur-driven car by Jules Stein, the boss of MCA. Raphael was determined not to have 'those ... parasites' join him and the Axelrods for supper. They dropped them off at the Beverly Hills Hotel.

On 11 May the Lord Chamberlain, Lord Maclean, presented to the Queen the Resolution and Judgment of the House of Lords in the case of the Barony of Ampthill and she gave her assent.

In her letter to David Russell of 13 April 1976, Mary Deane wrote:

'I waited to write to you about darling Christabel until this [the Lords hearing] was over, thank God, triumphantly for all of you – how she must be crowing on her cloud (unlicensed – I bet). That other lot have done themselves no good & their heads must be hanging in shame, & surely they can't have a friend left in the world?'

There was a sad footnote: on 21 May, the *Daily Mail* Diary reported that the third Baron's widow, Adeline, Dowager Lady Ampthill, was being forced to sell up her home in St John's Wood, London 'after that £40,000 battle'. The house was for sale at £65,000. 'Recently she revealed to friends that she was opposed to her son pursuing the claim to the barony,' the columnist added. 'Her fear was that another defeat would put a too-massive strain on family funds.'

In obedience to the sonorous and minatory command of the royal writ of summons, Geoffrey, 4th Baron Ampthill, took his seat in the House of Lords on 25 May 1976. A life peer had to be introduced by two peers in a flurry of ermine, but once a hereditary peer had received his writ of summons from the Queen, he just turned up.

Geoffrey took his seat as a cross-bencher – that is, as an independent peer. (He had left the Conservative Party over Suez in 1956). Not long after he took his seat, he was introduced to the seventy-year-old Lord Goschen – the Deputy Chairman of Committees – a grandson of the Lord Goschen whom Lord Randolph Churchill 'forgot'[96] Goschen beamed and said, 'I knew your father.'

'You have the advantage of me, sir,' said Geoffrey.

> # HOUSE OF LORDS
>
> *Tuesday, 25th May, 1976.*
>
> The House met at half past two of the clock: The LORD CHANCELLOR on the Woolsack.
>
> *Prayers—Read by the Lord Bishop of Bradford.*
>
> The Lord Ampthill—Sat first in Parliament after the death of his father.

He made his maiden speech in the Lords in the 'State of the Nation' debate on 14 July 1976. The speech began lightheartedly.

'My Lords, a funny thing happened on my way to the House, and if I may be granted that indulgence which your Lordships extend to maiden speakers, which I shall sorely need, I should like to take this first opportunity to apologise to the House for the immense amount of trouble occasioned by the dispute which preceded my arrival here.'

He went on to thank the whole House, in particular those peers who had sat on the Committee for Privileges, for their careful examination of the rival claims. He added: 'All I can do in return, and it is most inadequate, is to place myself unreservedly at the service of your Lordships' House.'

And that is exactly what Geoffrey did. It was soon realized that he had a good brain and application. He served on various committees and eventually became Lord Chairman of Committees – the highest office in the House after that of Lord Chancellor. Handsome tributes were paid to him from all sides of the House when he stood down as Lord Chairman in 1994 and he was still sitting as a Deputy Speaker in his mid-eighties, crisp in his rulings and often witty in his interventions, though he admitted he did not remember all the new peers' names.

Geoffrey Ampthill died on 23 April 2011, aged eighty-nine. His sons decided that he should be buried, not at Leeds Castle, but at Over Stowey, Somerset, where he had been so happy as a boy. A memorial service was held at St Margaret's, Westminster.

The story of the Russell Baby is the essence of all great stories, whether of the Greek and Roman classics, the Bible, Dante, Shakespeare, Tolstoy or fairy tales. A child of noble ancestry, handsome and virile, confronts incalculable obstacles; is disowned by his father; goes to war; woos a beautiful heiress in a huge, moated castle; marries her; resigns from a high, enjoyable and lucrative job on moral grounds; suffers the death of a beloved son. Another set of dragons' teeth rears up in his path. He triumphs. As with Einstein and academe, doors are slammed in his face; but, once inside, he rises as high in his destined firmament as he possibly can. He survives the 'Cull' of the House of Lords. The laws he has helped to pass may be broken or abrogated (though the Channel Tunnel might be rather hard to revoke); but his story will live on, an English *chanson de geste*.

Humbert Wolfe – a poet very popular at the time of the Russell divorce trials – has written:

> Not Helen's wonder
> nor Paris stirs,
> but the bright untender
> hexameters.
> And thus, all passion
> is nothing made,
> but a star to flash in
> an Iliad.[97]

(In this case, a Hilliad.) It was Wolfe, too, who wrote these much anthologized lines:

> You cannot hope
> to bribe or twist,
> thank God! the
> British journalist.
> But, seeing what
> the man will do
> unbribed, there's
> no occasion to.

It might seem traitorous of me to quote that, because I have been a journalist. In 1963 I was a reporter on *The Times,* whose front page was still covered by small-ads of the kind that had brought Christabel and John Hugo together half a century before. (Front-page news supervened in 1966.) I helped Philip Howard cover the funeral of Sir Winston Churchill in 1965. There was a gutter press then; but today the gutter is far deeper. From time to time, a journalist with nothing better to do will rake over the Russell Baby case, scavenging all the scurrilous clichés that have attached themselves to the story, over the years, like barnacles to a shipwreck's hull. Sponges, sleepwalking, virgin births (Christabel's was only a virgin *conception)* – every scurvy fiction is trotted out again. It would be sanctimonious to claim that the sole purpose of this book is to repudiate such tattle. The true story – and I have told it as truthfully as I know how – is extraordinary enough to need no fanciful embellishments. It wrenched human lives; it provoked a King of England; it changed the law, and the lesson of *Russell* v. *Russell* was drummed into generations of trainee barristers and solicitors. The story deserves to become part of English folk tradition, something like a Norse saga.

Whether – with all her wit, flair, vivacity and courage – the 'Nordic' Christabel can be considered its heroine, moralists may dispute; but Geoffrey Ampthill is undeniably its hero; and even in an unheroic age, heroes never quite go out of fashion.

Appendix I

The Slingsby Baby Case

The Times of 3 December 1914 carried an article under these headlines:
THE TITLE TO THE SLINGSBY ESTATES
REMARKABLE LEGITIMACY SUIT
AN ALLEGED CHANGELING

This was the report beneath:

'Mr Justice Bargrave Deane began the hearing today in the Probate, Divorce and Admiralty Division of a suit which raises the question of the right of succession to large estates in Yorkshire. It is alleged that the wife of the present holder of the estates substituted for a child of her own who died the son of another woman.

'The petition is made under the Legitimacy Declaration Act, 1858, by Charles Eugene Edward Slingsby, of Scriven Park, Knaresborough, Yorkshire, an infant, through his guardian, Charles Henry Reynard Slingsby. The petition prays for a decree that he is the lawful child of Charles Henry Reynard Slingsby and Dorothy Morgan Slingsby, and that he is therefore tenant in tail male in remainder expectant on the death of his father of the Slingsby estates. The respondents and parties cited allege that the petitioner, "so far as regards Charles Henry Reynard Slingsby and his wife, was a wholly suppositious child" and has been falsely passed off-since 1910 as the lawful child of Charles Henry Reynard Slingsby ...

'By their answer, Thomas William Slingsby and Alan Peter Slingsby, as respondents and parties cited and brothers of Charles Henry Reynard Slingsby, alleged, *inter alia*, that the petitioner was not a natural-born subject of the King, or domiciled in England; that there never had been any issue of the marriage of Charles Henry Reynard Slingsby and Dorothy Morgan Slingsby, and that the petitioner was not his child, either by the said marriage or at all; that the petitioner was born out of wedlock on or about 1 September 1910 in San Francisco; that his mother was one Lillian Anderson, then an unmarried woman; and his father was one Paul Colvin, of Santa Rosa, California, or some other man whose name was unknown; that on or about 10 September 1910, through one Dr W.W. Fraser, acting on behalf of Lillian Anderson, Dorothy Morgan Slingsby obtained the custody of the petitioner, and had ever since falsely passed him off as her own lawful child by Charles Henry Reynard Slingsby.'

Henry Duke KC [who later presided over the first *Russell* v *Russell* trial] acted for the petitioner, now four years of age.

Headlines in *The Times* of 4 February 1915 proclaimed:

'THE SLINGSBY JUDGMENT. CHILD DECLARED LEGITIMATE
A SCULPTOR ON FAMILY LIKENESS.'

Beneath them, the paper reported:

'A few years back the Rev. Charles Edward Slingsby succeeded to the estates in Yorkshire – the Slingsby estates. He was married and his wife was still living and there were three sons.'

The report recorded a dramatic development in the case: 'Sir George Frampton [the sculptor of "Peter Pan" in Kensington Gardens] had come to the court and had seen Mr and Mrs Slingsby as they sat in Court with the boy. Sir George Frampton had afterwards pointed out to the learned judge what he himself had previously noticed – namely, the extraordinary resemblance of the boy to his father.' [Frampton had particularly drawn attention to a similarity between the left ear of the boy and the left ear of his mother. Whereas in the Russell case it was important to establish that Geoffrey Russell was the son of his father, in the Slingsby case it had been important to prove that the boy was the son of his mother – and therefore not a changeling.]

The Court found in favour of the petitioner, adjudging him to be the lawful child of Charles Henry Reynard Slingsby and Mrs Dorothy Morgan Slingsby. The matter went to the Appeal Court, before the Master of the Rolls and Lord Justice Warrington [later prominent in the Russell case] and Mr Justice Bray. The appeal was allowed: on 14 March 1916 The Times ran the headlines 'CHILD DEPRIVED OF ESTATES UNANIMOUS DECISION OF THE COURT.' In giving the Court's judgment, the Master of the Rolls stated that 'We have held that the calling in of a distinguished sculptor friend, Sir George Frampton, to give his opinion, was wrong.' On another page *The Times* reported that the Slingsby estates were said to be worth £9,000 a year.

On 14 April 1916 *The Times* reported that the boy, through his guardian, was making an appeal to the House of Lords. On 15 December of that year, the paper ran the headlines 'THE SLINGSBY LEGITIMACY SUIT. APPEAL DISMISSED.'

The Lords hearing was before Lord Loreburn, Lord Mersey, Lord Atkinson, Lord Shaw of Dunfermline and Lord Sumner [the peer who also gave his opinion in the Russell case]. Lord Loreburn said that the calling of Frampton as a witness was 'irregular'; and Sumner agreed with him. Costs were awarded against the appellant.

Appendix II

Warren v Warren, 1925

There was much mention of *Russell* v. *Russell* in the *Warren* v. *Warren* divorce case which opened on 28 May 1925.

The parties in *Warren* v. *Warren* were married in May 1913; there was one child, born in January 1916. In the autumn of 1916 the husband had complained to his wife of her conduct with certain soldiers, and she confessed that she had committed adultery; her husband forgave her and the parties lived happily together at Marks Tey in Essex until June 1922. In that month the wife went to stay with her mother in Halesworth in Suffolk until the middle of July. After her return, she confessed to her husband that she had committed adultery during her absence and was pregnant in consequence.

In February 1923, the wife went away from her husband's house and stayed with an uncle at whose house the child was born on 5 April 1923. The wife registered the birth of this child without naming a father. On 15 January 1924, the husband filed a petition for a divorce on the ground of his wife's adultery. The only evidence of the adultery was the wife's confession, verbal and in certain letters, coupled with the assertion that the adultery resulted in the birth of the child. There was no evidence of non-access, or non-possibility of access, of the husband during the period within which the child must have been conceived. J.P. Gorman for the petitioner tendered the letters of the wife and evidence of her verbal confessions as sole evidence of her adultery.

SWIFT, J. 'How can I admit this evidence in face of the decision in *Russell* v. *Russell*?

'All that *Russell* v. *Russell* decides is that neither the father nor the mother can give evidence which would bastardize the child. This evidence could not bastardize the child, because unless you can prove non-access of the husband you cannot hope to bastardize a child. The wife's confession of adultery is good evidence against her, but what she says about the pregnancy is a mere uncertain inference. In the absence of evidence to show that there was no access by the husband this inference would not bastardize the child; it would not even be admissible in a case against a seducer for maintenance at quarter sessions.'

In his summing-up on 23 June 1923, Swift quoted what Lord Finlay had said in *Russell* v. *Russell*: 'There is a strong presumption that the child of a married woman was begotten by her husband. This, however, is not a presumption *juris et de jure*; it may be rebutted by evidence. The fact that the wife had immoral relations with other men is not of itself sufficient to displace the presumption of legitimacy; non-access by the husband at the time when the child must have been begotten must (unless there be incapacity) further be proved. Proof of non-access cannot be given for this purpose either by the husband or by the wife; neither of them can be asked any question tending to prove such non-access; it must be established entirely by the evidence of other witnesses.'

Swift continued his summing-up:

'A statement by a husband that he had not been near his wife and has not had sexual intercourse with her is inadmissible; a statement by a wife that her husband has not at the time of her impregnation had access to or intercourse with her is equally inadmissible. I find, however, no authority for saying that a statement made or evidence given by a wife to the effect that whilst her husband had access to her, and whilst presumably he was having intercourse with her, she committed adultery, is to be excluded.

'Mr Gorman in his very able argument convinced me that if the access of the husband was not disputed, the wife's possible belief and her allegation that the child was not the child of her husband were quite immaterial. Any woman may, and some do, have sexual intercourse with more than one man in the course of a few hours; and if a woman has within the period during which conception must have taken place had connection with more than one man, she is only guessing, on more or less data, as to which is the father of the child. But the law presumes that if one of those men is her husband, the child is his. Her guess, and any evidence she gives or any statement she makes about it, are immaterial. However many men she had had connection with, nothing can bastardize the child unless non-access of or proof of her conduct and statements are inadmissible unless and until it is sought to prove by these means non-access or non-intercourse. Until then the Court will listen to such testimony and may well come to the conclusion that some of it is absolutely true, and that the rest of it is a mere opinion or guess on her part. It does so in this case. I am quite satisfied on the evidence before me that this woman committed adultery.

'I do not accept her guess or opinion that the child she gave birth to in April 1923 was not her husband's; there is no evidence before me of non-access or non-intercourse between 1 June and 31 July, and I do not think *Goodright* v. *Moss* or *Russell* v. *Russell* in any way touch this case.

'I hold that the evidence of the statements made by the respondent to the petitioner and to Mr Charles Warren and the confessions in her letters are true in substance and in fact. On that evidence I believe that the respondent committed adultery, and I grant the petitioner a decree nisi.'

In legal textbooks, the rule in *Warren* v. *Warren* is summarised thus:

'A wife's admission that she had committed adultery, even if accompanied by a statement of her belief that a child, subsequently born, was the result of the adultery, cannot bastardize the child without evidence of the non-access of the husband. The confession of the wife, therefore, that she has committed adultery is admissible as evidence in a suit for divorce so long as she does not assert that the husband could have had no access at the time of conception.

'*Russell* v. *Russell* (1924) distinguished.'

Readers may consult four extra appendices (A – D), free of charge, on the internet, at www.hopcynpress.com/thevirginsbaby

They are as follows:

    A) Their Lordships' House
    B) The Russell Family
    C) Lord Odo Russell, 1st Lord Ampthill
    D) (Arthur) Oliver, 2nd Lord Ampthill.

By kind permission of the Bodleian Library, Oxford, the entire text of this book, including the extra appendices, is lodged in the Special Collections there in 'hard copy', with extra illustrations. The author is greatly indebted to Sarah Wheale and Dr Judith Priestman for this courtesy.

BH.

Notes

1 *The Times*, 1 May 1971

2 On Oakley House, see Simon Houfe, 'Furniture for a Hunting Box', *Country Life*, 14 March 1991, pp. 54-56.

3 Since this paragraph was written, Dr Lucy Bland has contributed to *History Workshop Journal* (Issue 73, 7 February 2012) a perceptive article about the Russell Baby case – '"Hunnish Scenes" and a "Virgin Birth": a 1920s Case of Sexual and Bodily Ignorance'. I understand that it will form a chapter of her book *Women on Trial: Sexual Transgression in the Age of the Flapper*, which is being published by the University of Manchester Press at about the same time as the present book.

4 As a result of the Russell Baby case, upper-class young ladies were warned by their mothers: 'Never take a bath in water that has been used by a man.' Bizarre and improbable as such a means of conception might seem, another still more outlandish was postulated in a television programme on the British 'Discovery' Channel on 12 July 2009. For full details of this extraordinary incident, see John Julius Norwich's *Christmas Cracker* for 2011.

> **6.00 Mythbusters** An investigation into the curious story of a woman who supposedly became pregnant after being struck by a bullet that had passed through a soldier's genitalia. *9315218*

5 The Hon. Robin Warrender (b. 1927), third son of the first Baron Bruntisfield and his wife Gillian, daughter of Leonard Rossiter. In 1986 Warrender was a director of London Wall Holdings Ltd.

6 Lees-Milne's wife Alvilde (*née* Bridges, formerly Viscountess Chaplin).

7 Geoffrey Ampthill was actually sixty-four then.

8 See our Extra Appendix A, 'Their Lordships' House'.

9 I wrote to John Russell to invite him to contribute to this book in one of two ways: I could interview him on the tape-recorder; or he could, if he wished, write his own Appendix to appear uncut and unaltered at the end of the book. He replied courteously that he preferred to stand by what he had written in his letter to *The Times* in 1976 after Geoffrey was declared the legitimate heir: that

he would say nothing further. However, he stated his continuing belief that 'a great miscarriage of justice' took place in the 1920s.

10 His son wrote to me that his father was infirm, and that in any case he always declined to make any additional comment on a case in which he had been involved in the past.

11 See Extra Appendix D, 'The Second Lord Ampthill'.

12 Lady Diana married Duff Cooper in 1919.

13 This was not a pun on the George Cross medal, as that was not instituted until 1940 (by George VI) for acts of conspicuous heroism, primarily by civilians.

   In later life, Cross rose to some eminence. He became a brigadier and secretary of the Commonwealth Press Union and was appointed CBE (*Who Was Who*).

14 An anonymous author contributed to *Fraser's Magazine* in December 1863 an article headed 'A Fortnight in Paris in the May of 1863'. He (or she) had written to his old friend, the manager of the Hôtel Mirabeau, to book his usual room there, but on arrival found she had died and that no booking had been made. He wrote:

   'I found capital quarters hard by, on the first floor at the Hôtel Chatham, 67 Rue Neuve St. Augustin, between the Rue de la Paix and the Boulevard des Capucins; and by no means dear as prices now run in Paris. The keeper of this house, which has been newly fitted up, is a very civil German, in the prime of life, of the Grand Duchy of Baden, of the name of Holzschuch, who, after showing me an apartment which I at once took, conducted me to the *salle à manger*, a lightsome room at the end of a spacious courtyard.'

15 I am grateful to Dr Stephen Cretney for the following information about Withers. He was born in 1863, the son of a solicitor. He was educated at Eton and King's College, Cambridge, where he read classics, became captain of the College boat club and was 'the life and soul of the newly founded Footlights Club' (L.P. Wilkinson, *Kingsmen of a Century 1873-1972* [1980]).He remained devoted to the college and active in its affairs, as its solicitor and in other ways. He was admitted a solicitor in 1890; after six years' partnership with his father, he set up a new practice in partnership with his younger brother, Thomas. They built up a clientèle partly through John Withers's King's connection and partly through his mountaineering friends. (In 1893 he was elected a member of the prestigious Alpine Club.)

   John Withers was fifty-nine at the time of the first *Russell* v. *Russell* trial of 1922. Eileen Hunter describes him as 'short, rosy [and] well-dressed' and records that he always wore a buttonhole. She states that Christabel Russell liked him enormously; it had apparently been necessary for him to explain 'various aspects of the "facts of life" that had escaped her wayward attention'. Also in 1922, at the same time that the Russell case was occupying the attention of the High Court and the press, Withers was fighting another much publicized case in the House of Lords, on behalf of his client Mrs Rutherford. Dr Cretney writes:

'The facts were put (not altogether dispassionately) by Lord Buckmaster, a former Lord Chancellor, and an active - it might almost be said obsessive - advocate of divorce law reform.

'Colonel Rutherford had committed "adultery, murder and robbery. He is found not to be too insane to plead and to be responsible for the action which he has committed; but after the trial he is found to be of unsound mind and is sent to a criminal lunatic asylum." Nevertheless, Mrs Rutherford's divorce petition was dismissed. She appealed to the House of Lords against the refusal to grant her a divorce but was unsuccessful. Lord Chancellor Birkenhead included in his Opinion a call for statutory reform: "It is an unfortunate circumstance that [Mrs Rutherford] should ... be tied for life to a dangerous, violent and homicidal lunatic, after having for many years suffered, both in body and in spirit, from his unfaithfulness and his cruelty." '

Withers, who became an MP in 1926 and was knighted 'for public services' in 1929, played a significant part in bringing about the divorce law reform that Birkenhead thought desirable. He was also a great supporter of women's suffrage and rights; successfully fought the English law which allowed a testator of sound mind to disinherit his wife and children; and worked tirelessly to ensure the regulation of solicitors' accounting procedures. He died in 1939.

16 Withers frequently acted for the aristocracy; and, when he did so, often the same legal *dramatis personae* were brought into play. In 1922 he instructed Sir John Simon when acting for the infant Earl of Shrewsbury in an application to set aside his grandmother's will. (*The Estate of the Earl of Shrewsbury and Talbot, The Times*, 23 June to 1 July 1922). In that case Simon led Sir Ellis Hume-Williams KC, D.Cotes Preedy and Bush James. The executors were represented by two leading counsel (one the future Lord Chancellor Douglas Hogg) and a junior. It was alleged that the will was not duly executed, that the testator did not know and approve its contents, that he lacked testamentary capacity, and that the execution had been obtained by the undue influence of his mistress Mrs Nellie Brownlee. The allegations of lack of testamentary capacity were based in part on the deceased's decision to 'sell everything' - including Alton Towers, now the popular pleasure resort.

In 1925 Simon and Hume-Williams again appeared together – instructed by Withers – representing the Duchess of Westminster in the case of *Grosvenor VMG (Duchess of Westminster) v. Grosvenor HRA (Duke of Westminster)* (*The Times*, 18 June 1925). Dr Stephen Cretney, to whom I am indebted for all the information in this footnote, writes:

'In 1925 the Duchess of Westminster began to suspect that the Duke (one of the richest men in the country) had been using his yacht at Monaco as base from which to carry on relationships with other women. When confronted, the Duke (according to the Duchess's evidence) was "very angry and refused to give them up". The Duchess left, and Withers presented a divorce petition in which, over some thirty paragraphs, "various matters" were alleged. The Duke formally denied most of the allegations but not that he had committed adultery with a named married woman.

'The case was undefended.'

[17] See Chapter 8, 'Disgusted, Buckingham Palace'.

[18] *The Oxford Dictionary of National Biography.*

[19] He meant a layette (a baby's set of clothing); trousseau means the clothes and household linen collected by a bride for her marriage.

[20] *Oxford Dictionary of National Biography.*

[21] In the *Times* reports, Welford's forename is misspelt throughout as 'Hylton'.

[22] Elfrida Shorten.

[23] Under cross-examination, the 'fortune teller' (Mrs Mary Naismith) corrected this to five months.

[24] *A Butterfly on the Wheel* (1922) was a four-act play by Edward George Hemmerde. The title was adapted from a line in Alexander Pope's 'An Epistle to Dr Arbuthnot' (1735) – 'Who breaks a butterfly upon a wheel?' – the phrase of which William Rees-Mogg, editor of *The Times*, made such effective use in his 1967 editorial deploring the prison sentence on Mick Jagger for drugs possession.

[25] See Appendix I 'The Slingsby Baby Case'.

[26] 'As pants the hart for cooling streams When heated in the chase ...'
Nahum Tate and Nichholas Hardy, *New Version of the Psalms* (1696) – Psalm 42. (The version of that psalm in *The Book of Common Prayer* begins: 'Like as the hart desireth the water-brooks: so longeth my soul after thee, O God ...')

[27] In 1940 Cross married Margaret, the daughter of Sir Robert Taylor. There were no children.

[28] See Appendix I, 'The Slingsby Baby Case'.

[29] For a fair and scholarly account of Duke's service in Ireland, see D.G. Boyce and C. Hazlehurst, 'The Unknown Chief Secretary: H.U. Duke and Ireland, 1916–18', *Irish Historical Studies*, 20 (1976–7), pp. 286–311.

[30] *Oxford Dictionary of National Biography.*

[31] In much of this chapter, I am greatly indebted to a masterly essay by Dr Gail Savage, 'Erotic Stories and Public Decency: Newspaper Reporting of Divorce Proceedings in England', *Historical Journal*, 41, 2 (1998), pp. 511-28. I have also found valuable Dr Stephen Cretney's book *Law, Law Reform and the Family*, Oxford 1998, in particular his Chapter 4, whose heading I have borrowed – with his permission – as the heading of this chapter.

[32] See B. Hillier, 'Nicholas Crisp and the Elizabeth Canning Scandal', *Transactions of the English Ceramic Circle*, vol. 16, part I (1996), pp. 7-43.

[33] Schuster was a great friend of Christabel Russell's solicitor, John Withers. They were fellow members of the Alpine Club; and Schuster contributed a eulogistic obituary of Withers to *The Alpine Journal* in May 1940.

[34] See Chapter 14, 'Swift to bless'.

35 In September 1923 Marshall Hall made the speech that saved Madame Fahmy from the gallows. Holding aloft the pistol with which she had shot her husband, he imitated the crouch of the stealthily advancing Egyptian, and declaimed: 'In sheer terror – as he crouched for the last time, crouched like an animal, like an Oriental – she turned the pistol and put it to his face, and to her horror the thing went off ...' He pointed the pistol straight at the jury, then let it fall with a terrific crash, 'symbolizing the fall of a beastly and brutal tyrant'. He later claimed that his dropping the gun had been an accident.

On the Fahmy case, see Andrew Rose, *Scandal at the Savoy*, London 1991, and his reconsideration of the case in *The Prince, the Princess and the Perfect Murder*, London 2013.

36 The authors' quotation is from the memoirs of Marshall Hall's chief clerk, A.E. Bowker, *A Lifetime in the Law*, London 1961.

37 John Mortimer, *The Summer of a Dormouse*, London 2000.

38 *Aliundi* (or *aliunde)*: from another source; from elsewhere.

39 George Kemp, first Baron Rochdale (1866-1945), Liberal MP for N.W. Manchester; created a peer 1913.

40 As noted before, the '7½ months' was later corrected to five months.

41 This part of the first trial does not appear in the newspaper reports which are our only record of the 1922 trial – presumably they were just too graphic for the press of that time, candid as the reports were in most other respects.

42 Christopher Sly: 'A keeper of bears and a tinker, son of a pedlar, and a sad drunken sot in the Induction of *The Taming of the Shrew* (1593). Shakespeare mentions him as a well-known character of Wincot, a hamlet near Stratford-on-Avon, and it is likely that he is an actual portrait of a contemporary.' Brewer's *Dictionary of Phrase & Fable*, London 2002 edn.

43 It would appear that Christabel Russell had four different nicknames for Elfrida Shorten: Freda, Frog, Frug and Rug.

44 This was probably Denis Friedberger (see p. 118).

45 Christabel Pankhurst (1880-1958) was co-founder of the Women's Social and Political Union, which fought for women's suffrage.

46 Denis was one of the names Christabel's baby was given.

47 'Lady Mab' of the *Sunday Express* wrote (18 March 1923):

'An actress? Mrs Russell is the worst actress in the world. She knows less about it than a simpering schoolgirl. If she had acted I am certain she would have won her case. Supposing she had shed a few tears every time Marshall Hall went a bit rough? Supposing she had swooned from exhaustion? Supposing she had summoned a maiden blush to o'erplant her cheek? Supposing her lips had quivered whenever the baby was mentioned? What would have been easier for any woman – and what effect would it have had on the jury?... In my opinion Mrs Russell largely lost her case because she chose to fight it with a rapier rather than a powder puff.'

The identity of the journalist who wrote the 'Lady Mab' column is not known, but Lucy Bland has pointed out that a character of that name had appeared in a recently performed play by Arnold Bennett, *Body and Soul*.

48 The Biblical quotation, from I Corinthians, Ch. 13, v.1, is *'through* a glass, darkly'.

49 Vaginismus: involuntary spasmodic contraction of the vagina. Symptoms can include difficult or impossible penetration because the muscles of the vagina have tightened; and intense fear of penetration and avoidance of sex.

50 See Chapter 8, 'Disgusted, Buckingham Palace'.

51 On Christabel as author, see Chapter 13, *'Afraid of Love'*.

52 See Chapters 16 and 18, 'The Young Pretender' and 'The Title Fight'.

53 On Arthur Ponsonby, see Chapter 8, 'Disgusted, Buckingham Palace'.

54 Elizabeth Ponsonby was one of the leaders of the 'Bright Young People', always in the gossip columns for some discreditable escapade or other, and a sore trial to her parents. On her, see D.J. Taylor, *The Bright Young People*, London 2007.

55 Ria was the wife of Sir Frederick (Fritz) Ponsonby, Arthur's brother, who worked for the royal family and wrote *Recollections of Three Reigns*, London 1951.

56 Magdalen (Maggie) Ponsonby was Arthur's sister. She was much involved in social work with the Rev Dick Sheppard at St Martin-in-the-Fields, London.

57 This letter is filed under 'Letters from Dorothea Ponsonby to Arthur Ponsonby' at Shulbrede Priory, Haslemere. I am grateful to the Hon. Laura Ponsonby for kindly permitting me to inspect it.

58 See Appendix I, 'The Slingsby Baby Case'.

59 In his 1987 biography of Wilde, Richard Ellmann suggested that this was 'probably a court reporter's error for "You are impertinent and insolent"'.

60 *Oxford Dictionary of National Biography*.

61 *Oxford Dictionary of National Biography*.

62 On how shocking this style could seem, see F. Scott Fitzgerald's short story, 'Bernice bobs her hair', which was first published in the *Saturday Evening Post* in May 1920.

63 VAD – (Member of the) Voluntary Aid Detachment.

64 See Chapter 17, 'The Life of Christabel'.

65 In his recent book on the Fahmy case, already alluded to, Andrew Rose convincingly suggests that Establishment pressure was brought to bear on Swift in that case, becase Mme Fahmy had been a mistress of the Prince of Wales (later Edward VIII) and held compromising letters from him. Rose notes that Swift told the prosecuting barristers that they were to make no mention of Mme Fahmy's early career as a common prostitute or her later one as a high-class call-girl. If that evidence had been allowed, the jury might well have convicted her; and if her career as a prostitute had been made public, she might have mentioned the Prince's letters.

66 On *Warren* v. *Warren*, see Appendix II.

67 On Roxburgh, see Noel Annan, *Roxburgh of Stowe*, London 1965; also Evelyn

Waugh, *A Little Learning*, London 1964; *The Diaries of Evelyn Waugh*, ed. Michael Davie, London 1976; David Niven, *The Moon's a Balloon*, London 1971; and Peregrine Worsthorne, *Tricks of Memory*, London 1993.

68 No such title is among White's books listed in the British Library catalogue.

69 There, too, collaborators were being arrested – among them, Hergé, creator of the Tin-Tin comic strips.

70 Sir Gawaine Baillie died in 2004. He had formed a large stamp collection, which was sold by Sotheby's.

71 Geoffrey's son Anthony disputes his father's version of his relations with Lady Baillie's two daughters. 'I always understood that he really wanted to marry Popsy – but she wouldn't have him.'

72 On Dorothy Paget, see Sidney Galtry, *Memoirs of a Racing Journalist*, London 1935, and Quintin Gilbey, *Dorothy, Queen of the Turf: The Dorothy Paget Story*, London 1973.

The present Lord Ampthill recalls: 'She once broke down on the way to the races and missed backing some horse she wanted to back. It duly won; so for evermore thereafter she took *two* cars to the races – the relief one followed behind. And she had two complete sets of staff in case she wanted a roast chicken with all the trimmings at four in the morning.

'Another of her eccentricities was that, whenever she was going to the races, she sent one of her attendant ladies on ahead, to sit on a lavatory seat for as long as the races lasted, to keep it warm for her in case she felt the call of nature.'

73 Ernest Thornton-Smith has a place in the history of design. In the early 1920s, as Selina Hastings records in her biography of Somerset Maugham (2009) he was head of Fortnum's antiques department. Maugham's young wife Syrie turned to him, 'asking him to take her on as an unpaid apprentice to teach her about furniture and restoration, how to deal with customers, and all the invaluable little tricks of the trade. It quickly became apparent that Syrie had found her vocation, not only in décor but as a businesswoman... In 1922 with borrowed capital of £400 she opened a shop, Syrie Ltd, at 85 Baker Street.'

74 In 1953 Ian and Ann Fleming stayed with Somerset Maugham at the Villa Mauresque in Antibes. Andrew Lycett writes: 'On the Flemings' departure, the famously mean Maugham took his secretary-companion, Alan Searle to task for the number of towels that had been used. Anthony Powell uncharitably recorded in his *Journals*, "It then appeared that the towels so prodigiously sent to the laundry were used to 'alleviate the smart where Ian Fleming whipped his wife during the sexual encounters taking place during their visit.""

75 Lady Charlotte Curzon, daughter of Earl Howe. She was born in the same year as James Russell, 1948. In 1988 she married John Barry Dinan, who, like Geoffrey Ampthill, had been a Captain in the Irish Guards.

76 Hugo Vickers, the biographer of royalty and of Cecil Beaton, lived in Egerton Terrace as a boy and attended Hill House prep school with Anthony Russell; he remembers Susan Russell, 'dressed in deepest black, with pure white hair',

walking her dog after James's death. He says: 'Colonel Remington Hobbs was always trying to marry rich women, and I rather think he succeeded on more than one occasion. You know the type – charming, pointless, amiable, harmless unless it is your wife they are after.'

77 As we have seen, only three of the children were surviving in 1970, James having been killed in 1969.

78 Christabel was right: in his will, her former husband provided that what Geoffrey called 'her pittance' (a £500 annuity) was to continue to be paid to her.

79 Eileen Petrovitch wrote to Geoffrey Russell on I July 1973:
'My dear Geoffrey,

'I was astounded to see in the press several reports that your half-brother ... means to challenge your right to the title. In one of the many talks I had with Chris while preparing the book, she mentioned to me that when your father in 1935 saw her for the purpose of asking her to divorce him, she told me he told her that he was "sorry about the case and that he absolutely believed you were his son".

'When I finished the book last year your father was still alive and after some thought I decided not to include this information in the book as I thought that although your father had told Chris he was "sorry" and believed you were his child, he might not have told his third wife and children and I was anxious to avoid causing him distress ...'

80 Lord Shackleton did not, in the event, sit on the Committee which ruled on the challenge by John Russell to Geoffrey Russell.

81 Although James Miskin had agreed to be Geoffrey Russell's counsel, his appointment as Recorder of London (1975) forced him to stand down and Sir John Foster undertook the task instead.

82 On 13 March 1974, John, thirteenth Duke of Bedford, wrote to Messrs Theodore Goddard and Company:
'The Barony of Ampthill
'I am writing as head of the Russell family to place on record my great regret that the succession to the barony, following the death of the late Lord Ampthill last June, should be a matter of dispute.

'The late Lord Ampthill was for a long period a Trustee of the Bedford Settled Estates and thus was well known to me. I have also known his elder son, Geoffrey, very well since I attended his marriage in 1946.

'There is not, and never has been, the slightest doubt in my mind that Geoffrey was the rightful heir of his father, nor did the late Lord Ampthill at any time indicate to me that Geoffrey would not be his lawful successor. The physical resemblance between Geoffrey and his father is strong, and that between my godchild, Geoffrey's elder son David, and his grandfather is even more striking. Many other of Geoffrey's characteristics unquestionably point to his Russell blood.

'It seems to me that for John Russell, who is also known to me, to contest the succession after the dispute between the late Lord Ampthill and his wife Christabel had been resolved in the House of Lords nearly fifty years ago, is despicable.

'Yours faithfully, Bedford'

[83] On 26 May 1974, in Ireland, an armed gang stole paintings worth £8m from a country house. On 3 May they threatened to destroy them unless the Nationalist Price sisters were released from jail. On 25 June Dr Bridget Rose Dugdale, a former debutante, was jailed for nine years for the art theft.

[84] See the record of facts in *Baroness Ampthill* v. *Baron Ampthill* (*The Times*, 26 November 1935).

[85] *The Times*, 20 and 22 January 1937.

[86] *The Matchgirls* by Bill Owen and Tony Russell (no relation) was a musical about a strike by the girls of a Victorian match factory. It was reviewed in *The Times* on 2 March 1966.

[87] Edward Wolfe, RA (1897-1982), artist. He had been part of the Bloomsbury Group's Omega Workshops.

[88] Presumably, Christabel was thinking of a badger's sett.

[89] Isaiah Berlin, *Flourishing: Letters 1928-1946*, ed. Henry Hardy, London 2004, p. 708.

[90] Richard Ollard, the editor of Rowse's *Diaries* (2003), appends a footnote on Foster: 'All Souls friend, in whose sex life ALR found a vicarious excitement'.

[91] In the early 1970s the television series *Upstairs, Downstairs* – about an aristocratic family and its servants from Edwardian to 1930s Britain – was popular on British television. It came to an end in December 1975.

[92] Idi Amin (Dada) (1925-2003), Ugandan soldier and politician. In a coup of 1971 he established a military dictatorship. He was overthrown in 1978.

[93] *Palmer's Peerage Laws of England.*

[94] As we have seen, Elisabeth was a Mallon, not a Mellon.

[95] The 21 Club, a fashionable restaurant run by the Kreindler and Bern families at 21 West 52nd Street in New York City.

[96] When, in 1886, Lord Randolph Churchill tendered his resignation to Lord Salisbury, he thought he was irreplaceable. But Salisbury had had enough of Churchill's tantrums, and appointed George Goschen Chancellor of the Exchequer in his place. Churchill ruefully commented: 'I had forgotten Goschen'.

[97] In 1924, the year of Christabel's triumph in the House of Lords, John Drinkwater brought out *Select Poems of Lord de Tabley*, who lived between 1835 and 1895. The opening of de Tabley's poem 'Sonnet' makes a case exactly the opposite to Humbert Wolfe's – Record is nothing, and the hero great.

Index